The Tudor Theatre

To my good friend, Ellis Jones, 'the very abstract of our time'.

The Tudor Theatre

1576-1642

Nicholas Fogg

First published in Great Britain in 2025 by
Pen & Sword History
An imprint of Pen & Sword Books Limited
Yorkshire – Philadelphia

ISBN 978 1 03613 068 8

A CIP catalogue record for this book is available from the British Library.

Typeset by Mac Style
Printed in the UK by CPI Group (UK) Ltd, Croydon, CR0 4YY.

The Publisher's authorised representative in the EU for product safety is Authorised Rep Compliance Ltd., Ground Floor, 71 Lower Baggot Street, Dublin D02 P593, Ireland.
www.arccompliance.com

For a complete list of Pen & Sword titles please contact

PEN & SWORD BOOKS LIMITED
47 Church Street, Barnsley, South Yorkshire, S70 2AS, England
E-mail: enquiries@pen-and-sword.co.uk
Website: www.pen-and-sword.co.uk
or
PEN AND SWORD BOOKS
1950 Lawrence Road, Havertown, PA 19083, USA
E-mail: uspen-and-sword@casematepublishers.com
Website: www.penandswordbooks.com

Contents

Acknowledgements vi
Introduction vii

Chapter 1 The Sumptuous Theatre Houses 1

Chapter 2 All Our Pageants of Delight 30

Chapter 3 Where the Infectious Pestilence did Reign 57

Chapter 4 'According to their Habilities' 86

Chapter 5 Great Inconveniences and Misrule 113

Chapter 6 These our Servauntes 142

Chapter 7 'The Whole Course of the Present Time' 170

Chapter 8 We are Such Stuff as Dreams are Made On 199

Chapter 9 Our Revels Now are Ended 229

Chapter 10 As it was Lately Acted 257

Notes 283
Bibliography 287
Index 289

Acknowledgements

Tom Axworthy, Robert Bearman, Richard Demarco, Kathy Hamilton, Mary and Lawrence James, John Hewitt, Sylvia Morris, David Sherratt. Lucy Calista, Laura Hirst, Karyn Burnham, Olivia Canozzio, Wilhelm Vossenkuhl, Roger Pringle, Mairi Macdonald, Sandy Holt, Rupert Alexander, James Paterson, Celia Tanner, Preston Witts, Chris Towner, Jon Wright, Angie Gowan, Clare Walton, Rob and Pat Lister and Edwina Fogg who endured my lunchtime discourses on the book.

Introduction

In the small town where I live, there is a narrow alley, leading off the high street, which opens onto a courtyard. If you walk down the alley, you may notice a small plaque on the wall – the outer wall of a neighbouring shop. If you stop to read it, you will learn that, in the late sixteenth century, the town hosted a group of actors from London. They were, presumably, moving around the country – perhaps the capital had been struck again by the plague and the company needed time away – and they had ended up in the West Country, entertaining the local townspeople. They probably put on their shows in the courtyard behind the high street. There is nothing exceptional about this – except for the fact that the company in question was the Lord Chamberlain's Men and that there is a possibility that William Shakespeare was travelling and performing with them. It could be argued, as Nicholas Fogg does in this exhaustive study, that the Lord Chamberlain's Men is the most influential theatre company in history. And there is, of course, no doubting the status and significance of William Shakespeare.

At the time of the visit to Wiltshire, he may well have already written some of the most famous plays in the English language – plays that would have a profound impact all over the world and for centuries to come. I was surprised by how excited I felt when I first discovered the plaque. Many people in the town seemed to take it for granted; but as a recent resident I was thrilled by the idea that Shakespeare – a hero of mine – might have walked the same streets where I now shopped, drank my morning coffee and downed my evening pint of beer in the local pub. This may seem trivial and, if I'm honest, it is. Like so much in Shakespeare's life, quotidian details are hard to locate and he may never have visited my home town, so to fantasise about his buying food in the market or patronising the inn across the road is frankly silly. But there were other reasons for excitement. The wording of the plaque places Shakespeare clearly within a group of working artists. In other words, it implies that he was a genuine collaborator, who must have understood the pressures felt by a working theatre company and adapted his work accordingly. By the late 1590s, he was certainly seen by many as one of the best playwrights in town – perhaps even exceptional. He was also regarded by some with suspicion – a sign, surely, of his blossoming talent. The first oblique reference to him in print is an acidic attack from another writer, who accuses Shakespeare of plagiarism and hints that a vulgar provincial like him should not presume to compete with more educated and skilled artists. People knew his work and recognised its power. But, as Shakespeare's importance grew over the years after his death, it became too easy to forget that, genius though he undoubtedly was, he was also a hard-working professional and had to respond carefully to other people's ideas and demands. I have known and loved Shakespeare's writing for most of my life. Like many English schoolchildren, I was introduced to him when I was very young and I was lucky that both my schools thought it important that pupils should act as well as read his plays. By the time I went to university, I had already presented, however inadequately, my versions of Hippolyta and Desdemona and King Lear. As a professional actor, I have appeared in around twenty of Shakespeare's plays. For many years, he was simply the man who wrote great works and great roles – the man who, in Dame Judi Dench's words, helped to 'pay the rent'. But then, about twenty years ago, I became interested in the world that Shakespeare inhabited. I found that there was so much to discover outside of the plays themselves – something that this book celebrates. His early life in Warwickshire; the writers that must have influenced him when he first arrived in London – like Thomas Kyd and Christopher Marlowe; the actors – including the great comics – that he knew and eventually wrote for; his dealings with both an urban audience and the courts of Queen Elizabeth and King James; learning about all this added immeasurably to my enjoyment of reading and re-reading his plays. I became fascinated, too, with the after-life of Shakespeare's work – how the great collection that is now known as the First Folio came into being, the lives of his close colleagues that he left behind him after his death, the closing of the theatres at the time of the Commonwealth and their reopening under the stewardship of men like Killigrew and Davenant. Nicholas Fogg touches on all these things in his book and manages to find a way through the byzantine complexities of the story with consummate ease. The plays stand by themselves, of course; but there is no harm (and a great deal of fun) in finding out more of how and why the were written and of how a true genius lived and worked.

Simon Russell Beale
February 2025

Chapter One

The Sumptuous Theatre Houses

The Gorgeous Playing Place

On the night of 28 December 1598, around sixteen men assembled in the London suburb of Shoreditch beyond the city walls. They were carrying saws and axes – the tools of demolition. Their bold project was to demolish nothing less than an entire theatre and carry its timbers away.

The eponymous name of The Theatre in question made sense, since it was the only one in existence when it was built. The force behind it was an actor named James Burbage. He was originally a joiner and carpenter by trade, useful skills in his third career as a builder and theatre manager. He was a leading member of an acting company under the patronage of Robert Dudley, Earl of Leicester, one of the most powerful men in England. It had become customary for leading noblemen to maintain troupes of players, a relationship of mutual benefit. The Lord had the prestige of the actors under his patronage, who performed for him on special occasions. For the actors, the relationship was even more valuable. Under the Poor Laws enacted in 1572, they could be classed as wandering vagabonds and fined or imprisoned. The patronage of a great aristocrat meant that they were officially his servants and thus immune from such charges.

A letter from Burbage to Robert Dudley written on 3 January 1572, reveals how the system worked. He requested that the actors be appointed as the Earl's 'household retainers'. They would not expect 'any further stipend or benefit'. They wanted the prestige and protection of his name while operating as an independent commercial entity. As John Stowe put it:

> Comedians and stage-players of former times were very poor and ignorant, but being now grown very skillful and exquisite actors for all matters, they were entertained into the service of diverse great lords.[1]

As the Queen's favourite, Robert Dudley used his influence at Court in 1574 to secure the first Royal Patent granted to a theatrical troupe. It authorised his company,

> to use, exercise and occupy the art and faculty of playing comedies, tragedies, interludes, stage plays and others such like … as well within our City of London and liberties of the same, as also within the liberties and freedoms of any of cities, towns, boroughs, etc. whatsoever … throughout our Realm of England.

Crucially, the warrant overrode earlier policies which enabled local officials to censure or ban plays. This power was now invested in royal authority through the Lord Chamberlain. Once the players had gained this approval, they could perform their plays without local interference. Even more importantly, it put the theatre on a professional basis and established the opportunity to create great drama.

One of five actors named in the Royal Licence was the Company's clown, Robert Wilson, noted for his 'quicke, delicate, refined, extemporal wit'. He was likley the author of *The Three Ladies of London*, which was published in quarto in 1584 and probably performed at The Theatre before that. The three Ladies in question are personifications of abstract qualities: Lucre, Love and Conscience. The play represents a transitional stage between the medieval morality play of popular tradition and the new, more realistic drama, featuring rounded characters. It must have been a success because a sequel, *The Three Lords and Three Ladies of London*, appeared soon after. Like many plays of its era, it is lost to posterity.

After graduating from Oxford in 1576, Stephen Gosson wrote a number of plays, including *Cateline's Conspiracies*, a tragedy, *Captain Mario*, a comedy, and *Praise at Parting*, a 'moral'. He established a reputation as a poet, Francis Mears regarding him as one of the 'best for pastorals'. All the works that bore his name are lost.

In his *The Schoole of Abuse*, Gosson names two plays, *The Blacke Smiths daughter*, and his own *Catiline's Conspiracies* and states that they had been 'brought in to Theater'.

> The first contayning the trechery of *Turkes*, the honourable bountye of a noble minde, and the shining of vertue in distresse: The last, because it is knowen too be a Pig of myne owne Sowe, I will speake the lesse of it; onely giuing you to vnderstand, that the whole marke which I shot at in that woorke, was too showe the rewarde of traytors in *Catilin*, and the necessary gouernment of learned men, in the person of *Cicero*, which forsees euery danger that is likely to happen, and forstalles it continually ere it take effect.

Leicester's Men performed at Court during the Christmas festivities in 1574 and 1575. They played a major part in entertainments provided by Robert

Dudley at Kenilworth Castle in 1566, 1572 and 1575. The latter occasion was an eighteen-day extravaganza in honour of the Queen, during which the clocks were stopped at the hour of feasting. The Company presented a waterborne pageant on the castle's mere, *The Delivery of the Lady of the Lake*. In one scene, a boy musician dressed as Arion rode a stage dolphin across the water. It is possible that William Shakespeare, aged 11, was among the crowd who saw this spectacle: Kenilworth is just twelve miles from Stratford. He may have recalled it two decades later in *Twelfth Night*.

> Where, like Arion on the dolphin's back,
> I saw him hold acquaintance with the waves.

Other noblemen possessed or acquired troupes of players: an important motivation was the hope of gaining influence through a performance at Court. With the example set by Leicester's Men, they began to appear in public. Among the most prominent were those of the Earls of Pembroke and Sussex. These were all surpassed in longevity by Oxford's Men. The troupe of players under the patronage of John de Vere, 16th Earl of Oxford, could trace its origins to the 7th Earl, whose performers were paid 6/8d for an entertainment in Canterbury around 1353. Successive Earls sponsored minstrels, acrobats, jugglers, animal acts and, occasionally, actors. Another John de Vere, the fiercely Protestant 15th Earl, realised the theatre's potential as a means of indoctrination, commissioning the anti-Catholic polemicist John Bale to write six plays between 1534 and 1536. Edward de Vere, the 17th Earl, broke this historic continuity when he discontinued Oxford's Men, in 1564, but he continued to patronise other forms of entertainment.

Although the building of The Theatre was a milestone in the history of the drama, it was not the first theatre of its era. The accomplishment of creating the first theatre in England since Roman times belongs to John Brayne, whose sister, Ellen, James Burbage had married. He was a prosperous grocer with a business in Bucklersbury. He was described as 'worth £500 at least, and by common fame worth a thousand marks'.

The City burgesses tended to be hostile to public performances. This was probably as much from a fear of the potential disturbances caused by large gatherings than from religious disapproval, although that was a factor with some. For this reason, nearly all the theatres founded over the next half century were erected outside the City walls, beyond their jurisdiction. In 1567, Brayne built the Red Lion Theatre at Mile End with the assistance of his actor brother-in-law. The first play was performed there on 8 July 1567, but apart from the title, *The Story of Samson*, nothing is known of it.

The Red Lion Theatre was not a success. As the name implies, the small settlement on the road to Colchester was a mile beyond the City boundary at Aldgate, probably too distant to draw a regular audience. Yet its importance in the history of the theatre cannot be underrated. Previously public performances had taken place in galleried inns. The audience stood around a stage erected in the centre of the courtyard while the better-heeled sat in the galleries above. Although no details survive of the form and shape of the Red Lion Theatre, it undoubtedly incorporated the familiar design of the inn. The theatre's shape governed the nature of the works written for its stage and the way they were performed. There was little, if any, scenery, the Elizabethan theatre was, above all, a theatre of the imagination, with the action played out in the minds of the audience. 'Let us, ciphers to this great account,' urges the Chorus in *Henry V*, 'on your imaginary forces work.' The creation of such imagery to set the scene was an important feature of the playwright's task. The Chorus urges the playgoers to 'piece out our imperfections with your thoughts'.

Despite the lack of theatres specifically created for the production of plays, there was a long history of dramatic production in England. Having its origins in the antiphonal exchanges of the medieval liturgies, the drama had transposed itself into the streets on the Feast of Corpus Christi when the Blessed Sacrament was exposed publicly for veneration. 'Mystery' plays were performed at points where the monstrance halted that recounted salvation history from Creation to Apocalypse. The word derives from the Latin '*mysterium*', meaning 'handicraft', and indicates that the plays were performed by various trades guilds, each with its own play. These performances survived into William Shakespeare's lifetime. He could have seen the plays of the Coventry Mystery Cycle before their suppression in 1579, when he was 15. In his advice to the players, Hamlet refers to two of the *grand guignol* characters in the old cycle. 'I would have such a fellow whipped for o'erdoing Termigant. It out-Herods Herod.'

The Morality Plays grew out of the Mysteries in the late fifteenth century. Again the name expresses the function. The human and divine characters of the Mysteries are replaced by ones representing abstract vices and virtues. In most the central figure represents 'Everyman' (the title of the best-known morality play), or 'Mankind', the proponent in another well-known play, *The Castle of Perseverence*, who is confronted with a moral dilemma and has to make a choice between Good and Evil. The prototype for Shakespearean tragedy is here, although the choice for Shakespeare's tragic heroes is infinitely more complex.

In the early 1550s, a new type of drama began to appear in educational foundations. A revival of interest in classical literature saw the production of comedies based on the style of the Roman dramatists, Terence and Plautus. Two plays typify the genre. *Ralph Roister Doister*, written around 1553 by the schoolmaster Nicholas Udall, was probably first performed by his pupils at Westminster School. *Gammer Gurton's Needle*, a Latinate comedy of the same period, was first performed at Christ's College, Cambridge, and probably written by one of the Fellows. Related to this was the emergence as a theatrical force of children's companies of actors, drawn from the choir schools of cathedrals and chapels. The noted composer, Richard Cornish, Master of the Children of the Chapel Royal at St James's Palace, wrote plays that were performed by the boys under his direction. At Christmas in 1515, they acted *The Story of Troylus and Pando* before Henry VIII at Eltham Palace. The choristers of St George's Chapel at Windsor were performing plays and pageants at Court by 1516 and those of St Paul's Cathedral by 1525. Under the Mastership of Sebastian Westcott, the Children of Paul's performed twenty-seven times at Court between 1557 and 1582, more than any other company. Queen Elizabeth's clear love of the theatre and the performances of the boys' companies were the subject of a fearsome Puritan denunciation entitled *The Children of the Chapel Stript and Whipt*, published anonymously in 1569. Despite his condemnatory attitude, the author was not immune to the erotic appeal of the choirboys.[2]

> Plaies will never be supprest while her maiesties unfledged minions flaunt it in silkes and sattens. They had as well be at their Popish service, in the deuils garments … Even in her maiesties chappel do these pretty vpstart youthes profane the Lordes day by the lascivious writhing of their tender limbs, and gorgeous decking of their appareil, in feigning bawdie fables gathered from the idolatrous heathen poets.

According to Richard Flecknoe,[3] the Children of the Chapel and the Children of Paul's performed plays on weekdays after vespers, the former at the old White Friars monastery outside the walls between Fleet Street and the river; the latter at Convocation House at the Cathedral.

The developing drama was dominated by respect for its classical predecessors. It was within these rigid modes that the first writers for the Elizabethan stage set their works. In 1562, law students known as the Gentlemen of the Temple performed a play called *Gorbuduc* before the Queen. It was written by two young courtiers, Thomas Norton and Thomas Sackville. It is a turgid piece, its chain of slaughter and revenge based on Senecan models. The Queen would be better entertained during her long reign. Yet it was highly significant because it introduced the form of blank verse to the English drama. It had a huge impact. Sir Philip Sidney found it 'full of stately speeches and well- sounding phrases, climbing to the height of Seneca his style, and as full of notable morality, which it does most delightfully teach.'

A favoured place for performances was the courtyards of inns. There were a number of such theatres operating in London. Most were first recorded around the time the Red Lion Theatre was established. Four were within the City Walls: the Bel Savage on Ludgate Hill, the Bull off Bishopsgate, the Cross Keys off Gracechurch Street and the Bell in Bell's Inn Yard. The earliest record of a play being performed at the Boar's Head in Whitechapel is in 1557.

The playwright turned preacher, Stephen Gosson, loved the performances at the Bel Savage, 'where you shall find never a word without wit, never a line without pith, never a letter placed in vain'. He admired two now-lost plays that he saw at the Bull, *The Jew* and '*Ptolome*'. The former may have given William Shakespeare inspiration for the *Merchant of Venice*, for he describes it as 'representing the greediness of worldly choosers, and bloody minds of usurers', and how 'false friends, with their own swords and rebellious commons with their own snares are overthrown'.

A Company that would play a major role in the development of the theatre first appeared in 1576. Lord Howard's Men was formed under the patronage of the Queen's cousin, Charles, 2nd Lord Howard of Effingham. An influential and rising man at Court, he had been appointed General of the Horse in 1569 and to the Order of the Garter in the year his theatrical company was founded. In July 1563, the 27-year-old Howard married Katherine Carey, who was around 13 years old, daughter of Henry Carey, 1st Baron Hunsdon, who was also a cousin of the Queen. These two men, ostensibly in charge of rival companies, would be the major patrons of the Elizabethan theatre.

Lord Howard's Company was an immediate success, performing a play called *Tooley* at Court during the Christmas season in December 1576/7 and, on 17 February, one called, *The Solitary Knight*. The Company toured the nation extensively over the next two years, playing as far afield as Bath and Nottingham. In 1585, Howard was appointed England's Lord High Admiral and the Company adopted the name reflecting his status – The Admiral's Men.

The lessons of the Red Lion Theatre were not lost on Burbage and Brayne. On 13 April 1576, Burbage signed a twenty-one year lease with Giles Allen, on a plot of land on Holywell Street in Shoreditch,[4] just north of the City walls, where he intended to 'erect or set up in the gardens or void ground a theatre or playing place'. It was the site of the Holywell Priory, a house of Augustinian sisters, which had been dissolved in common with other religious houses in 1539, The principal buildings were demolished soon after, although the gateway remained and, according to an account of 1600, a slaughterhouse, a brew house and 'low paultyre buyldinges'.[5]

The site was ideal. It was close to the City, but beyond the jurisdiction of the City Fathers. The rental was relatively low at 14/- per annum, reflecting the fact that the buildings were derelict. There was a 'fine' (down payment) of £20 with an opportunity for a ten year extension on the initial twenty-one year lease if Burbage spent the considerable sum of £200 on buildings and repairs beyond the cost of building the Theatre.

That Giles Allen was far from being a Puritan is demonstrated in a further clause in the contract:

> And further, that it shall or may[be] lawful for the said Gyles and for his wife and family, upon lawful request therefor made to the said James Burbage, his executors or assigns, to enter or come into the premises, and there in some one of the upper rooms to have such convenient place to sit or stand to see such plays as shall be there played, freely without anything therefore paying.

Another clause would be vital and was perhaps added because Burbage was already beginning to have doubts about Allen's integrity.

> And farther, the said Gyles Alleyn and Sara his wife did covenant and grant to the said James Burbage that it should and might be lawful to the said James Burbage in consideration of the imploying and bestowing the foresaid two hundred pounds in forme aforesaid at any time or times before the end of the said term of one and twenty years, to have, take down, and carry away to his own proper use for ever all such buildings and other things as should be builded, erected, or set up in or upon the gardens and void grounds by the said James, either for a theatre or playing place, or for any other lawful use, without any stop, claim, let, trouble, or interruption of the said Gyles Alleyn and Sara his wife.

The site was in a serious state of decay. In 1600, one Randolph May recalled that the buildings were 'rotten', adding that they were 'ould houfes of office and fome of them open that Roges and beggars harboured in them'. Yet, despite the dereliction, Burbage saw the potential. He fulfilled the clause in the lease by spending £200 on renovating the buildings. His commitment is demonstrated by the fact that he built a dwelling there for himself. Yet a number of contemporaries testify that he was not a wealthy man. An input of cash was needed and the obvious person to approach was his wealthy brother-in-law, John Brayne, who entered into the project with great enthusiasm.

According to Burbage's later testimony, he offered to 'bear and pay half the charges' in order 'that he might have half the moiety'. A subsequent deposition stated that, having joined Burbage, 'he began to slack his own trade', and gave all his energies to building the theatre, 'and the chief care thereof he took upon him and hired workmen of all sorts for that purpose, bought timber and all other things belonging thereunto and paid all.'

Brayne developed an obsession with the project. He saw it as a means towards great fame and wealth. Therefore he put forward initially a huge sum of around a thousand marks. He sold off the lease of his house in Bucklersbury for £100 and all his goods and chattels for a further £146. He paid one 'Kymbre', an ironmonger, £40 for work at the Theatre. As his obsession grew, 'he was driven to borrow money to supply the same, saying ... that his brother Burbage was not able to help the same, and that he found not towards it above the value of fifty pounds, some part in mony and the rest in stuff.'

According to one account, Brayne and his wife 'were driven to labor in the said work' to save some of the cost of employing two labourers, whereas James Burbage 'went about his own business', and 'when he did take upon him to do some thing in the said work, he ... was allowed a workman's hire as other the workman there had.' Burbage's contribution to the new building cannot be underrated. It was his concept. It was he who created the dimensions of the Elizabethan theatre. All the theatres built in that era were modelled on The Theatre.

Richard Farrant, a noted composer, was appointed organist and choirmaster of St George's Chapel, Windsor in 1564. This entailed putting on an annual play before the Queen with the choirboys, who were known as 'The Children of Windsor'. His talents led to his appointment as deputy to William Hunnis, Master of the Children of the Chapel Royal. He continued to put on dramatic performances with both sets of boys, sometimes combining the two. He was the first to realise the commercial potential of the children's companies. In 1576, he leased part of the former buttery of the old Dominican monastery of Blackfriars, situated between the Thames and Ludgate Hill, from the owner, Sir William More, for conversion as an indoor theatre. He appears to have convinced More – who was not happy with his property being used as a public theatre, but was ambitious for advancement – that the purpose of the lease was to provide rehearsal space for performances before the Queen. Like The Theatre, Blackfriars was beset with landlord difficulties. The eminent citizens who lived in the vicinity were to prove a bugbear and perhaps this animosity had already begun.

When Farrant died in 1580, the lease passed to his widow, Anne. A partner, John Newman, subleased the property from her, but the enterprise did not go well, which put him in arrears with the rent. To avoid legal action by the widow or by More, the partners transferred the sublease to a Welsh scrivener of somewhat dubious character called Henry Evans. This unauthorised transfer led More to take an action for repossession. Evans prevaricated to delay matters and finally sold the sublease in November 1583 to Edward de Vere, 17th Earl of Oxford, who was patron of a children's troupe known as 'Oxford's Boys'. There was no legal reason why More should not have continued his suit, but he probably considered de Vere to be influential at Court and someone who could further his hopes of advancement. In this he was mistaken, Edward de Vere had lost favour after impregnating Anne Vavasour, one of the Queen's Maids of Honour, who gave birth to a son in March 1581. Like her noted successor, the Queen was not amused.

Edward de Vere was too beset by his personal and financial problems to give much attention to his playhouse, so he handed it over to his secretary, John Lyly, although the combined companies were still sometimes known as Oxford's Boys. Lyly was most noted in his lifetime as the author of *Euphues, or the Anatomy of Wit*, which was published in 1578 and put a new word into the English language. 'Euphuism' denotes the mannered and elaborate style much in vogue in the 1580s.

A sermon preached by John Stockwood, the Puritan Headmaster of Tonbridge School, in 1578 attests the huge popularity of the drama. 'Will not a filthy play, with the blast of a trumpet, sooner call thither a thousand than an hour's tolling of the bell bring to the sermon a hundred?'

The Red Lion Theatre appears to have inspired others. Around the time that The Theatre opened (it may even have preceded it), Jerome Savage, an actor with the Earl of Derby's Men, acquired the sub-lease of a tenement at Newington Butts, a village a mile south of London Bridge. It was not a success, probably for the same reason as the failure of the Red Lion Theatre, its distance from the City contributing to the 'tediousness of the waie' for playgoers.

The Theatre was erected rapidly. Performances were staged even before it was completed. It was an economic necessity to do so. John Grigges, a carpenter employed on the site, later deposed that Burbage and Brayne 'had finished the same with the help of the profits that grew by plays there used before it was fully finished'.

In 1635, James Burbage's son, Cuthbert, recalled the original terms under which the actors were engaged. 'The players that lived in those first times had only the profits arising from the doors, but now the players receive all the comings in at the doors to themselves, and half the galleries.'

The first reference to The Theatre as a working institution came in an order of the Privy Council dated 1 August 1577, which refers to continuing concerns about the playhouses. It was ordered that letters[6] be sent to Lord Wentworth, the Master of the Rolls and 'Mr Lieutenant of the Tower',

> Signifying unto them that for the avoiding of the sickness likely to happen through the heat of the weather and assemblies of the people of London to plays, her highness's pleasure is that as the Lord Mayor hath taken order within the City, so they immediately … shall take order with such as are and do use to play without the Liberties of the Citee … as the Theatre and such like, shall forbear any more to play until Michaelmas be past at the least.

Raising funds was the top priority for The Theatre management. A sum estimated at around £700 had been expended on erecting the building and with its opening, costs would have been high. Part of this would have been offset by a lucrative trade in refreshments. James Burbage was the proprietor of an alehouse in nearby Holywell Street, which may have provided sustenance for thirsty playgoers.

A year after The Theatre opened, another playhouse – the Curtain – opened some 200 yards to its south. It was located close to a plot of land known as Curtain Close. Excavations have shown that the building was rectangular and a conversion from a previous tenement on the site. In 1585, Henry Lanman, its proprietor, made an agreement with James Burbage that his theatre should become a supplementary house, or 'teaser', to The Theatre.

A German traveller, Samuel Kiechel, who visited London in the autumn of 1585, described the playhouses, as having 'about about three galleries, one above the other'. Recent archaeological investigations of the foundations of London's early Elizabethan theatres has revealed that the thrust stage was probably tapered, wider at the back than at the front. The structure was not particularly robust. On 3 May 1583, the Lord Mayor wrote to Sir Francis Walsingham, warning of 'the perils of so weak buildings' as The Theatre, the Curtain 'and other like places'. It was a tenable viewpoint. In January that year, part of the seating had collapsed at the Bear Garden, killing a number of spectators. According to an Act of Common Council passed on 6 December 1574, such disasters were not infrequent.

Even the enemies of the playhouses regarded them as exotic places. 'Behold the sumptuous Theatre houses, a continual monument of London's prodigality', fumed the Anglican Divine, Thomas White, in *A Sermon Preached at Pawles Crosse, on Sunday the Thirde of November 1577*. The Revd John Stockwood referred to The Theatre as 'the gorgeous playing place erected in the Fields'.

Given Burbage's association with them, it is likely that Leicester's Men were the first permanent company to play at The Theatre. The documentary record is sparse, so it is difficult to discern what plays were performed and by which companies. That Richard Tarlton was one of its great draws is revealed by Sir

John Harrington in his *Metamorphosis of Ajax*, who states that the famous clown used the word 'prepuce' (foreskin), during a performance there in 1583. 'Which word was afterwards admitted with great applause by the mouth of Master Tarlton, the excellent comedian, when many of the beholders, that were never circumcised, had as great cause as Tarlton to complain of their Prepuse.'[7]

A member of the Earl of Sussex's Company, Tarlton was the greatest comic actor of the age. John Stowe eulogised about his 'wondrous plentifull pleasant extemporall wit',[8] adding 'hee was the wonder of his time'. 'Tarlton, so beloved that men use his picture for their signs', wrote a contemporary. By 1579, he had become a favourite of Queen Elizabeth. 'Our Tarlton was master of his faculty', wrote Thomas Fuller.

> When Queen Elizabeth was serious, I dare not say sullen, and out of good humour, he could un-dumpish' her at his pleasure. Her highest favourites would, in some cases, go to Tarlton before they would go to the Queen, and he was their usher to prepare their advantageous access to her. In a word, he told the Queen more of her faults than most of her chaplains, and cured hermelancholy better than all her physicians.

Years later, Henry Peacham recalled the effect of his first appearance on an audience:

> Tarleton when his head was only seen,
> The tire-house door and tapestry between,
> Set all the multitude in such a laughter,
> They could not hold for scarce an hour after.

Other early performers at The Theatre were Oxford's Men, which Edward de Vere, re-formed in 1580. He poached a number of players from the Company under the patronage of Ambrose Dudley, Earl of Warwick. The defection of the leading actors, John and Laurence Dutton and their fellows appears to have been resented by Dudley, despite his increasing infirmity and Puritan leanings. It also caused a stir in the wider world. A scurrilous verse circulated at Court, whose preamble reads: 'The Duttons and theyr fellow-players forsakying the Erle of Warwycke theyr mayster, became followers of the Erle of Oxford, and wrot themselves his COMOEDIANS, which certayne Gentlemen altered and made CAMOELIONS.'

Oxford's Men shared their patron's tempestuous habits. Soon after their re-formation, they got into a brawl with students from the Inns of Court while performing there. Several members of the Company were jailed, but were soon released.

Oxford persuaded two of the most powerful men in the nation, his father-in-law – the Queen's Chief Minister, Lord Burghley – and the Lord Chamberlain, the Earl of Sussex, to commend the Company to the Vice-Chancellor of Cambridge University, pending a four or five day tour there. Burghley's letter is dated 9 June 1580:

> Where the bearers hereof servauntes to the Right honorable my very good Lord the Erle of Oxford are desierous to repaire to that universitie and there to make shewe of such playes and enterludes as have bene by them heretofore played by them publykely, as well before the Queens majestie as in the Citie of London, and intend to spend iiij or v. daies there in Cambridg as heretofore they have accustomed to do with other matters and arguments of late yeres, and because they might the rather be permitted so to do without empeachment or lett of yow the vicechauncelor or other the heades of howses, have desired my lettre unto yow in their favor.

The authorities were not happy with the development in Shoreditch and a major public disturbance at The Theatre soon added to their concerns. On 21 February 1579/80, 'John Braynes of Shoreditch, yeoman, and James Burbage of the same parish', were summoned to appear before the Clerkenwell Sessions. They were charged with

> bringing together unlawful assemblies to hear and to see certain colloquies … called playes or interludes … at a certain place called the Theatre at Holywell in the county of Middlesex, by reason of which great affrays, assaults, tumults and quasi-insurrections and divers other enormities … were perpetrated to the danger of the lives of divers good subjects.

As so often happened with James Burbage, nothing seems to have come of the matter.

'Not a Turd for Conscience'

The complicated financial arrangements between Burbage and Brayne led to a falling out. Given the intense commitment each had to the project, this was, perhaps, inevitable. Brayne seems to have considered he should be indemnified for the money he had put into the project in excess of Burbage's contribution. Accusations flew back and forth. In the end, the two men agreed to take their disagreement to a Notary Public, but, when they appeared, they 'fell a reasoning together'. Brayne claimed that he had paid at least three times as much towards the project as Burbage. When he hinted that his brother-in-law was guilty of 'ill-dealing', Burbage struck him with his fist, 'and so they went together by the ears, in so much', declared the Notary, 'that this deponent could hardly part them'. When things had calmed down, they agreed to refer the matter to arbitration and each signed a bond for £200, pledging to abide by the decision.

The arbiters, John Hill and Richard Turnor, were 'men of great honesty and credit'. They summoned witnesses to the hearing in the Temple Church. On 12 July 1578 they delivered their verdict, 'having thoroughly heard' both sides. The profits from The Theatre should be used first to pay the debts on the building and then to pay Brayne the money he had spent above that spent by Burbage. Thereafter, the profits were to be shared 'in dividens equally concerning the said Theatre, that then the said James Burbage and the said John Brayne should *join* in pawning or mortgageing of their estate and interest of and in the same'. Such an occasion soon arose. On 26 September 1579, the two partners mortgaged The Theatre to John Hide for the sum of £125 8*s*. 11*d*. They were clearly short of ready money and had failed to meet the mortgage repayments, so the title of the property passed to Hide. There must have been some cleverly-worded clauses in the contract, for he was unable to take possession. Instead he was reduced to issuing warrants for the arrest of Burbage and Brayne. This put further pressure on the already tenuous relationship between the brothers-in-law. There can be little doubt that Burbage was ruthless in his dealings. When challenged about his behaviour, he replied that he cared 'not a turd for conscience'.[9]

Brayne's continuing obsession with the drama was demonstrated in 1580 when he took a twenty-four year lease on the George Inn at Whitechapel, in partnership with a City Alderman, Robert Myles. Perhaps he hoped that Myles' civic standing would help his cause. The reverse would prove the case.

In 1581, another serious threat to The Theatre's survival emerged. Its roots went back to the reign of Henry VIII. In 1544, following the Dissolution of the Monasteries, Holywell Priory had been granted to Henry Webbe, Gentleman Porter of the Tower of London. Sir Edmund Peckham proposed a match between his son George, and Webbe's only daughter and sole heir Susan, a *marriage de convenance* uniting wealth with social standing. Webbe made it a condition that George declare that he was marrying Susan willingly. When he did so, Webbe settled his property on his daughter and her heirs. A few months after their marriage, the Priory was sold for £533 6*s*.8*d*. to Christopher Bumsted, who mortgaged it to Christopher Allen and his son Giles for £600. On the death of his father, Giles Allen charged Bumsted with breaking the covenant. He was apparently seeking an opportunity to foreclose on the deal and in this he seems to have succeeded. It was a presager of things to come.

Susan Peckham died in December 1555, one day after giving birth to a son, who was named Edmund. In 1581, this Edmund took an extraordinary legal action, claiming that his father's sale of the property was invalid. According to Edmund, George had not married Susan willingly; nor was he married on the day allotted, and although Susan was the owner under the terms of the marriage agreement, she was never a party to the sale. He now claimed the return of the property, even finding a jury to agree with him. Burbage was again under threat. While, in an age of arranged marriages, the first two pleas would not have been taken too seriously, the third might prove telling. Peckham attempted to create facts by seizing the building, so Burbage 'was fain to find men at his own charge to keep the possession thereof from the said Peckham and his servants'. Things turned violent. Burbage was 'once in danger of his own life by keeping possession thereof'. He was obliged to keep guards on duty day and night to keep out Peckham's men. The aim was to terrorise the proprietors into submission – and it almost succeeded. Burbage was 'much disturbed and troubled in his possession of The Theatre, and could not quietly and peaceably enjoy the same'.

The campaign of physical coercion went beyond the proprietors to all involved. Such was the harassment that 'the players forsook the said Theatre', to Burbage's great loss. To offset this, he withheld £30 of the rental owed to Giles Allen. Naturally, this increased Allen's animosity. When Burbage sought to renew the lease in 1585, Allen claimed he had failed to carry out the £200 worth of repairs required under the original agreement. Burbage strenuously denied this and engaged three skilled artisans to survey the buildings and estimate what he had spent. They signed a declaration that at least £220 had been expended. Burbage then tendered 'Alleyn a new lease devised by his counsel, ready written and engrossed, with labels and wax thereunto affixed, agreeable to the covenant', but Allen still refused to sign, maintaining that the new lease was not a verbatim copy of the old one, that £200 had not been spent on repairs and that Burbage owed him rent. Although the latter claim was probably true, it represented considerable deviousness. Allen knew The Theatre was flourishing and wanted to increase the rent.

On 18 July 1586, Burbage engaged another six skilled artisans to estimate his expenditure. Their report was similar to the first. They estimated that £240 had been spent. Again Allen rejected the findings. Despite this rebuff, Burbage tried an irenic approach that was out of character. According to his son, Cuthbert, he 'did often in gentle manner solicit and require the said Gyles Alleyn for making a new lease of the said premises according to the purporte and effect of the said covenant', but Allen continued to prevaricate.

John Brayne died in June 1586, allegedly as a result of blows from Robert Myles, his partner in the George Inn enterprise. The Coroner's Court indicted Myles for murder, but he seems to have come out of the affair unscathed.

Things at The Theatre worsened after Brayne's death. John Hide, probably realising that it would be more difficult to deal with the stubborn Burbage alone, redoubled his efforts to collect the considerable debts owed him. He transferred the leasehold to his father-in-law, George Clough, whose fearsome reputation is confirmed by the fact that 'the said Clough … did go about to put the said defendant out of The Theatre, or at least did threaten to put him out'. After Burbage invoked the clause in the mortgage preventing his eviction, Clough embarked upon a campaign of harassment, paying visits to The Theatre 'diverse and sundry times'. This had its effects on performances and attendances, but Burbage continued to hold out.

The harassment paid off. It transpired that Burbage could cover the debt after all. He had allowed Brayne's widow to take half the profits of The Theatre. 'Then on a sudden he would not suffer her to receive any more of the profits there, saying that he must take and receive all till he had paid the debts.' He told Hide he would pay the debt if the title deeds were made out to his son, Cuthbert. The widow Brayne made the same offer if the deeds were made out to her. Hide stated that, since the deeds involved both parties, he could only deal with them jointly. This was sensible. To have settled with just one for the whole amount might have left him liable to a legal action by the other. He changed his mind when the money was still not forthcoming. In 1589, he declared that 'since he had forborne his money so long, he could do it no more, so as they that came first should have it of him.' Cuthbert Burbage brought the money immediately, together with a letter from Sir Walter Cope, Gentleman Usher to the Lord High Treasurer, the 1st Lord Burghley, requesting Hide to make over The Theatre to Cuthbert. In return he would use his influence with Butghley to Hide's advantage.

Cuthbert Burbage was baptised at St Stephen's, Coleman Street in the City of London on 15 June 1565. His brother, Richard, was baptised in the same church on 7 July 1568. In 1635, Cuthbert recalled that 'for 35 yeares paines, cost and Labour', Richard had 'made meanes to leave his wife and children, some estates'. This would mean that he made his stage debut around 1584. His acting talents must have been early recognised, but in the confusion of the theatrical record, it is impossible to delineate his progress. The first play in which he is known to have appeared was *The Dead Man's Fortune*. Although the text is lost, the stage plot, or 'platt' – the paper that was hung backstage to indicate to the actors when to respond to their cues – survives. Most actors are referred to by the names of the characters they played. Burbage's name appears after the third music cue as 'a messenger'. It seems curious that an actor who was to create so many great parts appeared in such a minor role.

Cuthbert was as essential to the Company's survival and progress as his famous brother. He possessed the acumen to keep the budgets balanced through good times and bad. This had been apparent from an early age. His father had found him a position with Sir Walter Cope, the writer of the letter, most likely as a clerk to the Treasury..

Villaines, Rascals and Knaves

There were reasons for attending the theatre other than to see the show. 'In the playhouses of London', Stephen Gosson wrote in *Plays Confuted in Five Actions* around 1581:

> It is the fashion for youths to go first into the yard and to carry their eye though every gallery, then, like unto ravens, thither they fly, and press as near to the fairest as they can .... They give apples, they dally with their garments to pass the time, they minister talk upon odd occasions, and either bring them home to their houses on small acquaintance, or slip into taverns when the plays are done.

Philip Stubbes considered that the encounters were not limited to the heterosexual, although how he knew what occurred between consenting adults in private is uncertain.

> Then these goodly pageants being done, every mate sorts to his mate, every one brings another homeward of their way very friendly, and in their secret conclaves (covertly) they play the sodomites, or worse. And these be the fruits of plays and interludes, for the most part.

Yet the new form of entertainment soon acquired at least quasi-respectability. It was given a huge boost in 1585 when Queen Elizabeth's Men were formed under Royal patronage. The Queen's Principal Secretary, Sir Francis Walsingham, was tasked with assembling the company. He did it with aplomb, using his influence to suborn leading actors. His greatest coup was to secure Richard Tarlton from Sussex's Men, but he also recruited leading actors from other companies, including Robert Wilson and two other long-standing members of Leicester's Men, John Laneham and William Johnson, John Adams, the leader of Sussex's Men and the brothers, John and Laurence Dutton from Oxford's Men. Due acknowledgement was made of their newly exalted status. 'They were sworn the Queenes servants, and were allowed wages and liyeries as grooms of the cham'r.' Others in the Company were John Singer and John Bentley – who was described by Thomas Dekker as 'inimitable'. Bentley was a poet of some note, although his works are lost, for Dekker describes him as 'a register to the Muses'. Another early star was William Knell, who created the part of the King in *The Famous Victories of Henry V* at the Bull in Bishopsgate. The play was a prototype for Shakespeare's Henrician trilogy, containing a number of the same scenes and characters. A description of the business is contained in the book *Tarlton's Jests*, published in 1600. The actor playing a judge was supposed to take a box on the ears from the King, but failed to appear. Tarlton, 'ever forward to please', took on the part, in addition to the main clowning role as Derick, a tailor. 'Knel, then playing Henry the fift, hit Tarlton a sound boxe indeed, which made the people laugh the more because it was he.

> Anon the judge goes in, and immediately Tarlton in his clownes cloathes comes out, and askes the actors, 'What newes?' 'O' saith one, 'hadst thou been here, thou shoudst have seene Prince Henry hit the judge a terrible box on the ear.' 'What man!' said Tarlton, 'strike a judge!' 'it is true, yfaith,' said the other. 'No other like,' said Tarlton, 'and it could not be but terrible to the judge, when the report so terrifies me that methinkes the blow remains stil on my cheeke that it burnes againe!' The people laught at this mightily.

Knell and Tarleton may be regarded as the first 'superstars' of the Elizabethan Theatre. Apart from his appearance in *The Famous Victories*, little is known of Knell except for his marriage, on 30 January 1586, to the 15-year-old Rebecca Edwards. His date and place of birth are unknown, but, it would appear he achieved celebrity at an early age. Thomas Heywood in his *Apology for Actors*, published in 1615, mentions him, with five others, who,

> since I never saw them, as being before my time, I cannot (as an eyewitness of their desert) give them that applause, which in no doubt, they worthily merit, yet, by the report of many judicial auditors, their performance of many parts have been so absolute, that it were a kinde of sinne to drown their worthe in Lethe, and not commit their (almost forgotten) names to eternity.

Thomas Nashe, in *Pierce Penniless* avowed that the talents of 'Knell, Tarlton, Edward Alleyn and John Bentley should be recognised throughout Europe as surpassing those of the famous actors of ancient Rome'.

The founding of the Queen's Men was a significant milestone in theatrical history. It was the first company employing a considerable number of actors – twelve leading players, 'hired men' playing smaller parts, and boy actors in the women's roles. Sussex's Men, by contrast, consisted of just six. This increase opened the way for the presentation of such plays as *The Famous Victories...*, which has twenty speaking parts in the first 500 lines. This, in its turn, opened the way for the dramas of Shakespeare's era.

The Queen's Men were given license to perform in two City locations: the Bel Savage and Bell Inns. The two other City theatres in inns – the Cross Keys and the Bull – were licensed at the same time. The Cross Keys and the Bell were indoor venues: the Bel Savage and the Bull, outdoor ones, so the Queen's Men anticipated the King's Men by two decades by providing winter and summer venues.

The rise of the drama was meteoric and remarkable. That the leading Elizabethan acting companies were highly professional and talented is evinced by the work they performed. Many roles require actors of the highest calibre. As well as acting, performers were skilled in fencing and dancing and probably singing and musicianship.

This so Infamous Art

The nascent theatre soon attracted the serious opponents who would eventually bring it down. It has been suggested that the implacable opposition of the Corporation of London to the staging of plays within its jurisdiction was due to its dominance by Puritans. There is no great evidence for this. Of the Lord Mayors between 1586 and 1613, Sir Richard Martin – who held the office in 1588 and 1594 – is clearly so definable. He and Dorcas, his wife, a translator of Calvinistic works, were active in such radical religious causes as the 'Admonition Controversy', concerning the wearing of vestments in worship. Sir Wolstan Dixie, Lord Mayor in 1585, endowed scholarships and fellowships at Emmanuel College, Cambridge, founded in 1584 by the Puritan, Sir Thomas Mildmay. He was no friend to the theatre, remarking that 'to play in plague time increases the plague by infection: to play out of plague time calls down the plague from God.' Sir Richard Saltonstall, Lord Mayor in 1597, was the uncle of his namesake, a founder of the Puritan Massachusetts Colony.

Yet, whatever the views of the incumbent, the tradition of 'the Lord Mayor's Show', on 8 November, was highly theatrical. The new Lord Mayor went to Westminster on his gilded barge. On his return, he was greeted with a series of pageants, often devised by such noted playwrights as Thomas Dekker, John Webster, Anthony Munday and Thomas Middleton. One of the earliest scenarios for such a pageant was written by the dramatist, George Peele, for the inauguration of Wolstan Dixie. On that day at least there was interchange between City and theatre.

A goodly selection of clerics, not all Puritans, opposed the theatre. To the Puritan preacher, John Field, the very presence of such arenas as playhouses was likely to produce a mini-apocalypse of God's judgement. In *A Godly Exhortation...*', a pamphlet addressed to the Lord Mayor and Magistrates', written after the collapse of scaffolding at the Bear Garden had caused widespread injury and death, he warned that due to the presence of 'these Heathyenishe Enterludes and Players...,

> surely it is to be feared, beesides the destruction bothe of bodye and soule, that many may be brought into, by frequenting the Theatre, the Curtin and such like, that one day those places will likewise be cast downe by God himselfe, and be drawen with them a huge heape of such contempurs and prophane persons utterly to be killed and spoyled in their bodies.

The most celebrated and effective of the Puritan assaults was contained in the *Anatomie of Abuses* by Philip Stubbes. He lambasted the stage in the chapter graphically entitled *Of Stage-Playes and Enterluds, with their wickedness*:

> Who will call him a wise man that playeth the part of a fool and a vice? Who can call him a Christian that playeth the part of a devil, the sworn enemy of Christ? Who can call him a just man that playeth the part of a dissembling hypocrite? And, to be brief, who can call him a straight dealing man, who playeth a cozener's trick? And so of all the rest. Away therefore with this so infamous art.

Here, in essence, is the Puritan objection to the theatre, a variation on the second commandment. 'Thou shalt not make unto thee any graven image.' It is a place where actors assume roles and emotions that are not their own and this was a form of idolatry. Most outrageous of all was the practice of boys dressing as women on the stage. In *Th' Overthrow of Stage Plays*, John Rainolds, warned of 'the filthy sparks of vice ... that ... the putting of women's attire on men may kindle in unclean affections'. The anonymous author of *The Rich Cabinet* inveighed on similar lines, despite his admiration of the actor's dexterity,

> Plaiers practises can hardly be warranted in Religion: for a man to put on womans apparel, and a woman a mans, is plaine prohibition ...

> ... Player hath many times, many excellent qualities: as dancing, actiuitie musicke, song, elloqution, abilitie of body, memory, vigilancy, skill of weapon, pregnancy of wit, and such like.

Thomas Heywood, made a robust defence of the boy actors in *An Apology for Actors*. 'To see our youths attired in the habit of women, who knows not what their intents be? Who cannot distinguish them by their names, assuredly knowing they are but to represent such a lady, at such a time appointed.'

It is difficult to calculate the level of spleen against the theatre that must have been uttered from pulpits in sermons that have not survived to posterity, but their influence was considerable. 'Amongst many other thinges tolerated in this peaceable and florishing State,' Heywood complained:

> It hath pleased the high and mighty Princes of this Land to limit the use of certaine publicke Theaters, which since many of these ouer-curious heads haue lauishly violently slandered, I hold it not a misse to lay open some few Antiquities to approue the true vse of them, with arguments (not of the least moment) which according to the weaknes of my spirit and infancy of my iudgment I will (by gods grace) commit.

There were those who defended eloquently the theatre on the grounds that the drama represented a morality. In *Pierce Penniless*, Thomas Nashe argued that plays are a way to escape from sins such as sloth and represent the triumph of virtue over vice:

> In plays, all cozenages, all cunning drifts over-gilded with outward holiness, all stratagems of war, all the cankerworms that breed on the rust of peace, are most lively anatomized; they show the ill success of treason, the fall of hasty climbers, the wretched end of usurpers, the misery of civil dissension, and how just God is evermore in punishing of murther.

Sir Thomas Overbury took up this theme in his *New Elegies*:

> By his action hee fortifies morall precepts with example; for what we see him personate, we thinke truly done before us: a man of deepe thought might apprehend the Ghosts of our ancient Heroes walk't againe, and take him (at severall times) for many of them

Although Nashe's plea that visits to the theatre kept men away from vices in which they might otherwise have indulged is somewhat unconvincing, it gives an insight into some of those constituting the audience:

For whereas the afternoon being the idlest time of day, whereas men that are their own masters (as gentlemen of the court, the Inns of Court and the numbers of captains and soldiers about London) do wholly bestow themselves upon pleasure, and that pleasure they divide (how virtuously, it skills not) either into gaming, following of harlots, drinking or seeing a play; is it not then better (since of four extremes all the world cannot keep them but they will choose one) that they should betake them to the least, which is plays?

The satirist, Samuel Rowlands, expressed the choice:

Speak gentlemen, what shall we do today?
Drink some brave health upon the Dutch carouse?
Or shall we to the Globe and see a play?
Or visit Shoreditch for a bawdy house?
Let's call for cards or dice, and have a game.
To sit thus idle is both sin and shame.

The theme was developed further by another satirist, William Goddard, whose analogy Stubbes would have endorsed:

Go to your play-house you shall actors have,
Your bawd, your gull, your whore, your pander knave.
Go to your bawdy–house, y'ave actors too,
As bawds, and whores, and gulls, panders also.
Besides, in either house (if you enquire)
A place there is for men themselves to tire.
Since th'are so alike, to chose there's not a pin
Whether bawdy-house or play-house you go in.

According to Thomas Dekker, prostitutes were so often in the theatre that they knew the plays word for word – 'every punk and her squire, like the interpreter and her puppet, can rant out by heart'. Thomas Platter, a 25-year-old Swiss visitor, noted the 'great swarms' of prostitutes frequenting the taverns and playhouses.

Large audiences, packed together, inevitably attracted criminal elements. The clown, Will Kempe, revealed what happened in the theatre when two such 'dy-doppers' were taken at Brentwood during his famous Morris Dance to Norwich.

The officers bringing them to my Inne, I justly denyed their acquaintance, saying that I remembred one to be a noted Cut-purse, such a one as we

> tye to a poaston on the stage, for all the people to wonder at, when at a play they ae taken pilfering.

It is unlikely that an actual performance would be disrupted by such rough justice. Most likely the malefactor would be held until the close of the play when he would be pelted with the refuse of the day.

John Davies, around 1595, commented on the diversity of the theatre audience:

> For as we see at all the play house dore
> When ended is the play, the daunce, and song,
> A thousand townsmen, gentlemen, and whores,
> Porters and serving men together throng.

At some point Stephen Gosson turned against the theatre, describing it as 'a generall Market of Bawdrie' and declaring that the players should be brought to account 'for the abuses that grow by their assemblyes'. In this, he was at one with the City Fathers. Indeed, his pamphlet, the gloriously-entitled *The Schoole of Abuse, conteining a plesaunt iniective Poets, Pipers, Plaiers, Iesters and such like Caterpillars of a Commonwaealth* .... was dedicated to the Lord Mayor, Sir Richard Pipe. As might be expected from a man who was considering taking Holy Orders, he considered that the theatre should be a moral force, in which it was largely failing. Yet he conceded that plays and players could have their merits. 'And as some of the Players are farre from abuse, so some of their Playes are without rebuke.'

Gosson anticipates the criticism that he was attacking the very institution in which he had once hoped to succeed. He hints that this hope was not fulfilled, which may have been a cause of his disillusion:

> If any man aske me why my selfe haue penned Comedyes in time paste, and inueigh so egerly against them here, let him knowe that *Semel insaninimus omnes*: I have sinned, and am sorry for my fault: hee runnes farre that neuer turnes, better late than neuer. I gaue my self to that exercise in hope to thriue, but I burnt one candle to seek another, and lost bothe my time and my trauell, when I had doone.

Despite this apparent, even if circumscribed, approbation for the drama, Gosson's movement towards a Puritan view of the stage is epitomised in his next published assault on the theatre, *Plays Confuted in Five Actions*, in 1582. He has modified his previous antipathy. Now it is morally permissible to read plays, but not so to see them performed:[10]

> If it should be Plaied, one must learne to trippe it like a Lady in the finest fashion, another must have time to whet his minde unto tyranny that he may give life to the picture hee presenteth, whereby they learne to counterfeit, and so to sinne. Therefore whatsoever such Playes as contein playd, without a manifest breach of Gods commaundement.... Action, pronuntiation, apparel, agility, musicke, severally considered are the good blessings of God, nothing hurtfull of their owne nature, yet being bound together in a bundle, to set out the pompe, the plaies, the inventions of the divell, it is abhominable in the sight of God, and not to be suffered among Christians.

The rebukes of the poet Edmund Spenser were somewhat different. He may have been the very first to regret, in literary form, the sentiment expressed in the title of the 1950s Cockney musical, *Fings Ain't Wot They Used T'Be*. In Spenser's view, the theatre wasn't what it was:

> O all is gone, and all that goodly glee,
> Which wont to be the glorie of gay wits,
> Is layd abed, and no where now to see;
> And in her roome vnseemly Sorrow sits,
> With hollow browes and greisly countenaunce,
> Marring my ioyous gentle dalliaunce.

What some believed to be a censure on The Theatre from an even higher source than the Clerkenwell Sessions came on 6 April 1580, with one of the most severe earthquakes recorded in England. The epicentre was somewhere off the Straits of Dover, but such was its power that its effects were felt in London. Chimney stacks and a pinnacle on Westminster Abbey came down. Two children were killed by stones falling from the roof of Christ's Hospital. The brief quake took place during theatrical performances. 'At the play-houses,' wrote Anthony Munday, 'the people ran forth surprised with great astonishment.' Philip Stubbes said that many were 'sore crushed and bruised', possibly in the panic to exit. The same theme was picked up by a contemporary ballad.

> Come from the Plaie,
> The House will fall so people saye,
> The earth quakes, lett us haste awaye.

Just six days after the earthquake, The Theatre was again under threat. On 12 April, Sir Nicholas Woodroffe, the Lord Mayor, complained to the Privy Council that 'some great disorder was committed at The Theatre' on the previous Sunday. This was the day of the earthquake, so it may relate to the crushing and bruising, or even to looting that followed the disturbance. Sir Nicholas sent his Under Sheriff to summon the players before him. He reveals that part of the motivation for the harassment of the playhouses was a sense of frustration on the part of the authorities that large numbers of people could assemble just beyond their jurisdiction. 'These playes doe make assemblies of citizens and their families of whom I have control,' he complained. On hearing that the House of Lords was considering the matter, he 'surceased to proceed', but could not resist firing a condescending and somewhat unctuous shaft at the actors:

> The players of playes which are used at the Theatre and other such places ... are a very superfluous sort of men, and of such facultie as the lawes have disallowed, and their exercise of these playes is of great hindrance to the service of God, who hath with his mightie hande so lately admonished us of our earnest repentance.

If James Burbage was one of those summoned before the Lord Mayor, he again escaped unscathed, but his enterprise was not unimpaired for long. On 13 May, following another outbreak of plague, the Privy Council ordered all playhouses closed until Michaelmas – throughout the vital summer months. To recompense for at least part of his losses, Burbage may have taken his company on tour. He possessed great resilience, performing as usual at Court during the Christmas Revels.

In a letter written on 28 July 1597, the Lord Mayor, Richard Saltonstall, revealed another reason for hostility to the theatre.

> Divers apprentices and other servants, who have confessed unto us that the saide Staige-playes were the very places of their randevous appointed by them to meete such others as wear to joigne with them in their designes and mutinous attemptes, being allso the ordinarye places for maisterless men to come together to recreate themselves.

Those in authority had good reason to be wary of large gatherings. In 1583, the Lord Mayor banned the then (and now?) unruly pastime of football, which involved hundreds of men chasing a ball through the streets. On this issue, William Shakespeare seems to have shared his distaste for the future national sport. In *King Lear*, the worst insult that Kent can hurl at Oswald is 'base football player'. Disturbances among the disaffected were frequent. Professor

Ian Frederick Moulton[11] estimates that there were thirty-five such outbreaks between 1581 and 1602.

The authorities clearly considered that this burgeoning scene had to be brought under control. A Royal Commission in 1581 gave the Master of the Revels, Edmund Tilney, extensive regulatory powers over the theatre. His office can be traced back to the medieval Court. As the name implies, its main function was the arranging of Court entertainments. Now it achieved greater significance. Tilney could license plays, acting companies and theatres. Before public performances could occur, scripts had to be presented to him. He could accept, refuse, or, edit them. All companies being considered for a performance at Court were required 'to presente and recite' before him the plays they were hoping to stage.

The Revels Office occupied the old Clerkenwell Priory of the Order of St John of Jerusalem. There were several rooms 'for artificers to work in together with a convenient place for rehearsals and setting forth of plays and other shows'.

'The Wonder of his Time'

Elizabethan clowns were noted for their dexterity in ad libbing, at which Richard Tarlton was the master. An anecdote in *Tarlton's Jests*, reveals that a little bawdy was inherent to his act:

> A Gentlewoman merrily disposed, being crossed by Tarlton and half angry, said, 'Sirrah, a little thing would make me requite you with a cuff.'
>
> 'With a cuff, lady?' said Tarleton. 'So would you spell my sorrow forward, but spell my sorrow backward, then cuff me and spare not.'
>
> When the gentlemen by considered of the word, their laughing made the simple meaning gentlewoman to blush for shame.

Tarlton was a skilled fencer. In 1585, he was admitted Master of Fence, the highest degree, to the School of Defence, a process that took fourteen years. He was one of five judges when another Master, James Cranydge, staged a bout at the Bel Savage Inn with nine separate opponents on 21 November 1587. 'A sundry variety of weapons' was employed: longsword, backsword, sword, rapier and dagger. The performance was a great success because it was repeated throughout the following January.

Regular fencing displays occurred at The Theatre. On 25 August 1578, 'Edward Harvie played his provost's prize…, at three weapons, the two-hand sword, the back sword, and the sword and buckler.'

Swordsmanship was not just a matter for plays and competitions, but an everyday skill for Elizabethan men. Audience would be cognisant of the finer points of the art and could have seen a demonstration of such exceptional skills in the very week a fight might be staged as part of a play. Tarlton's skills would have been employed in training his fellows and in devising the elaborate choreography to ensure that fights were both exciting and safe. He was famous for another talent – his legendary jig. This involved far more than dancing. Cross-dressing, singing, masks, extempore asides (frequently scurrilous) and slapstick were all part of it. It occurred at the end of the play. It could involve a number of performers and last up to twenty-five minutes.

The only surviving image of Tarlton shows him in jig mode. He wears his stock-in-trade country bumpkin cap and plays a pipe and tabor. His social status is reflected in his gentlemanly title – 'Mr Tharlton' [*sic*].

To Tarlton is attributed one of the most successful works of the day. The text of *The Seven Deadly Sins*, first produced around 1585, is lost, but this take on the morality plays of the previous generation was clearly a vehicle for his comic genius. It continued to attract audiences to The Theatre into the 1590s. The author was identified by Gabriel Harvey in 1592, as Tarlton's 'famous play of the seaven Deadly sinnes'. He was 'verie gently inuited thereunto at Oxford, by *Tarleton* himselfe, of whome I merrily demaunding, which of the seauen, was his owne deadlie sinne, he bluntly aunswered after this manner; By God, the sinne of other Gentlemen, Lechery.'

Her Majesties Poor Players

During 1584, an unnamed person described as the owner of The Theatre, claimed to be under the protection of Lord Hunsdon, a Privy Councillor. He had been the patron of small troupes of actors for some twelve years. Now The Theatre came under his patronage. That James Burbage was the 'owner' so cited is confirmed by Cuthbert Burbage. In his account of his brother Richard's stage career, he mentions that he had become an actor in the 'year that father declared himself to be Hunsdon's man'.[12]

Henry Carey was born in 1526, the son of Mary Boleyn and a courtier, Sir William Carey. Mary had been a mistress of King Henry VIII. On her death, he became the ward of her sister, the ill-fated Anne Boleyn. He was 10 years old when she was executed. There were thos1e who suggested that he was the King's son, but the affair was over at the time of his begetting. Even if he was not Queen Elizabeth's half-brother, he was certainly her cousin. She had raised him to the peerage soon after her accession. Such was her trust in him that she appointed him Captain of the Gentlemen at Arms, effectively her personal bodyguard, in 1564. He won her lasting gratitude for his part in the suppression of the Northern Rebellion in 1571.

The connection with Hunsdon was to be crucial to the future success of Burbage's Companies, not least on 18 June 1584, when Thomas Pullyson, the Lord Mayor, sent two Alderman to seek the permission of the Privy Council 'for the suppressing and pulling down of The Theatre and the Curtain. All the Lords agreed thereto saving my Lord Chamberlen and Mr Vice Chamberlen.' This followed a serious incident a few days before when a serving man named Brown 'did at the Theater quarrel with certain poor boys, handicraft prentices and struck some of them, and lastly he with his sword wounded one of the boys upon the left hand.' The incident drew a crowd of some 1,000 riotous people.[13] The Aldermen probably achieved more than they'd expected, obtaining an injunction suppressing all public dramatic performances. That evening, the Recorder, William Fleetwood, sent for the Queen's and Lord Arundel's Players and informed them of the injunction, which they agreed to obey. James Burbage was not present at this meeting and clearly the rival companies did not wish him to gain any advantage from his absence. 'The chiefest of Her Highness' Players advised me to send for the owner of The Theatre … and bind him,' wrote Fleetwood. The actor, who may have been Robert Wilson, warned that Burbage was 'a stubborn fellow'. As a former colleague in Leicester's Men, he would know him well. His assessment proved correct. Burbage refused to obey the summons, replying that 'he was Lord Hunsdon's man, and that he would not come to me, but he wold in the morning ride to my Lord'. Fleetwood realised that the dignity of the law was at stake and despatched the Under Sheriff to summons Burbage to his presence.

When the actor arrived, he was very short with the Recorder, but quietened down when he showed him Lord Hunsdon's name on the order. Despite this, Burbage was as stubborn as ever, declaring that he would rather die than be so bound. The Theatre was his creation and his livelihood. Its destruction was unthinkable. Fleetwood determined to send him to prison because of his refusal to be bound by the order but Burbage, whose career had given him a good knowledge of the law, said he had the right to appear in court. Fleetwood agreed to his request to go 'where he shal be sure to be bownd or else do worse. He was wrong about this, at least in the long term. The Theatre was saved, although by what means is unknown. Perhaps Burbage persuaded Hunsdon that he been unaware of what he was signing.

Nevertheless, the Lord Mayor was enabled to lay down highly-restrictive circumstances under which performances would be permitted:

> It is to be noted that it is not convenient that they present before Her Majestie such playes as have been before commonly played in open stages before all the basest assemblages in London and Middlesex, for their exercise and more for the place that ... they make their exercise of playing only in private houses. That they be not suffered from playing in the throng of a multitude, Also, it lyeth within the dutieful care of her Majestie's Royal person and of some infected, to presse so nere to the presence of her majestie.[14]
>
> That they hold them content with playing in private houses, at weddings etc., without public assemblie.
>
> That they play not openly till the whole deaths in London have been by 20 daies under 50 a weeke, nor longer shal it so continue.
>
> That no playes be on the Sabbath.
>
> That no playing be on Holy daies but after evening prayer, nor any received into the auditorye till after evening prayer.
>
> That no playeing be in the dark, nor continue nor continue any such time but as any of the auditorye till after evening prayer.

The restrictions had a disastrous effect on the Queen's Players and, doubtless, other companies. They were constrained to observe the regulations about the times they could perform, which excluded the Sabbath Day. It was probably around this time that they petitioned the Privy Council 'for the better helpe and relief in our poor lyvinge':

> The season of yere beyinge past to playe att any of the houses without the cittye of London, as in our articles annexed to this our supplication maye more at large appeere unto your Lordships. Our most humble peticion ys that yt maye please your Lordships to vowchsaffe the reading of these fewe Articles and in tender Consideracion of the matters therein mentioned, contayninge the verie staye and good state of our livinge to graunt unto us the confermacion of the same or of as manye or as much of them as shalbe to yor honors good lykinge. And therewith all your Lordships favorable letters unto the Lord Mayor London to permit us to exercise within the cittye according to the articles, and also that the said letters maye contayne some order to the Justices of Middlesex as in the same is mentioned, maybe wherbie as wee shall cease the continewell troublinge of yor Lordships for your often letteres in the premises, So shall wee daylie be bounden to praye of your Lordships in honor helthe and happiness long to cintinewe.
>
> Your Lordships most humblie bownden and dailie Orators
>
> Her Majesties poor Players

Again, the threat lessened. The Lord Mayor's attempt to dictate what the Queen could or could not see would not have gone well. Nor would would his effort to use the players' royal status as a weapon against them.

Life in the theatre was never easy.

Chapter Two

All Our Pageants of Delight

Great and Horrible Oathes

The Burbages' campaign of attrition won the day. Brayne's widow was legally excluded from any share in the ownership of The Theatre. Her attorney, Robert Myles (the alleged murderer of her husband!), deposed in 1592 that from henceforth Burbage 'would not suffer her to meddle in the premises, but thrust her out of all'. On 16 November 1590, armed with an order from the Court of Chancery in her favour, he called at the Burbages' house near The Theatre and, in a 'rude and exclamable sort', demanded 'the moiety of the said Theatre'. James Burbage, 'hearing a noise ... went to the door, and there found his son ... and the said Myles speaking loud together'. A heated argument ensued, until Burbage, provoked by Myles 'with great threats and words that he would do this and could do that', physically threatened him. Myles was unfazed by these threats. He soon returned, with a retinue of supporters including Margaret Brayne. They were met by Mistress Burbage, who 'charged them to go out of her grounds, or else she would make her son break their knaves' heads'. Aroused by the noise, her husband, looking out of a window, called the Widow Brayne 'a murdering whore' and her companions, 'villaines, rascals, and knaves'. When she spoke of the Court Order, 'he cryed unto her, ... "I will obey no such order, nor I care not for any such orders, and therefore it were best for you and your companions to be packing betimes, for if my son come he will thump you hence!' Just then Cuthbert Burbage arrived, 'and in very hot sort bid them get thence, or else he would set them forwards, saying "I care for no such order. The Chancery shall not give away what I have paid for."' After more 'great and horrible oathes' from the Burbages, their antagonists departed.

All was not over. Myles tried a new tactic. He, the widow, her son Ralph and his business partner, Nicholas Bishop, went 'to the Theatre upon a play-day to stand at the door that goeth up to the galleries ... to take and receive for the use of the said Margaret half of the money that should be given to come up into the said gallery'. They were met by Richard Burbage and his mother, who 'fell upon the said Robert Myles and beat him with a broom staff, calling him murdering knave'. Nicholas Bishop later deposed that when he protested at this contemptuous treatment of the Court Order, Richard Burbage, 'scornfully and disdainfully playing with this deponent's nose, said that if he dealt in the matter, he would beat him also, and did challenge the field of him at that time'. An actor arriving for the performance, John Alleyn, brother of the soon-to-be famous Edward, 'found the foresaid Richard Burbage ... there with a broom handle in his hand'. When he asked what the fuss was about, he replied 'in laughing phrase' that they came for a moiety, 'But,' he said, holding up the broom handle, 'I have, I think, delivered him a moiety with this, and sent them packing.' Alleyn warned that Myles could bring an action of assault and battery against them. 'Tush,' replied the father. 'I warrant you; but where my son hath now beat him hence, my sons, if they will be ruled by me, shall at their next coming provide charged pistols with powder and hempseed, to shoot them in the legs.'

Despite the Burbages continuing determination to defend what they considered theirs, the controversy was having its effect on the company. A witness in a legal action in 1592 recalled that 'James Burbage lost much money by that controversy and trouble, for it drove many of the players thence because of the disturbance of the possessor'.

Oxford's Boys

John Lyly's first act at Blackfriars was to place Henry Evans in charge. Presumably this was to give him time to write plays for 'Oxford's Boys'. His first effort was probably *Campaspe*, a romantic and euphuistic comedy set in classical times, which includes a characteristic debate between contending philosophers. It was presented at Court during the 1583/4 Christmas revels. Within three months, Lyly had written and produced *Sappho and Phao*, an elaborate allegory of Queen Elizabeth, full of flowery language, with a modicum of wit, but light on plot. A third play, *Gallathea*, demonstrates considerable dramatic development. It broke the mould by being set in a village on the banks of the Humber, although the names of the shepherds, Tyleres and Melebeus and their respective daughters, Gallathea and Phillada, are not ones normally associated with Humberside. Nor was the annual sacrifice of a virgin to appease the sea-god, Neptune, a custom generally observed in the ancient district of Lindsey. Yet Lyly pioneers an obvious ploy, which would be utilised by William Shakespeare. If the heroine is to be played by a boy, why not turn him back into a boy by the simple means of disguise? Gallathia/Tylerus II and Phillada/Melebeus II are the theatrical forebears of Rosalind/ Gannymede, Portia/Balthazar, Nerissa/Stephano and Viola/Cesario.

Gallathia was staged before the Queen by the Children of Paul's on 1 January 1587–8, but it was never performed at Blackfriars. Sir William More obtained a repossession order in June 1584, so Oxford's Boys had to vacate the premises. This was a setback, although they continued to perform.

The Little Rose

In 1587, Philip Henslowe built the Rose Theatre on Bankside, south of the river, the first to be constructed in the area that is most associated with the Elizabethan theatre. It was built on a messuage called 'The Little Rose' that Henslowe leased from St Saviour's parish. Little is known of its early years, but the Admiral's Men arrived there from The Theatre in 1591.

Henslowe's origins were humble. He is described as 'but a poor man ... servant unto one Mr Woodward'. His situation improved markedly when he married his master's wealthy widow. He probably used her legacy to take out the lease on the Little Rose. His motivation appears mainly financial, but it is unlikely that anyone would build a theatre without artistic interest in it.

At some point Edward Alleyn – who, together with Richard Burbage, became a leading actor of the day – became associated with Henslowe.

Alleyn was born in 1566, in St Botolph's parish, the son of the landlord of the Pye Inn in Bishopsgate. His father died when he was 4, and his mother remarried an actor named Brown. It may have been his stepfather who inspired 'Ned' to take to the stage. At the age of 16, he was with 'Worcester's Men', one of the earliest acting Companies. Under the patronage of William Somerset, 3rd Earl of Worcester, it had toured as early as the mid-sixteenth century. By 1587, Alleyn was 'a servant to the Lord Admiral', the company most associated with Henslowe's Rose. The huge demand for new plays and the commercial factors involved in commissioning them meant that the company tended to work in a markedly different way from that later adopted by the Lord Chamberlain's Men. To get plays onto the stage as quickly as possible teams of writers were employed, each writing a section.

An early such collaborator was Anthony Munday. He was baptised at St Gregory by St Paul's on 13 October 1560, the son of Christopher Munday, a stationer, and his wife, Jane. In 1576, he was bound apprentice to a stationer, but soon obtained his release. On his own account, he went abroad to see 'strange countreies' and learn foreign languages. He lived in the English Catholic Seminary in Rheims under an assumed name and later resided in the English College in Rome. It is unclear whether he was employed as a government spy or whether he used the knowledge he had gained to turn informer on his return. Certainly he capitalised on his experiences by publishing an account of his experiences entitled *The English Romayne Life*. His earliest play, *Fidele and Fortunio*, an Italianate comedy, was written in 1584, probably for performance by Oxford's Boys. He was to spend a great deal of time and energy seeking the Earl's patronage. A prolific author in various genres, including a number of virulently anti-Catholic pamphlets, he set the pattern of collaboration that Henslowe favoured, working with many authors over an extensive career.

Henslowe's single-mindedness in the pursuit of his interests and willingness to ignore the niceties of the law is revealed in an order of the Privy Council to the Justices of Surrey on 27 October 1587:

> Whereas the inhabitants of Southwark had complained unto their Lordships declaring that the order by their Lordships set down for the restraining of plays and interludes within that county on the Sabbath Days is not observed, and especially within the Liberty of the Clink, and in the Parish of St Saviours …

A highly significant development in theatrical history occurred in 1588. The Company under the patronage of Ferdinando Stanley, Lord Strange, which had been founded in 1564 as a troupe of jugglers and tumblers, began staging dramatic performances. This represents the foundation of the Company which, under various titles, became the most significant in theatre history. One of its earliest productions was *Fair Em, the Miller's Daughter of Manchester*. Of uncertain authorship, it has been attributed to Robert Greene, Robert Wilson, Anthony Munday and even William Shakespeare. The latter attribution is extremely unlikely, but it does feature a ploy he later favoured – that of the mistaken bed-partner. The play was popular. The undated first quarto states it was 'sundrie times publiquely acted in the honourable citie of London, by the right honourable the Lord Strange his seruaunts'.

In the absence of a direct heir to Queen Elizabeth, Ferdinando Stanley had a strong claim to the throne. Under the Third Act of Succession of 1543, his mother, the Countess of Derby, was heiress presumptive as the granddaughter of Henry VIII's sister, Mary.

Seven Deadly Sins

On the death of the Earl of Leicester in 1588, a number of his leading actors transferred to Lord Strange's Men. In 1590, the company became directly associated with the Admiral's Men. Whether this was an amalgamation or just a temporary alliance is unclear, but it brought together briefly, the great acting talents of Richard Burbage and Edward Alleyn. On 6 March 1592, Henslowe recorded that Lord Strange's Men performed 'Four Plays in One' at his Rose Theatre. This was a revival of the first part of Richard Tarlton's *Seven Deadly Sins* – i.e. four of the seven sins are featured. The natural follow-up was the second part, dealing with the other three, which might have been described as 'Three Plays in One'.

Although the text of both plays is lost, the 'platt' for the second part survives. It gives some indication of the actors who appeared and the parts they played. Tarlton is not in the cast, so the performances for which the platt was created presumably occurred after his death. Just three of the deadly sins – Envy, Sloth and Lechery – are personified in this production. The other four – Pride, Gluttony, Wrath and Covetousness – appear briefly at the opening of the play, but are pushed off the stage by the other Sins.

The fourteen men and six boys in the cast include a number of William Shakespeare's future colleagues. Richard Burbage appears in the prominent role of Gorboduc, but he is not the leading member of the Company. These were three actors who are graced with the honorific title of 'Mr': George Bryan, who played the dual roles of Warwick and Damascus; Thomas Pope, who played a character representing Sloth, and another named Arbactus.

Even then, Richard Burbage must have possessed rare dexterity as an actor. Not much more than 20 at the time, he plays a King with two grown-up sons, Ferrex and Porrex. In a scene anticipating *King Lear*, he abdicates his regal powers with disastrous consequences. The brothers quarrel and attempt to kill one another. The personified sin is Envy.

Ferrex is played by an actor referred to as 'Harry'. This may be the first mention of one of the future Company's greatest stalwarts, Henry Condell. If it is Henry, he would have been 16 years old in 1592. He was a Norfolk man. His will refers to family in New Buckenham. David Kathman has demonstrated convincingly that the Henry Condell baptised at the church of St Peter Mancroft in Norwich on 5 September 1576 was the actor.[1]

Nothing is known of the background of William Sly, who played Porrex. Like Richard Cowley, who played seven different minor roles in the production, he would become a sharer in the Lord Chamberlain's Men. John Sinkler (or Sinklo) played at least three parts, as well as featuring as a musician. He would appear in a number of companies, but mainly those associated with William Shakespeare. From the parts he played and other references, it is clear he was a notably skinny fellow.

The play features two dumb shows, with Lydgate as commentator. In the second, the unnamed boy actor playing Philomel enters, bearing 'Itis head in a dish'; Mercury also appears, presumably played by another boy actor. There was flamboyance in the costume department. Augustine Phillips first appears on stage as Sardanapalus, King of Assyria, 'with as many Jewels, robes and gold as he can carry'.

John Duke was with Shakespeare's companies as a hired man until 1602, when he joined Worcester's Men. He is not assigned a particular part. Perhaps he played King Henry VI or the poet John Lydgate, who were on stage throughout the performance.

An actor referred to merely as 'Kit', who plays a soldier in the Envy play and a Captain in the Sloth one, may be Christopher Beeston, another who would have a long career in the theatre. If so, he couldn't have been much more than 14 years old, but the Company as a whole was youthful, so a mature adolescent could have filled the bill.

One boy actor, named tersely as 'R. Go.', played Aspatia, the wife of Pericles, in the play called 'Sardanapalus', representing Sloth. This must be Robert Gough, who would have been aged around 12.

Another boy actor referred to merely as 'Nick' has been identified as Nicholas Tooley. If so, he would have been no more than 11 years old. He came from a very different background from most of the boy actors. His father was William Tooley, a Freeman of the Leathersellers' Company, whose dealings extended to Antwerp where he married the daughter of Hans Loquart, a wealthy and influential merchant. He died at his father-in-law's mansion in 1583, expressing a desire that his baby son be brought up in England and instructing his wife, Susan, to take him to live in London within ten months of his death. He clearly felt that his son needed more sureties in his boyhood than the care of his mother, who would be a foreign woman in an unfamiliar land. Guardianship of the boy was placed with the Court of Orphans of the City of London, according to their 'Lawdable vse and custom'. Susan soon provided the boy with a stepfather. On 14 January 1583/4, she married Thomas Gore, a member of another prominent merchant family, at the Church of St Stephen Walbrook. The rapidity of the match raises the possibility that her previous husband had arranged it on his deathbed to ensure that his widow and child were properly supported, hence his desire to get them to London. Within two years, Susan Gore was again widowed. On 16 December 1585, her husband was laid to rest in the church where he had been married. If Tooley had indeed intended that the Gore family should have a protective oversight of his young son, he chose well. Family members were assiduous in ensuring that 'Orphan Tooley' received his rightful inheritance.

A year after the death of her second husband, Mistress Gore married a third, Christopher Humfrey, a Freeman of the Grocers' Company. After his death, she married Roger Gwyn, her final husband, a prominent apothecary, who became Warden of the Grocers' Company. What became of young Nicholas during this succession of matrimonies is unknown, but it would appear his mother was happy for him to become a member of the Burbage family. In his last will and testament, four decades later, he leaves 'the somme of tenn poundes' to Cuthbert Burbage's wife, Elizabeth, 'as remembraunce of my love in respect of her motherlie care to me'. Cuthbert Burbage had married Elizabeth Cox, the daughter of John Cox, gentleman, on 8 July 1594 at St Mary-le-Strand. The couple were of comparatively mature years, the bridegroom 29, the bride, 26. Perhaps Elizabeth had been Nivholas's nanny. He began his career on the stage as Richard Burbage's apprentice.

Robert Tallant and John Holland were to feature in the Lord Chamberlain's Men and other companies. Most intriguing are the actors named as 'Ned' and 'Will'. Ned was the familiar name of Edward Alleyn. If this performance took place at the time of the temporary amalgamation of the companies, he could well have taken part. It is not impossible that the 'Will' was William Shakespeare, though it was more likely the famous comedian Will Kempe. Although it is not clear which part Tarlton played, another comedian would have taken it on.

The University Wits

A new wave of dramatists was emerging who had attended the universities of Oxford or Cambridge who were later to be dubbed the 'University Wits'.[2] Most senior was Robert Greene, who was born in Norwich around 1558. He was probably an innkeeper's son. He attended the local grammar school and St John's College, Cambridge. After doing the Elizabethan equivalent of the Grand Tour in Italy, he got married around 1585. His wife bore him a son, but he left her as soon as the marriage portion was spent. This prolific author was probably the first to make a living entirely from writing. Between 1583 and 1592, he published over twenty-five prose works. He was among the first writers to discover the commercial potential of descriptions of low life, to the extent that many contemporaries assumed, perhaps correctly, that he was recounting his own debaucheries. 'Glad was that printer,' wrote Thomas Nashe, 'that might bee so blest to pay him deare for the very dregs of his wit.' His plays were presented by Queen Elizabeth's Men at their two houses in the City. His comedy, *Friar Bacon and Friar Bungay*, was performed at Court in 1602, some thirteen years after its first staging. It introduced the concept of a multi-plot structure. Greene was a prolific writer for the stage, producing five plays in around five years. His *The Scottish Historie of James IV* appears to take up the historical themes which would be followed notably by Shakespeare, but it is a romantic comedy, remarkable for introducing the fairies taken up by Shakespeare in *A Midsummer* Night's Dream. It even includes an Oberon.

As well as reporting on contemporary vice, Greene was not beyond a little skulduggery himself. In his 1592 play, *The Defence of Conny Catching*, he accused himself of the very double-dealing of which he wrote:

> Aske the Queen's Players if you sold them not Orlando Furioso for twenty nobles, and when they were in the country sold the same play to the Lord Admiral's Men for as much more. Was this not plain conny-catching, R.G.?[3]

The History of Orlando Furioso, was loosely based on Sir John Harrington's translation from the Italian of Ludovico Ariosto's epic poem. Philip Henslowe's diary reveals it was performed at the Rose Theatre by Lord Strange's Men in February 1591/2, when that company was associated with the Admiral's Men. The lead part was played by Edward Alleyn. At the age of 25 he was coming into his ascendency. In the following year Thomas Nashe wrote in *Pierce Penniless* that 'not Roscius, nor Aesope, those admired tragedians that have lived ever since Christ was born, could ever perform more in action than the famous Ned Allen'.

Aside from Greene's alleged double-dealing, the play is notable for the fact that the part of Orlando is the only surviving example of an individual script. Rather than being given the entire text, actors just received their own parts. 'Good masters,' says Peter Quince, 'here are your parts, and I am to entreat you, request you, and desire you to con them by tomorrow night.' This was probably to frustrate attempts by stationers to publish pirated versions of plays. A number of such editions appear to be based on an individual actor's recall, rather than the entire text. The part was copied out from the author's manuscript by a scribe, but it has been amended by Alleyn. The quarto of 1594 differs considerably from that amended by Alleyn. This may be an example of a 'bad quarto', the material being provided by an actor or actors in the original production, or it may simply indicate that plays changed during the course of performance.

According to his Puritan adversary Gabriel Harvey, Greene's death was precipitate. On 3 September 1592, he overindulged in pickled herring and wine at his lodgings with a poor shoemaker in Dowgate Ward. He was tended by the shoemaker's compassionate wife and two other women, one of whom was the mother of his illegitimate son, Fortunatus. The other, 'Em' was 'a sorry ragged quean', a prostitute who was the sister of the notorious cutpurse, 'Cutting Ball'. Shortly before his death, Greene wrote to his misused wife about a bond for £10 he had given the shoemaker. 'Doll, I charge thee by the love of our youth and by my soul's rest that thou wilt see this man paid, for if he and his wife had not succoured me, I had died in the street.'

The best-known of the 'University Wits' is Christopher Marlowe. Born in 1564 – the same year as William Shakespeare – he came from a similar artisan background. His father was a member of the Guild of Shoemakers in Canterbury. He attended the King's School in that city and went up to Christ's College, Cambridge, in 1579. In the following year, he was awarded a six-year scholarship that had been endowed by a previous Master of the College and later Archbishop of Canterbury, Matthew Parker. It was implicit that the recipient should study for Holy Orders. That may or may not have been Marlowe's intention, but subsequent events demonstrated that he would not have been an ideal candidate for that vocation. His career assumes an air of mystery. It appears he was recruited into the extensive system of surveillance and espionage that had been established by Sir Francis Walsingham, although his role is uncertain. Secret agents by definition live in a twilight world. Whatever it was involved him leaving Cambridge for weeks on end. It was probably due to these prolonged absences that the Master of his College declined to award him a degree. The importance of his assignments was revealed when six members of the Privy Council wrote to the University requesting that he 'should be furthered in the degree he was to take'. He had,

> ever behaved orderlie and discreetlie whereby he had done her majestie good service and deserued to be rewarded for his faithfull dealing .... It was not her Majestie's pleasure that anie one employ'd as he had been in matters touching the benefit of his countre should be defamed by those that are ignorant in th' affaires he went about.

Marlowe's scholarship made him worthy of the degree. He translated the first book of Lucan's *Pharsalia* and Ovid's *Elegies* into English. Yet nothing known of his life comes from himself, but from the hostile statements of his enemies, or those disapproving of his attitudes and morals. Yet their consistency is a statement in itself. Three strands abound: he was a government agent, a homosexual and a militant atheist.

The first of Marlowe's works for the stage was probably *Dido, Queen of Carthage*. Its source was the *Aeniad*, but he already shows discernment in the use of his material, adding and deleting scenes to Virgil's work. It also demonstrates the homoerotic tendencies that emerged in *Edward II* and *Hero and Leander*. According to the quarto published in 1594, it was performed by the Children of the Chapel Royal. Authorship is attributed to Marlowe and Thomas Nashe, but the extent of the collaboration is difficult to gauge. They could have known each other at Cambridge. Nashe graduated from St John's College in 1586, two years after Marlowe. Whatever his contribution may have been, it ranks among the earliest of his works to be published. He was to become the most influential pamphleteer of the era, while dabbling with the theatre. He also purveyed such witty pornography as his erotic poem, *The Choise of Valentines*. It was not published in his lifetime, but was dedicated to 'Lord S'. (Strange? Southampton?) so it was probably written in the hope of patronage. Copies must have circulated extensively because he was rebuked for writing such a lewd work, notably by the future Bishop of Norwich, Joseph Hall, and the poet, John Davies. His response was to be echoed by others over the centuries. He needed the money.

> When … the bottom of my purse is turnd downeward, & my conduit of incke will no longer flowe for want of reparations, I am faine to let my Plow stand still in the midst of a furrow, and follow some of these new-fangled *Galiardos* and *SeniorFantasticos*, to whose amorous *Villanellas* and *Quipassas* I prostitute my pen in hope of gaine.

The success of *Dido, Queen of Carthage* seems to have brought Marlowe to the attention of Philip Henslowe. The two parts of *Tamburlaine the Great, Dr Faustus* and *The Jew of Malta* were first performed at his Rose Theatre. As the leading actor in the Admiral's Men, Edward Alleyn would have created the title roles. His close ties with Henslowe were further cemented on 22 October 1592, when he married Joan Woodward, the impresario's stepdaughter. He shared his father-in-law's entrepreneurship. In 1594, he bought the lease of the Bear Garden for £200, 'There be the two Beare-gardens,' wrote John Stowe in 1598, 'the old and new places wherein be kepte Beares, Bulles, and other beastes, to be bayted. As also Mastiues in seurall kenels are there nourished to bait them. These Beares … are … bayted in plottes of grounde, scaffolded about for the beholders to stand safe.'

Theatrical performances took place at the Bear Garden as well as blood sports. Such was the growing popularity of the drama that a law enacted in 1591 closed all theatres on Thursdays to give animal-baiting spectacles the opportunity to gain a sufficient audience.

With the two parts of *Tamburlaine the Great*, Marlowe bursts onto the theatrical scene. Although they incorporated the *grand guignol* element so beloved of Elizabethan audiences, they possessed an unprecedented vigour of language. The Prologue to Part One is an inspirational explosion of blank verse.

> From jigging veins of rhyming mother wits,
> And such conceits as clownage keeps in pay.
> We'll lead you to the stately tent of war;

The influence on contemporary drama was huge, although there were critics from the first. Robert Greene, in his preface to *Perimedes the Blacksmith*, delivered an oft-repeated theme, accusing Marlowe of 'daring God out of heaven with that Atheist Tamburlaine or blaspheming with the mad preest of the Sonne'. The criticism is underwritten by Gabriel Harvey, in *A New Letter of Notable Conceits*, in 1593:

> The graund Dissease disdain'd his toade Conceit,
> And smiling at his tamberlaine contempt,
> Sternely struck-home the peremptory stroke.
> He that nor feared God, nor dreaded Diu'll,
> Nor ought admired, but his wondrous selfe:

A related criticism to such charges of idolatry and egotism was that Marlowe's plays lack humanity: in his *Timber: or, Discoveries*, Ben Jonson criticised 'the Tamerlanes and Tamer-chams of the late age, which had nothing in them but the scenical strutting and furious vociferation'.

Such criticism may be applied to another of Marlowe's highly-successful plays, *The Jew of Malta*, in which he follows a contemporary stereotype of Jews – that they dabbled in poison. 'As for myself,' says Barabbas, the Jew, 'I walk abroad a-nights / And kill sick people groaning under walls / Sometimes I go about and poison wells.'

Given Marlowe's apparent militant atheism, *Dr Faustus* seems a curious choice of subject. This Germanic legend of the learned doctor who sells his soul to the Devil in return for worldly knowledge and pleasure first appeared in an English translation in 1592. *The History of the damnable life, and deserved death of Doctor Iohn Faustus* by one 'P.F., Gent' is the likely source. The nature of repentance and redemption is an important theme. A good and a bad angel compete for Faustus' soul. In selling his soul to the Devil, has Faustus forsaken any hope of redemption? The issue was germane to contemporary religious debate and would have been grasped by the audience in a way that few today would comprehend. The rising force of Puritanism espoused Calvinistic doctrine, which included the concept of predestination – that salvation was reserved for an 'Elect' and whether a soul went to Heaven or Hell was predetermined. The doctrine had a strong following in Marlowe's university. He would have been familiar with the name, if not the person, of William Perkins, an eminent Puritan divine and Fellow of Christ's College at the time he was at Cambridge. Perkins was an advocate of the Calvinistic doctrine of 'double predestination': the belief that some people actively choose damnation. Faustus is condemned by his rejection of the path to redemption:

The reward of sin is death? That's hard.
Si peccasse negamus, fallimur, et nulla est in nobis veritas
If we say that we have no sin,
We deceive ourselves and there is no truth in us.[4]

He exercises necromancy to summon devils:

Why then belike we must sin,
And so consequently die.
Ay, we must die an everlasting death.
What doctrine call you this? *Che sarà, sarà!*
What will be, shall be! *Divinity, adieu!*
These metaphysics of magicians,
And necromantic books are heavenly!

The play caused a huge sensation. It was widely believed that the necromancy scenes could summon devils to the stage. In his *Histriomastix*, the Puritan polemic published in 1632, William Prynne claimed that this occurred during a performance at the Bel Savage Inn in 1604, 'to the great amazement of both the actors and spectators, an event so horrifying' that several members of the audience were driven 'distracted with that fearful sight'.

A similar manifestation supposedly occurred 'while certain players at Exeter[were] acting on stage the tragical story of Dr Faustus the conjurer'. A person referring to himself as G.J.R. recorded the incident, although it appears he was not present himself:

> As a certaine number of Devels kept everie one his circle there, and as Faustus was busie in his magical invocations, on a sudden they were all dasht, every one harkning other in the eare, for they were all persuaded there was one devell too many amongst them; and so after a little pause desired the people to pardon them, they could go no further with this matter; the people also understanding the thing as it was, every man hastened to be first out of dores. The players (as I heard it) contrary to their custom spending the night in reading and in prayer got out of the town the next morning.

Indications of the stage effects in such a production were given by John Melton in *The Astrologaster* of 1620:

> Men go to the Fortune in Golding Lane to see the Tragedy of Dr Faustus. There indeed a man may behold shag-haired devils roaring over the stage

> with squibs in their mouths, while drummers make thunder in the tiring house and … the twelve penny hirelings make artificial lighting in their heavens.

The satirist, Samuel Rowlands, gave a curious indication of Alleyn's costume.

> The gull gets on his surplus,
> With a crosse upon his breast,
> Like Allen playing Faustus,
> In that manner was he dressed.

Perhaps we are looking at the penitent Faustus attempting to escape his inexorable damnation.

It is difficult for a modern audience to envisage the effect scenes of necromancy and incantation would have had on the Elizabethans. These were not imagined terrors, but concrete realities. Around the time of the first production of *Dr Faustus*, King James VI of Scotland sailed to Denmark to bring back his bride, the Princess Anne. On the return voyage, the fleet was scattered by storms. Convinced that this natural phenomenon was caused by witchcraft, he had some seventy suspects arrested. On 23 July 1590, Robert Bowes, the English Ambassador, reported that 'it is advertised from Denmark that the admiral there hathe caused five or six witches to be taken in Coupnahaven, upon suspicion that by their witche craft they had staied the Queen of Scottes voyage into Scotland and sought to have staied likewise the King's returne'. On 28 November, he further wrote: 'The King and Counsaill is occupied with the examinaciouns of sundry witches taken in this conttye, and confessing both nombers and also strange and odiouse factes done by them.' Many confessed under torture, a procedure on which Portia (or Shakespeare) had a view.

> Ay, but I fear you speak upon the rack
>   Where men enforcèd do speak anything.

An account of the North Berwick witch trials appeared in London, as *Newes from Scotland*. It is likely William Shakespeare obtained a copy. The witches' rituals and language in *Macbeth* mirror the confessions of the accused at North Berwick. The invocations of the First Witch recall the voyage of King James. 'Though his bark cannot be lost, / Yet it shall be tempest-tossed.'

Hotspur (or Shakespeare) was sceptical on the issue.

Glendower: I can call spirits from the vasty deep.
Hotspur: Why, so can I, so can any man,
But will they come when you do call for them?

The best-known dramatic representation of necromancy occurs in *Dr Faustus*. The eloquence of Marlowe's verse is typified in the scene where Faustus encounters Helen of Troy. He has selected to have carnal knowledge of this beauty summoned from the depths by 'Mephistophilis', a demon he has invoked:

> Was this the face that launch'd a thousand ships
> And burnt the topless towers of Ilium?
> Sweet Helen, make me immortal with a kiss.
> [kisses her]
> Her lips suck forth my soul: see, where it flies!
> Come, Helen, come, give me my soul again.
> Here will I dwell, for heaven is in these lips,
> And all is dross that is not Helena.

Tamberlaine, Barabbas the Jew and Faustus are characters beyond the moral norms, who prey on the society they blame for their condition. Marlowe may have been such a man. He had a history of violence. On 18 September 1589, he engaged in a sword and dagger fight in Hog Lane with a man called William Bradley. His friend and fellow poet, Thomas Watson, intervened and stabbed Bradley to death. The two men were arrested on suspicion of murder. At their trial on 3 December at the Middlesex Sessions, it must have been decided that they struck in self-defence, for they were discharged with an order to keep the peace. Further troubles followed. On 9 May 1592, Allen Nicholls, the Constable, and Nicholas Elliott, the sub-Constable, of Holywell Street in Shoreditch, appealed for protection from Christopher Marlowe, who was bound over to keep the peace in the huge sum of £20. On 15 September, he allegedly attacked a local tailor, William Corkine, with a stick in his native Canterbury. Five days later the tailor sued for damages of £5. The outcome is unknown.

Nor is Marlowe diffident about homosexuality, despite the fact that sodomy carried the death penalty under an Act of 1563. 'Here the curtains drawn', read the stage directions for the opening scene of *Dido, Queen of Carthage*, 'there is discovered Jupiter dandling Ganymede upon his knee.' His uncompleted narrative poem *Hero and Leander* is laden with such themes. 'In his looks,' he wrote of Leander, 'were all that men desire.' As he swims to visit Hero, he provokes the lasciviousness of the sea god, Neptune.

The lusty god embraced him, call'd him 'Love'...
He clamped his plump cheeks, with his tresses played.

By the end of the 1590s, a reaction had set in against Marlowe's vigorous language. Shakespeare parodies Tamburlaine's bombast in the character of Pistol in *Henry V*.

O braggart vile and damned furious sight!
The grave doth gape, and doting death is near.
Therefore exhale.

The Turk Play

The two parts of *Tamburlaine the Great* are early examples of the genre known as the 'Turk Play', which portrayed ruthless eastern rulers who rose to power in a sea of blood, devoid of mercy or integrity. The Turks were regarded as a continuing threat to western Christendom. Thus these somewhat extravagant dramas often concerned the conflict between Christianity and Islam, 'Turk' being virtually a generic term for a Moslem. Something of the heritage of hostility to Islam which was a feature of the medieval drama may be seen in this. In the Turk Plays, tales of derring-do saw heroes defeating the Saracens in remarkable feats of combat. Such plays tended to be presented at theatres like the *Red Bull*, where the audience appreciated their rumbustious qualities. The heroic character of 'Great Edward Longshanks' in George Peele's *The Famous Chronicle of King Edward I* of around 1592, is demonstrated by reference to his deeds in the Holy Land in the opening scene:

...That famous prince of Wales
Who at Damasco beat the Saracens
And broughtst home triumphs on thy launces point.

A feature of the 'Turk plays' is that the heroes are virtually all Catholics. This is inevitable, given it was the Catholic powers that stood as the bulwark of Western Christendom against the Turks, but it meant that Catholics – who, domestically, were officially regarded as subversive of the state – in the wider scheme were regarded as saviours of civilisation. Such was the case with Sir Thomas Stukeley. Reputedly an illegitimate son of Henry VIII, this noted adventurer had served in Ireland. Having persuaded Queen Elizabeth to equip six ships to found a colony in Florida, he turned privateer and raided commerce off the coast of Munster. Fleeing to Spain, he aligned himself with the Catholic cause and sought to raise an army to invade Ireland. He commanded a squadron at the decisive naval victory of the Holy League over the Turks at Lepanto. He later joined King Sebastian of Portugal in a disastrous invasion of Morocco. Both were killed at the Battle of Alcazar against the Moors. In death, he became an English folk-hero. His treasonous activities were erased from the historic account and ballads were composed in his honour. In the play, the Spanish King, Philip II, remarks of him:

> If England have but fifty thousand such
> The power of Spain their coast shall never touch.

Alcazar was regarded as a brave attempt to stem the advance of Islam. The fall of King Sebastian was a highly pertinent issue because it enabled England's arch-enemy, Philip II, to 'usurp' Portugal's throne. The dramatic version of these events, generally attributed to George Peele, was published in 1594 as *The Battel of Alcazar, fought in Barbari betweene Sebastian king of Portugall, and Abdelmelec, king of Morocco*. The sub-title is *With the Death of Thomas Stukeley*, and he is given a long speech in which he recounts his life. In 1596, he was the subject of a play bearing his name. Philip Henslowe probably referred to the anonymous play, *The Famous historye of the life and death of Captaine Thomas Stukeley With his marriage to Alderman Curteis Daughter, and the valiant ending of his life at the Bataile of Alcazar* on 8 December 1596 when he paid 3/- 'for stewteleyes hosse'. Three days later, he noted the Admiral's Men had performed a new play called 'Stewtley'. It proved highly popular, running to at least ten performances, the last recorded on 27 June 1597. It was entered onto the Stationers' Register on 11 August 1600, although it was not published until five years later. This quarto may not entirely reflect the play that Henslowe originally presented, although it demonstrates the scale of the production. It presents a huge geographical sweep and a plethora of fifty-three speaking parts, as well as many walk-on roles, although there would have been much doubling. The American critic John Quincy Adams jr regarded it as 'an excellent drama of adventure, celebrating the career of one of the most daring soldiers of fortune known to the Elizabethan age'.[5]

There was huge interest in Sebastian, whose fate Stukeley, had shared. This was enhanced by the appearance in Venice in 1598 of a man claiming to be the supposedly dead King. Sebastian who had been succeeded by his great uncle, Henry, the Cardinal Archbishop of Braga, who died without issue after seeking a papal revocation of his vow of celibacy. On his death, Dom Antonio, the illegitimate son of Sebastian's brother, the Duke of Beja, seized the throne,

He too had fought at Alcazar but had survived by subterfuge. He was captured and held to ransom, but released after persuading his captors he was of no value.

Dom Antonio was ousted after a reign of just twenty days by Philip II, who had a genuine dynastic claim. He provided a useful foil against the Spanish for the French and English. The play of Stukeley takes up the cause of Antonio. He is declared to have been killed, but the possibility of his survival is posited. 'Suppose the soldiers who you saw surprised,' announces the Chorus, 'The poor dismayed prince Antonio / Have sold him to the wealthy Moore they talked of.'

A now-lost book, *Strange newes of the Retourne of Don SEBASTIAN Kinge of Portugal*, was entered on the Stationars' Register on 1 February 1599. It tells the story of the supposed return of the lost monarch. Another book on the topic, a translation by Anthony Munday of *The Strangest Adventure that Ever Happened* by a Dominican friar, José Teixeira, was published in 1601. Henslowe again saw the potential. On 18 April 1601, he paid 70 shillings 'unto Thomas deckers & harey chettell in earneste ... of a Boocke called kinge sebastiane of portugalle'. This was the down-payment. On 16 May, he paid them a further 40/-. Six days later, he made a final payment to Dekker of £3 'at the a poyntment of E Alleyne'. At 35 years old, his son-in-law could well have played the 24-year-old King.

The most extra-ordinary of the Turk plays is *The Tragedy of Soliman and Perseda*, which is set around the Turkish conquest of Rhodes in 1523. It is a full rendering of the play-within-a-play in *The Spanish Tragedy*. It may have been written by Thomas Kyd in response to that play's popularity. All the elements – betrayed young lovers and a ruthless and treacherous Islamic conqueror are expressed in the full title of the play, as published in 1592: *Tragedie of Soliman and Perseda, wherein is laide open Love's Constancy, Fortune's Inconstancy and Death's Triumphs*. The personified characters of Love, Fortune and Death act as Chorus.

Kyd was among the most successful of the new wave of playwrights. Born in London in 1558, the son of a scrivener, he attended the newly founded Merchant Taylors' School. Edmund Spenser and Thomas Lodge were among his fellow pupils. He may have worked as a pamphleteer and translator, but nothing is known of his progression into the world of theatre. At some time in the 1580s he created a sensation with his *Spanish Tragedy*, arguably the most popular play of the era, which established the cult of the revenge tragedy, based on Senecan models, but referring back to the morality plays through the personification of Revenge, whose representation of an acceptable reaction to a visited atrocity is expressed in the simple statement of the leading character, Hieronimo – *Vindicta mihi* – 'Vengeance is mine'. That Richard Burbage created this part is evidenced in the undergraduate play, *Return To Parnassus*. 'I think your voice would serve for Hieronimo,' Burbage tells a 'scholar', 'observe how I act in it, and then imitate.' 'Old Hieronimo' is listed as one of his parts in an anonymous valedictory poem of 1619. The influence of *The Spanish Tragedy* is evidenced by the number of contemporary writers referring to it. It influenced William Shakespeare, particularly in *Hamlet*, with which it shares a ghost, a play-within-a-play and a character called Horatio. In the Induction to *Bartholomew Fair*, written in 1614, Ben Jonson refers to it as 'five and twenty or thirty' years old, which would mean it was first performed at some point between 1584 and 1589.

Thomas Kyd is often cited as the probable author of the lost play, known to scholars as the *ur-Hamlet*.[6] Thomas Nashe makes a punning reference to 'Kidde' in his Preface to Greene's *Menaphon* in which he refers to the play:

> Yet English Seneca read by candlelight yields many good sentences, as 'Blood is a beggar' and so forth, and if you entreat him faire in a frosty morning, he will afford you whole Hamlets, I should say handfuls of tragical speeches.

He further states that English imitators of Seneca 'imitate the kid in Aesop'. It is significant that, as early as 1587, he considered Senecan revenge tragedy a declining force. The phrase 'Blood is a beggar' must be quoted from the *Ur-Hamlet*. One other line survives in *Wit's Misery and the World's Madness*…, a pamphlet by Thomas Lodge which reveals where the play was performed. He mocks a character 'who walks for the most part in black under cover of gravity, and looks as pale as the vizard of the ghost who cried so miserably at the Theatre like an oyster wife, *Hamlet, revenge*!' It is noteworthy that the leading character in the *Ur-Hamlet* established the tradition that Hamlet be dressed in black. He also gives a clue to the appearance of the ghost. A vizard is a mask, so the spectre would have the paleness of a corpse. The popularity of the play is indicated by the fact that two leading writers freely refer to it without feeling it necessary to explain the allusion. There may have been at least one other version based on *Ur-Hamlet*. In *Satiromastix*, Thomas Dekker alludes to Ben Jonson acting in a play called *Hamlet's revenge*, in which he 'ranst mad at the death of Horatio'.

Around 1591, Kyd seems to have retired, at least temporarily, from the theatre and become the secretary to a great nobleman, probably the Earl of Sussex. At the time, he shared lodgings with Christopher Marlowe: an arrangement that would have disastrous consequences.

At some point – it is impossible to do more than speculate when – a promising and aspiring young man arrived in London from the provinces. William Shakespeare must have appeared on the theatrical scene some time after 1584, when he was engaged back in Stratford-upon-Avon in begetting twins with his wife, Anne. Hopefully, he was still around when they were born, on 24 February 1584/5. Why he left Stratford is unclear. Popular legend says he fled to escape the wrath of the local magnate, Sir Thomas Lucy. Professor Mark Eccles discovered that the Queen's Men were two actors short when they arrived in Stratford in 1587; their leading actor, William Knell, had been killed by his fellow, John Towne, during a brawl at Thame, in Oxfordshire. Towne was arrested, but, since he had struck in self-defence, was later pardoned.[7] In the meantime, had his place been taken by a young man of theatrical enthusiasm from Stratford-upon-Avon? He must have possessed some dramatic experience. It is likely that his first essays into acting occurred at school. There are records of plays being performed at St Paul's, Merchant Taylors, Eton and Westminster Schools. It is likely that the same happened at Stratford. Ben Jonson mentions the vogue of the school play, in the context of the Latin-dominated curriculum in his *Staple of News*:

> They make all their scholars play-boys. Is't not a fine sight to see all our children made interluders? Do we pay our money for this?
>
> We send them to learn their grammar and their Terence and they learn their playbooks.

It is an engaging thought that Richard Tarlton might have been with the Queen's Men when they visited Stratford. Many of the leading acting companies passed through the town during William Shakespeare's youth. The Stratfordians were not always spectators. In 1593, 13/4d was paid to 'Davi Jones and companye for his pastyme at Whytsontyde'. David Jones was a saddler, whose second wife was a cousin of Anne Hathaway. Did William Shakespeare, aged 19, take part in this performance at the Corporation's annual feast? His daughter Susannah was born in the same month, so it is likely that he was in Stratford 'at Pentecost,

> When all our pageants of delight were played.
> Our youth got me to play the woman's part
> And I was trimm'd in Madame Julia's gown,
> Which served me as fit, by all men's judgements.
> … I did play an honourable part,
> Madam. 'Twas Ariadne passioning
> For Theseus' perjury and unjust flight,
> Which I so acted with my tears,
> That my poor mistress, moved there withal,
> Wept bitterly.

John Aubrey gives a further clue to the poet's youthful dramatic activity. He makes the dubious claim that the young William was apprenticed to a butcher and 'when he killed a calf he would do it in high style and make a speech'. This curious tale gains credence with the knowledge that 'Killing the Calf' was a popular charade, played behind a curtain, in which the performer acted the parts of both butcher and beast.

William Shakespeare first emerges in London as the result of an attack on him, supposedly by Robert Greene, in 1592, but, by then, he was a successful dramatist. What his initial role in the theatre may have been is unknown. A story that was first written down in 1753, but which had something of a pedigree, claimed that he was employed in holding the horses of playgoers. Whether this unlikely tale be true or not, it suggests he had an early association with the theatre. Certain it is that he was an actor before he became a playwright. In the attack on him attributed to Robert Greene, he is described as such. In view of his subsequent association with the Burbages, there can be little doubt that one of the venues in which he performed would have been The Theatre. Nor is it clear with which acting company he was first associated. That actors and plays moved easily between the various companies is borne out by the first quarto edition of his early play, *Titus Andronicus*, which states that it had been played by 'the Right Honourable the Earle of Darbie, Earle of Pembrooke and the Earl of Sussex their servants'.

The Earl of Derby in question was Ferdinando Stanley. The Company's name had changed with his accession to the title in 1594. Since William Shakespeare's name appears as a playwright whose works Derby's Servants performed, it is reasonable to speculate that he might have been involved with them as an actor. The company included a number of those with whom he would be closely associated.

We do not know the process by which William Shakespeare was transformed from actor into actor/playwright. Clearly his writing abilities would have soon been recognised. His earliest known literary output was in the classical mode that was deemed the theatrical norm. *Titus Andronicus* is a Senecan tragedy full of blood and gore. To most modern theatregoers it is little more than a ghastly period piece, rarely performed, mainly of interest because of its authorship. Yet it was in the style of its time and it is an indication of Shakespeare's creative genius that he realised that there were better ways than slavish adhesion to the classics. The indication of the dating of *The Spanish Tragedy* in the Induction to *Bartholomew Fair*, also serves for *Titus Andronicus*. The *Ioronimo* mentioned by Jonson is an alternative name for *The Spanish Tragedy*:

> Hee that shall sweare *Ioronimo* or *Andronicus* are the best plays yet, shall pass unexcepted at, here, as a man whose Iudgement shewes it is constant, and hath stood still, these five and twentie, or thirtie yeares.[8]

Bartholomew Fair was written in 1614, so, if Ben's dates are taken literally, *Titus* was also written between 1584 and 1589, which fits on both biographical and stylistic grounds. It was certainly in existence in 1592 when an allusion was made to it in the play called *A Knack to Know a Knave*.

The Induction tells us that *grand guignol* was highly popular in the late 1580s, but is now regarded, by Jonson at least, as passé. *Titus* clearly retained its popularity for some time before becoming a period piece.

It seems strange to modern sensibilities that such a blood-soaked form of drama should become a cult when the horrendous spectacles of public executions, involving the severing of genitals and disembowelling while the victim yet lived and hanging by strangulation were frequently available. We can only recall the familiar words of L.P. Hartley. 'The past is a foreign country; they do things differently there.'

Shakespeare used the classical models for *The Comedy of Errors*. As Seneca was the model for tragedy, so were the Latin dramatists, Terence and Plautus, for comedy. The play is closely modelled on two comedies by Plautus: the *Menaechmi*, in which two sets of long-separated twins are mistaken for each other and finally reunited and the *Amphitruo*, in which masters and servants become confused. An English translation of the *Menaechni* by William Warner was not entered onto the Stationers' Register until 1594, but Shakespeare was probably familiar with both plays from his schooldays. He may even have acted in them. The main source of the play is stated in the earliest record of a performance – at Gray's Inn, probably on Holy Innocents' Day (28 December) in 1594. After various revels, 'a Comedy of Errors (like to Plautus his Menaechmus) was played by the Players'. Given the circumstance of its presentation, it is likely the performers were members of the Inn. With a length of just 1,787 lines, it is Shakespeare's shortest play. This contrasts with the 1,422 lines that constitute the role of Hamlet, although the full version is rarely performed. To the modern audience, Shakespeare's touch is surer with this play than with *Titus Andronicus*, although it is still a work in progress. Together with the much later *The Tempest*, it is his only play to observe the 'Classical Unities' – Unity of Action: a play should have just one action, with a minimum of sub-plots; of Time: the action should occur over a period of no more than twenty-four hours; and Unity of Place: the action should take place in a single location. *The Comedy of Errors* is actually set in three, but all are in the same locale, Ephesus.

Rigid insistence on adherence to these 'Unities' was based on a misinterpretation of Aristotle's *Poetics* by Renaissance scholars in France and Italy, which had been reiterated as recently as 1570 by the Italian neo-classicist, Lodovico Castelvetro. Aristotle does not even mention the Unity of Place, but was more forthcoming on the Unity of Action:

> the plot, being an imitation of an action, must imitate one action and that as a whole the structural union of the parts being such that, if any one of them is displaced or removed, the whole will be disjointed and disturbed. For a thing whose presence or absence makes no visible difference, is not an organic part of the whole.

His only reference to the Unity of Time is in defining the contrast between epic poetry and the tragic drama:

> Epic poetry agrees with Tragedy in so far as it is an imitation in verse of characters of a higher type. They differ, in that Epic poetry admits but one kind of metre, and is narrative in form. They differ, again, in their length: for Tragedy endeavours, as far as possible, to confine itself to a single revolution of the sun, or but slightly to exceed this limit; whereas the Epic action has no limits of time.

Given that Aristotle appears to be recording the practice as it was, not necessarily as it should be, it is extraordinary that the theory should have had such a hold over drama in France and Italy. Although the style of English theatre was influenced by the Classics in its themes and formats, its commercial basis ensured that it possessed a healthy pragmatism. Yet the Unities had their advocates. Ben Jonson was highly critical of those such as Shakespeare, who failed to adhere to them. Sir Philip Sidney was scathing about the effects of a failure to observe them, although his parody of the standard plots is too exaggerated to be effective:

> You shall have Asia of the one side, and Affrick of the other, and so many other under-kingdoms, that the Player, when he cometh in, must ever begin with telling where he is: or els, the tale will not be conceived. Now ye shall have three Ladies, walke to gather flowers, and then we must beleeve the stage to be a Garden. By and by, we heare news of shipwracke in the same place, and then wee are to blame, if we accept it not for a rock. Upon the backe of that comes a hideous Monster, with fire and smoke, and then the miserable beholders are bounde to take it for a Cave. While in the meantime, two Armies flye in, represented with foure swords and bucklers, and then what harde heart will not receive it for a pitched fielde? Now, of time they are much more liberall, for ordinary it is that two young princes fall in love.
>
> After many traverces, she is got with childe, delivered of a faire boy, he is lost, groweth a man, falls in love, and is ready to get another childe, and

> all this in two hours' space: while how absurd it is in sence, even sence may imagine, and Arte hath taught and all auncient examples justified.

The answer of the finest Elizabethan dramatists to the issues of time and space was to build the play in the minds of the audience. The Chorus in *Henry V* answers the point about four swords and bucklers representing two armies:

> O, pardon, since a crooked figure may
> Attest in little place a million.
> Into a thousand parts divide one man,
> And make imaginary puissance.

Thus Shakespeare and others broke free of the tyranny of the Unities. He has paid his tribute to the Ancients and can move on to more complex matters.

The Unperfect Actor

There can be no theatre without actors. The 'many excellent qualities' required by the player were described in a book of etiquette of 1616, attributed to Thomas Gainsford, based on the *Galarea* of Giovanni Della Casa, charmingly entitled *The Rich Cabnett furnished with a varietie of excellent Discriptions, exquisite charracters, witty discorses, and delightful histories, deuine and morral*:

> Dancing, actiuitie, musicke, song, elloqution, abilitie of body, memory, vigilancy, skill of weapon, pregnancy of wit, and such like: in all which hee resembleth an excellent spring of water, which growes the more sweeter, and the more plentifull by the often drawing out of it: so are all these the more perfect and plausible by the often practice.

By the time this treatise was written, acting had become a fine art, garnished with such names as Knell, Alleyn, Burbage and Lowin. In three decades, the profession had transformed itself from the style cited by Shakespeare in *Hamlet*, although, by implication, there were still actors who performed as if they were in *The Mysteries*:

> Speak the speech, I pray you, as I pronounced it to you, trippingly on the tongue. But if you mouth it, as many of our players do, I had as lief the town crier spoke my lines. Nor do not saw the air too much with your hand, thus, by use all gently, for in the very torrent, tempest, and (as I may say) whirlwind of your passion, you must acquire and beget a temperance that

may give it smoothness. O, it offends me to the soul to hear a robustious periwig-pated fellow tear a passion to tatters, to very rags, to split the ears of the groundlings, who for the most part are capable of nothing but inexplicable dumb shows and noise.

Shortcomings of some actors are delineated in *Essayes and Characters* by John Stephens the Younger of Lincoln's Inn, published in 1615. He is critical of the 'common player' who, 'when he doth hold conference upon the stage and should looke directly in his fellow's face, hee turnes about his voice into the assembly for applause sake, like a Trumpeter in the fields that shifts places to get an echo.'

Sir Thomas Overbury defined the qualities apparent in an 'excellent actor'.

Whatever is commendable in the grave orator, is most exquisitely perfect in him, for by a full and significant action of body, he charmes our attention.

Sit in a full Theater, and you will thinke you see so many lines drawne form the circumference of so many eares, whilst the Actor is in the *Center.*

His skills enhanced the work of the playwright:

Hee addes grace to the Poet's labours: for what in the Poet is but ditty, in him is both ditty and musicke. He entertaines us in the best leasure of our life, that is betweene meales, the most unfit time, either for study or bodily exercise.

There are echoes of Shakespeare's 'Ages of Man' speech – that 'one man in his time plays many parts':

All men have bene of his occupation: and indeed, what he doth fainedly that doe others essentially: this daie one playa a Monarch, the nexte a private person. Heere one Acts a Tyrant; on the morrow, an Exile: A Parasite this man to night, tomorrow a Precisian, and so of divers others.

That Sir Thomas regarded Richard Burbage as the epitome of artistic talent is made clear by his view that the 'excellent Plaier' was also 'an exquisite painter'. Richard Flecknoe, in the next generation, recalled his supreme qualities. 'He was a delightful Proteus,[9] so wholly transforming himself into his Part, and putting off himself with his Cloathes, as he never (not so much as in the Tyring-house) assum'd himself again until the Play was done.'

Tarlton's Jests

The Queen's Men were struck another blow in the year after Knell's death. Richard Tarlton made his last will and testament on 3 September 1588. He died and was buried before the day was out. His last thoughts were for the future care of his son, who was still a minor. It is almost possible to hear him dictating the will. 'Greetings in the Lord everlasting, knowe yee that I, the saide Richard, for the naturall love and fatherly affection that I doo beare unto my natural and wel beloved sonne, Philip Tarlton, and to the intent that he maje be mainteyned and brought upp in the feare of God'. He left him to the care of 'my most loving mother, Katherine Tarlton, widowe, and my very lovinge and trustie frendes, Robert Adams, gentleman … and my fellow, William Johnson, also one of the grooms of her Majesty's Chamber.' Adams was the Queen's Surveyor of Buildings, Johnson one of the five actors named in the Royal Patent granted to Leicester's Company in 1576. Tarlton lived in Holywell Street, Shoreditch, as did the Burbages. He was buried in his parish church of St Leonard.

Despite these losses, the Queen's Company flourished a while longer, performing a number of Robert Greene's plays and such unattributed works as *King Leir and his Daughters*, *Sir Clyomon and Sir Clamdyes*, *The Troublesome Raign of John, King of England* and *The True Tragedie of Richard the Third.*

The publication of *Tarlton's Jestes* in three parts around 1600 demonstrates that the clown's legend lived beyond his lifetime. This collection of jokes, quips and anecdotes is not entirely attributable to him. Some clearly predate him. Yet much has an authentic feel. Let one such anecdote stand for the whole. Jest No.17 tells 'How Tarlton deceived an innholder … upon a time when the plaiers were put to silence'; presumably when the theatres were closed by the plague. Tarlton and his boy stayed at an inn in Sandwich 'at great charge', and 'frolickt so long in the countrey that all their money was gone'. They were 'a great way from London, they knew not what to do. But as want is the whetstone of wit, Tarlton gathereth his conceit together, and practised a trick to beare him up to London without money.'

On the third morning, he sent his boy downstairs to 'content himself before his host and his hostesse, and mumbling, saye to himself "Lord, Lord, what a scald master doe I serve."' The mumblings convinced the innkeeper that his master was a seminary priest, so he summoned the constable and took him to Tarlton's chamber. The door was locked, but when they peered through the keyhole, they saw Tarlton on his knees, crossing himself. They 'made no more ado, but in they rushed, and arrested him'. The innkeeper forewent Tarlton's bill (he had no choice) and, with the constable, bore the charge of escorting the two up to London, to present the supposed seminarian to Mr Fleetwood, the Recorder.[10]

> But now, marke the jest: when the Recorder saw Tarlton and knew him passing well; entertained him very courteously, and all to be fooled the Inn-holder and his mate, and sent them away with fleas in their eares but when Tarlton sawe himself discharged out of their hands, he stood jesting and pointing at their folly, and so taught them by cunning more wit and thrift against another time.

The anecdote says much about Tarlton's uninhibited cheek, his impromptu wit and his confidence that his fame, status and ability could turn the incident into an elaborate joke at the expense of innkeeper and constable. As the most famous man-of-the-theatre of his time, his doings off-stage were as much recounted as those on it.

A Pleasant Conceited Historie

Four other comedies conspicuously date from Shakespeare's early career as a playwright: *The Taming of the Shrew*, *The Merchant of Venice*, and *The Two Gentlemen of Verona*. *The Taming of the Shrew* was written before June 1593, when the *Beauty Dishonoured* of the poet and pamphleteer, Anthony Shute, was published. It contains the line, 'He calls his Kate and she must come and kiss him', which is not only a clear reference to the play, but indicates its popularity. References are only made to lines in plays if it is known they will be recognised and, of course, the line in question gave rise to the title of a musical in modern times – *Kiss me Kate*. Today, with the growth of the feminist movement, doubts are cast on the play's approach to sexuality, but such issues are unlikely to have disturbed an Elizabethan audience that would have seen it as little more than a comedy of the perpetual war between the sexes.

A puzzling issue is the relationship between *The Taming of the Shrew* and a play with virtually the same name. On 2 May 1594, *A Pleasant Conceited Historie called The taming of a Shrew* was entered onto the Stationers' Register. It has many parallels with its near namesake and many perplexing differences. The setting is Athens rather than Padua. The only names in common are those of Kate and Sly. Petruchio in *The Shrew* is Fernando in *A Shrew*. It has been suggested that it is a pirated version of the original, but it had a life of its own. The quarto states that 'it was sundry times acted by the Right Honourable the Earle of Pembrook his servants'. This was a well-established company, with which Shakespeare was certainly involved. That it performed the play indicates that was not just a pirated version of the original. That it was 'sundry times acted' indicates its popularity, as does the publication of two further quartos in

1596 and 1607. On 11 June 1594, Richard Henslowe recorded a performance of 'the taming of a shrowe' at the Newington Butts Theatre.

A further complication arises from clear verbal parallels with both *Shrews* and *A Knack to Know a Knave*, which Henslowe noted was performed by Lord Strange's Men at the Rose Theatre on 10 June 1592, so both plays were in existence by then. There is no extant record of a performance of *The Shrew* until it was played at Court before Charles I and Queen Henrietta Maria on 26 November 1631, when it was described as 'likt'. No quarto edition was published in Shakespeare's lifetime. It was not seen in print until it was included in the First Folio of 1623. Yet there are indications that the play was popular. A quarto edition of this 'Wittie and Pleasant Comedie' was produced in the same year as the royal performance. The title page states that it had been 'acted by His Maiestes Seruants at Blacke Friers and the Globe'. The King's Men did not play at the Blackfriars Theatre until 1609, so this, together with the royal performance, indicates that the play was in repertory for at least forty years. That John Fletcher wrote a sequel further indicates its popularity.

Another mystery is the fact that both *Shrews* are plays within a play. The drunken tinker, Christopher Sly, is persuaded that he is a noble lord and the play is performed for his entertainment. The curiosity is that, whereas *A Shrew* sustains the Sly scenario throughout the play, in *The Shrew*, it only features in the first two scenes. There is no simple explanation for this, other than that there must have been a fuller Induction that for some reason was lost to the editors of the First Folio. Thus, when productions of *The Shrew* include the full Induction, all the scenes apart from the first two are taken from *A Shrew*. Interestingly, in the Induction to *The Shrew*, Shakespeare invokes his Warwickshire roots. Christopher Sly is 'old Sly's son of Burton Heath': a reference to the village of Barton-on-the-Heath, in the south of the county, where lived his Aunt Joan and her husband, Edmund Lambert. He speaks of 'Marion Hacket, the fat ale-wife of Wincot', and her daughter Cicely. Wincot is a hamlet some four miles south of Stratford, or perhaps it is his mother's home village of Wilmcote to which Shakespeare is referring. That there was a Hacket family resident in Wincot at the time makes it more likely, although whether they kept an alehouse is unknown.

In *The Taming of the Shrew*, Shakespeare abandons the Aristotelian principles of *The Comedy of Errors* and indulges in a lively sub-plot involving the suitors of Kate's younger sister, Bianca. This skilfully contrasts with the main action; one fulfilling the intentions of the title, the other, the reverse.

Chapter Three

Where the Infectious Pestilence did Reign

Martin Marprelate

An extra-ordinary controversy arose in October 1588, when the first of seven Puritan tracts appeared under the pseudonym of Martin Marprelate. The anonymous author claimed they were 'printed oversea in Europe', presumably to confuse pursuers. 'All our Lord Bishops, I say, are petty popes and petty usurping Antichrists,' the anti-clerical rant declared. In 1586, the authoritarian Archbishop of Canterbury, John Whitgift, had secured from the Star Chamber, a decree banning the publication of books, pamphlets or tracts not authorised by himself or the Bishop of London. Puritan literature, if distributed at all, was produced in more sympathetic places like Holland and Scotland, but this was different. These tracts were produced on a secret printing press that had been established at East Moulsey in Surrey by John Penry, a Welsh Puritan who had been University Preacher at Cambridge. To avoid detection, the press was moved from place to place.

The author's style was distinctive. Rather than the usual polemic, he employed the popular language of the streets in his scathing attacks on what he denounced as the hypocrisy and ineffectiveness of the Anglican Establishment. In obvious puns, but ones unexpected in a Puritan tract, he refers to vicars as 'fyckers' and 'fickers', and to Whitgift as 'John Cant'. The assault was personal as well as doctrinal and frequently demonstrated an intimate knowledge of the foibles and shortcomings of the Episcopal bench. One particular target was Thomas Cooper, Bishop of Winchester, who had written a somewhat feeble riposte to the tracts. Martin labelled him a hypocrite with a face 'made of seasoned wainscot'. He was ignorant of biblical languages and a plagiarist. He dubbed him 'Mistress Cooper's husband' and spread scurrilous gossip about the wife's supposed extramarital affairs. Further ripostes from the hierarchy tended to confirm Martin's view of its ineffectiveness.

More strident strictures issued from the secret press, mocking the pomposity of the counter-attack. Richard Bancroft, a future Archbishop of Canterbury, hit upon a strategy to 'stop Martin and his Fellow mouths: we have to have them answered after their own vein in writing'. Men of the theatre, John Lyly, Thomas Nashe, Anthony Munday and Robert Greene were engaged to give anonymous ripostes to Marprelate. The result was a public furore in which the theatres became involved in mocking the Puritans. 'Everie stage Plaier made a jest of him,' one anti-Martinist tract recorded.

Although it might be thought that the ecclesiastical and political establishment would welcome such support, when Lord Strange's Men put on performances in which Marprelate's style was lampooned, it was reported to the Privy Council as causing 'great offence ... [by presuming] to handle in their plaies certen matters of Divinitye and of the state unfit to be suffred'. The lawyer, Francis Bacon, condemned the players for exceeding their authority. 'Whatsoever be presented the people is no meet judg[e] or arbitratour.' John Harte, the Lord Mayor of London, described such performances in a letter to Lord Burghley as giving 'greate offence of the better sorte'. In 1589, Edward Tilney, the Master of the Revels, closed the theatres because of the affront these dramatic barbs were causing. The employment of playwrights to tussle with Marprelate proved an instrument rebounding on those who engaged them.

Despite the ripostes, the tracts continued to pour out, with the press moving to Fawsley in Northamptonshire, on to Coventry and other parts of Warwickshire before being seized in Manchester in August 1589. Penry had fled to Scotland, but later secretly returned, living in the hamlet of Ratcliffe, just east of the City of London. He joined a secret Brownist[1] congregation, but was arrested after being recognised by a local vicar. The authorities may have thought they had caught Martin, although Penry's turgid prose style in other documents argues against this, as does his vehement denial of the allegation. Nevertheless, he was charged with sedition on the basis of an inflammatory petition to the Queen found among his papers. Although it had never been presented, he was found guilty and hanged. The authorities clearly felt that the time had come for a crackdown on Separatists. Two other leaders of London's Underground Church, John Greenwood and Henry Barrow, had been executed at Tyburn in the previous months, for 'devising and circulating seditious books'. A third prisoner, John Udall, died in custody. When cross-examined, he denied all knowledge of the identity of the author of the tracts. 'I for my part, have been inquisitive, but could never learn who he is.'

Among the companies censured for engaging in the controversy were the Children of Paul's. *Pappe with a Hatchet*, a satirical tract by their resident dramatist, John Lyly, may have been adapted for the stage. The school's High Master, John Harrison, had reason to be cautious. In 1584, he had composed an 'allegory or dreame' to be performed before the members of the Mercers' Company, whose foundation the school was. Rightly or wrongly, they concluded that it was castigating them for being stingy with funding and were deeply offended.[2] Harrison's headship was in doubt, but he retained his position after promising that he would 'deale no more with such dialogue'. Despite this, the Children of Paul's were placed in abeyance for the entire decade.

For Lyly, the demise of the Children of Paul's spelt the fading of his dramatic star, but this was probably more due to the changing tastes represented by the rise of a new wave of dramatists. His play, *Mother Bombie*, 'sundry times acted by the children of Paul's' may have been his last for them. He had made some effort to adjust away from classical mythology towards the taste for Latin comedy. In the homely setting of Rochester, the play is reminiscent of the *Comedy of Errors* with its comic touchstone of mistaken identity. Later he tried to accommodate himself to the new genres by writing a play in blank verse. His stock was still high enough for *The Woman in the Moon* to be performed at Court, although there is no indication which company performed it, or on which public stage it was presented. That it was presented before the Queen must have raised Lyly's hopes of preferment to an influential position such as the Master of the Revels, but this was unfulfilled. He became a Member of Parliament, the only dramatist of the era to do so, a position carrying a certain cachet, but not one delivering significant financial resource. In desperation, he petitioned the Queen, 'Thirteen years your highness servant but nothing…A thousand hopes, but all nothing: a hundred promises, but yet nothing.' He was not entirely forgotten. Francis Meres' list of the 'best for comedy' of 1598 included the 'eloquent and witty John Lyly'.

Upstart Crow

Shortly after the death of Robert Greene, Henry Chettle, a writer and printer, published a pamphlet entitled *Greenes Groatsworth of Witte, bought with a million of Repentance*. The title gives the clue to the work. It is a somewhat rambling cautionary tale describing the low life encountered by the author during his exotic career. It advises the reader to take heed of his unfortunate example and avoid bad company. He particularly warns three of his 'fellow Schollers about this Citie' about the ingratitude of actors, scathingly dismissing them as 'Puppets … that spoke from our mouths … Anticks garnished in our colours.' One actor is the subject of especial vitriol:

> Yes, trust them not, for there is an Upstart Crow beautified with our feathers, that with his *Tygers Hart wrapt in a players hide*, supposes he is as well able to bombast out a blanke verse as the best of you, and being an absolute *Johannes Factotum*, is in his own conceit the only Shake-scene in a countrey.

The reference to William Shakespeare is unmistakable. As happens so often, the attack falls tantalisingly short of the full story, but provides enough information to enable the conclusion that Shakespeare's work is popularly admired. The misquotation from *Henry VI, Part III* – the line should read, 'Tiger's heart wrapped in a woman's hide' – shows that his lines were so well-known that they could be quoted without reference to source, which was probably the 'harey the vj' that Henslowe entered as a new play performed by Lord Strange's Men at the Bear Garden on 3 March 1592. Since Greene and the playwrights to whom the diatribe is addressed were university men, the phrase 'supposes he is as well able to bombast out blank verse with the best of you' may refer to Shakespeare's comparative lack of classical learning, an accusation that dogged him for the rest of his life – and beyond. 'Beautified with our feathers' implies that he was a plagiarist. Although the context is unclear, there is an element of truth in it. Like Montaigne, Shakespeare believed the function of the poet was to gather 'other men's flowers'. Few of his plots are original.

'*Johannes Factotum*'? He is an actor who has been writing plays. In other words, he will turn his hand to anything. The phrase gives a clue as to what he was doing for much of the seven missing years between the birth of his twins and Greene's attack. He was exercising the actor's trade before making the transition to playwriting that so disturbed the author of *Groatsworth*. It has been suggested that his first essays in drama consisted of revising other men's work. This may explain 'beautified with our feathers'. The number of his plays, more those of any other writer, that existed in a previous form, may be significant. Nor do two of his fellow playwrights escape the onslaught. 'The famous gracer of Tragedians' (almost certainly Marlowe) is attacked for his atheism and his devotion to the works of Machiavelli. The other, probably Thomas Nashe, this 'young Juvenal, this byting satirist', is reproached for 'too much liberty of reproofe'.

It is sad that Robert Greene, a powerful and innovative literary figure, should be best remembered for this intemperate attack, but it was rumoured that he had not written it even when *Groatsworth* was published. When it was suggested that Thomas Nashe was the author, he reacted with fury. Within a month, his pamphlet, *Pierce Penilesse*, vehemently denied the suggestion.

> Other news I am advertised of, that a scald trivial lying pamphlet, cald Greens groatsworth of wit, is given out to be my doing. God never have care of my soule, but utterly renounce me, if the least word or sillible in it proceed from my pen, or if I were in any way privie to the writing or printing of it.

Marlowe also seems to have reacted angrily. The public charge of atheism could have grave consequences. Shakespeare made no public reply, but sensibly enlisted others in his support. Henry Chettle was constrained to make amends. His pamphlet *Kind-Hartes Dream* is ostensibly a riposte to Nash's remarks. He claims to be pained by the furore he has caused:

> About three months since, died *M. Robert Greene*, leauing many papers in sundry Booke sellers hands, among others his Groats-worth of wit, in which a letter written to diuers play-makers is offensively by one or two of them taken, and because on the dead they cannot be auenged, they wilfully forge in their conceite a living Author, and after tossing it to and fro, no remedy, but it must light on me.

Chettle must have made his peace with Nashe, for he escapes mention. Concerning Marlowe, he adds further insult. 'With one of them I care not if I never be,' he writes scathingly. Marlowe's reputation had gone before him. The other playwright was a different matter. He had met him since the attack. 'Because my selfe haue seene his demeanor no lesse civil than he exelent in the qualitie he professes.' 'Divers of Worship' had taken up Shakespeare's cause and stressed 'his uprightness of dealing, which argues his honesty, and his facetious grace in writing which approoues his Art'.

Rumours were circulating that Chettle himself was the author of the attack – a charge he indignantly denied. 'I protest it was all Greene's, not mine nor Maister Nashes, as some most vnjustly haue affirmed.' Modern textual analysis tends to uphold the charge. Chettle was frequently in debt and the temptation to add a sensational dimension to Greene's pamphlet may have been irresistible. Indeed, he had greater grounds for jealousy than Greene, who died a highly esteemed writer. Chettle never achieved such success and little survives of his work. Philip Henslowe regularly 'lent' money to those he employed, probably in the way of advances. Chettle borrowed from him more often than any other writer. On 17 January 1599, he even paid to get him out of the Marshalsea – the debtors' prison. On 3 March 1603, he paid to get one of his plays out of pawn. If the attack was indeed Chettle's, he calculated well. *Groats-worth* must not only have sold well, it gave him the opportunity to launch another pamphlet in response. That some of the mud flung by *Groatsworth* stuck is demonstrated by the appearance of a pamphlet entitled *Greene's Funeralls*. It contains a short verse that indicates continuing admiration for Greene's works and that Shakespeare was not the only one who plagiarised them:

> Greene is the ground of everie painter's die;
> Greene gave the ground to all that write on him'
> Nay, more, the men that so Eclipst his fame,
> Purloynde his Plumes, can they deny the same?

The charge had little effect. Shakespeare was to find in Greene's *James IV* inspiration for *A Midsummer Night's Dream* and his sources for *A Winter's Tale* in the same author's hugely popular novel, *Pandosto.*

'Divers of Worship'

Chettle's apology indicates that William Shakespeare was already associated with people of influence – 'divers of worship'. They may have been members of the 'Essex Circle', the smart set of noblemen that surrounded the Earl of Essex: a prominent member was Henry Wriothesley, the 3rd Earl of Southampton, soon to be Shakespeare's patron. *Love's Labour's Lost*, one of only two of Shakespeare's plays with no known source, appears to allude to this group. It presents difficulties to the modern reader, unable to grasp its in-jokes. The convoluted plot suggests a playwright still finding his way. Modern scholarship tends to date it to around 1595 on stylistic grounds, but there is evidence that the text, as it has come down to us, is a revision at that period by the author himself. The names of the characters indicate that the play was probably first written in the late 1580s. The three main protagonists – the Lords Berowne (or Biron), Longueville (or Longaville) and Dumaine – bear the names of soldiers prominent in the Wars of Religion then being waged in France. The proximity of the play's original drafting to the momentous events of 1588, is further indicated by the name of the fantastical Spanish character – Don Adriano de Armado. The 1598 quarto states that it was 'Newly corrected and augmented by W. Shakespere'. Another note indicates the purpose of the revision: 'As it was presented before her Highnes this last Christmas'. If this courtly play was to go down well anywhere, it was most likely the royal court.

The Chronicle History

The Classical Unities certainly did not accord with the project Shakespeare was developing – to write a dramatic sequence of a key sweep of English history. There had been a number of history plays staged previously, although perhaps not enough for the genre to be described as a vogue.

Like much contemporary drama, the Chronicle History play had roots in the medieval religious cycles. The embryonic example is contained in John Skelton's play, *Magnyfycence*. The play of *Kynge Johan* is probably the earliest example of a play about a specific non-Biblical figure. Although it represents the new vibrant force of Protestantism, it is firmly based within the medieval tradition. The character of King John, who has defended England and her Church against papal tyranny, is assailed and supported by allegorical figures of personified virtues and vices such as Verity and Sedition. The play lauds 'our late Kynge Henrye [who] Clerely brought us out in to the lande of mylke and honye'. This it has in common with Shakespeare's history plays. It has a political purpose. The author, John Bale, was a man of the new era, an apostatised Carmelite Prior, he had been advanced in the Anglican Church to an Irish Bishopric.

A number of subsequent plays such as *Gorboduc* featured historical characters or supposed ones, but the chronicle history per se was derived from a number of contemporary works. Edward Hall's *The Union of the Two Noble and Illustrate Famelies of Lancastre and Yorke* was published in 1548. In that year, London printer Reginald Wolfe conceived the idea of creating a 'Universal Cosmography of the whole world, and therewith certain particular histories of every known nation'. He engaged Raphael Holinshed and William Harrison as assistants. Wolfe died in 1573 with the work incomplete. The project was taken over by a consortium of three London stationers. Sensibly, it was decided to restrict its scope to the British Isles. Holinshed was appointed to continue the great work, with the help of four assistants, one of whom was the future martyr and saint, Edmund Campion. The huge volume finally appeared in 1577, as *The Chronicles of England, Scotlande and Irelande*.

The works of Hall and Holinshed reflect a growing interest in the nation's history, born of the surging patriotism of a land under threat. This enthusiasm for the past made its way into the theatre. A second play of King John. *The Troublesome Reign ...* was performed by the 'Queen's Majesties Players' around 1588. As is appropriate to a play written for a company inaugurated by the Protestant enthusiast, Sir Francis Walsingham, the play, like its predecessor, is noted for its anti-Catholic polemic. The Chronicle History could be a version of events to suit the Courtly interest. *The Famous Victories of Henry the fifth*, presented by the company around the same time, was a patriotic effusion for a nation at war. The Queen's Players also performed *The True Tragedie of Richard III*, a play of debated provenance, but which fulfils its purpose of exalting the Tudor dynasty.

Holinshed died in 1580, but a second, revised, edition of his *Chronicles* was published in 1587. This edition was used extensively by William Shakespeare in his history plays, as was Hall's *The Union....* Shakespeare was a voracious reader; as well as Holinshed, he drew on at least five other documentary sources in writing *Henry VI, Part II.* Christopher Marlowe also appears to have possessed a copy. Much of the material in *Edward II* comes from that source.

Such plays as *The Troublesome Reign of King John, The Famous Victories of Henry V* and *The Contention of the Two Famous Houses...* appear prototypes for William Shakespeare's later revival of their themes. The question is whether he had a hand in their creation and subsequently revised them. If so, the chronicle history play of *The Raigne of King Edward III* may give an indication of the way such collaborations worked. No playwright's name was attached to it when it was first published in 1596, but the stationer Cuthbert Burby recorded that 'it hath bin sundrie times plaied about the Citie of London'. This success led him to publish another edition in 1599. The balance of critical opinion now considers that the play was co-authored by Shakespeare. Various names have been suggested as its co-author: Marlowe, Kyd and – for many scholars' the front-runner – George Peele.

That the historical play was a call to the nation in dangerous times was indicated by Thomas Nashe:

> What if I prove plays to be no extreme, but a rare exercise of virtue? First, for the subject of them (for the most part, it is borrowed out of our English chronicles, wherein our forefathers valiant acts (that have long been buried in rusty brass and worm-eaten books) are revived and they themselves raised from the grave of oblivion; and brought to plead their honours in open presence; than which, what can be a sharper reproof to these degenerate effeminate days of ours?

Shakespeare's *Henry VI* trilogy is the first fruit of a unique saga of English history, stretching from the tragic reign of Richard II to the rise of the House of Tudor. This great work was not written in chronological order. The *Henry IV* plays were written in the mid-1590s. *Henry V*, the last play in the cycle, dates from 1599. It is unlikely that William Shakespeare had conceived the entire history when he wrote the three parts of *Henry VI.* Yet the themes that dominate the cycle are present in the earliest play. The heroine is England herself. The theme is expressed in a history play that is not part of the cycle, *King John* – 'Naught shall make us rue / If England to herself do rest but true.'

In *Henry VI, Parts I and II*, the English Crown loses its French possessions. The land becomes divided against itself through the rival houses of York and Lancaster. The divisions are revealed in the highly stylised fourth scene of Part I. York and Lancaster pluck red and white roses as the emblems of their causes in the garden of the Inner Temple. The Earl of Warwick, a major protagonist in the quarrel, foresees impending disaster:

> … this brawl to-day …
> … Shall send between the red rose and the white
> A thousand souls to death and deadly night.

Civil war is the greatest evil that can befall a nation. It sets brother against brother, father against son. Yet the history plays represent something more than a plea for national unity. They are an essay on the institution of monarchy. In the series, Shakespeare goes some way to espousing the doctrine of the Divine Right of Kings. At his Coronation, the monarch is anointed, so conferring a priesthood upon him. To usurp this prerogative is a crime against the divine order. Regicide was a heinous offence. There is a biblical theme to the Histories: that the sins of the fathers will be visited on the sons, even to the third and fourth generation. Society, the history plays tell us, is hierarchical and pyramidical. Every man has his place and there's a place for every man. Throughout his canon, Shakespeare shows contempt, not for the humbler classes as such, but for the chaos that will ensue when the designated social order is overstepped. Such is the case with Cade's rebellion in *Henry VI, Part II*. Then, as now, the familiar line must have brought delighted cheers from the audience – 'The first thing we do, let's kill all the lawyers.'

Despite the crudity of the characterisation of Cade and his fellows, a reflection on history shows that Shakespeare had a point. The examples of France and Russia show us that if revolutions turn wrong, they can become instruments of irrational oppression. The pograms that such upheavals can unleash are lauded by Jack Cade:

> And you that love the commons, follow me.
> Now show yourselves men; 'tis for liberty.
> We will not leave one lord, one gentleman.
> Spare none but such as go in clouted shoon;
> For they are thrifty honest men, and such
> As would, but that they dare not, take our parts.

The privileges of the governing classes bring huge responsibilities. No onus is greater than that of the monarch. His is the moral burden of the entire nation. His subjects bear no such responsibilities. Following classical tradition, the shepherd is an exemplar of this order; a perspective demonstrated by the highly stylised and hugely effective scene which occurs during the Battle of Towton in *Henry VI, Part III*. The King, alone on stage, takes his seat upon a molehill and contemplates his divided nation. He concludes:

Gives not the hawthorn bush a sweeter shade
To shepherds looking on their silly sheep
Than doth a rich embroider'd canopy
To kings that fear their subjects' treachery?
O, yes, it doth, a thousand-fold it doth.
And, to conclude, the shepherd's homely curds,
His cold, thin drink, out of his leather bottle,
His wonted sleep under a fresh tree's shade,
All which seemly and secure he enjoys,
Is far beyond a prince's delicates ….

The scene moves on to express deep horror at the division of families caused by civil war. The stage direction reads: '*Alarum. Enter a son that has killed his father, dragging in the dead body,*' 'Who's this?'

O God! It is my father's face,
Whom in this conflict I unawares have killed.
Oh, heavy times, begetting such events.

The scene is paralleled on the other side of the stage: '*Enter a father that hath killed his son, bringing in the body.*'

Thou that so stoutly hath resisted me,
Give me thy gold, if thou hast any gold:
For I have bought it with a thousand blows
But let me see: is this our foeman's face?
Ah, no, no, no, it is mine only son!
Ah, boy, if any life be left in thee,
Throw up thine eye! See, see what showers arise,
Blown with the windy tempest of my heart,
Upon thy words, that kill my eye and heart!
O, pity, God, this miserable age!
… O boy, thy father gave thee life too soon,
And hath bereft thee of thy life too late!

The King's distress at the divisions of his nation is expressed in a further stylised scene:

Son: How will my mother for a father's death
Take on with me and ne'er be satisfied.

Father: How will my wife for slaughter of my son
Shed seas of tears and ne'er be satisfied.
King: How will the country for these woful chances
Misthink the king and not be satisfied!
Son: Was ever son so rued a father's death?
Father: Was ever father so bemoan'd his son?
King: Was ever king so grieved for subjects' woe?
Much is your sorrow; mine ten times as much.

Shakespeare wrote fewer such scenes as his skills developed. Two other notable examples occur in *Richard III*, the sequel to the three parts of *Henry VI*. Indeed the text assumes the audience's familiarity with the previous trilogy. In Act IV, Scene 4, Queen Margaret recites a litany of deaths, a theme picked up by Queen Elizabeth and the Duchess of York:

I had an Edward, till a Richard kill'd him;
I had a Harry, till a Richard kill'd him.
Thou hadst an Edward, till a Richard kill'd him.
Thou hadst a Richard, till a Richard kill'd him.

Similarly, Richard's victims parade through his nightmare before the Battle of Bosworth. The scene is highly stylised, with Richard and Richmond in their tents on each side of the stage. The politics loom large. The future Henry VII will found the Tudor dynasty and restore the equilibrium of a nation at peace with itself. The theme is expressed in the words of the Princes, murdered in the Tower:

Sleep, Richmond, sleep in peace, and wake in joy.
Good angels guard thee from the boar's annoy!
Live, and beget a happy race of kings!
Edward's unhappy sons do bid thee flourish.

'Boar's annoy'? Shakespeare was still honing his craft…

The main source for *Richard III* is Holinshed's Chronicles. Its account of the reign was based on Thomas More's *History of Richard III*. More distorted history: Richard's vanquisher, Henry Richmond, was no less steeped in dynastic blood, but it suited the purpose to portray him as the nation's deliverer. Nor is Shakespeare beyond changing his sources to increase the dramatic impact. In reality, Queen Margaret of Anjou returned to France after the death of her son and the deposition and murder of her husband. This was fourteen years before the scenes depicted in Shakespeare's play, in which she remains a figure around the Yorkist court. She serves as the commentator on Richard's evil acts, the counter-balance to his scheming. 'Then forth the kennel of thy womb hath crept,' she tells Queen Elizabeth, 'a hellhound that doth haunt us all to death.' In contrast with Marlowe's attitude towards his anti-heroes, Shakespeare does not admire Richard.

The part of Richard III is the first title role to be linked with the name of Richard Burbage. The company with which the 23-year-old actor was most associated at this time was Lord Strange's Men and it is highly likely that it was for that company that Shakespeare wrote this play. An anecdote recorded by the law student, John Manningham in 1602, recounts that Burbage so provoked the passion of an early 'groupie', 'that she appointed him to come to her that night by the name of Richard the 3':

> Shakespeare overhearing their conclusion went before, was entertained and was at his game ere Burbage came. The message being brought that Rich. The 3 was at the door; Shakespeare caused return that William the Conqueror was before Rich. the 3.

We are more likely in the presence of a contemporary joke than an actual incident.

It may have been the success of the *Henry VI* trilogy and *Richard III* that inspired Christopher Marlowe to turn to English history. *Edward II* is his finest play – and his last. The King is the most effectively created of his title-roles. Like Tamburlaine, Faustus and Barabbas, he is an outsider. His homosexuality makes him another anti-hero attempting to impose his will on the world, but he is a different, more-rounded character than the previous creations. In this he anticipates Shakespeare's great tragedies. His own foibles bring about his downfall, rather than external circumstance. His character is three-dimensional.

In the opening scene, the King's favourite, Piers Gaveston, elaborates on the homoerotic joys he intends to set before him:

> Music and poetry is his delight;
> Therefore I'll have Italian masques by night,
> Sweet speeches, comedies, and pleasing shows;
> And in the day, when he shall walk abroad,
> Like sylvan nymphs my pages shall be clad;
> My men, like satyrs grazing on the lawns,
> Shall with their goat-feet dance an antic hay.
> Sometime a lovely boy in Dian's shape,
> With hair that gilds the water as it glides,

Crownets of pearl about his naked arms,
And in his sportful hands an olive tree
To hide those parts which men delight to see,
Shall bathe him in a spring; and there, hard by,
One like Actaeon, peeping through the grove,
Shall by the angry goddess be transformed,
And running in the likeness of a hart
By yelping hounds pulled down and seem to die.
Such things as these best please his majesty.

The play was popular. It was entered onto the Stationers' Register on 6 July 1593. The earliest edition published in 1594 states that it was 'sundrie times publiquely acted in the honourable citie of London by the right honourable the Earle of Pembrooke his seruants'. This raises an intriguing possibility. William Shakespeare had worked with Pembroke's Men. A version of *Henry VI, Part III*, entitled *The True Tragedie of Richard Duke of Yorke as it was sundrie times acted by the Right Honourable the Earle of Pembrooke his Servants* was published in an octavo version in 1595. Thus it is possible that Shakespeare and Marlowe worked for the Company at the same time and that Shakespeare, the actor, took a part in *Edward II*. The most likely creator of the lead role is Richard Burbage, who was probably then acting with the Earl of Pembroke's Men. Perhaps Marlowe, a volatile character, had fallen out with Henslowe and the Admiral's Men and thrown in his lot with the other Company.

In *Richard III*, Shakespeare explores his recurrent theme of the disasters that ensue when place is usurped, one that he will take up in both *Hamlet* and *Macbeth*. In the background is a clear awareness of the political statecraft of Niccolo Machiavelli. Although *The Prince* was a banned book – it was not translated into English until 1636 – it had a huge influence on English thought, not least in the writings of Christopher Marlowe. In *The Jew of Malta* it is Machiavelli, or Machiavel, as Marlowe calls him, who acts as Chorus. In Machiavelli's view, the government of states takes various forms. It can be hereditary or elective. It can be acquired by conquest, or by skilful and ruthless manipulation. The audience is left in no doubt that it is the latter that Richard represents from his first soliloquy:

Plots have I laid, inductions dangerous
By drunken prophesies, libels and dreams,
To set my brother Clarence and the king
In deadly hate, the one against the other.

The theme is that of Chapter 8 of *The Prince*: 'Concerning Government: Those Who Have Obtained Principalities by Wickedness.' 'These methods are,' wrote Machiavelli, 'when, either by some wicked or nefarious ways, one ascends to the principality, or when by the favour of his fellow citizens a private person becomes the prince of his country.' Richard pursues both strategies. When the Lord Mayor and citizens urge Richard to take the crown, he appears between two bishops. 'See where he stands between two clergymen,' exclaims the Lord Mayor. This is consistent with Machiavelli's advice to Lorenzo the Magnificent in the final chapter of *The Prince*:

> It is unnecessary for a Prince to have all the good qualities I have enumerated, but it is very necessary to appear to have them. And I shall dare to say this also that to have them and always to observe them is injurious, and that to appear to have them is useful, to appear merciful, faithful, humane, religious, upright and to be so, but with a mind so, you may be able and know how to change to the opposite.

The ensuing scene is all that Machiavelli required of a prince as Richard is propelled towards the throne by the voices of the citizens.

Much of Shakespeare's history is distorted, but that is not the point. He was a dramatist not an historian and changed facts to suit his purpose, but there were other reasons for so doing. His early history plays were a vehicle for propaganda on behalf of the House of Tudor, which represents legitimacy, the rule of justice and the unity of the realm, concepts expressed in Richmond's speech in the last Act of *Richard III*:

> We will unite the white rose and the red.
> Smile heaven upon this fair conjunction,
> That long have frown'd upon their enmity
> What traitor hears me and says not amen?
> England hath long been mad and scarr'd herself.
> The brother blindly shed the brother's blood,
> The father rashly slaughter'd his own son:
> The son, compell'd, been butcher to the sire:
> All this divided York and Lancaster,
> Divided in their dire division.
> O, now, let Richmond and Elizabeth,
> The true succeeders of each royal house,
> By God's fair ordinance conjoin together,
> And let their heirs, God, if thy will be so,

Enrich the time to come with smooth-faced peace,
With smiling plenty and fair prosperous days!

'The father rashly slaughter'd his own son' – that stylised scene of fratricide and filicide must have so impressed the audience that Shakespeare can refer to it in the knowledge that the allusion will be grasped.

The play closes with a dire warning against those who would bring such desperate divisions to England again:

Abate the edge of traitors, gracious Lord,
That would reduce these bloody days again
And make poor England weep in streams of blood!
Let them not live to taste this land's increase,
That would with treason wound this fair land's peace!
Now civil wounds are stopp'd, peace lives again
That she may long live here, God say amen!

While the sentiment expressed is a clear rallying call for the Tudor monarchy, it contains an element of doubt. Civil strife did not end on the battlefield of Bosworth. Uprisings and insurrections occurred periodically over the next century. Within William Shakespeare's lifetime, the North of England had risen in rebellion and Lord Hunsdon had played a prominent part in its suppression. Even as Shakespeare wrote his histories, the confident force of Puritanism was gathering strength. The appeal to the unity of the nation was immediate. Yet beyond such anxieties, it is clear that, by the late 1580s, William Shakespeare was established as a celebrated man-of-the-theatre, but nemesis was soon to strike.

Fly, fly and Never Return

On 11 May 1593, what the Privy Council described as 'divers lewd and mutinous libels' intended to inflame opinion against Protestant refugees from France and Holland were posted on the walls of the Dutch Church at Austin Friars and elsewhere in the City. Unfortunately for Christopher Marlowe, the 'libel' concluded 'Fly, fly, and never return', followed by the words '*per* Tamburlaine'. The play was invoked as a threat to the immigrants that the vengeance to follow would be as ruthless and bloody as that meted out by Marlowe's eponymous character. The authorities may not have realised that Marlowe was no longer sharing lodgings with Thomas Kyd. It may have been nothing more than what is now known as a 'routine enquiry', but, for whatever reason, Kyd's lodgings were searched. Nothing was found to link him with the scurrilous graffiti, but the findings were potentially as bad for him. 'Vile heretical conceits denying the eternal deity of Jesus Christ' were discovered among his papers. This was serious business. The Queen was divinely anointed of Christ. To deny His divinity was to deny her authority and tantamount to treason. Just a month before the libels, three Cambridge scholars had been hanged for propounding the cause of Separatism – the doctrine that the Church should not be ruled by the State – another denial of the divine prerogative of the monarch. Kyd was arrested and imprisoned in the Bridewell. The Privy Council was determined to unravel the matter. On 11 May, the Commissioners were authorised to put to torture 'those who refuse to confess the truth ... and by th' extremity thereof to be used ... as often as you think fit, draw them to discover their knowledge concerning the said libells'.

When interrogated, under torture or otherwise, Kyd claimed the papers were shuffled, 'unbeknown to me', among his own 'two years since'. The implication was that they were Marlowe's. A warrant was issued for his arrest on 18 May; he was not in London but at Scadbury Manor, the home of Sir Thomas Walsingham, who – like his cousin, Sir Francis – had played a role in the Queen's spy system. Marlowe appeared before the Privy Council two days later. He was ordered to report daily to one of its officials. He must have realised the precariousness of his situation as he faced a potentially capital charge. He told Kyd he intended to flee to Scotland, a safe refuge for those dissenting from the doctrines of the Church-by-Law established. On 30 May 1593, he met with Ingram Frizer, Nicholas Skeres and Robert Poley – all three described as 'gentlemen' at the house on Deptford Strand of a widow named Eleanor Bull. This was probably what is known as a 'safe house'. All four who gathered there had been in Walsingham's service. It may have been intended that Marlowe undergo a 'debriefing' before embarking aboard a ship bound for Scotland, and safety. The four had dinner, a walk in the garden and supper. There was then a dispute about 'le recknynge'. In a state of fury, Marlowe seized Frizer's dagger and inflicted two head wounds. Frizier grabbed back the knife and stabbed Marlowe through the temple, two inches above his eye, as they struggled together. At the Coroner's inquest, the jury was impressed that Frizer had stood his ground and not fled. In view of Marlowe's record of unprovoked violence, it is reasonable to accept the jury's verdict, 'delivered upon view of the body of Christopher Marlowe, there lying dead and slain', that Frizer had struck in self-defence.

Marlowe's death was a sensation. Rumours and confusion abounded. Gabriel Harvey referred to him as dead of the plague. According to Francis Meres, he was 'stabbed to death by a bawdy servingman, a rival of his in his lewd love'. The Puritan, Thomas Beard, interpreted the death of 'this barking dog' as a divine judgment, but mistakenly thought that it had occurred in a street brawl. His account of Marlowe's last moments is reminiscent of the fate of Dr Faustus:

> The manner of his death being so terrible (for he even cursed and blasphemed to his last gasp and together with his breath an oath flew out of his mouth) that it was not only a manifest sign of God's judgment but also an horrible and fearful terror to all that beheld him.

William Shakespeare was familiar with the Coroner's verdict. 'Where a man's verses cannot be understood,' states Touchstone in *As You Like It*, 'nor a man's good wit seconde with the forward child's understanding, it strikes a man more dead than a great reckoning in a little room.' The jester is referring to Marlowe's admired line in *The Jew of Malta* – 'infinite treasures in a little room'. That the reckoning was 'great' gives the cause for the quarrel. Marlowe may have assumed that the bill was on Walsingham and reacted with characteristic violence when he found it was not.

Marlowe was on Shakespeare's mind when he wrote *As You Like It*. He pays touching tribute to the dead poet with a reference to his poem, *The Passionate Shepherd to his Love* and quotes directly from *Hero and Leander*:

> Dead shepherd, now I find thy saw of might,
> He never loved who loved not at first sight.

The Topical Broadsheet

As may be expected, William Shakespeare's name generated a large apocrypha of works attributed to him, often on flimsy evidence. A type of play that does not appear in his accepted opus is what might be described as 'the topical broadsheet' – the telling of some shocking contemporary event such as a murder.[3] The 1580s saw a huge surge in the production of pamphlets on such sensations, often published within days of the incidents they described. They included accounts of trials and executions, particularly those of Catholic 'traytours', and a wide spectrum of events overseas, such as *A true discourse of the assault committed upon William Prince of Orange* in 1582, or, *Newes from the Englishe armye out of Britanne the thirde of June 1591*.[4] It is not surprising that such events were brought to the stage. A probable early prototype is the now-lost *The History of Murderous Michael*, performed at Court by Sussex's Men in 1578. The best-known such work is *Arden of Faversham*, a play of undetermined authorship that was published in 1592. It is based on the true story of Thomas Arden and the failed attempts of his wife Alice, and her lover Mosby, to murder him.

Eventually they engage two villainous ex-soldiers, Black Will and Shakebag, to do the job. Together with Alice, they stab Arden to death in his own home and dump his body in a field in a snowstorm, in the hope that it will appear that he was attacked by 'footpads'. In a scene worthy of a Victorian melodrama, a trail of footprints in the snow leads directly back to Arden's house. Justice is done ... well, not exactly. Two of those arraigned and executed were guilty merely by association, and innocent of the crime. Nor is Arden an admirable character. He had made a fortune by unscrupulously trading in monastic properties after the dissolution, including those at Faversham. It may be wondered whether the anonymous author was not expressing disapproval of the destruction of the monastic system with its inherent works of charity and its replacement by entrepreneurial greed.

There has been much speculation on who the author, or authors, of *Arden of Faversham* was. The quality of the script is reflected in the fact that the three leading playwrights of the day, Marlowe, Kyd and Shakespeare, have had their advocates. The play is almost certainly the product of a collaboration and some commentators have detected Shakespeare's hand in its middle scenes.

Because the subject matter of such plays tended to be the latest gory sensation – and so not long remembered – it was not usually a genre of great longevity. Such plays formed little part in the repertory of the King's Men, but they presented *A Yorkshire Tragedy* in 1608. It recounts the story of the horrific murders perpetrated by Walter Calverley on his family on 23 April 1605. A broadsheet about his awful crimes appeared in June and a ballad in July, even before he had been put on trial. Like *Arden of Faversham*, the subject gained interest because it dealt not with the actions of the criminal classes, but with those of social standing. *The Miseries of Enforced Marriage* by George Wilkins was performed by the King's Men at around the same time. The title reflects the fact that Calverley had been persuaded to abandon a romantic attachment with a local lass and marry a granddaughter of Lord Cobham, whom he heartily disliked.

A Yorkshire Tragedy is restricted to ten scenes. Uniquely, apart from three servants, the characters bear no names, but are known by their roles – Wife, Husband, Master, Knight, etc. This may have been through pressure from Lord Cobham to protect the name of his family. The same pressures may have caused the murders to be dropped from Wilkins' play and a reconciliation substituted.

The theme of the play is one of an eternal domestic tragedy. The husband is a spendthrift, running through the family fortune in debaucheries. When he hears that a cousin has been arrested for a debt for which he is responsible, he blames his wife for his self-inflicted disasters, claiming that his three sons aren't of his begetting. Four gentlemen intervene and the husband is wounded in the resultant brawl. One gentleman tells him their intention was not to kill him but to save him from himself. He calls on him to remember the example of his distinguished forebears:

> Alas, that hate should bring us to our grave!
> You see my sword's not thirsty for your life.
> I am sorrier for your wound than yourself;
> Y'are of a virtuous house; show virtuous deeds;
> Tis not your honour, 'tis your folly bleeds.
> Much good has been expected in your life:
> Cancel not all men's hopes: You have a wife
> Kind and obedient: heap not wrongful shame
> On her, your posterity. Let only sin be sore,
> And by this fall, rise never to fall more.

As may be expected in this psychologically-observed drama, this well-intentioned intervention only makes things worse for the wife. 'I'm to be reveng'd!' he shouts.

> My strumpet wife,
> It is thy quarrel that rips thus my flesh,
> And makes my breast spit blood! But thou shalt bleed.
> Vanquished? Got down? Unable e'en to speak?
> Surely 'tis want of money makes men weak.
> Ay, 'twas that o'erthrew me; I'd ne'er been down else.

The Master of an unnamed college arrives and tells the husband, 'that hopeful young gentleman, your brother, whose virtues we all love dearly through your default and unnatural negligence, lies in bond executed for your debt, a prisoner, all his studies amazed, his hope strook dead, and the pride of his youth muffled in those dark clouds of oppression.'

The husband goes back into the house. His little son enters, carrying a top and a scourge. A heart-rending scene ensues. 'What ails you, father? Are you not well? I cannot scourge my top as long as you stand so.'

In a touch of terrifying realism, the little boy thinks his father is playing a game with him with his fearsome looks. 'Puh,' he says. 'You cannot make me afear'd with this. I fear no Vizards.'[5]

The stage direction reads: '*Husband takes up the child by the skirts of its long coat in one hand and draws his dagger with the other.*' A motivation is offered for his crazed actions.

He is seeking to kill his children to spare them the disgrace of living in penury.

'Up sir, for here thou hast no inheritance left.'
'Oh, what will you do father?' cries the son plaintively. 'I am your white boy.'[6]

As he stabs his son, the father declares that in killing him, he is saving the family honour by saving him from having to beg for his living:

Bleed, bleed, rather than beg, beg;
Be not thy name's disgrace.
Spurn thou thy fortunes first if they be base:
Come view thy second brother. Fates,
My children's blood shall spin into your faces!
You shall see
How confidently we scorn beggary!

The Husband carries his mortally wounded son upstairs with the intention of killing his younger brother who is with his mother. When the Maid tries to defend the child, he throws her down the stairs with an allusion that the audience would have recognised:

So, the surest way to charm a woman's tongue
Is break her neck: a politician did it.

The reference is to the supposed incident when the Earl of Leicester, who sought to marry Queen Elizabeth and enhance his power in the land, had his wife pushed down the stairs, breaking her neck. It would not have passed the censor in the previous reign.

The Husband stabs his second child who is in his wife's arms. He then takes off with the intention of killing his youngest son, who is with his wet nurse, but he falls from his horse and is taken into custody.

A Yorkshire Tragedy was entered onto the Stationers' Register on 2 May 1608. Its authorship was ascribed to 'William Shakespere'. The published quarto repeats this attribution and states that the play was performed by the King's Men at the Globe Theatre. The attribution is repeated in 1619 as part of an ambitious project, never completed, by Thomas Pavier, to publish a compilation of Shakespeare's complete works. This type of domestic tragedy is not a genre with which Shakespeare is generally associated, but that is not in itself a reason why he should not have turned his hand to it. He is credited with the authorship by three reliable sources and there is no other attribution. The quality of the work makes it worthy of his pen, yet the weight of modern scholarly opinion credits Thomas Middleton as the most likely author. If this was the case, why was Shakespeare so accredited? The obvious answer that the stationer was attempting to capitalise on his name is unlikely, since the text comes with the apparent approbation of the Company.

A possible explanation for Shakespeare's name on the title page is that, as the senior resident dramatist to the Company, he may have been responsible for assessing plays that were presented for potential production. That he had such a role is suggested by the story that it was his insistence that brought Ben Jonson's *Every Man in His Humour to* the stage. On other occasions, he may actually have rewritten whole parts of plays. This seems to have been the case with *Pericles*, of which he appears to have composed about half, the remainder probably being the work of George Watkins.

Whoever the author of *A Yorkshire Tragedy* was, he was a writer of talent and introspection, capable of interpreting the drama to levels of psychological depth. When the Wife tells the Husband that she has persuaded her uncle to rescue him from his financial troubles, he does not react with joy, as might be expected, but with furious wounded pride that his difficulties have been revealed:

> Thou politick whore, subtler than nine devils, was this thy journey to *Nunck*, to set down the history of me, of my state and fortunes? Shall I that dedicated myself to pleasure be now confin'd in service to crouch and stand like an old man i' th' hams, my hat off?[7]

The Husband is about to stab her when he is interrupted by a servant who announces the arrival of a visitor. The plaintiff lament of the wife on his departure has echoes of Desdemona:

> Was ever wife so wretchedly beset?
> Had not this news stepp'd in between, the point
> Had offered violence to my breast.
> That which some women call great misery
> Would show but little here, would scarce be seen
> Amongst my miseries. I may compare
> For all wretched fortunes with all wives that are;
> Nothing will please him, until all be nothing.

As with Shakespeare's great tragedies, it is the Husband's personal foibles that bring him down, and others with him. He has self-knowledge of where his indulgencies have brought him, but it is pride in his ancient line and the dread of penury that drive him on his homicidal path:

> Terrible, horrible misery! How well was I left, very well, very well! My lands showed like a full moon about me, but now the moon's i' the last quarter, waning, waning. And I am mad to think that moon was mine and my father's, and my forefathers, generations, generations. Down goes the house of us, down, down, it sinks. Now is the name a beggar, begs in me that name which hundreds of years has made this shire famous: in me, and my posterity runs out. In my seed five are made miserable beside myself. My riot is now my brother's jailer, my wife's sighing, my three boys' penury, and mine own confusion.

'I that ever did in abundance dwell', he reflects, 'For me exceeds the throes of Hell!'

This harrowing play was not without its *bon mots*. 'If marriage be honourable,' says the Husband, 'then cuckolds are honourable, for they cannot exist without marriage.'

And Let Those that Play Your Clowns

It is a matter of conjecture how and when the character sometimes described as 'the Clown' became an important part of the *dramatis personae*. Certainly Richard Tarlton was part of this transition. It is a development likely to have been enhanced by William Shakespeare. That Kempe and his colleagues were regarded as being associated closely with the process is revealed in the undergraduate play, *The Pilgrimage to Parnassus*: 'Clownes have bene thrust into playes by head and shoulders ever since Kempe could make a scurvey face.'

No Company could be without its clown, although the relationship had its moments of ambivalence. The popularity of the breed is revealed in a piece of contemporary doggerel:

> Why, I would have the fool in every act.
> Be 't comedy or tragedy, I've laugh'd
> Until I cried again, to see what faces
> The rogue will make. Oh it does me good
> To see him hold out 's chin, hang down his hands,
> And twirl his bauble. There is ne'er a part
> About him but breaks jests.

This popularity is further revealed in *Return to Parnassus*, the final part of the undergraduate trilogy, in a scene in which 'Kempe' boasts to the 'scholars' of the riches to be had from the theatre and claims equality of fame with Richard Burbage:

> But be merry, my lads, you have happened on the most excellent vocation in the world for money: they come north and south to bring it to our play- house; and for honours, who is of more report than Dick Burbage and Will Kemp; there's not a country wench that can dance Sellenger's Round[8] but can talk of Dick Burbage and Will Kemp.

Nothing is known of Kempe's early life. He performed at Leicester House in 1585, probably as jester to Robert Dudley. He accompanied the Earl on his ruinous military expedition to the Netherlands that year. Sir Philip Sidney sent letters home from there with 'Will, my Lord of Leicester's jesting player'. Later he complained that Kempe had delivered them to Lady Leicester rather than Lady Sidney. After this brief return to England, he went on a great adventure with two other future Lord Chamberlain's Men, George Bryan and Thomas Pope. They played before King Frederick II of Denmark at Elsinore, a name redolent in Shakespeareana, and before Christian I, Elector of Saxony, on an extensive tour.

Kempe fulfilled the role of the large and merry clown. A quarto records that he played Peter, the servant, in *Romeo and Juliet*, a small part, but one that would have given scope for extemporising. The First Folio records that he played Dogberry in *Much Ado about Nothing* and that Richard Cowley played Verges.

According to *Tarlton's Jestes*, that famous clown recommended that Robert Armin should take his place on his retirement. The son of a tailor from King's Lynn, at the age of 13, he was taken on as an apprentice at the Royal Mint by the Master of Works, John Lonyston, a friend of his father. On one occasion he was sent to collect money from a lodger at an inn kept by Tarlton.[9] When the man defaulted, young Armin wrote verses satirising him on the wall:

> Oh world, why wilt thou lye?
> Is this Charles the Great! That I deny.
> Indeed Charles the Great before,
> But now Charles the lesses, being poore.

Tarlton was so amused by the verse that he wrote a riposte beneath it:

> A wagge thou art, none can prevent thee;
> And thy desert shall content thee.
> Let me devine. As I am
> My adopted sonne therefore be,
> To enjoy my clownes suite after me.

He was true to his word and took on the youth as his apprentice and successor. Armin could have had no better mentor. He may already have had something of a literary reputation when he completed his apprenticeship in 1592 (if he ever did so). In 1590 his name was affixed to the preface of a religious tract entitled, *A Brief Resolution of the Right Religion*. Both Thomas Nashe and Gabriel Harvey mention that he was a writer of ballads, but none has survived. At some point he joined the theatre company under the patronage of William Brydges, 4th Baron Chandos, Little is known of this company, which seems to have toured southern England. He wrote a number of plays, including *The History of the Two Maids of More clacke*... which may have been written during his time with the Chandos Company and regularly revised to provide contemporary allusions. He implies this in his preface to the quarto of 1609.

Armin created a different kind of Fool, a melancholy and cryptic commentator on the events around him. He was noted for his singing. According to Catherine A. Henze, the average number of songs in Shakespeare's plays after his arrival increased from 1.25 per production to 3.44.[10] He was noted for his ability to extemporise doggerel on subjects suggested by the audience. If not to the collectivity of clowns in general, it might well have been Armin to whom Shakespeare was referring in his advice to the players in *Hamlet*:

> And let those who play
> Your clowns speak no more than is set down for them.

Sir Philip Sidney questioned whether clowns should be on stage at all.

> But, besides these gross absurdities, how all their plays be neither right tragedies nor right comedies, mingling kings and clowns, not because the matter so carrieth it, but thrust in the clown by head and shoulders to play a part in majestical matters, with neither decency nor discretion; so as neither the admiration and commiseration, nor the right sportfulness, is by their mongrel tragi-comedy obtained.

Lord have Mercy on Us

At the time of Marlowe's death Shakespeare was living in the parish of St Helen's in Bishopsgate within the City Walls. Nearby was the impressive Crosby Place. Built in 1466 as the home of a wealthy merchant, it was the largest house in London. It had been home to the Duke of Gloucester, later King Richard III. It features in the play of that name. 'When you have done, repair to Crosby Place,' he tells the murderers of Clarence. To reach The Theatre, Shakespeare would pass through the Bishop's Gate in the City walls which gave the area its name. A bishop's mitre was carved in stone high above the portico. Beyond was the street called Bishopsgate. Along its breadth were numerous inns – the *White Hart*, *Dolphin*, *Green Dragon*, *Wrestlers*, *Angel*, *Catherine Wheel* and the *Black Bull*, a theatrical venue, where the Queen's Players sometimes performed. He would have passed the hospital known as Bedlam, where those declared insane were incarcerated. The stench from the drains was noxious and the noise of the inmates 'so hideous, so great that they are more able to drive a man that hath his wits rather out of them'. Beyond were 'baseless tenements and houses of disorderly resort … as namely poor cottages and habitations of beggars and people without trade, stables, inns, alehouses, taverns, garden houses converted to dwellings, ordinaries, dicing houses, bowling alleys and brothel houses'. Needless to say, 'these noisesome and disorderly houses' harboured a 'great number of dissolute, loose and insolent people'.

The corollary to such overcrowding was plague. One of London's worst epidemics erupted in 1593. The immediate reaction of the authorities was to close all public places of entertainment. Rosemary, believed to be a disinfectant, was scattered in the streets. For the same purpose, people saturated their clothing with vinegar. The afflicted were obliged to carry a long white rod if they ventured abroad, those who tended them, a red one. Physicians wore bizarre masks with long beaks filled with oil of bergamo as a disinfectant. A red cross and the words 'Lord have mercy on us' were painted on the doors of infected houses. We begin to understand the force of Mercutio's 'A plague on both your houses.'

Puritan preachers and polemicists regarded the outbreak of plague as a punishment for sin. Others considered that a malignant alignment of the planets created 'miasma', or 'bad air', a poisonous vapour, or mist filled with particles from decomposed matter. Shakespeare refers to both these supposed causes in *Timon of Athens*:

A planetary plague, when Jove
Will o'er some high-vied City, long hang his poison
In the sick air.

Many must have doubted whether the theatre would ever return to its former state. The Earl of Pembroke's Men went on an extensive tour during 1592–3 to places as far apart as York, King's Lynn and Rye, but it did not end well. In a letter to Edward Alleyn on 28 September 1593, Philip Henslowe wrote that he had heard that the Company had been forced to pawn its costumes. The Burbages would have had to continue paying for the lease of The Theatre, with no hope of a return. A growing antagonism with their landlord may date from this time.

Early in 1594, leave was given for the playhouses to reopen. The Earl of Sussex's Men opened a six-week season at the Rose Theatre on 24 January, with the performance of a play which Henslowe recorded as *Titus & Ondronicus.* The 'take' – £3 8*s.* 0*d.* – was high, which demonstrates the enthusiasm with which the public greeted the return of the drama. The choice of play indicates that, understandably, the Company had nothing new in its repertoire. Further performances on 23 January and 6 February reflected the continuing taste for *grand guignol.* On 4 February, the company performed *The Jew of Malta*. On 6 and 8 April, it joined forces with the Queen's Men to present *The Moste Famous Chronicle historye of Leire King of England and his Three Daughters.* This was a version of a British folk tale that had been recorded by Geoffrey de Monmouth as early as 1135. The anonymous author of the play expanded this old tale into a five-act drama, adding new characters and situations, which was to provide the background to William Shakespeare's version.

A New Patron

No sooner were Derby's Men back in business than another blow fell. On 15 April 1594, the Earl died under circumstances that can only be described as suspicious. He had succeeded to the title on the death of his father just seven months before. According to John Stow, a man named Richard Hesketh attempted to persuade him to advance his claim to the throne. He threatened him with a terrible death if he did not concur. The Earl, 'fearing lest some trappe were laid for him', rejected the idea. He died under mysterious and painful circumstances a few months later. 'He expired in floure of his youth', wrote William Camden:

> Not without suspicion of poyson, being tormented by cruel paynes, by frequent vomitings of a dark colour like rusty yron ... The matter vomited up stayned the silver Basons in such sort, that by no art they could possibly be brought up againe to their former brightnesse ... No small suspicion lighted upon the Gentleman of his horse, who as soone as the Earl took to his bed, tooke his best horse, and fled.

Derby's Men were on tour in East Anglia at the time of his death. The loss of their patron and the influence he could exert on their behalf represented a serious crisis. The process by which a new patron was found is uncertain, but there can have been no better choice than Henry Carey, the 1st Lord Hunsdon. In late

1594, the Lord Chamberlain's Company was formed. His connections with James Burbage went back at least till 1584 when the creator of The Theatre had 'declared himself 'Lord Blunsdon's Man'. As the holder of the hugely-influential office of Lord Chamberlain, he was in charge of Edmund Tilney, whose task as Master of the Revels, as the name implies, was to organise Court entertainments. Over the years the role had evolved so that he became, in essence, the official censor of plays. He was a force for tolerance, tending to exercise his authority only over material that might be deemed subversive or offensive. His support protected the players from the hostile civic authorities. William Webbe, Lord Mayor in 1592, named him as an obstacle to ending public performances in the City. His importance for the Company was increased further in 1594, when he was made responsible for licensing playhouses.

The pressing need for the theatre companies was to raise money. One way to do this was to get the plays whose scripts they owned into print. On 6 February 1594, the printer, John Danter, entered *A Noble Roman Historye of Titus Andronicus* onto the Stationers' Register. It was the first of Shakespeare's plays to be published. On 12 March, *Henry VI, Part II* was likewise registered.

Another theatrical collaboration occurred that summer. Two years of neglect as the theatres stood idle in all weathers necessitated refurbishments at both The Theatre and the Rose. Indeed the Rose was ordered closed by the Privy Council between 16 May and 18 June, possibly for that reason. So, the Lord Chamberlain's Men and the Admiral's Men collaborated, or perhaps merely performed within the same venue. Henslowe put on a season of plays at the Newington Butts Theatre between 3 and 13 June. Again, the productions were revivals and like *King Leir*, *Hamlet* and *The Taming of a Shrew* were of plays that were prototypes of later Shakespearean works. A further production of *Titus Andronicus* demonstrates its continuing popularity.

Henslowe's season was the swansong of the Newington Butts playhouse. In July 1594, the freeholders, the Dean and Chapter of Canterbury Cathedral, granted the lease to one Paul Buck on condition that he convert it to another use. Plays were not to be performed there after Michaelmas Day (29 September), which is probably when Henslowe's rental expired. This would seem an unnecessary codicil. The theatre was on the brink of collapse. According to the the Privy Council, 'of large tyme plaies have not there bene used on working daies'. Given that performances were not permitted on the Sabbath, the implication is that the theatre only opened on public holidays, if at all.

The value to the Lord Chamberlain's Men of its patron was demonstrated on 8 October 1594, when Lord Hunsdon addressed a letter to the Lord Mayor, Sir Richard Martin. His 'nowe Company of Players' was seeking to use the Cross Keys Inn as its winter base, but the Corporation had rejected its licensing application. He wrote in conciliatory style. 'Thankes be to god there is nowe no danger of the sicknes'. The letter indicates the length of a contemporary dramatic performance – between two and three hours. It also reveals that performances were generally announced by the beating of drums and the blast of trumpets.

> They have undertaken to me that, where heretofore they began not their Plaies til towardes fower a clock, they will now begin at at two & haue don between fourer and fiue and will nott vse anie Drumes or trumpettes att all for the callinge of peopell together and shalbe contributories to the poore of the parishe where they plaie accordinge to their habilities.

The outcome is uncertain, but the letter confirms that the objections of the City Fathers to theatrical performances were not entirely theological, but could be related to the disruption they caused.

With the reopening of the Rose Theatre, the Admiral's Men embarked upon a strenuous schedule. Henslowe recorded that, between June and September in 1594, the company performed seventeen plays, eight of which were 'ne' (new?), in 105 performances. On 19 July 1594, he recorded that 'an enterlude entituled Godfrey of Bulloigne with the conquest of Jerusalem' was performed by the Admiral's Men. This must be Thomas Heywood's *The Four Prentices of London*, a romantic extravaganza with a long stage history. 'As it hath bene diverse times Acted at the Red Bull by the Queenes Maiesties Servants', the subtitle stated when it was first printed in 1615. The four prentices of the title are the sons of the Earl of Boloigne, who has lost his inheritance to a usurper. Despite their aristocratic antecedents, they are all London apprentices. Godfrey is a mercer, Guy a goldsmith, Charles a haberdasher and Eustace, a grocer. In contrast to the contemporary image of apprentices as riotous and subversive, Heywood's characters bring to their trades the aristocratic qualities that they are heirs to and to which, by implication, every apprentice has the potential to aspire. Godfrey, the eldest, expresses this clearly:

> I hold it no disparage to my birth,
> Though I be born an Earl, to have the skill
> and the full knowledge of the Mercers trade,
> and were I to create anew,
> It should not grieve me to have spent my time,
> The secrets of so rich a trade to know,
> By which advantage and great profits grow.

He demonstrates that not all apprentices have bad attitudes:

Bound I must obey: since I have undertook
To serve my master truly for seven years,
My duty shall both answer that desire,
And my master's profit in every way.

After various preposterous escapades, Robert of Normandy succeeds to the English throne on the death of his father, William the Conqueror. It is his duty to crown a King of the newly conquered Jerusalem. Godfrey declines the offer, which Guy then accepts. Charles becomes King of Cyprus and Eustace, King of Sicily. The rightful inheritance as sons of the Earl of Boilogne was more than restored.

That the play is wildly historically inaccurate almost goes without saying. Robert of Normandy never became King of England. There was indeed a Count of Boulogne, Eustace II, who acquired estates in England in return for his part in the Norman Conquest. He had three sons, none of whom followed the unlikely career (for them) of becoming London apprentices. Eustace, the oldest, succeeded his father as Count of Boulogne. Godfrey, the second son, was created King of Jerusalem on its capture by the Crusaders. On his death, the youngest brother, Baldwin, became King. But this is to miss the point, which was to provide a rumbustious entertainment while at the same time warning of the perils of Islamic perfidy.

Chapter Four

'According to their Habilities'

'A Bounty Very Great'

The backbone of the new company was the former Lord Strange's Men. It was a bold response to the crisis. Until now, the Burbages had owned the company exclusively, but they had received little or no income for two years and had many outgoings. They needed to spread the load. The way forward was to form a 'super-troupe' of top performers. The incentive of being a 'sharer' may have been a means of attracting them into the Company. Although there was an initial outlay and always the possibility of indemnifying losses, becoming a sharer was the surest route to wealth in the theatre. This was the first time that members of a theatrical company had joined the management. The arrangement ensured the life-long loyalty of many of the leading participants in the enterprise. It underwrote its excellence and stability. Over the years, other members of the Company achieved the status of 'sharers'. To raise the necessary funds, Cuthbert and Richard Burbage brought in six others. Each would own 10 per cent of the freehold. It was vital to secure William Shakespeare. His participation could not be assumed. His name had been associated with at least three other companies. With the deaths of Marlowe, Kyd and Greene he became unchallenged as the leading living dramatist. That he was also an actor was a bonus. He had become affluent by the mid-1590s, when the average payment to a playwright for a play was £8 – a goodly sum, but not enough to make a man wealthy. Yet, in this period, Shakespeare bought into the company, bought and refurbished the second biggest house in Stratford, embarked on the costly business of acquiring a coat of arms and probably set up his brother Gilbert as a London haberdasher. A major factor in this wealth may have been the generous support of a patron. He had dedicated the two narrative poems written in the plague year, *Venus and Adonis* and *The Rape of Lucrece*, to the 3rd Earl of Southampton. It was suggested by his early biographer, Nicholas Rowe, that the Earl was so pleased with the poems that he gave the poet a lavish reward:

> There is one instance so singular in the magnificence of this Patron of Shakespeare's that if I had not been assur'd of it by Sir William D'Avenant, who was probably acquainted with his Affairs, I should not have ventur'd to

> have insert'd, that my Lord Southampton, at one time, gave him a thousand Pounds, to enable him to go ahead with a Purchase when he had a mind to. A bounty very great and very rare at any time.

The story has a tenable pedigree. Rowe's informant was probably the leading actor of the Restoration period, Thomas Betterton, whose informant was probably Sir William Davenant, Shakespeare's godson. Although he was but a child when the poet died, his parents had known him well, so we are but three whispers from the poet. Southampton was a noted and lavish patron of poets, a backer of colonial ventures and a considerable benefactor of his Cambridge college. As a devotee of the theatre he might well have responded to a request to help the company restore its fortunes. He would also have had a debt of honour to William Shakespeare as the dedicatee of his poems. The expected collateral from patron to poet was financial largesse. As for so many, the plague years would have been lean ones for Shakespeare.

Will Kempe was another whom it was important to secure. As one of the most renowned clowns of his day, it was a considerable coup to have recruited him. His position as a sharer may have been the price to be paid for his services. That he had assumed a pre-eminence in his art and was regarded as the natural successor to Richard Tarlton, is indicated by Thomas Nashe's dedication of his pamphlet, *An Almond for a Parrot* to him as 'viceregent general to the ghost of Dick Tarlton'.

Kempe's confreres on his European adventure of a decade before, George Bryan and Thomas Pope, had strong pedigrees in a number of companies. Both were in Lord Strange's Men as was Augustine Phillips, a key member of the Company who was also a musician and had a role in the training of the Company's apprentices, musical and otherwise. In his will in 1605, he left his cistern, bandora and lute to James Sands, on the 'expiration of his term of years in his indenture of apprentice-hood'. His bass viola he left to his 'late apprentice', Samuel Gilborne, and a 30/- gold piece to each of his 'servants' the actors, Christopher Beeston and Alexander Cooke. He was probably the composer of a jig, *Phillips His Slipper*, which was entered on the Stationers' Register in 1595. He also had involvement in the Company's financial affair.

Phillips' wife Anne bore him at least five children. In 1594, he was living in Paris Gardens on Bankside, a convenient location for the future Globe Theatre. He was the stepbrother of Thomas Pope, and his sister married Robert Gough, whose name is listed among the Company's twenty-six principal actors in the Shakespeare First Folio. Such close family ties reflected the close relationships within the circle, rather like modern fairground and circus folk, and may represent a continuity with the travelling entertainers of previous generations.

It is not over-fanciful to suggest that many Elizabethan actors and musicians were following the trade of their forebears.

Henry Condell and John Heminges were to be long-serving members of the company. Heminges was baptised on 26 November 1556, at the church of St Peter de Witton in Droitwich. He came to London at the age of 12 to serve as a grocer's apprentice, becoming a Freeman of the Grocers' Company on 24 April 1587. He capitalised on this status to found a business as a wholesale grocer. He may well have cornered the healthy trade in refreshments at the theatres where the Company played. On 13 December 1608, he was admitted to the lucrative position of one of the ten sea coal meters appointed to measure the amount of coal imported into the City. Between 1595 and 1628 he took on ten apprentices; ostensibly these were with the Grocers' Company, but eight appear to have performed in the theatre.

Heminges was another marrying within the circle. In March 1588, he wed Rebecca Knell (née Edwards), the 17-year-old widow of William Knell who had been killed in the brawl in Thame the year before. The wedding took place at the church of St Mary, Aldermanbury, where Rebecca had married Knell. Heminges was to become its churchwarden. His wife would bear him fourteen children.

Henry Condell was just 18 when the new company was formed. He must already have acquired a high reputation as an actor. He had the resources to buy into the role, although he would have been legally a minor and there would have been difficulties for him in taking it on. Through family circumstance, he was to inherit considerable property in London. On 24 October 1596, he married Elizabeth Smart at the Church of St Laurence Pountney. Her father is described as a 'gentleman', again indicating the rising status of the theatre. She bore her husband nine children, but only three survived to adulthood. They lived in the parish of St Mary Aldermanbury where, like his colleague, he became a churchwarden.

The formation of the Lord Chamberlain's Men left a number of actors behind. Derby's Men continued as a company under the patronage of Ferdinando Stanley's heir and brother, William, the 6th Earl. The troupe was led by the actor, Robert Browne. It spent much of its time touring the provinces, but received payments for performances at Court in 1600 and 1601. Robert Browne ran the Boar's Head Theatre in the City of London between 1601 and 1603. He was a figure of some standing. In October 1603, Joan Alleyn wrote to her husband, telling him the news of his death. Despite the loss of their leading performer, Derby's Men continued to tour until 1620.

Whether William Shakespeare had continued to write plays during the plague years in the expectation of the reopening of the theatres is unknown, but given the scale of his subsequent outpourings, it is likely. His relationship with the new Company is different. Rather than being a journeyman actor and playwright working for whosoever chose to employ him, he is a force within it. Such was his dominance of the work with the Lord Chamberlain's Men that the company must almost have seemed to exist solely to perform his works. In future, all his plays were written for the Company. Each part is drafted for a particular actor. It is not over-fanciful to detect a new confidence and a distinctive style in his work. The norm was collaboration – churning out collective works at great rapidity to fulfil the almost insatiable demand for new plays. Shakespeare did collaborate – but rarely. He could dictate his literary terms and metier, breaking out of the classical straitjacket to develop his own style. While it is difficult to date most of the early plays precisely, there is a pre- and post-plague feel to his output.

Through Thicke and Thin

The other companies were still reeling from the effects of the plague and with the temporary fall in popularity of the children's companies, the Lord Chamberlain's Men established an ascendancy over the popular stage. Its first act was to embark on a provincial tour which took it as far as York. The prosperous market town of Marlborough may have been the first place to see this exciting new venture. The reward was not great; a mere 2/8*d*, but the Company may have welcomed this chance to set its wares out in public before moving on to more lucrative locations. They would have secured the usual permission of the Mayor to present a further performance in the White Hart next to the Guildhall. This was the first of a number of visits by the Company to the town, so they must have expected a friendly welcome. They were probably on their way to Bristol; an obvious target, since it was the third largest city in Britain and one of the wealthiest. There they would have played in the lofty Guild Hall and moved on to Bath, to the Guild Hall near the Abbey. On the same tour they visited Ipswich, where they were paid a handsome forty shillings. Later, 'Rich Burbage' received payment for two comedies performed at Court during the Christmas Revels on 26 and 28 December.

The touring companies were adept at adapting their productions to a wide variety of settings: Guild Halls, inns, colleges and mansions of the wealthy. Over the years, the Lord Chamberlain's Men covered the length and breadth of the country, visiting, among many other places, Cambridge, Faversham, Rye, Dover, Oxford, Shrewsbury, Coventry, Wilton, Barnstaple, Maidstone, Dunwich, Hythe, New Romney, Folkestone, Stafford and Nottingham.

Travelling could be tough, through all weathers, along roads that were little more than cart tracks. Will Kempe described an incident on the road between

Chelmsford and Braintree on his famous 'jig' from London to Norwich in 1600. 'My taberer strucke up,' he wrote, 'and lightly I tript forward, but I had the heaviest way that ever mad Morrice dancer trod':

> With hey and ho, through thicke and thin,
> the hobby horse quite forgotten,
> I follow'd as I did begin,
> although the way were rotten

> This foule way I could finde no ease in, thicke woods being on eyther side of the lane: the lane likewise being full of deep holes, sometimes I skipted up to the waste: but, it is an old Proverb. That it is a little comfort to the miserable to have companions, and amidst this merry way, I had some mirth by an unlookt for accident.
>
> It was the custome of honest Country Fellows, my unknowne friends, upon hearing my Pype ... to get up and beare mee company a little way. In this foule way two pretty plaine youthes watcht me, and with their kindness somewhat hindred me. One a fine light fellow would be still before me, the other ever at y heeles. At length coming to a broad plash of water and mud, which could not be avoyded, I fecht a rise, yet fell in over the anckles at the further end. My youth that follow'd me, tooke his jump, and stuck fast in the midst, crying out to his companion, come George, call yee this dauncing. Ile go no further: for indeede hee could goe no further, till his fellow was faine to wade and help him out. I could not chuse but lough to see howe like two frogges they laboured: a hartye farwell I gave them, and they faintly bad God speed me, saying if I daunst that durties way this seaven yeares againe, they would never daunce after me.

That touring had its hazards is demonstrated by the incident in Thame that led to the death of William Knell. On 15 June 1583, the Queen's Men were performing in the courtyard of the Red Lion Inn in Norwich. Richard Tarlton, John Bentley and John Singer were on stage, armed with swords, when a man named Wynsdon tried to enter without paying. In a struggle with the gatekeeper, money was spilt. The three actors leapt off the stage. After Wynsdon was struck on the head with the hilt of his sword by Bentley he ran off, pursued by the actors. A bystander was attacked after throwing a stone at Bentley, which hit him on the head. He later died of his wounds. Presumably the actors entered the usual plea of self-defence and nothing seems to have come of it.[1]

'Star crossed Lovers'

Hunsdon's role as the man ultimately in charge of the Queen's Revels soon paid off for the new Company. During the 1594/5 Christmas season, on St Stephen's Day and Holy Innocents Day, they played 'two severall comedies or interludes' at Court for a fee of £13 6*s*. 8*d*. On 15 March 1595, the royal accounts recorded payments to 'William Kempe, William Shakespeare and Richard Burbage'. Her Majesty appears delighted with what she saw. The accounts record the payment of an additional £6 13*s*. 3*d*. – half as much again as the original sum: perhaps a bonus for an outstanding performance?

There is a strong case for making *Romeo and Juliet* an early example of Shakespeare's new confidence. It was his most successful work to date. The title page of the first quarto in 1597 stated that it 'hath been often (with great applause) played publiquely'. That the plague was fresh in his mind is demonstrated by his reference to the 'Searchers of the Dead', the elderly women who examined corpses to ascertain whether they had died of plague. If so, the house was boarded up and the inhabitants forbidden to go abroad until there are had been no further outbreaks for forty days. Thus Romeo does not receive the message about Juliet's feigned death because the priest who is supposed to convey it is confined to a house in which an outbreak of plague has been identified by the searchers.

> Going to find a barefoot brother out
> One of our order to associate me
> Here in this city, visiting the sick
> And finding him, the searchers of the town,
> Suspecting that we both were in a house
> Where the infectious pestilence did reign,
> Seal'd up the doors and would not let us forth,
> So that my speed to Mantua was stayed.

Romeo and Juliet is a 'Revenge' tragedy with a difference. The feud between the two houses is the focus of the action. That Tybalt kills Romeo's friend Mercutio, and is then killed by Romeo, appears to set up the classic cycle of retribution, but it is not to be. The play moves beyond such nemesis to a Christian theme of growth and reconciliation through suffering. The fate of the lovers expiates the fallen world of Verona and gives future hope. Their love brings about their destruction, but in the process it leads to the reconciliation of the warring houses. As the Prince expresses it:

Where be these enemies? Capulet? Montague?
See, what a scourge is laid upon your hate,
That heaven finds means to kill your joys with love.
And I for winking at your discords too,
Have lost a brace of kinsmen: all are punish'd.

Capulet: O brother Montague, give me thy hand:
This is my daughter's jointure, for no more
Can I demand.

Montague: But I can give thee more:
For I will raise her statue in pure gold;
That while Verona by that name is known,
There shall be no figure at such rate be set
As that of true and faithful Juliet.

Capulet: As rich shall Romeo by his lady lie;
Poor sacrifices of our enmity.

This theme of expiation is one to which Shakespeare will return in his great tragedies. Here circumstance is the overriding theme. Romeo is 'fortune's fool' and the lovers are famously 'star-crossed'.

In *Romeo and Juliet* Shakespeare develops a technique characteristic of his innovative genius. He gives his characters a life beyond the stage, even in the backdrop to the plot. The cause of the 'ancient quarrel' between Montague and Capulet is deep-rooted, but its origins are lost in history. Only the hate remains, carrying its own volition. As the opening scene demonstrates, it has even communicated itself to the servants of the respective houses. Shakespeare even creates a credible character who is not seen on stage. Romeo's first passion is not for Juliet but for Rosaline, another young lady of Verona. 'Be rul'd by me,' advises his cousin, Benvolio, 'forget to think of her.' She emerges as a personality in her own right. Romeo tells Benvolio that she has rejected him because she has sworn to be 'chaste' forever, but, as Friar Lawrence tells him later, she adopted this attitude because she was uncertain of the maturity of his love. 'Oh, she knew well / Thy love did read by rote that could not spell.' Benvolio realises that Romeo, in the flush of love, cannot objectively judge her qualities. 'Compare thy love with some that I shall show,' he tells him. 'And I will make thee think thy swan a crow.' Yet she is the catalyst for the action. 'At this same ancient feast of Capulet's,' Benvolio tells Romeo, 'Sups the fair Rosaline whom thou so loves.' It is here that Romeo meets Juliet, but it is also here that Tybalt makes Romeo the focus of the blood feud, leading to inevitable nemesis.

Shakespeare creates a life beyond the stage for the nurse. She is a widow who has lost her only child – Juliet's exact contemporary:

Susan and she – God rest all Christian souls! –
Were of an age: well, Susan is with God;
She was too good for me.

Another credible character not seen on stage is introduced – the widowed nurse's husband. She recounts an incident from Juliet's infancy:

I remember it well;
'Tis since the earthquake now eleven years;
And she was wean'd – I never shall forget it, –
Of all the days of the year, upon that day;
For I had then laid wormwood to my dug;
Sitting in the sun under the dove-house wall;
My lord and you were then at Mantua: –
Nay I do bear a brain; – but, as I said,
When it did taste the wormwood on the nipple
Of my dug and felt it bitter, pretty fool,
To see it tetchy and fall out with the dug!
'Shake!' quoth the dove-house. ''Twas no need I trow;
To bid me trudge:
And since that time it is eleven years;
For then she could stand alone; nay, by the rood;
She could have run and waddled all about;
For even the day before, she broke her brow;
And then my husband – God be with his soul!
A was a merry man – took up the child;
'Yea,' quoth he, 'dost thou fall upon thy face?
Thou wilt fall backward when thou hast more wit;
Wilt thou not, Jule?' and, by my holy dame,
The pretty wench left crying and said 'Ay';
To see now, how a jest shall come about;
I warrant, an I should live a thousand years,
I never should forget it: 'Wilt thou not, Jule?' quoth he;
And, pretty fool, it stinted and said 'Ay'.

Lady Capulet grows exasperated with the Nurse's repetitions. 'Enough of this, I pray thee, hold thy peace', but the Nurse is in full flight and unstoppable:

Yes madam; yet I cannot choose but laugh;
To think it should leave crying and say 'Ay'.

And yet, I warrant, it had upon its brow
A bump as big as a young cockerel's stone;
A parlous knock; and it cried bitterly:
'Yea,' quoth my husband, 'fall'st upon thy face?'
Thou wilt fall backward when thou comest to age;
Wilt thou not, Jule? it stinted and said 'Ay'.

Juliet shares her mother's frustration at the Nurse's wittering. 'And stint thou too, I pray thee, nurse, say I.' This exasperation as understandable – the Nurse has recounted the anecdote no less than four times, but the audience is entering the wider world that Shakespeare is creating. Through the Nurse's yattering, Juliet, becomes a fully rounded and conceivable character. We even learn the diminutive name by which she was known in infancy – 'Jule'.

We also note the system of relationships characteristic of aristocratic houses. It is the Nurse who has breast-fed and weaned Juliet, who holds her in the love she bore for her lost daughter. Lord and Lady Capulet have affection for their daughter, but look upon her as the means to a dynastic alliance. 'Tell me, daughter Juliet,' Lady Capulet asks, 'How stands your disposition to be married?' Shakespeare sets the scene for her coming encounter with Romeo in her reply. 'It is an honour that I dream not of.' In one short scene, Shakespeare roots his characters in their past and in their destinies. No other dramatist did that.

That the part of Romeo was written for the 28-year-old Richard Burbage is confirmed by an elegy written on his death twenty-five years later: 'Poor Romeo never more shall tears beget / For Juliet's love and cruel Capulet.'

The most likely boy actor to have created the part of Juliet was Robert Gough. The youth of the boy actors is frequently reflected in the parts they played. Juliet is 'fourteen come Lammastide': Lady Capulet, usually portrayed on the modern stage as a mature matron, reveals that she gave birth to Juliet when she was much the same age as her daughter is now, so she is around 28 years old. The Elizabethan stage was a youthful place.

Sir Thomas More

William Shakespeare's antipathy to mob rule, exemplified in his treatment of the Cade rebellion, is made more explicable by a proclamation issued in London in 1590 which promulgated a curfew after 9 pm 'upon pain of imprisonment'. This followed 'a very great outrage lately committed by some apprentices and others being masterless men and vagrant persons' after a concerted assault on Lincoln's Inn, no less. The injunction had little effect. In the following year there were 'sundry great disorders' propagated by 'unlawful great assemblies of multitudes of a popular sort of base condition'. This invoked even more extreme measures. Unlawful assemblies were banned under martial law. Offenders were to be 'execute upon the gallows'.

The riots were frequently directed against immigrants, who were victims of the perennial accusation of undercutting the job market and taking away the livelihoods of native workers. Folk memory recalled the 'Ill' or 'Evil' May Day riots when apprentices launched fearsome attacks on the resented foreigners. On 11 June 1592, a particularly virulent outbreak confirmed the worst fears of the City Fathers. A mob of apprentices rioted outside the playhouses. Eleven days later, 'for avoidinge of theis unlawfull assemblies in those quarters', the Privy Council ordered 'that there be noe playes used in anye place neere thereabouts, as the Theater, Curtayne, or other usual places'.

Given the circumstances of these anti-immigrant riots and the Dutch Church Libel, it seems odd that a play dealing with such a topic should be presented to the Master of the Revels. The manuscript of *Sir Thomas More* is a rare surviving Elizabethan script. There are several contributors. The principal hand is that of Anthony Munday. Those of Henry Chettle, Thomas Dekker and Thomas Heywood have also been recognised. Most intriguing are three pages of manuscript that scholarly opinion has long identified as being in the hand of William Shakespeare.

The play is conceived on a grand scale. There are fifty-nine speaking parts, twenty-two of which appear in the first 500 lines. Even with complex doubling, it would have taxed the ability of any company to have presented it. The part of More, at over 500 lines, is the fourth longest to have then been written for the stage.

Topicality may have been a motive in its writing, but it was unlikely that the censor would look kindly on such a production. Sir Thomas More had been arraigned and executed on the orders of the Queen's father, Henry VIII. The controversial nature of the subject was increased by the fact that More had been set on the path to beatification, thereby implying that the Queen's father was responsible for slaying a saint. In 1579, the Papal Bull, *Quoniam Divinae Bonitati* had proclaimed More and John Fisher, Bishop of Rochester, Catholic martyrs.

The choice of subject is curious for another reason. During Munday's sojourn at the English College, a fresco had been commissioned from the artist, Nicolo Pomarancio, depicting the martyrdoms of More, Fisher and Margaret Pole. On his return to England, he had been a hostile witness at the trials of former seminarians he had known, including Edmund Campion. He had even engaged in disputes with Catholic priests on their way to execution, yet, in the play, the character of More is treated sympathetically. He is devoted to his family and sympathetic to the refugees whose presence has caused 'Ill May Day', yet he pleads for clemency for the rioters. While it is acknowledged that he is in dispute with the King, the nature of the dispute is never specified; Perhaps Munday's attitudes had changed with time and reflection.

There is no indication of when the play was written. The size of the cast indicates that it may have been intended for production during the period in 1590–1 when the Admiral's and Lord Strange's Men collaborated at The Theatre.

The manuscript provides the name of just one actor. A scribe wrote in the margin of the manuscript: 'Mess T Goodal', opposite a direction for the entrance of a messenger. This is Thomas Goodale, a player of minor parts. He was a member of Lord Berkeley's Company in 1581 when that nobleman's players were involved in a fracas with some gentlemen of Gray's Inn. He appeared in *Seven Deadly Sins* in a number of roles, including a precursor to his designated part in *Sir Thomas More* by playing a messenger.

The play ran into trouble with Edmund Tilney, Master of the Revels, who struck his quill through chunks of it. 'Leave out ye insurrection and ye causes thereof,' he wrote in the margin, but he does not seem to have entirely discounted the possibility of a production.

It may have been Shakespeare's ability to work with Tilney that inspired the possessor of the, by now, somewhat tawdry script to ask him to rewrite the 'Ill May Day' passages. It may even have been Tilney who suggested he do so. The choice was a wise one. Shakespeare uses his familiar arguments against the stirring of civil unrest and conceding power to mob rule. He also sympathises with the plight of the refugees and condemns the cruelty of those who would expel them:

> Imagine that you see the wretched strangers
> Their babies at their backs, with their poor luggage,
> Plodding to the ports and coasts for transportation.
> ... What would you think,
> To be thus used? This is the stranger's case
> And this your mountainous inhumanity.

Although there is no evidence that the play was ever performed, the mention of a specific actor in a specific role indicates that it may have been. More likely, the many alterations and delays ensured its hour had passed. Certainly the logistics of a production on such a grand scale may well have caused any company to baulk at the prospect. Apart from its value as a document that gives the intriguing sight of Shakespeare's handwriting and his working method, the manuscript demonstrates the process by which a play could be brought to the stage, showing the way in which writers cooperated towards producing a finished work.

Sir Thomas More is an example of another type of drama that was a feature of the Elizabethan stage – plays about noted contemporary or near-contemporary personalities. Such works could run into trouble with the Master of the Revels, because they could push political or religious content beyond the limits of the permissible. As early as the first year of Elizabeth's reign – 1559 – a statute had defined the restrictions on subject matter for public performances:

> No play shal be permitted to be played wherein either…

> matter of religion or of govrernance of the State of common weal shal be handled or treated on danger of arrest and imprisonment.

Sir Thomas More is one of several plays that present the lives of prominent courtiers of Henry VIII's reign, a time within living memory. *Thomas, Lord Cromwell* was printed in 1602. 'As it hath beene sundrie times publikely Acted by the Right Honorable Lord Chamberlain his Servants', the title page stated. The theme of the conflict between the King and Wolsey was taken up in Samuel Rowley's play, *When You See Me, You Know Me*, which was published in 1605. It was this element that attracted playwrights to the reign, most notably in Shakespeare and John Fletcher's[2] play of *The Famous History of the Life of King Henry the Eighth*. In this the antagonisms are more complex, as gradually more characters take exception to Wolsey, culminating with the King himself.

'Applauded Merriments'

Despite the demise of Newington Butts, Henslowe's accounts from the Rose Theatre confirm that the playhouses boomed in the period after the plague. The populace had been starved of public entertainment for the best part of two years. At first he presented revivals. Both parts of *Tamburlaine* and *Dr Faustus* grossed the goodly sum of £3, but new plays were returning as playwrights picked up their quills again. A now lost play entitled *The Wise Man of West Chester* may have been a revival of Anthony Munday's *John a Kent and John a Cumber*, which had been performed as early as 1587. Another lost play entitled *The Grecian Comedy* was performed on 10 January. On 13 January, 'A Pleasant Conceited Comedie, Called *A Knacke to Know an Honest Man*', was premiered. It was probably a riposte or sequel to a play entitled *A Knack to Know a Knave*, which had been performed at the Rose by Lord Strange's Men on 10 June 1592. It too was highly popular, being performed on several occasions and taking £3 12*s*. 0*d*.[3] The only known text is a quarto published in 1596. It is extremely confused and appears to be a 'memorial edition' – one which actors sold to stationers, incorporating what they knew of the script. It is the first edition of a play that mentions specific actors. It is described as 'newly set forth as it hath been played by Ed. Allen and his company', with Kemp's 'applauded merriments of the men of Gotham'. This was a folk tale from the reign of King John. If the King were to travel through the village of Gotham, it would make the local road an official highway, something the villagers did not want, so whenever Royal Messengers arrived, they would feign imbecility and get up to all sorts of silly tricks like trying to drown an eel in the duck-pond, rolling cheeses downhill in the hope they'd get to Nottingham Market, or planting a hedge round a tree where it was intended to place a cuckoo so that it wouldn't escape and would sing all the year round.

These were all good vehicles for Will Kempe's comic talents and clearly created much 'applauded merriments', yet all the quarto contains of such scenes is one short piece of dialogue. Kempe probably extemporised.

Folk tales were in vogue at the Rose. A play entitled *The Life of Long Meg of Westminster* presented on 14 February was another great success: by the following October, it had been performed a dozen times and netted over 34/-. It was entered onto the Stationers' Register in 1590 and ran through many editions. The original is lost but subsequent editions tell much the same story – of a Lancashire lass of uncommon height who came to London and worked in a tavern. She accompanied the army of Henry VIII to France in 1544, probably as a laundress. Later she married and kept an inn. The blurb of the edition of 1635 indicates the nature of the play. It contains 'the mad merry pranks' Meg 'played in her life time, not only in performing sundry quarrels with divers ruffians about London, but also how valiantly she behaved herself in the warres of Bolloigne'.

A Pleasant Conceyted Comedie of George a Green, Pinner of Wakefield, further demonstrates the popularity of plays about English folk heroes. One of the earliest plays that Henslowe staged at the Rose after the resumption of performances, it appears to have been staged by all three companies there at the time. According to the quarto of 1599, it had been acted by Derby's, Pembroke's and Sussex's Men. There was no author's name on the title page. When the Master of the Revels, George Buck, bought a copy of the play some time later, he asked two leading men of the theatre who he might have been. He noted their replies on the title page of his edition:

> Written by ... a minister who ac[ted]
> the pinners part in it himself. Teste W. Shakespea[re].
> Ed. Iuby saith that this play was made by Rob. Gree[ne]

The reference to Shakespeare is intriguing. 'A minister' implies a minister of religion, but no such person is known to have written plays at this time, let alone one who acted the lead role. The former playwright Stephen Gosson just about fits the bill, but he was long into his Puritan phase by then. Perhaps Buck misunderstood what Shakespeare told him.

Edward Juby was an actor who was with the Admiral's Men in 1594. He seems to have had some sort of liaison role in terms of the company's court performances, so Buck would have known him well. He may even have performed in *George a Green* himself, so he would have been in a good position to know the name of the author. Robert Greene was adept at selling the same play to different companies, so any or all of those performing it could have received it from him.

The play of is one of several in the era focused around the figure of Robin Hood. The topic was a link with a half-forgotten pagan past. Robin Hood and Maid Marian were traditionally the King and Queen in the May Day celebrations. William Shakespeare would have been familiar with such traditions which were anathema to the Puritans. There was a crackdown on such activity in Stratford in the 1620s when one Francis Palmer of Shottery was presented before the Vicar's Court 'for being the Maid Marrion'.

That the May Day revels could turn riotous is revealed in an Act of the Scottish Parliament of 1555 which forbade citizens to assemble together to celebrate 'Robert Hood, a wild or uplandish man'.

That there were more Robin Hood plays than have actually come down to us is revealed in lines from one that survived, *The Downfall of Robert Earl of Huntingdon*. In announcing what play they are to play before the King, in a play within a play, the Friar says:

> For merry jests they have been shown before
> As how the friar fell into a well
> For love of Jenny, that fair bonny belle;
> How Greenleaf robbed the Shrieve of Nottingham,
> And other mirthful matter full of game.

Two Robin Hood plays published around 1560 are linked to May Day. *Robin Hood and the Friar* was described as 'a newe playe for to be played in Maye games very plesaunte and ful of pastyme'. It is based around the folktale of the first encounter of Robin Hood and Friar Tuck in which each demands that the other carries him across a stream. The play differs from the traditional tale in one detail. Robin makes the Friar an offer he cannot refuse:

Robyn Hode: How sayest thou, frere, wylt thou be my man,
To do me the best servyse thou can?
Thou shalt have both golde and fee.
And also here is a lady free.
I wyl geve her unto the,
And her chapplayn I the make
To serve her for my sake.

The Friar is more interested in the woman's mortal body than her immortal soul:

Fryer: Here is an huckle duckle[4]
An inch above the buckle.
She is a trul[5] of trust,
To serve a frier at his lust.
A pryker,[6] a prauncer,[7] a terer of sheets,[8]
A wagger of ballockes[9] when other men slepes.
Go home, ye knaves and laye crabbes in the fyre,[10]
For my lady and I wil daunce in the myre,
For veri pure joy.

This is the lewd aspect of 'Maying' to which Puritans objected so strenuously. It places aspects of the drama within the English folk traditions. 'They say he's already in the Forest of Arden' says Charles of the Banished Duke in *As You Like It*. 'And as many merry men with him and there they live like the old Robin Hood of England.' The Friar's rumbustious bawdy has its heir in the character of Falstaff, while his dance with the woman prefigures the jig that completed theatrical performances.

The tradition of the Robin Hood masquerade is a feature of George Peele's play published in 1593 with a lavish title:

> *The Famous Chronicle of King Edward the First, sirnamed Edward Longshankes, with his returne from the holy land. ALSO THE LIFE OF LLEVELLEN rebell In Wales. Lastly, the sinking of Queen Elinor, who sunck at Charingcrosse, and rose againe at Pottershith, now named Queenehith*

The part of Friar Tuck in the masquerade is played by a lascivious Welsh religious, Friar Hugh ap David. The randy friar was a feature of the Robin Hood tradition. The play is part history, part raucous fantasy. In terms of the history, it has the underlying theme of uniting Britain as a nation under the English Crown. Edward seizes Wales from its hereditary prince, Lluellen (Llewellyn), and makes John Baliol, King of Scotland, his vassal. Yet the historical perspective is blurred by farcical scenes involving Edward's Queen, Eleanor of Castille. After she blasphemes against Heaven, she is swallowed up in a sinkhole at Charing Cross and spat out a mile away at Queenhithe. On her deathbed, she confesses that only the heir to the throne, Prince Edward, is the King's son. It is no surprise to find that all the others were 'baselie borne begotten of a frier'.

An anonymous Pleasant Pastoral Comedy of Robin Hood and Little John was entered in the Stationers' Register in 1594, but has not survived. On 15 February 1598, Henslowe paid Anthony Munday 'for a playe booke called the firste parte of Robyne Hoode'. This was *The Downfall of Robert Earl of Huntingdon*, afterward called *Robin Hood of merrie Sherwodde*, which elevates the outlaw into the ranks of the aristocracy. Appropriately, given the hero's rise in status, it is set in the court of Henry VIII. On 20 and 28 February, and Henslowe made further payments to Munday for 'the second pte of Roben Hood', but he also recorded a payment made to Henry Chettle on 25 February 'for the second pte of Robart hoode'. Given the short time between the commissioning of the two plays, it is likely that Chettle was called upon to assist Munday with the script for the second part. On 25 November, Chettle was paid for 'mending' a Robin Hood play for a performance at Court. The two plays were published in quarto in 1601, which reveals why Chettle had been called in. The second is called *The Funeral of Richard Couer de Lion*. The text contains many discrepancies and a lack of continuity. Presumably it constitutes Munday's original version, taken from his 'foul papers'. It is odd that the 'mended' version was not published.

In 1598, the Lord Admiral's Men presented around thirty plays. Of these only Munday's two of Robin Hood survive. That so much was lost is another indication that the work done by that Company was more ephemeral than that of the Lord Chamberlain's Men. It is difficult to escape the supposition that Shakespeare's Company had an eye on posterity.

Of course the best-known play of the forest in Elizabethan drama is *As You Like It*. Although it pays due to the classical Arcadia, it too represents the pastoral tradition in English folklore. Either way, Shakespeare mocks those who romanticise the forest life through the cynical (or realistic) Jacques. His response to Amiens' song lauding life 'Under the Greenwood Tree' is a lyric expounding his version of reality.

> If it do come to pass
> That any man turn ass,
> Leaving his wealth and ease
> A stubborn will to please.
> Ducdame, ducdame, ducdame.
> Here shall he see

Gross fools as he
An if he will come to me.

The Robin Hood plays not only represent an invocation of 'Merry England', but increasingly a lament for it. Ben Jonson's sole pastoral play, the unfinished *The Sad Shepherd*, contains Robin's regrets for the age that has passed.

... 'twas a happy age, when on the Plaines,
The Wood-men met the damsells and the Swaines
The Neat'ards, Plow-men and the Pipers loud
And each did dance, some to the Kit, or Crowd,
Some to the Bag-pipe, some to the Tabret-mov'd
And all did love, or were belov'd.

Parnassus

Undergraduate enthusiasm for the theatre is attested by the trio of plays around the theme of Parnassus, the literary name for Cambridge, that were presented at St John's College, in successive Christmas seasons. *The Pilgrimage to Parnassus* was written during or after 1596 because it mentions books published in that year. It may have been intended as a one-off and then extended with further parts over subsequent Christmases because it proved so popular. In the character blatantly named 'Stupido', the Puritans are satirised. The Marprelate controversy still reverberated.

The author of the second and third plays, the two parts of *The Return from Parnassus*, is more familiar with London than Cambridge, although he mentions the Granta, the local name for the River Cam. He knows two noted Cheapside inns, the Nag's Head and the Pegasus. He is familiar with the booksellers in St Paul's Churchyard and the possibility of buying volumes in foreign languages there. He knows Ram Alley, a notorious passage between Fleet Street and the Temple, the haunt of low characters – a traditional place of sanctuary from arrest, and Shoe Lane, another low place noted for its squalor and dirt and containing a much-frequented cockpit. He refers to a prison called the Counter. The Wood Street Counter was a small debtors' prison, which also held people convicted of drunkenness; the Poultry Counter was where Thomas Dekker was imprisoned for debt in 1599. He knows the London literary scene. He abhors the minor poets who were foisting their wares upon an unsuspecting public to the detriment of such finer authors as Edmund Spenser, Henry Constable, Samuel Daniel, Michael Drayton, John Davies, Thomas Lodge, 'Kit' Marlowe, Thomas Watson, Ben Jonson and William Shakespeare. He mentions the lutenist and composer, John Dowland. He refers to John Marston as 'Monsieur Kinsayder' – this was the name attached to an epigram that satirist Joseph Hall, a Fellow of Emmanuel College, had pasted into the copies of Marston's acerbic collection of poems, *The Metamorphosis of Pigmalion's Image* and *Certaine Satyres* that were sold in Cambridge. It means a castrator, 'stone' being contemporary slang for a testicle, hence 'mar-stone'. The connotation of stray dogs invokes Marston's misanthropy. 'What Monsieur Kinsaydor,' says a line in *The Return*, 'lifting up your leg and pissing against the world? Put up man!' It is unclear whether Hall was the source of this witty name, or Marston himself, since he attaches it to his collection of satirical poems, *The Scourge of Villanie*, published in 1598. Lampoons and satire had found fertile ground in pamphlets, which could be produced rapidly in response to events, but this vogue had its effect in riling the authorities. The machinery of official censorship was revived. The censors John Whitgift, Archbishop of Canterbury, and Richard Bancroft, Bishop of London, ordered Marston's pamphlet to be burnt by the public hangman, together with other offending works, including those of Joseph Hall. It may have been this that decided Marston to give up pamphleteering and write for the stage, as a renewed outlet for his satire. On 28 September 1599, Henslowe 'lent' (his familiar word) 'unto Mr Maxton, the new poete ... the sum of forty shillings'. This may have been for *Histriomastix*, the play that began the War of the Theatres. Marston's talent for controversy continued unabated.

Nor does Ben Jonson escape the Cambridge onslaught. The old jibe is revived. He is 'the wittiest fellow of a bricklayer in England'. There are references to the *Isle of Dogs*, the ill-fated play he wrote with Thomas Nashe. William Shakespeare is subjected to what may have been a frequent comment about his much-admired *Venus and Adonis*:

> Could but a graver subject him content,
> Without love's foolish languishment.

The Character Judicio shares what must have been a common view of Christopher Marlowe:

> Alas unhappy in his life and end,
> Pity it is that wit so ill should dwell,
> Wit lent from heaven, but vices sent from hell.

The character Ingenioso has written a book entitled *A Catalogue of Cambridge Cuckolds* and is meeting a printer called John Danter in the hope of getting it published. In 1594, Danter had printed *Titus Andronicus*, having entered it onto the Stationers' Register in the proper way. Subsequently, his affairs and his standards deteriorated. He was printing books without the authority of the Stationers' Company, which, in retaliation, seized and destroyed two of his presses early in 1596. In the following year, he produced a pirated version of *Romeo and Juliet.* That Ingenioso is seeking to get his book published by a printer with a dubious reputation and no printing presses was something of an in-joke.

The author is familiar with contemporary events. He refers to the lengthy defence of Ostend by Prince Maurice of Nassau and to the eminent recusant lawyer, Sir Edmund Plowden, who coined the phrase (and legal principle), 'the case is altered', the title of a play by Ben Jonson. He knows Thomas Nashe has died. He refers to the Catholic exile, William Allen:

> Nor Rome nor Rheims, that wonted are to give,
> A Cardinal's cap to discontented clerks,
> That have forsook the home-bred thatched roofs.

Allen was instrumental in founding English mission colleges in Rheims and Rome. He was created a Cardinal by Pope Sixtus V in 1587. He died in 1594. Edmund Plowden had died in 1585, so neither would have been an immediate figure to Cambridge undergraduates. Such factors, together with the sophisticated style of the work, make it likely that the third *Parnassus* play at least was written by a dramatist working in London, possibly with some input from the undergraduates with such lines as 'Ah, sweet Mr Shakespeare. I'll have his picture.' He has clear knowledge of the contemporary theatrical scene. He places Will Kempe among the Lord Chamberlain's Men. His movements in that period can be retraced. He was with the Company around 20 September 1598 when he performed in *Every Man in His Humour*. If indeed he played Falstaff, for which the circumstantial evidence is strong, the part was written out of *Henry* V, so it is likely that he was not with the Company when it was first performed in the spring of 1599. His absence almost certainly meant that Shakespeare employed a ploy familiar to producers of modern soap operas. If a character leaves, kill him off. From the epilogue to *Henry IV, Part 2*, it would appear that he had pondered this intention before writing *Henry V*, a play in which he promises that Falstaff will appear, but may not last through the action:

> One word more, I beseech you. If you be not too
> much cloyed with fat meat, our humble author will
> continue the story, with Sir John in it, and make
> you merry with fair Katharine of France: where, for
> any thing I know, Falstaff shall die of a sweat,
> unless already a' be killed with your hard opinions.

Although Falstaff does not appear in *Henry V*, the play includes Mistress Quickly's memorable account of his death. Instead the actor who played Pistol, found his part elevated, as evidenced by the billing in the 'bad quarto' of 1600:

The Cronicle
Hiftory of *Henry the fift*,
With his battel fought at *Agin Court* in
France. Togither with *Auncient*
Pistoll

Yet Kempe was to tread the boards at the Globe. *A Pit to Purge Meloncholy* reveals that his fellow clown, Robert Armin is cited as attending 'One pleasant comedy or another of Monsieur de Kempe on Monday next at the Globe.' He refers several times to 'the Ass's burden', a probable reference to Dogberry's line: 'Gentlemen, remember that *I am an ass*; even though it's not written down, don't forget that I'm an ass.' The play may have been first performed in the summer of 1599 and Kempe, a huge theatrical draw, persuaded to return to take part in it.

If *The Return, Part 2* is accurate (and there is no reason to believe otherwise),[11] Kempe was with the Company in 1601 and so could have created the part of the Gravedigger in *Hamlet*, which was very much his métier. On 26 July 1602, the play was entered on the Stationer's Register as 'latelie Acted by the Lo.Chamberleyne his servantes', so it could have been played at the time *The Return Part 2* was written. It was published in the following year in a quarto entitled *The Tragicall Historie of Hamlet Prince of Denmark, By William Shakespeare. As it hath beene diurse times acted by his Highnesse seruants in the Cittie of London as also in the two Universities of Cambridge and Oxford and else-where*. Thus, both Burbage and Kempe had recently appeared before a Cambridge audience. The stage direction for the opening of Act V, Scene 1, reads: 'Enter Clown and an other', who is described as the '2nd Clown' in the voice cues. Did Will Kempe and Robert Armin come on stage in that earliest production of the play?

If Kempe indeed created the part of the Gravedigger, it was likely to have been his swansong with the Company. Why he quit is a mystery. Possibly he just wanted to do something different. Throughout his career he embarked on rare adventures. By 1599, he had been with the Company for over seven years. He was now embarking on his 'Nine Daies Wonder', the Morris dance between London and Norwich that took place over several weeks in February and March 1599/1600. Towards the end of the pamphlet recounting his exploit, which was entered on the Stationers' Register on 22 April 1600, he writes of the 'great journey he pretends [intends]' and gives an indication of to where it might be. 'Imploy not your little wits in certifying the world that I am gone to Rome, Jerusalem, Venice, or any other place at your idle appoint.' A number of references associate him with Italy. Around 1601, *The Retvrne from Pernassvs: or The Scourge of Simony*, the third play, contains the line: 'God save you, M. Kempe, welcome M. Kempe, from dancing the morrice over the Alpes.' *The Travailes of Three English Brother...*, a play by John Day, William Rowley and George Wilkins published in 1607, features an encounter – with characteristic bawdy dialogue – between Kempe and Sir Anthony Shirley, the Ambassador of the Safavid Empire to the Venetian Republic.

After Edward Somerset, 4th Earl of Worcester, was appointed the Queen's Master of Horse, he sought to elevate the status of his players. In 1602, the Earl of Worcester's Men became the third Company licensed to play in London when they took over the Rose Theatre in cooperation with Henslowe. Kempe was with that Company by then; he may have received an irresistible offer. It was a coup to have secured him, but it was necessary to equip the new star. On 10 March 1602, Philip Henslowe 'lent unto m kempe ... in Redy money twentye shellenges for his necessary uses'. On 22 August, he 'lent' him money, 'to buy buckram to macke a payer of gyents hosse'. On 3 September, he paid 'into the company ... to buy a seute for wm kempe'. Next day he paid a 'tyerman, for mackinge of wm kempe sewt and the boyes'.

With the right to perform obtained, the services were secured, not only of a giant of the stage, but of three promising younger actors from the Lord Chamberlain's Men. John Duke and Robert Pallant had appeared in the *Seven Deadly Sins* as boy actors. If Christopher Beeston is identified with the boy actor named Kit, then he too appeared in that production. Their presence at the Rose was not without tensions. In the spring of 1599, Robert Shaw of the Admiral's Men sought sureties of the peace against Christopher Beeston and Robert Pallant. Beeston's change of company might have been related to events earlier that year. Margaret White, a clothier's widow, was charged with giving birth to an illegitimate child. In her defence, she claimed that she had been raped by Christopher Beeston on the previous Midsummer's Eve. 'Hee did it forciblie,' she claimed, 'for said hee, I have lyen with a hundred wenches in my tyme.' On 13 November, Beeston was brought before the court. He brought his colleagues with him:

> The said Beeston and others his conferedates plaiers did very undecentlie demeane themselves to certen governors and much abused the place and yett upon some reports made known to this court[Beeston was] greatlie suspected to have committed the crime.

Beeston's rowdy court appearance coincided with his departure from the Lord Chamberlain's Men, so he may have become an embarrassment and it was thought politic for him to leave. Rape was a capital offence so the unseemly behaviour of Beeston and his coteries in court would imply confidence of acquittal, possibly through denigration of the defendant's history and character, but he may have been obliged to perform public penance and pay towards the upkeep of the child. He worked closely with the Admiral's Men's prolific resident dramatist, Thomas Heywood. In 1603, the Company presented Heywood's masterpiece, the domestic tragedy, *A Woman Killed with Kindness.*

Beggar's Bush

Henslowe commissioned plays with great rapidity to keep up with the demand in the post-plague era. The haste with which the playwrights wrote and the pressure they were under was deplored by Thomas Heywood who protested that he had no time to revise his works for publication.

Other than William Shakespeare, there were few dramatists who never worked for Henslowe. Most who did had in common a state of penury. This may have been due to poor returns from their literary efforts, or to the extravagant lifestyle of a man-of-the-theatre. Henslowe was always lending them money, but whether this was an act of personal generosity or a means of control is unclear. It is confusing that he appears to use the word 'lent' to mean a down-payment rather than a loan.

Henry Chettle is virtually entirely remembered today for his part in *A Groatsworth of Wit*, but he enjoyed a considerable reputation among his contemporaries, Francis Meres describing him as 'best for comedy'. He was a prolific writer. Henslowe paid him for thirty-six plays between 1598 and 1603, and he may have contributed to over fifty, thirteen of which are attributed to him alone. In addition he wrote pamphlets, including *Kind Heart's Dream*. Chettle was possessed of an ample figure and was short of breath and sweaty; in his *Knights Conjurer*, Thomas Dekker describes him as 'sweating and blowing by reason of his fatness'.

Dekker was probably the most successful of Henslowe's playwrights after Marlowe's death. That his surname suggests his family origins may have been Dutch, and this is confirmed by his use of the language in his best-known play, *The Shoemakers' Holiday*. He too was hugely prolific. Between 1598 and 1602, he was involved in some 40 plays for Henslowe, usually in collaboration. He enjoyed a good measure of popularity; some twenty of his plays survive. Of all Henslowe's dramatists he was the most impecunious. He was imprisoned for debt in 1599 and spent seven years in the King's Bench Prison after failing to repay £40 he owed the father of John Webster. His output was undiminished by his incarceration.

Little is known of Richard Hathwaye's life. For obvious reasons much effort has been spent on vain attempts to discover whether he was related to Shakespeare's wife. He wrote eighteen plays for Henslowe, but only received sole accreditation for one, *King Arthur*. Francis Meres lists him as 'best for comedy'.

William Haughton was another playwright rescued by Henslowe from a debtors' prison. On 10 March 1600, he lent him 10/- 'to release him out of the Clink'. He was a prolific writer, fitting the pattern of Henslowe's playwrights, but only two plays, *Englishmen for my Money* and possibly *Grim, the Collier of Croyden* appear to come from his sole hand.

Henslowe describes Henry Porter as a 'poor scholar', but also as a 'gentleman'. Little is known of him. Henslowe records payments to him for several plays, but only one, *The Two Angry Women of Abington*, survives. Francis Meres describes him as 'one of the best for comedy amongst us'. In 1598, he and Henry Chettle were paid twenty shillings for the second part of a play called *The Second Part of the Black Batman of the North*. He delivered his last IOU to Henslowe on 26 May 1599. The money was never repaid. Eleven days later, he was dead.

While never apparently bankrupt on the scale of Decker or Haughton, John Day was frequently 'lent' sums ranging from two to five shillings from Henslowe. Born in Norfolk, he was at Caius College, Cambridge, in 1592, but was sent down in the following year for stealing a book. He was another prolific and versatile author, working in collaboration with others. His finest work was probably his lengthy poem, *The Parliament of Bees*. He was probably the 'John Daye, yeoman' who stabbed his fellow dramatist, Henry Porter, in the left breast with a rapier, 'of the value of two shillings', on 6 June 1599 in Southwark. Porter died next day. Day was charged with murder, but pleaded he acted in self-defence. His testimony is reminiscent of John Towne's after he killed William Knell. He pleaded that 'he fled to a certain wall beyond which…'. His plea succeeded. He was either acquitted or pardoned. He lived on to the late 1630s. Ben Jonson described him as a 'rogue', (together with Thomas Decker and Edward Sharpham) and later as 'a base fellow' (together with Thomas Middleton and Gervase Markham).

As with many contemporary dramatists, little is known of the background of Thomas Heywood. There are many 'ifs' and 'maybes'. He may have been born in Lincolnshire in the early 1570s and his father may have been a clergyman. He may have attended Cambridge University. It is probable that, like William Shakespeare, he entered the world of theatre as an actor. According to the poet, William Winstanley, he said that he acted every day at this stage of his career. He is first mentioned as a playwright on 14 October 1596, when Henslowe paid members of the Admiral's Men 30/- 'for hawodes bocke'. He was another prolific writer. In his preface to *The English Traveller*, published in 1633, he claimed that it was 'one reserved amongst two hundred and twenty in which I have had either an entire hand or at least a maine finger'.

Wentworth Smith's main contribution to posterity may have been his initials. Three plays were published over a decade from 1595, including *Thomas, Lord Cromwell*, citing the author as 'W.S.' The stationer probably wished to give the impression that this was William Shakespeare, but it could have been Wentworth Smith. He appears rare among Henslowe's dramatists in that the impresario never records lending him money. This may have been because, unlike most of his fellow dramatists, he enjoyed a second income as a scrivener. Michael Drayton was another prolific writer in Henslowe's stable. Like William Shakespeare, he was a Warwickshire lad, born at Hartshill, near Nuneaton, in 1563. Unlike many of his colleagues, he was highly successful at obtaining support from those in high places. Poetry was his main interest, although his dramatic output was considerable. He contributed to twenty-three plays over nearly five years, for which Henslowe paid him £50 16*s*. 3*d*. In the ten months between 13 March 1597/8 and 20 January 1598/9, he contributed to sixteen, for which he received £32 6*s*. 8*d*. This was good money, so Henslowe must have rated him highly not only for his writing ability, but his capacity to deliver.

Smith and Drayton excluded, things were clearly hard going for most jobbing playwrights. In his *Peregrinato Scholastica, or Learning's Pilgrimage*, a collection of twenty-two *morall Tractes* looking back over his life, John Day lamented that 'notwithstanding ... Industry ... he was forct to take a napp at Beggars Bushe', The average payment for a play of £8 was not enough to make a man wealthy, especially if the money was divided between several authors. In order to sustain a living, most writers were driven to prodigious industry. Robert Wilson, the playwright-cum-clown, worked with other members of Henslowe's dramatic entourage on sixteen plays in just over two years. Thomas Heywood's claims may have had a touch of hyperbole, but it cannot be doubted that his output was vast, particularly if it is considered together with his huge number of other works – masques, pageants, pamphlets, chronicles and poetry. A great deal of his work is lost, just twenty-three surviving plays and eight masques are generally acknowledged as his.

Little is known of George Chapman's early life. He was born around 1559 at Hitchin in Hertfordshire into a long-established and well-connected family. His father, Thomas Chapman, was a local landowner, his mother the daughter of Henry VIII's Sergeant of Buckhounds. His classical learning has led to speculation that he might have attended Oxford University but there is no record of that. That he was the first writer to translate Homer's *Iliad* into English may be the source of the speculation – an achievement memorably commemorated in Keats' poem *On First Looking into Chapman's Homer*. He is also noted for completing Christopher Marlowe's narrative poem *Hero and Leander* after the poet's death. He came late to the theatre, perhaps motivated by a desperate need for money. He shared the impecuniousness of many of his colleagues. Like them, his penury was, in a measure, self-inflicted, but it was also born of ill-luck. In 1585, he signed a bond for a loan, but never received the money. He was plagued for years by suits for the recovery of debts from which he had gained no benefit but for which he was legally entailed. He would have blessed his good fortune when he obtained the patronage of Robert Devereux, but his hopes were dashed when the Earl was executed for High Treason. He later obtained the largesse of Henry, the Prince of Wales. This must have seemed a surer proposition, but sadly the heir to the throne died in 1612 at the age of 18.

Anthony Munday was another rare among Henslowe's dramatists in not being plagued by debt. It was helpful to an aspirant writer to come from an affluent background and have an additional occupation beyond writing. It was perhaps, his father's status as a Freeman of the Stationers' Company that enabled Munday to establish himself in the City. He is described on his monument at St Stephen's, Coleman Street, as 'a citizen and draper'. In the latter role he provided costumes for the Lord Mayor's Show. He was in a good position to secure these deals, since he held the lucrative position of chief pageant-writer between 1605 and 1616.

Thomas Middleton, who produced *The Triumphs of Truth*, the pageant of 1613, was also well-connected in the City. His father had been a Freeman of the Guild of Tylers and Bricklayers, was awarded a coat of arms and could call himself 'Gent.'. He died when Thomas was 5, and Thomas' mother subsequently remarried. Just two weeks into the marriage, her second husband, Thomas Harvey, a grocer who had lost money in Sir Walter Raleigh's Roanoke venture, tried to secure the inheritance of her children to himself. Thomas was called upon to give evidence in the fifteen-year legal wrangle that followed – which probably inspired his bitter satires against lawyers. He was commissioned to produce a series of ten 'Honourable Entertainments compos'd for the service of this Noble Citie' between Easter 1620 and Easter 1621. He was appointed the City's first paid Chronologer on 6 September 1620.

Most dramatists moved between companies, selling their work where they could. Thomas Heywood worked with at least four. He is the most likely author of the two parts of *Edward IV*, which were published in quarto in 1599. The title page states that it was performed by 'the Earl of Derby his servants', so he was working as a playwright for another company while contracted as an actor with Henslowe. The play is not a recounting of a monarch's reign like Shakespeare's history plays or Marlowe's *Edward II*. Its main theme is the love affair between the King and Jane Shore, wife of a City goldsmith. Successful plays often produced a raft of successors on the same theme from other companies. Henslowe's Diary reveals that Henry Chettle and John Day were working on a play about Jane Shore for Worcester's Men in May 1603.

In 1595, the campaign against the theatre achieved a great success when the Lord Mayor succeeded in banning performances at inns. The link between the theatre and its place of origin was broken. There were other troubling matters. An economic crisis was striking at London's populace. Food shortages and the familiar resentment against immigrants were causing unrest. During June, there were twelve days of disturbances and martial law was proclaimed, which ensured the closure of the theatres.

As if the domestic situation were not sufficient cause for despondency, news arrived in London that would have made the nation's very existence seem precarious. The defeat of the Spanish Armada was not the end of a war but the beginning. The seemingly interminable conflict dragged on throughout the 1590s. On 23 July 1593, four Spanish galleys landed troops in Cornwall, sacking Mousehole, Newlyn and Penzance. England seemed vulnerable again.

The plight of the nation had its impact on the well-honed theatrical instincts of William Shakespeare. Like the Hollywood filmmakers during the slump years of the 1930s, he realised that, in a time of economic and social depression, escapism is the order of the day. Just as Hollywood responded to the Great Depression with Busby Berkeley's extravaganzas, so Shakespeare responded to the Great Dearth with a series of sparkling comedies. Amid the pangs of scarcity, it is more comfortable to stretch the imagination to 'a wood near Athens' than to the apprentices' riots of *Sir Thomas More*. Who would want to go to the theatre to see the same distressing sights that existed around the corner? Although the subject of history continued to be addressed, it was the comic muse that dominated, playing its part even in the history plays of the period.

Four Amphitheatres worth a Visit

In 1589, Francis Langley purchased a plot of land for the huge sum of £850 in the Bankside district of Southwark. Paris Gardens was a Royal Liberty – part of the estates of the Abbey of Bermondsey that had passed to the Crown at the Dissolution of the Monasteries. He was a wealthy goldsmith who held the Office of 'Alnager and Searcher of Cloth' – one responsible for the trading standards of fabrics. He determined to build a theatre on the site. It helped that he had connections in the right places. His brother-in-law was Clerk to the Privy Council. The Swan Theatre was the grandest yet built. A Dutch visitor, Johannes de Witt, visited it around 1596, writing an invaluable account of the enchanting London theatre scene. He regarded the playhouses as among the wonders of the age:

> There are four amphitheatres in London that are worth a visit, which are given different names from their different signs. In these theatres, a different play is offered to the public every day. The two most excellent of these are situated on the other side of the Thames, towards the South, and they are called the Rose and the Swan from their signboards. There are other theatres outside the City towards the North, on the road that leads through the Episcopal Gate, called Bishopsgate in the vernacular. There is also a fifth, but of a different structure, intended for fights of animals, in which so many bears, bulls and dogs of stupendous size are held in different cages and behind fences, which are kept for the fight to provide a most pleasant spectacle to the people. The most outstanding of all the theatres, however, is that whose sign is the swan ... as it holds 3,000 people. It is built out of flintstones stacked on top of each other (of which there is a great store in Britain), supported by wooden pillars, which, by their painted marble colour, could deceive even the most acute observer.

'I have made a drawing of it,' he wrote. What he drew was the most important sketch in the history of the theatre. The original is lost, but his friend Aernoit van Buchel copied it into his commonplace book. It is the only known depiction of the interior of an Elizabethan theatre. Whereas de Witt was a skilled draughtsman, van Buchel drawing lacks perspective. The doors that he places at the back of the stage could only be used if the actors crawled through them on their hands and knees. Yet he purveys a clear idea of the basic mechanics of the contemporary theatre: the projecting stage, with its intimate contact with the audience: the inner stage under a projecting roof; the area above that can be occupied by a band or by spectators if not required for Juliet's balcony or the walls of Harfleur, and the two inner doors mentioned in the stage directions to *A Midsummer Night's Dream*: 'Enter a FAIRY at one door and ROBIN GOODFELLOW at another.'

It is noteworthy that de Witt only mentions The Theatre in passing. The building was over twenty years old and had been exceeded in grandeur by the Swan. If the Lord Chamberlain's Men were pondering relations with their difficult landlord, here was another reason to decamp to more salubrious premises.

Chapter Five

Great Inconveniences and Misrule

'Without the City are Some Theatres'

Evidence of a connection between William Shakespeare and Francis Langley, the proprietor of the Swan Theatre, comes with curious and unexplained legal proceedings in 1596. That November, Langley issued a prejudgment writ of attachment against William Wayte and William Gardiner. Wayte retaliated with a writ against Langley, William Shakespeare and two women, Anne Lee and Dorothy Soer. The court could order such a writ if the appellant demonstrated fraud on the defendant's part, or if it was shown that he was attempting to hide assets. Thus, the writ preserved the status quo pending a final resolution. It also provided a means of financial recovery for the plaintiff, who normally had to post a surety note up to twice his claim.

Gardiner's name was a byword for corruption and avarice. A property dealer and money-lender, he had cheated many clients, including his wife's relations. As a result he had acquired great wealth, which enabled him to boost his social status. He had acquired the preferment of Ewell in Surrey but failed to pay an adequate stipend to the parson, so the place was clergyless. His record included menacing and violent behaviour, for which he was briefly imprisoned. Nevertheless, he had attained the position of a Justice of the Peace for Southwark. His wealth, rather than his reputation, enabled him to become the High Sheriff of Surrey and Sussex in 1594/5.

Wayte was Gardiner's stepson and an equally dubious character. In one legal action he had been described as a 'loose person of no reckoning or value, being wholly under the rule and commandment of the said Gardiner'. It may well have been Gardiner who put him up to an action against the four plaintiffs petitioning for sureties of the peace, 'for fear of death'. The pairing of the names of Shakespeare and Langley further implies that the Company was performing at The Swan. Nor need the fact that Gardiner and Wayte were conspicuously villains mean that they were villainous on this occasion. Gardiner, as a magistrate, might have felt it necessary to emulate his colleagues in the City and crack down on the various activities occurring on Bankside. Dorothy Soer owned cheap lodging houses in Paris Garden Lane known as 'Soer's Rents'. Perhaps she and Anne Lee were engaged in a different form of entertainment from the theatre.

In 1598, another visitor arrived in London. 'Without the city are some theatres,' wrote the German traveller, Paul Hentzner, 'where English actors represent almost every day tragedies and comedies to very numerous audiences: these are concluded with excellent music, variety of dances and the excessive applause of those that are present.' He must have visited at least one of these theatres, but it did not seem to make as much impression on him as the bear baiting he attended, of which he wrote a full description, but he does shed light on a habit of the audience at both the Bear Pit and the theatres:

> At these spectacles, and everywhere else, the English are constantly smoking tobacco, and in this manner – they have pipes on purpose made of clay, into the farther end of which they put the herb, so dry that it may be rubbed unto powder, and putting fire to it, they draw the smoke into their mouths, which they puff out again through their nostrils like funnels, along with a plenty of phlegm and defluxion from the head. In these theatres, fruits, such as apples, pears and nuts, are carried about to be sold, as well as ale and wine.

Smoking had not yet caught on in Brandenburg!

Such shaping Fantasies I

In 1586, Timothy Bright, a physician at St Bartholomew's Hospital, published his *A Treatise on Melancholy*. Being a medical man, he ascribes the cause of melancholia to dietary and physiological issues. 'As all natural humours rise of nourishment, so melancholie being a part of the bloud, from thence it springeth also.'

Melancholia, to the Elizabethans, was more than condition. It was a cult, the extent of which was expressed by John Lyly in his play *Midas* of 1586:

> Melancholy is the creast of Courtiers armes, and now euerie base companion, beeing in his muble fubles, sayes he is melancholy.

Melancholic characters in Elizabethan drama fall into three types: the lover, the malcontent and the thinker. The Duke Orsino, in *Twelfth Night*, epitomises the melancholic lover. He invokes the anatomical aspects of the humours to express his aspirations in his love for Olivia:

> How will she love, when the rich golden shaft
> Hath kill'd the flock of all affections else

That live in her; when liver, brain and heart,
These sovereign thrones, are all supplied, and fill'd
Her sweet perfections with one self king!

That love is akin to a kind of lunacy is expressed by Duke Theseus in *A Midsummer Night's Dream*, but in both conditions it gives a special insight:

Lovers and madmen have such seething brains,
Such shaping fantasies, that apprehend
More than cool reason ever comprehends.

Polonius, reflecting the norms of his time, interprets Hamlet's odd behaviour as a manifestation of his love for Ophelia.

Ophelia: My lord, as I was sewing in my closet,
Lord Hamlet, with his doublet all unbrac'd,
No hat upon his head, his stockings foul'd,
Ungart'red, and down-gyved to his ankle;
Pale as his shirt, his knees knocking each other,
And with a look so piteous in purport
As if he had been loosed out of hell
To speak of horrors – he comes before me.
Polonius: Mad for thy love?
Ophelia: My Lord, I do not know.
But truly, I do fear it.

The Duke Orsino suffers from the imbalance produced by love:

For such as I am, all true lovers are
Unstaid and skittish in all motions else
Save in the constant image of the creature
That is beloved.

Music was a major force in the cult. The composer John Dowland wrote a consort entitled *Semper Dowland, Semper Dolens* (*Always Dowland, always doleful*). It is music that calms Orsino's melancholy, as he declares in the opening lines of the play:

If music be the food of love, play on.
Give me excess of it, that surfeiting,
The appetite may sicken and so die.

Later he calls on Feste to sing:

That old and antique song we heard last night.
Methought it did relieve my passion much,
More than light airs and recollected terms
Of these most brisk and giddy paced times.

Feste sings, but the beautiful song is unlikely to stir anyone from melancholia, unless by the kind of aversion therapy of which the Duke had spoken:

Come away, come away death,
And in sad cypress let me be laid.
Fly away, fly away, breath;
I am slain by a fair cruel maid.
My shroud of white, stuck all with yew,
O, prepare it!
My part of death, no one so true
Did share it.

The melancholic deals with another persistent theme of the Elizabethan theatre – the role of the outsider in established society. He can be a melancholic like Jacques in *As You Like It*. His disillusion can lead to acts of motiveless malignancy. Don John in *Much Ado About Nothing* is imbued with such solitary melancholia. 'I cannot hide what I am…

I must be sad when I have cause and smile at no man's jests, eat when I have stomach and wait for no man's leisure, sleep when I am drowsy and tend on no man's business, laugh when I am merry and claw no man in his humour.

'Will it serve for any model to build mischief on?' he asks when he hears of 'intelligence of intended marriage'. In his pursuit of motiveless destruction, he is a prototype for Iago.

The outsider can be part of a minority group. Often the treatment was not sympathetic. In *Grim the Collier of Croydon*, a play attributed to William Haughton, Honoria is aghast at a proposal of marriage from a supposed Spaniard:

Base Alien! Mercenary fugitive!
Presumptuous Spaniard! That with shameless pride,

Dur'st ask an English lady for thy wife.
I scorn my slave should honour thee so much.

A similar sentiment is expressed by Doll, in *Sir Thomas More*:

Now let me tell the women of this towne,
No stranger yet brought doll to lying downe;
So long as I an Englishman can see,
Nor ffrenche nor dutche can get a kisse of me.

The Pedlar's Prophecy, attributed to the clown and playwright Robert Wilson, is virulent about immigrants to the point of being inflammatory. 'Three Parts in London are already Alians,' says the Pedlar.

Other mongrels, Alians children, mischievously mixed,
And that with detestable Barbarians,
Which here forever have their dwellings fixed:
Still you Mariners bring them daily,
So you may have pence.
You may make yourselves rich and go gaily,
I would you were so readie to carry them hence.
You would bring in the divell for pence and groates:
You shall see them one day play their parts gaily,
When we thinke least, they shall cut our throates.

In *The First part of the Tragicall raigne of Selimus*, Selimus, in plotting the murder of his father, Bajazet, repeats the allegation made in *The Jew of Malta* – that Jews were skilled at preparing poisons to use malignantly:

Bajazet hath with him a cunning Jew
Professing physicke; and so skill'd therein,
As if he had pow'r over life and death
Withall a man so stout and resolute
That he will venture anything for gold.
The Jew with some intoxicated drinke,
Shall poison Bajazet and that blind Lord;
Then one of Hydraes heads is cleane cut off.

The same image is iterated by John Marsden in *The Malcontent*:

Mendoza: Canst thou impoyson? Canst thou impoyson?
Malevole: Excellently – no Jew, pothacary or polititian better.

This image led to the downfall of Roderigo Lopus, the best-known medician in England. A Portuguese Jew who had converted to Catholicism as a *Christiano Nuevo*, a 'New Christian', he came to England in 1559. He underwent a second conversion to Anglicanism and became a physician at St Bartholomew's Hospital. He assembled a circle of influential patients becoming personal physician to the Queen's favourite, Robert Dudley. Even then his name was smeared with associations popularly attributed to his ancestry. *Leicester's Commonwealth*, a libellous pamphlet published in 1584, suggested that he distilled poisons for Dudley and other noblemen. Despite this, he reached the pinnacle of his profession in 1586, when he was appointed the Queen's physician. His position in society seemed secure, but the previous libels contributed to his downfall. The erratic and volatile Earl of Essex became convinced that he was at the centre of a plot to poison the Queen. He was arraigned on extremely flimsy evidence, tried, condemned and executed. It has been suggested that Shakespeare based the character of Shylock on him. This is unlikely. Lopus was a sophisticated physician, an arriviste who moved in the highest circles. Shylock is a usurer who is treated as a pariah by those with influence. It is possible that Shakespeare never encountered a practicing Jew. They had been expelled from England as long ago as the reign of Edward I and the official ban on them remained until the Commonwealth period. That there was a population of artisan Jews in London during Shakespeare's time is revealed in *The World Tost at Tennis*, a masque by Thomas Middleton and William Rowley published in 1620:

I'll show you, sir, –
And they are men are daily to be seen.
There's Rabbi Job, a venerable silk weaver;
John, a throwster dwelling i' the Spitalfields.
There's Rabbi Abimelech, a learned cobbler,
Rabbi Lazarus, a superstichous tailor,
These shall hold up their shuttles, needles, awls,
Against the gravest Levite in the land,
And give no ground either.

The little community fulfilled the Talmudic injunction that Jews should learn a trade. Shakespeare had some knowledge of Judaism. He was aware that Orthodox Jews would not eat with those not of their faith. Although Shylock negates this tenet by going to supper at Bassanio's, this is necessary to get him out of his house to enable Jessica's escape. He appears to know nothing of Venice's Ghetto quarter – the original one – where Jews were compelled to live under a strict curfew. Shylock comes and goes as he pleases.

A significant figure in the portrayal of both Jews and Moslems onstage was the *grand guignol* character of Herod in the Mystery Plays. There was some confusion as to whether he was a Jew or a Moslem. 'By gracious Mahound more myrthe never have I had,' he exclaims in the Coventry cycle when he hears of the Massacre of the Innocents. Both Marlowe's Tamburlaine and his Jew may owe something to this stage character with whom Shakespeare was familiar. 'It out Herod's Herod,' says Hamlet in his warning to the players against over-acting.

Shakespeare spares Shylock the fiendish tricks of Barabbas. He is a straightforward usurer who is upset because Antonio has undercut the market by lending money free of interest. He is not intended to be a sympathetic character. 'With the extreame crueltie of Shylock the Jew towards the sayd Merchant,' reads the blurb to the first quarto of the play in 1600. Yet Shakespeare brings out the human aspects of the character by famously giving Shylock motives beyond avarice for his hatred.

> If you prick us, do we not bleed? If you tickle us, do we not laugh? If you poison us, do we not die? And if you wrong us, shall we not seek revenge?

The audience is party to some of the wrongs against Shylock. 'Signor Antonio, many a time and oft…,' he recalls, when Antonio seeks to borrow money from him,

> …In the Rialto you have rated me
> About my moneys and my usances;
> Still I have borne it with a patient shrug,
> For sufferance is the badge of all our tribe.
> You call me misbeliever, cut-throat dog,
> And spit upon my Jewish gaberdine,
> And all for the use of that which is mine own.
> Well then, it now appears you need my help.
> Go to, then; you come to me and you say
> 'Shylock, we would have moneys.' You say so!
> You, that did void your rheum upon my beard
> And foot me as you spurn a stranger cur
> Over your threshold! Moneys is your suit.
> What should I say to you? Should I not say,
> 'Hath a dog money?' Is it possible

A cur can lend a thousand ducats? Or
Shall I bend low, and in a bondsman's key,
With bated breath and whispering humbleness,
Say this: 'Fair sir, you spet on me on Wednesday last;
You spurned me such a day; another time
You called me "dog" – and for these courtesies
I'll lend you thus much monies?'

Shakespeare gives Shylock a motive for his desire for revenge. His fault lies not in his seeking retribution for his wrongs, but that he carries it too far. Yet despite his 'extreame crueltie', Shakespeare reveals a tender and human side. Shylock's daughter and his ducats are not his only losses resulting from Jessica's elopement. When he bewails the loss of a ring, he refers only to its deep emotional value. 'Thou torturest me Tubah: it was my turquoise; I had it of Leah when I was a bachelor. I would not have given it for a wilderness of monkeys.' Leah is presumably Jessica's dead mother, another example of Shakespeare's ability to create characters beyond those seen on stage and retrospective lives for those upon it.

Dreaming on Naught but Idle Poetry

At some point, Ben Jonson arrived in the theatrical firmament. Like William Shakespeare, he was an actor before he became a playwright. It was as such that Philip Henslowe recorded a loan on 28 June 1597 to 'Bengemen Jonson, player'. In December he advanced him 20 shillings for 'a Boeke wch he was to write for vs befor crysmas next after the date thereof wch he showed the plotte vnto the company'. The classical learning he acquired at Westminster School under the tutelage of the great scholar William Camden was to be an inhibiting factor in his dramatic career, although he never realised it. He claimed to be the posthumous son of a clergyman whose mother had married a master bricklayer after his father's death. He never lived down his apprenticeship in his stepfather's trade, as the epithet 'bricklayer' was flung at him by his enemies (and there were many of those). According to his own account, he served with the Earl of Leicester's expedition to the Low Countries. On his return he eschewed his trade for the hazards of a life on the stage. John Aubrey recorded that he 'acted and wrote, both ill, at the Green Curtaine, a kind of nursery or obscure playhouse, somewhere in the suburbs" Although his reputation as an actor did not to pass to posterity, he played some significant parts. One other reference to his acting career comes in Thomas Dekker's *Satiromastix*, written during the war of words between the two playwrights. Horace was a name Jonson gave himself, in obvious reference to the Latin poet. 'Thou hast been in Parris garden hast not?' Horace is asked, to which he replies that he had played the part of Zulziman there. This is probably the part of Soliman in *The Tragedy of Soliman and Perseda* and the venue in Paris Garden would have been the Swan Theatre. He had also played 'mad Ieronimo'. This was the lead part in the *Spanish Tragedy*, whose published version had the sub-title: *Hieronimo is Mad Again.*

When, in 1598, Francis Mere's wrote his compendium of English poets and playwrights, he described Ben Jonson as 'one of our best in tragedy'. Such works as he may have written at that time are lost, but they mark his emergence as a playwright. It was probably in the year of his loan from Henslowe that he wrote his first surviving play, *The Case is Altered.* It does not seem to have been a great success. It was first published in three variant quartos in 1609. All state that the play had been performed by the Children of the Blackfriars – a company of boy actors for which Jonson had worked when it was known as the Children of the Queen's Revels, but they were not active around 1597, when it is most likely the play was first performed by Pembroke's Men, so the quartos must refer to a revival.

It appears not to have been a play that Ben was proud to have written. He did not include it in the First Folio of his works in 1616. In many ways it is the antithesis of his subsequent rigid adhesion to the classical unities, although the plot is borrowed extensively from two plays by Plautus. Multiple plots and subplots were subjects against which he was to wax vehemently, but the play does contain some archetypal Jonsonian elements, although it can hardly be described as 'humours' comedy, the genre for which he was to become noted. The concept of humours may have originated in ancient Egypt, but it was the Greek physician Hippocrates who first cast it into a physiological theory. He considered that certain human moods, emotions and behaviours were caused by the vital bodily fluids or 'humours': blood, yellow bile, phlegm and black bile; an imbalance of these produced extremes of temperament. In the 2nd century AD, another Greek physician, Aelius Galenus, searched for physiological reasons for human behaviour. He related the humours to a matrix of hot and cold and moist and dry taken from the four elements of earth, water, air and fire. The balance between these qualities could yield a total of nine temperaments. In the ideal personality, the complementary characteristics of warm and cool, and dry and moist are perfectly balanced. In the four less ideal types, one of the four qualities dominates. These are the temperamental categories that Galenus named 'sanguine', 'choleric', melancholic' and 'phlegmatic after the bodily humours. The words have passed into the English language, as has 'temperament', from the Latin, *temperare*, 'to mix'.

The element of **sanguine** is air; its organ, the liver; its bodily substance, the blood; its qualities, hot and moist; the personality, courageous, happy, hopeful, irresponsible, amorous, lustful and generous. 'This argues fruitfulness and liberal heart,' says Othello, as he takes Desdemona's hand.

The element of **choleric** is fire; its organ, the gall bladder; its bodily substance, yellow bile; its qualities, hot and dry; the personality, violent, vengeful, short-tempered, ambitious. 'I scarce can speak, my choler is so great,' says York in *Henry VI, Part II*. 'O, I could hew up rocks and fight with flint.'

The element of **melancholic** is earth; its organ, the spleen; its bodily substance, black bile; its qualities, cold and dry; the personality, sadness, contrariness, deliberation. In *Twelfth Night*, Viola tells the Duke Orsino of her supposed sister who pined away for the love of a man:

> She never told her love,
> But let concealment, like a worm i' th' bud,
> Feed on her damask cheek. She pined in thought,
> And with a green and yellow melancholy
> She sat like Patience on a monument'
> Smiling at grief.

The element of **phlegmatic** is water; its organ, the brain; its bodily substance, phlegm; its qualities, cold and moist; the personality, idleness, apathy, cowardice, peaceful. In *Henry IV, Part I*, Prince Hal upbraids his phlegmatic companions:

> I know you all and will awhile uphold
> The unyoked humour of your idleness.

Since most drama is about foibles of character, it is difficult to categorise precisely which plays may be defined as 'humours comedies', but Ben Jonson expressed the issue succinctly in his Induction to *Every Man in His Humour*:

> As when some one peculiar quality
> Doth so possess a man, that it doth draw
> All his affects, his spirits, and his powers,
> In their confluctions, all to run one way:
> This may be truly said to be a *humour*.

The earliest plays that may be characterised as coming within this definition were by George Chapman. *The Blind Beggar of Alexandria* was first performed by the Admiral's Men at the Rose Theatre on 12 February 1595/6. It was a popular success, performed twenty-two times during April 1597, three performances taking over 40 shillings, which compared to the best returns of the season. Some of the more farcical elements in the play may be the work of another hand, perhaps reflecting the script as it had been adapted during performance. Chapman does not appear to have been happy with this. In the dedication to his comedy *All Fools*, he implies that he has edited the play for publication himself to prevent it being 'patch'd with others' wit'.

The Blind Beggar is a 'disguise' comedy as well as a humours one. The title page announces that the actor playing the Duke Cleanthes, will be 'most pleasantly discoursing his variable humours in disguised shapes full of conceit and pleasure'. The characters he played in disguise – Irus, the blind beggar of the title, Count Hermes and Leon the Usurer, each represent a different humour. Appropriate costumes convey each mood. The complexity of the action and the rapid costume changes must have represented a tour de force of staging. Irus describes this fusion of character and costume as he dons the robes of Count Hermes, representing the volatile humour of yellow bile:

> Now to my wardrobe for my velvet gown;
> Now doth the sport begin.
> Come, gird this pistol closely to my side,
> By which I make men fear my humour still,
> And have slain two or three, as 'twere my mood,
> When I have done it most advisedly,
> To rid them, as they were my heavy foes.
> Now am I known to be the mad-brain Count,
> Whose humours twice five summers I have held.

The earliest play with such multi-disguises was Anthony Munday's *John a Kent and John a Cumber*. It set the precedent for subsequent complicated plots. It also proved popular, being played thirty times between July 1594 and December 1597.

Sometime in May 1597, a City gent, John Chamberlain, attended a performance by the Admiral's Men at the Rose Theatre. He wrote to his friend, Dudley Carleton, that he had resolved to go to the theatre because of the 'common applause' the play he saw was receiving. It was 'in very great request'. Despite this, he did not care for it, 'as the fellow saide of the shearing of hogges, that there was a great crie for so litle wolle'. He had probably seen a performance of the 'comedy of umers' that Henslowe recorded as first enacted on 11 May. This was probably Chapman's second extant comedy. *An Humorous Day's Mirth* owes much to Plautus and Terence. A central character, Lemot, serves as commentator on the others' follies, which are caused by their extremes of humour, which he defines in each of them. 'I sit,' he says, 'like an old king in an old-fashion play … and point out all my humorous companions.' Dowceter is a model of melancholy, but the character of Labesha is a satire upon that cult. Henslowe's inventory of the Company's properties lists the appropriate costumes worn by each character. The play was published in 1599 but, like its predecessor, the text is corrupt.

Humours comedy was not without its critics. Around 1601, Ben Jonson revised *The Case is Altered.* He maintained his delight in lampooning his fellow dramatists by incorporating a character called Antonio Balladino, as a satire on Anthony Munday, a character who rails against the humours cult.

On 28 July 1597, the very day on which he obtained his loan from Henslowe, Ben Jonson ran into severe trouble. The newly reconstituted Earl of Pembroke's Men performed *The Isle of Dogs*, a play he co-authored with Thomas Nashe, at the Swan Theatre. This lost play caused outrage in royal circles. The Isle of Dogs is situated on the tip of the Poplar peninsular opposite the royal palace of Placenta in Greenwich. It was where the royal hounds were kept – hence the name. It does not take much imagination to realise that the play was probably a satire on the royal court. On 28 July, an order went out informing the Justices of Middlesex and Surrey that:

> No plays shal be used within London or about the city, or in any public place during the time of summer, but also that those playhouses that are erected and built for such purpose shall be plucked down.

The City Fathers must have been delighted, seizing the opportunity provided by the affair to petition for the 'final suppressing of the saide stage playes, as well at the Theatre, Curten and bankside, as in all other places in and about the Citie'. In one swoop, Jonson, Nashe and Pembroke's Men appeared to have achieved what they had plotted unsuccessfully for years. For innocent parties such as the Lord Chamberlain's Men, it represented disaster. Their friends in high places, such as Hunsdon, must have sought the Queen's ear. As a lover of the theatre, she may have become more amenable once her initial fury abated. On 15 August, Hunsdon attended a meeting of the Privy Council at which *The Isle of Dogs* was condemned as a 'lewd play … containing very seditious and slanderous matter'. The offence was compounded by the fact that it had not been submitted to the Master of the Revels. It was decided that justice demanded blame should be accorded to the perpetrators of the outrage rather than the theatre as a whole. The authors and principle actors in the play were to be detained immediately. Nashe fled to Great Yarmouth: 'I was glad to run from it', but Jonson and two of the leading actors, Gabriel Spencer and Robert

Shaa, were incarcerated in the Marshalsea Prison, where they were interrogated with some severity. By 8 October, the rage had cooled sufficiently for them to be released. Persons of influence must have intervened for the order came directly from the Privy Council. For Langley, the episode was a disaster. It was ordered that only two companies – the Lord Chamberlain's Men at the Theatre and the Admiral's Men at the Rose – be licensed to perform in London. This effectively finished the Swan as a theatrical location, although it staggered on by presenting such other entertainments as bear-baiting and swashbuckling displays for another two decades.

The Privy Council may have taken the opportunity to deal with Langley, who was under suspicion of fencing a valuable Portuguese diamond. Spencer, Shaa and three other actors of Pembroke's Men threw in their lot with Henslowe and were promptly sued for £500 by Langley, who claimed they had agreed to appear exclusively at The Swan. Since this was no longer possible, this piece of blatant opportunism sheds more light on his character.

It was to comedy of the humours that Ben turned next. This was a predictable step. He saw himself as the heir to the great Latin dramatists and here was a genre in their tradition. Lack of success had tainted him. There would appear to have been a split with Henslowe, who may have decided, in the light of the *Isle of Dogs* affair, that Ben was not good news. Thus he offered *Every Man in His Humour* to the Lord Chamberlain's Men. According to the assiduous Nicholas Rowe, it was not initially well received, 'At that time altogether unknown to the world' appears unlikely. Shakespeare must have been aware of the furore Ben had caused with his *Isle of Dogs*:

> Mr Johnson [sic], who was at that time altogether unknown to the world, had offered one of his plays to the players, in order to have it acted, and the persons into whose hands it was put after having turned it carelessly and superciliously over, were just upon returning it to him with an all-natured answer, that it would be of no service to their company, when Shakespeare luckily cast his eye upon it, and found something so well in it as to engage him first to read it through, and afterwards to recommend Mr Johnson and his writings to the public.

That the play was a success is indicated by its rapid entry onto the Stationers' Register. It was a play that Jonson considerably revised. In the quarto, its setting is Florence, but, in his later revision, that became London and the names of the characters changed accordingly. It was first performed before 20 September 1598, when a letter from Toby Matthews to Dudley Carleton describes how a German visitor had lost 300 crowns at 'a new play called Every Man's Humour'.

William Shakespeare's name leads the cast of 'principal comedians' in Jonson's First Folio, together with Burbage, Phillips, Heminges, Condell, Pope, Beeston and Kempe. There is a theatrical tradition that Shakespeare specialised in playing the parts of old men. If so, it's likely he played Signior Lorenzo di Pazzi, father of Lorenzo Junior, who was most likely played by Burbage. In the later version, he becomes Old Knowell, father of the young gallant, Edward. If he did play this part (and the top billing makes it likely), he must have got a laugh with the lines:

> Myself was once a student, and indeed,
> Fed with the self-same humour he is now,
> Dreaming on nought but idle poetry,
> That fruitless and unprofitable art,
> Good unto none, but least to the professors;

In the autumn of 1597, Henslowe made 'a note of all such goods as I have bought for playing since my son Edward Alleyn left [p]laying'. Why Alleyn had decided to retire from the stage is unclear; he was at the height of his fame. Spencer may have been intended as his replacement, but his time with Henslowe was short The *Isle of Dogs* episode may have been the cause for him to hold a deep animosity towards Jonson. He had not written the offending lines, merely spoken them, and had suffered for it, but perhaps the antipathy was the other way. Years later Jonson told William Drummond that 'in the tyme of his close Imprissonment under Queen Elisabeth his judges could gett nothing of him to all their demands but I and No, they placed two damn'd Villans to catch advantage of him, with him, but he was advertised by his Keeper, of the Spies.' Were they Spencer and Shaa? Whatever the cause, Spencer challenged Jonson to a duel. It was fought on 22 September 1598 on Hoxton Fields. Spencer was a formidable opponent. As well as the dexterity with the sword he would have possessed as a leading actor, he had a record of violence. On 3 December 1596, a Coroner's Inquest found he had killed James Feake with a rapier at a house in Southwark. This time he did not triumph. 'Now to let you understand news, I will teall you some, but yt is for me harde and heavey'. Henslowe wrote to Alleyn on 26 September. 'Sence you weare with me, J haue lost one of my company wch hurteth me greately that is gabrell for he is slayne in hoges den fylldes by the hands of benge honson bricklayer.'

Although he avowed that Spencer had struck first, wounding him in the arm, Jonson was charged with 'feloniously and wilfully' killing Spencer with 'a certain sword of iron and steel called a rapier, of the price of three shillings, which he then and there ... held drawn in his right hand'. He was arraigned at the Old Bailey on 6 October and confessed to manslaughter, for which the penalty was death, but he had a ploy to save himself from the gallows. He pleaded 'Benefit of Clergy'. Under this archaic[1] legal device, anyone who was proficient in Latin could claim clerical status and was exempt from the jurisdiction of the civil courts. The level of proficiency was not high, consisting of reading an entirely appropriate verse from Psalm 50 in the Vulgate. *Miserere mei, Deus, secundum misericordiam tuam et secundum multitudinem miserationum tuarum dele iniquitatem meam* – 'Have mercy upon me, O God, according to thy loving kindness: according unto the multitude of thy tender mercies blot out my transgressions.' Occasionally, to catch out those who had merely memorised the verse, the authorities demanded a different recitation, but, as a classical scholar, this would hold no fears for Ben. Once he had invoked what was known as 'the neck verse', he would have appeared before an ecclesiastical court where he would have sworn his innocence on oath, supported by a dozen 'compurgars', who would vouch for his integrity. He would have had to perform an act of penitence. The guilty verdict remained. He had escaped the noose by pleading Benefit of Clergy, but the plea could only be made once. 'T' – for 'Tyburn' was branded on his thumb to enable identification in case of further offending.

Jonson's penchant for finding trouble manifested itself even in the Marshalsea. He converted to Catholicism, 'by trust of a priest who visited him in Prisson'. This was probably Fr Thomas Wright, a Jesuit who was kept in a kind of partial detention in various jails. The sincerity of the decision is not in doubt, but it might be regarded as reckless. One of his interrogators during the *Isle of Dogs* affair had been the notorious persecutor of Catholics, Richard Topcliffe. He had been suspended by the Queen for his excessive use of torture, but he would be back to wreak his cruelties on adherents of this proscribed religion. It was a bold decision by Jonson to follow his conscience, probably occasioned by the prospect of his potential shameful demise.

Henslowe's scathing reference to Ben Jonson's artisan trade was much-flung, but it had its uses. His stepfather was probably Robert Brett, no mere bricklayer, but an affluent contractor, who became Master of the Tylers and Bricklayers Company. Jonson's apprenticeship gave him the status of a Freeman of the City. He was still paying dues to his Livery Company as late as 1611. Membership of a Guild carried a certain cachet. During the occasional, and sometimes lengthy, enforced closures of the theatres, it might have been handy to return to his old trade. In 1618, Jonson was welcomed to Edinburgh, not as a noted writer, but as 'inglisman burges and gildbrother'.

City Comedy

Jonson's institutional connection to London was of great value to him as a writer. He became a leading exponent of what became known as 'City Comedy'. He defined its essence in *The Alchemist*:

> Our Scene is London, 'cause we would make knowne,
> No countries mirth is better then our owne.
> No clime breeds better matter, for your whore,
> Bawd, squire, impostor, many persons more.

As the verse implies, 'City Comedy' was about the citizens in all their diversity and included elements of criminality and licentiousness. References to familiar locations around the City made the audience feel part of the show. The earliest known example is *Englishmen for my Money*, for which Philip Henslowe paid William Houghton in May 1598. It sets the themes others will follow. One was mocking foreigners and the way they spoke English. Pisaro, a Portuguese merchant living in London, was what would now be called a venture capitalist and the play has no inhibitions in presenting a radical critique of the potential for wealth and the resultant capacity to bring others to penury of that trade.

> And by the sweete loude trade of *Usurie*,
> Letting for Interest, and on Morgages.
> Doe I waxe rich, though many Gentlemen
> By my extortion comes to miserie:

Pisaro has three daughters by his English wife, Laurentia, Marina and Mathea. They have three suitors, all of whom the father approves because of their wealth – Vandalle, a Dutchman, Delion, a Frenchman and Alvare, an Italian. There are also 'three *English* Gentlemen' in contention, Harvie, Ferdinand and Walgrave (otherwise known as Ned), who Pisaro reveals:

> Haue pawnde to mee their Liuings and their Lands:
> Each seuerall hoping, though their hopes are vaine,
> By mariage of my Daughters, to possesse
> Their Patrimonies and their Landes againe:

Pisaro has hired Anthony, a schoolmaster, to instruct his daughters in moral philosophy, but he is reluctant to do so. 'Morall *Philosophy* is a kind of art', he tells the daughters:

The most contrary to your tender sexes;
It teacheth to be graue: and on that brow,
Where Beawtie in her rarest glory shines,
Plants the sad semblance of decayed age:

He is conveying messages from the three English suitors, whose affections the daughters reciprocate; Pisaro discovers this and dismisses him. In his place, he orders his servant, Frisco, to hire a speaker of Dutch and Italian, who is 'a Frenchman borne'. This gives the clown the opportunity to mock foreigners. 'I remember my great Grandfathers Grandmothers sisters coosen told mee, that Pigges and *French-men*, speake one Language, *awee awe*.' When a Dutchman speaks, he sounds as if his mouth is 'full of meate'. An Italian possesses 'a wanton eye, Pride in his Apparel and the Devil in his countenance'. Yet, beyond this mockery, the play reflects the growing commercial power of the City of London in terms of international trade and speculation. Of course, the foreigners and the miserly Pisaro are outwitted, but the play's lack of quality demonstrates why comparatively little of the output from Henslowe's dramatic stable survived.

In Thomas Dekker's *The Shoemaker's Holiday*, there are no less than eighteen references to specific London locations. The play was first performed by the Admiral's Men in 1599. It 'was acted before the Queen's most excellent Majesty on New Year's Day at night'. It is a satire on the contemporary class structure. Rose Oatley and Roland Lacy are deeply in love. His uncle, Sir Hugh Lacey, Earl of Lincoln, vows to stop the wedding. Her position is too lowly for such an alliance, although her father, Sir Roger Oatley, is Lord Mayor of London. 'Too mean is my poor girl for his high birth. Poor citizens must not with courtiers wed.' To break up the affair, Sir Hugh has Roland drafted into the army. It is set at the time of Henry V's expedition into France, so Dekker's choice of scenario may have been influenced by the success of Shakespeare's play. Roland relinquishes his command to his cousin, Askew, and learns the craft of shoemaking in Wittenberg. He returns to London disguised as a Dutch shoemaker, Hans Meulter. He secures an apprenticeship with Simon Eyre, 'the mad shoemaker of Tower Street', who makes shoes for the King and other notables. Rose, to evade her father, devises the pretext of having him fit her with a pair of shoes. Sir Hugh is delighted to hear that Rose is attached to someone other than Roland. 'Her love turned shoemaker? I am glad of this.' The situation is reversed. Previously, Sir Hugh had objected to Rose marrying above herself. Now her father objects to her marrying beneath herself:

A fleming butterbox, a shoemaker,
Will she forget her birth? Requite my care
With such ingratitude? Scorned she young Hammon,
To love a honnikin, a needy knave?
Well, let her fly. I'll not fly after her.
Let her starve if she will, she's none of mine.

'Young Hammon' is a character in the skilfully interwoven sub-plot. He falls in love with Jane Damport, who refuses to marry him until she is convinced that her husband, Ralph, has been killed in the French War – but, wounded, not dead, he returns to London. In a general contretemps, the protagonists gather at St Faith's Church, where it is believed the two weddings will take place. Ralph arrives in the church in time to prevent the wedding of Jane and Hammon and she pledges her renewed troth to him. Rose and Roland got warnings of the arrival of those seeking to prevent their union and celebrate their nuptials elsewhere. Sir Hugh resolves to go to the very top to get the match annulled:

... Come, Sir Roger Oatley,
The King will do us justice in this cause,
Howe'er their hands have made them man and wife,
I will disjoin the match, or lose my life.

He neither loses his life, nor disjoins the match. Nor does the King do him justice in his cause. In fact, Henry is dining with Simon Eyre, who has acquired great wealth through the financial advice of 'Hans Meulter'. He is to become Lord Mayor in succession to Sir Roger and is giving a huge breakfast for all the shoemakers' apprentices to celebrate the Feast of St Hugh, Patron Saint of Shoemakers. He persuades the King to pardon Roland for his desertion. 'Her blood is too base', Sir Hugh says of Rose, but the King differs. 'Dost thou not know,' he tells him, 'that love respects no blood?'

Cares not for difference of birth or blood;
The maid is young, well born, fair, virtuous:
A worthy bride for any gentleman!
Besides, for her sake your nephew did stoop
To bare necessity, and as I hear,
Forgetting honours, and all courtly pleasures,
To gain her love, became a shoemaker.

Since the King sits on top of the social pyramid, it may seem strange that he takes a less rigid view of the class system than the Lord Mayor and the Earl, but that is not the point. The King is all classes and none. He bears the moral responsibility for the well-being of his nation, a role well-realised in the part of the same King created by William Shakespeare:

> Upon the king! Let us our lives, our souls,
> Our debts, our careful wives,
> Our children and our sins, lay on the king!
> We must bear all. O hard condition,
> Twin-born with greatness, subject to the breath
> Of every fool, whose sense no more can feel,
> But his own wringing! What infinite heart's ease
> Must kings neglect, that private men enjoy!

One place where the social classes mingled was the theatre. Although there was a division based on wealth, between those seated in the galleries and the 'groundlings', it was the same play they saw, which often received royal approbation by being performed at Court, but it was the men-of-the-theatre who were the most socially mobile. Many came from artisan backgrounds. William Shakespeare's father was a glover; Christopher Marlowe's, a shoemaker; Edward Alleyn's, an innkeeper; Richard Burbage's, a joiner; Henry Condell's, probably a fishmonger; Richard Tarlton's, probably a pig farmer, and Ben Jonson's stepfather, a bricklayer. Yet they mixed in the highest ranks of the aristocracy. They were of all classes and none.

One City Comedy was unique, if only because it was based on a person actually living in London. *The Roaring Girl* by Thomas Decker and Thomas Middleton was presented by Prince Henry's Men at the Fortune Theatre around 1608. The central character, 'Moll', was modelled on Mary Frith, aka 'Moll Cutpurse', a criminal cross-dresser who was a familiar figure around theatre-land. A pamphlet by John Day entitled *The Mad Merry Pranks of Merry Moll of the Bankside* was entered onto the Stationers' Register on 10 August 1610, probably reflected the play's popularity. Mary Frith's celebrity and notoriety was further demonstrated in a city comedy by Nathan Field, *Amends for Ladies: with the Merry Prankes of Moll Cut-Purse, or the Humour of Roaring*. 'As it was acted at the Blacke-Fryers, both by the PRINCES Servuants, and the Lady ELZABETHS' states the quarto of 1616.

The popularity of *The Roaring Girl*, a characteristic city comedy in familiar London settings, with the usual tales of covert affairs and liaisons, mistaken identities and ultimately requited love, may have not entirely have been due to its dramatic qualities. Mary had a habit of appearing on stage during performances, dressed in men's clothing singing bawdy songs to a lute and smoking a long clay pipe, arguably the first woman to appear in an English public theatre. This led to her being charged with wearing 'indecent and manly apparel' and sentenced to stand dressed in a white sheet at St Paul's Cross during sermon time. 'She wept bitterly and seemed very penitent,' wrote John Chamberlain. 'It is since doubted she was maudlin drunk; being discovered to have tippled off three quarts of sack before she came to her penance.'

Despite featuring so rumbustious a character, the portrayal of Mary Frith in *The Roaring Girl* is strangely muted. She is indeed a cross-dresser who behaves mannishly in challenging an antagonist to a duel, but otherwise she is demure and pointedly chaste. Her character makes but a cameo appearance in *Amends* which does not feature too many 'mad merry prankes'. It is an engaging thought that the authors, aware of Mary's potential to ad-lib on stage, might have left a space for her to engage and delight the audience. Since such an appearance was illegal, it explains why she was brought to St Paul's Cross.

William Shakespeare had little to do with City Comedy, although *The Merry Wives of Windsor* might come under that definition. It is his only play in which all the characters are of humbler origin – with the exception, of course, of Sir John Falstaff. Shakespeare's lower-class characters are either comic parodies like those who frequent the Eastcheap Tavern and Mistress Overdone's brothel, or servants following the will of their masters like those in the opening of *Romeo and Juliet*. Otherwise, his world – and that of many other contemporary dramatists – is populated by those of position and rank.

Very Great Annoyance and Trouble

Giles Allen was continuing to be difficult about the lease of The Theatre. James Burbage frequently urged him to fulfil the original agreement, but in vain. Finally, Allen, 'according to his own will and discretion, did cause a draft of a lease to be drawn, wherein were inserted many unreasonable covenants'. The rental would increase from £14 annually to £24. The new lease would last just five years, after which Burbage would be obliged to convert the building to other uses, when it would revert to Allen. Such was James Burbage's keenness to ensure the company's future that he was prepared to accept the rent increase and the eventual reversion of the site to Allen, but the idea that The Theatre could only exist for another five years was firmly rejected. This is likely to have led to negotiations about finding a new home for the company. In a bold move, Burbage bought the freehold of the *dorter* and surrounding rooms of the old Blackfriars Priory from the executors of a former Master of the Revels, Sir

Thomas Cawarden, for the hefty sum of £600. This large hall had been the friars' dormitory in a different part of the extensive site from where the Children of the Chapel Royal had performed. It seemed an ideal location. Its status as a Liberty put it beyond the jurisdiction of the City fathers. It was on the north bank of the Thames, so there was no necessity for the audience to cross the river. Most of all, it was an indoor location, so performances were not dependent on the weather. It gave scope for special effects and for securing a better-heeled clientele who would pay more than the groundlings at The Theatre. Burbage began the extensive works to turn the building into a working theatre. Yet what had seemed a masterstroke became a near-catastrophe. It is an indication of the status of the theatre and the rowdy behaviour associated with it that the prospect of Blackfriars being so-utilised caused great alarm among the upmarket local residents. In November 1596, they petitioned the Privy Council. No argument was spared:

> The said Burbage … meaneth very shortly to convert and turn the same into a comon playhouse, which will grow to be a very great annoyance and trouble, not only to all the noblemen and gentlemen thereabout inhabiting but also a generall inconvenience to all the inhabitants of the same precinct, both by reason of the great resort and gathering togeather of all manner of vagrant and lewd persons that, under cover of resorting to the playes, will come thither and worke all manner of mischeefe, and allso to the great pestring and filling up of the same precinct, yf it should please God to send any visitation of sicknesse as heretofore hath been, for that same precinct is already grown very populous; and besides, that the same playhouse is so neare the Church that the noyse of the drummes and trumpets will greatly disturbe and hinder both the ministers and parishioners in tyme of divine service and sermons. In tender consideracion whereof, as allso for that there hath not at any tyme heretofore bean used any common playhouse within the same precinct, but now that all players being banished by the Lord Mayor from playing within the Citie by reason of the great inconveniences and misrule that followeth them, they now thinke to plant them selves in liberties.

The petition was signed by twenty-six local inhabitants, including Shakespeare's fellow Stratfordian and printer of his narrative poems, Richard Field, the formidable and influential Lady Russell – a friend of the Queen and sister-in-law of Lord Burghley, her Chief Minister, and even more ominously, by the 2nd Lord Hunsdon. Sadly for the players, their influential patron had died at his residence at Somerset House on 23 July 1596. His son, George Carey, succeeded him as their patron, so the Company became 'Lord Hunsdon's Men'. The Blackfriars Priory had been divided in the 1570s. One half became the Playhouse: the other, was acquired by Lord Hunsdon. We are in the presence of what is now known as 'nimbyism'.

In response, the 'owners and players' of the Blackfriars Theatre petitioned the Privy Council 'for permission to finish the reparations and alterations begun at their own expense'. The Privy Council supported the residents. It must have betokened a potential financial disaster for James Burbage, who had laid out large amounts of money with little prospect of a return. He did not long suffer the qualms of failure. He died in the extremely cold winter of 1596/7 and was buried on 2 February in his parish church of St Leonard's, Shoreditch, within sight of the theatre he had created. He left the Blackfriars Theatre, once the focus of his future hopes, now seemingly an expensive foible, to his son, Richard. With the lease about to expire on The Theatre and with little prospect of its renewal, both possessed little value. When his widow presented an invoice for his estate it came to just £37, not an inconsiderable sum, but a pittance for a man whose success in the theatre had been great, but who had apparently lost a fortune on enterprises that were not to be.

The incident had no lasting effect on relations between the company and its patron. Like his father, George Carey had a deep enthusiasm for the theatre. It was the father or the son who built a playhouse in Tonbridge,[2] where they were Lords of the Manor. Doubtless, a performance was *de rigeur* for the Company during its occasional tours into Kent.

Richard Burbage offset at least some of his father's losses on 2 September 1600 when he leased the Blackfriars Theatre to Henry Evans for twenty-one years for an annual rental of £40. Evans had been one of those evicted by Sir William More in 1584. He now returned to the vast building, in partnership with Nathaniel Giles, the Master of the Children of the Chapel Royal.

The petitioners of 1596 seem to have accepted this new development without protest. The children's companies were a different proposition from the turbulent groundlings in the public theatres, a point made in John Marston's, *Jack Drum's Entertainment*:

Sir Edward Fortune: I would haue had a play; I'faith I would.
I saw the Children of Powles last night,
And troth they pleasde mee prettie well.
The Apes in time will go it handsomely.
Planet: I' faith, I like the audience that frequenteth there
With much applause. A man shall not be choakte
With the stench of Garlicke; not be pasted

To the barmy jacket of a Beer-brewer.
Brabant Junior: 'Tis a good, gentle audience, and I hope the Boyes
Will come one day into the Court of Requests.

The social superiority of the Blackfriars Theatre over the public playhouses was reflected in the admission prices. The standard cost of attending a play there was sixpence, with higher prices according to vantage point, with a top rate for actually sitting on the stage. It was a theatre where it was as important to be seen as to see.

The Old Lad of the Castle

With the death of the 1st Lord Hunsdon, not only had the players lost a valued friend and patron, but his successor as Lord Chancellor, William Brooke, the 10th Lord Cobham, proved indifferent in their support, possibly because he was ailing – he died just seven months later. His accession to the office gave the City Fathers new energy in their campaign against the drama. Thomas Nashe, writing to a friend later that year, complained that the players were 'piteously persecuted by the Lord Mayor and Alderman, and however in their old Lord's time, they thought their estate settled, it is now so uncertain that they cannot build upon it'.

Cobham may have had a personal grievance against William Shakespeare. It has been claimed that he was a descendent of Sir John Oldcastle, the name under which Shakespeare's most celebrated comic character first appeared, but the relationship was tenuous. He was descended from Joan Braybrooke and her first husband, his thrice great-grandfather, Thomas Brooke, the 5th Lord Cobham. She was four times widowed. Sir John was her third husband. As a result of this alliance, Oldcastle assumed the courtesy title of Lord Cobham. Despite this slender link, the current Cobham seems to have taken umbrage at the portrayal of his forebear by marriage. Around 1625, the Puritan antiquary, Dr Richard James, wrote to Sir Henry Bouchier that offence was 'worthily taken by personages descended from his title'. As well as old Lord Cobham's successor, Henry Brooke, the 11th Lord Cobham, he may be referring to his brother, the Revd. Sir George Brooke, Prebendary of York and, significantly, their brother-in-law, Robert Cecil, who had married Elizabeth Brooke in 1588.

Dr James' letter is attached to a manuscript he wrote entitled *The Legend and Defence of ye noble Knight and Martyr Sir John Oldcastle*. His knowledge of the plays is shaky – Falstaff is referred to as being in *Henry V*, a play in which he features but does not appear. He considers the offence was taken 'as peradventure by manie others allso whoe ought to have him in honourable memorie'. The date of the letter reveals, that the slur on this revered name was long remembered.

The historic Oldcastle was a courtier of Henry V who served the Crown with distinction during the Owain Glyndwr rebellion. He became an adherent of the Lollards, a millennialist sect that condemned contemporary society as corrupt and unjust. The Second Coming of Christ would see the establishment of the Kingdom of God on Earth. It was the duty of its adherents to work to bring this about. Thus, Lollardy was an active political movement whose object was the destruction of the status quo. Oldcastle's commitment led to allegations of heresy, but the King, mindful of his past services, used his influence to protect him. His response was to formulate a plot to seize the King and his brothers at Eltham Palace. He would then become the Regent of a Lollard commonwealth, in which, presaging the Protestant Reformation, the monasteries would be dissolved and their wealth seized. When the plot was discovered, he went into open rebellion, waging guerrilla warfare on the Welsh Marches. He was probably a party to the plot to assassinate the King on the eve of his famous expedition to France, which Shakespeare dramatises in *Henry V*. He was eventually captured and hanged for treason at Smithfield before his corpse was burnt as that of a heretic. In an extraordinary rewriting of history, Oldcastle became a Protestant hero. His treason was wiped from the record by polemicists like William Tyndale, John Bale and John Foxe and he was presented as a victim of Catholic tyranny. According to Dr James, he 'gave witnesse vnto the truth of our reformation with a constant and resolute martyrdom, vnto which he was pursued by the Priests, Bishops, Moncks and Friers of those dayes.'

That the original name for Falstaff was Oldcastle is beyond doubt. Prince Hal refers to 'My old lad of the Castle' in *Henry IV, Part I*. In *Part II*, a speech prefix escapes alteration. By then Cobham was probably dead. We do not know what stirred the controversy that led Shakespeare (or his Company) to change the character's name. It was inherited from his main source, *The Famous Victories of Henry V*, in which Oldcastle is one of a bunch of dissolute ne'er-do-wells who are the companions of the young Prince Hal. It is tempting to speculate that Shakespeare could not resist having a pot at this Protestant icon (if that is not a contradiction in terms). Given his interest in history and his noted caution about offending authority, it is difficult to conceive that he would not have realised the reverence militant Protestants bestowed upon Oldcastle.

'Oldcastle' had to go and Falstaff' was substituted. It is the name of a cowardly knight called Sir John Fastolf who flees the battlefield in *Henry VI, Part II*. His descendants were living in Suffolk, but perhaps were not theatregoers and never heard of this slight on their ancestor. It must have been decided that it would be injudicious to retain the names of Russell and Harvey, Oldcastle's rowdy companions. Both were the surnames of prominent courtiers. They survive in a scene direction in *Henry IV, Part II*. Even this did not appease Dr James. 'The post was putt, to make an ignorant shifte of abusing Sr Jhon Fastolphe, a man not inferior of vertue though not so famous in pietie as the other.'

It may be pondered why Shakespeare's exploitation of that name should arouse such fury when it had already been employed in the *Famous Victories* without apparently arousing comment. It may be that 'Oldcastle' was such a consummate comic creation that the assumed slight on his memory could not go unnoticed.

A letter written by Rowland Whyte to his employer, Sir Robert Sidney, on 8 March 1599/1600, describes the entertainment provided for the delegation led by Louis Vereken, the Ambassador of the Archduke of Austria, who was a member of the delegation to conduct peace negotiations on behalf of the Hapsburg Empire. These were important people on a vital mission, so Hunsdon accorded them appropriate courtesy:

> All this Weeke the Lords have bene in London and past away the tyme in feasting and plaies … upon Thursday my Lord Chamberlain feasted him, and made him a very great and delicate dinner, and there in the afternoon his players acted before Vereken Sir John Old Castile, to his great contentment.

Since it was a private performance, the Company may have chosen to revert to the play's original script.

In 1599, Henslowe sought to take advantage of any discomfort caused to the Lord Chamberlain's Men by the Oldcastle affair by commissioning Anthony Munday, Michael Drayton, Richard Hathwaye and Robert Wilson to write a play on the same topic. In the production by the Admiral's Men, Oldcatle is no drunken rogue, but the hero beloved of the Puritans. The roguish figure was not forgotten, however. In the context of this play, it is not surprising that he is a Catholic priest called Sir John of Wrotham. The Prologue launches a swipe at the character of Falstaff:

> It is no pampered glutton we present,
> Nor aged Councellor to youthful sinne,
> But one whose vertue shone above the rest,
> A valiant martyr and a virtuous peere.

Shakespeare does not seem to have been in the habit of responding to provocations, at least not in his dramatic works. Nevertheless, someone in the company added a disavowal in the epilogue to *Henry IV, Part II* – 'For what I have to say is of my own makin,' he tells the audience, 'for Oldcastle died a martyr, and this is not the man.' It is unlikely that William Shakespeare would have described his own play as 'very displeasing' as does the speaker of the epilogue – who admits Shakespeare did not write the words. 'If you look for a good speech now, you undo me,' he tells the audience, 'for what I have to say is of my own making.' The intention to close the performance with a dance suggests the speaker could have been Will Kempe, whose jig would have ended the show. 'If my tongue cannot entreat you acquit me,' he pleads, 'will you command me to use my legs? And yet that were but light payment, to dance out of your debt.' This was but a few months before Shakespeare wrote the line: 'And let those who play your clowns speak no more than is set down for them.'

News of the furore reached Robert Persons, Head of the English College in faraway Rome. In his 1603 work, *A Treatise of Three Conversions of England*, written under the pseudonym of R. Dolman, he described Oldcastle as 'a ruffian knight, as all England knoweth, and commonly brought on by comedians on their stages'. Thomas Middleton appears unaware of the change of name. In his play of 1604, *The Meeting of Gallants at an Ordinarie*, his character, Signor Shuttleworth, tells his companions:

> Now Signors, how like you Mine Host? Did I not tell you he was a mad round knave, and a merrie one too, and if you chaunce to talke of fatte Sir John Oldcastle, he will tell you he was the great grand-father and not much unlike him in Paunch, if you mark him well by all descriptions.

The jibe continued to fester among Puritans. In *The History of Great Britain*, published in 1611, the cartographer John Speed registered his offence about what he considered a gross libel against a Protestant hero. 'R.Doleman' had made Oldcastle 'a Ruffian, a Robber and a Rebell':

> His authority, taken from stage-plaiers, is more befitting the pen of his slanderous report than the Credit of the judicious, being only grounded from this Papist and his Poet, of like conscience for lies, the one ever feigning, and the other ever falsifying the truth.

The controversy continued even after the theatres were closed during the Interregnum. Thomas Fuller took it up in *The Church History of Britain*, published in 1655:

> Stage poets have themselves been very bold with, and others very merry at, the memory of Sir John Oldcastle, Whom they have fancied a boon

> companion, a jovial royster, and yet a coward to boot, contrary to the credit of all chronicles, owning him a martial man of merit. The best is, Sir John Falstaff hath revived the memory of Sir John Oldcastle, and of late is substituted buffoon in his place, but it matters little what malicious papists have written against him.

Even after the Restoration, Fuller was still fulminating about the misuse of Fastolfe's name in his *Worthies of England*, published in 1662: 'Since the stage hath been over-bold with his memory, making him a thrasonical puff and emblem of mock virtue.'

When Nicholas Rowe wrote the first formal biography of Shakespeare in 1709, the issue was still live, despite it being over a century since the play was first performed. He adds the detail that the change in the character's name was the result of a Royal Decree:

> It may not be improper to observe that this part of Falstaff is said to have been written originally, under the name of Oldcastle; some of the family being there remaining, the Queen was pleased to command that he alter it; upon which he made use of Falstaff.

The Queen's role in the affair is a tenable hypothesis. As Lord Chancellor and a Privy Councillor, Cobham would have had her ear. Even more so would his brother-in-law, Robert Cecil, her most trusted minister.

Yet theatrical tradition has it that Elizabeth delighted in the character of Falstaff. 'I know very well that it hath pleased one of the greatest queens that ever was in the world,' wrote John Dennis in the preface to *The Comical Gallant: or the Amours of Sir John Falstaffe*, his adaptation of *The Merry Wives of Windsor* of 1702. Five years later, Nicholas Rowe elaborated on the story:

> She was so pleas'd with the admirable character of *Falstaff*, in the two Parts of *Henry* the fourth, that fhe commanded him to continue it for one Play more and and to fhew him in love. This is faid to be the occasions of his writing *The Merry Wives of Windsor*.

'About midnight my Lord Chamberlain died,' reported Rowland Whyte, Sir Robert Sidney's agent in Flushing on 6 March 1596/7. 'The court is now full of who shall have this and that office.' On 17 April, he wrote further, 'Lord Hunsdon this day made Lord Chancellor to her Majesty and by Her Majesty's express command was sworn in of her Majesty's Privy Council this afternoon.'

This appointment of George Carey to his father's former office enabled his theatre company to revert to its previous title – the Lord Chamberlain's Men.

Another honour came to Hunsdon on 23 April when he was appointed one of five Knights of the Garter during the St George's Day celebrations in Whitehall. The Queen attended this occasion, but it was not her custom to attend the Garter ceremony, which took place at Windsor on 24 May. The occasion began with the candidates processing from London to Windsor in a great cavalcade in which each sought to outdo the others by the magnificence of his retinue. Rowland Whyte heard that 'it was agreed between themselves that they would have only fifty men apiece, but now I hear that my Lord Chamberlain will have 300 and Sir Henry Lee 200'.

On the day, the retinue of Sir Henry, the Queen's Champion, led the way, followed by the train of Charles Blount, 8th Baron Mountjoy. After him came the grandest cavalcade of all:

> my Lord chancellor with a brave company of men and gentlemen, his servants and retainers with all his men in blue coats faced with orange colour taffeta and orange colour feathers in their hats, most part having chains of gold, besides a great number of knights and others that accompanied his Lordship.

Hunsdon's 'brave company' would have included his 'servants', his company of players. Such was their status that they may have had pride of place in his entourage. The fourth cavalcade was that of Lord Thomas Howard, the vice-admiral in the expedition against Cadiz in the previous year. Always impecunious, he maintained the agreement to limit his followers to fifty.

Next day, each new knight was escorted into the choir of St George's Chapel to swear the oath before the Registrar, Henry Percy, the 9th Earl of Northumberland and be installed in his stall. 'Service being done,' wrote Rowland Whyte, 'they all went into the Castle to dinner, where honourable fare was prepared at the charge of the four new installed Knights, whose servants attended and served us'.

Since it is probable that the Lord Chamberlain's Men were among these 'servants', it is likely that they were called upon to put on a theatrical performance and the most likely play to have been presented is *The Merry Wives of Windsor*. There are a number of references to the absence of German visitors in the text. It had been intended that Prince Frederick of Mompelgard, heir to the Duke of Württemberg, should be installed into the Order that day, but he could not be present. Everything about the play pleads for a Windsor setting. 'There comes my master, Master Shallow,' says Peter Simple, 'from Frogmore, over the stile,' Slender 'came yonder at Eton to marry Mistress Page.' John Taylor, the ubiquitous water poet, mentions the Garter Inn in the town in 1636, so the Host in *Merry Wives* was likely to be based on a real person. The legend of the ghost of Herne the Hunter and his old oak tree would not be grasped by a London audience but would be familiar at Windsor.

That the play was in some way bound up with the Garter ceremony is supported in the final scene. In a speech reminiscent of the fairies blessing the bridal bed in *A Midsummer Night's Dream*, the pseudo fairies of *The Merry Wives* bless Windsor Castle, the stalls of the Knights of the Garter and their motto:

> Search Windsor Castle, elves, within and out:
> Strew good luck, ouphes,[3] on every sacred room:
> That it may stand until perpetual doom;
> In state as wholesome as in state 'tis fit,
> Worthy the owner and the owner it.
> The several chairs of order look you scour
> With juice of balm and every precious flower:
> Each fair instalment, coat, and several crest,
> With loyal blazon, evermore be blest!
> And nightly, meadow-fairies, look you sing;
> Like to the Garter's compass, in a ring:
> The expressure that it bears, green let it be,
> More fertile-fresh than all the field to see;
> And 'Honi soit qui mal y pense' write
> In emerald tufts, flowers purple, blue and white …

This speech does not appear in the edition of the play published in 1602. This was a 'bad' quarto, one of those referred to by John Hemings and Henry Condell in the preface to the First Folio as 'divers stolen and surreptitious copies'. It was probably produced from the memory of one of the actors.[4] 'As it hath been diuers times Acted … Both before her Maiestie and else-where', the title page announces, so it had been performed at Court, and the fairies' epilogue could have been added for the Garter performance. It is included in the First Folio, when it would have been copied from the original text.

According to the tradition picked up by Dennis, the play was written with great rapidity. The Queen was so eager to see it acted that it was written in fourteen days. It appears to have been written in haste and Oldcastle was not entirely expurgated. In the final act, Falstaff is required to call out the first letter of his name – 'O, O, O', which signifies Oldcastle rather than Falstaff.

Chapter Six

These our Servauntes

The Great Globe Itself

On 29 September 1598, Cuthbert Burbage made his final appeal to Giles Allen, who proffered a new lease, but he would not 'accept thereof' because of the 'very unreasonable covenants therein contained'. Allen's ploy appeared to have succeeded. Soon after, he contended that since Cuthbert had 'suffered the same there to continue till the expiration of the said term ... the right and interest of the said Theatre was both in law and conscience absolutely vested in him'. Accordingly he planned to pull it down and take the timbers, but he must have spoken too freely because Cuthbert 'got intelligence' of his intention. Meanwhile, the empty Theatre languished unvisited: a sight noted by the satirist, Edward Guilpin:

> But see yonder,
> One like an unfrequented Theatre
> Walks in dark silence and solitude.

Although Allen owned the freehold, the timber frames of The Theatre had been erected by the Burbages' father and, as long as the lease was current, belonged to them. On the night of 28 December 1598, they made their move, taking advantage of Allen's absence in the country. According to a deposition lodged by a still-furious Allen four years later, they 'armed themselves with divers and manye unlawful and offensive weapons: as namlye swordes, daggers, billes, axes and such like. And soe armed did then repayre unto the sayd Theater.' The party included the skilled master carpenter, Peter Street and some dozen of his workmen.

According to Allen, 'divers ... servauntes and farmers then goinge aboute in peacable manner', entreated the party to desist from their 'unlawfull enterpryse', but they, with

> greate violence not only then and there resisted them ... pulling breaking and throwing downe the sayd Theater in verye outrageous violent and riotous sort to the great disturbance and terrifying not onlye of your

subjectes sayd servauntes and farmers but of divers others of your majesties loving subjectes there neere inhabitinge.

The materials were conveyed to Street's warehouse on the Thames near the Bridewell. When Allen learned his plot had been foiled, he brought a bill of complaint in the Easter Term of 1599 against the Burbages and their contractors for trespass, demolishing the Theatre and taking away the timbers, but his language was so intemperate and his charges so reckless that he weakened his case. The suit dragged on for three years. In the summer of 1601 it was dismissed. Finally, the Court of Requests declared Allen to be what became known as a vexatious litigant. Thus the history of London's first playhouse, a story of quarrels, litigation (and some theatre too), came to a close.

Where the Company went after quitting The Theatre is uncertain. They could have found a temporary home at The Curtain a few yards away. It is unlikely that they would have gone in with Henshaw at the Rose, but an arrangement with Francis Langley is a possibility. That the Company had some sort of agreement with him is suggested by the famous drawing of the interior of the Swan Theatre made by Johannes de Witt around 1596. Three actors are on stage, two in women's roles. The third is an affected figure, making a low obeisance. The scene shouts out '*Twelfth Nigh*t: Act III: Scene 4.' Olivia is seated, as befits the mistress of the house, behind her stands Maria, as befits a maid. Is it Malvolio who is making the exaggerated bow? His dress appears extravagant and he carries the steward's staff of office.

Since Leslie Hotson discovered in the papers of the Duke of Northumberland, a record of the entertainment of the Muscovite ambassador and an Italian nobleman, Virginio Orsini, Duke of Bracciano, at Court on 6 January 1601/02, there has been something of a consensus that this was the occasion of the play's first performance.[1] It has been suggested that the name of a leading character – Orsino – was chosen to honour the Duke. If so, it was an odd gesture. The character is full of foppish melancholia: not one that would be complimentary to an eminent foreign dignitary. In any case, Orsini was not the guest-of-honour that evening. It was the representative of Tsar Boris Godenov, Grigory Ivanavich Milulin. The English Government was keen to expand trade and so 'it was ordered that the Embassador for the mershants of Moscow should in confirming the League dine or eate Bread and Salt, [the traditional way of confirming a treaty], with the Queenes Maiestie'.

The Queen had requested the Master of Revels 'to make choyse of the play that shal be best furnished with rich apparel, have great variety and change of musicke and duances, and of a subject that may be most pleasing to her majestie.' *Twelfth Night* features music, but not dances.

The 'clown' most associated with the part of Feste is Robert Armin, although there is no record of his playing it. It is likely that he was with the Lord Chamberlain's Men when *As You Like It* was first performed. Since it was not mentioned by Francis Meres on his list of Shakespeare's plays of 1598 and was entered onto the Stationers' Register in 1600 as a forthcoming publication, 1599 seems a likely date for its premier. Armin is often speculatively associated with the part of Touchstone, but if the putative date is correct, then the robust Kempe would have still been with the company and he is a more likely candidate for the role. If Armin was in the production, more likely he would have played the melancholy Jacques, or Amiens, the chief singer in the play. Thomas Morley's *First Book of Ayres*, published in 1600, contains a setting for the song from the play, 'It was a Lover and his Lass'.

It is unlikely that William Shakespeare was part of the 'riotous' assembly that gathered at The Theatre on that December night, but he would surely have been aware of Cuthbert's intentions. On 21 February following, he was a party to the formal thirty-one-year leasehold agreement with Sir Nicholas Brend for a parcel of land on Bankside, south of the river. The Burbage brothers would own half the value of the proposed building, five actor-sharers, the other half. The rental was £14 10*s*. 10*d*. per annum. The land on which the theatre was to be built and its provenance is precisely described in the lease. It reveals the semi-rural nature of the area. The land had only recently been enclosed and formed into four separate garden plots. From east to west it was 220 feet long. To the south lay Maiden Lane and, to the east, Horseshoe Alley. John Stowe's *Survey of London* tells us more. 'Maiden Lane, a long straggling place, with ditches on each side, the passage to the houses being over little bridges, with little garden plots before them, especially on the north side, which is best both for houses and inhabitants.' The Globe was approached over a bridge from at least one direction. In February 1606, the Sewer Commission ordered that 'the owners of the playhouse called the Globe … shall before the 20 day of April next pull up and take clean out of the sewer the props or posts which stand under their bridge on the north side of Maid Lane'. Ben Jonson described the Globe, as 'the glory of the Banke … Flanck'd with a Ditch, and forc'd out of a Marish'.[2]

Despite the terrain, the site had huge advantages. It was accessible from the City, by foot over London Bridge, or by crossing the Thames by ferry. The area of Bankside known as the Liberty of the Clink was, like Shoreditch, beyond the remit of the City Fathers. Its status as a 'peculiar' under the easygoing jurisdiction of the Bishops of Winchester ensured that it became a pleasure ground of Elizabethan London.

Although, the scope of ownership was probably extended to raise funding for the huge task in hand, it had the effect of binding the company together.

The five new sharers asked William Leveson, a mercer who was churchwarden of St Mary Aldermanbury and Thomas Savage to allocate their shareholdings. Savage was a Freeman of the Goldsmiths' Company who owned considerable property, including the house in which John Heminges lived. Like Heminges, he was one of the ten sea-coal meters. The two merchants must have been completely trusted. The purpose of the exercise is revealed in one of the clauses:

> William Shakespeare, Augustine Phillips, Thomas Pope, John Heminges, and William Kempe did shortly after grant and assign all the said moiety of and in the said gardens and grounds unto William Levison and Thomas Savage, who regranted and reassigned to every one of them severally a fifth part of the said moiety of the said gardens and grounds.

The key phrase is 'every one of them severally'. They have delivered their shares to their two friends as individuals. Now they are returned to them as a collectivity. No sharer could sell his holding without first offering it to the others. Kempe was important enough within the Company to have been asked to participate at the heart of its fortunes, but it was an opportunity he soon declined, selling his share to the others. That he had to do so demonstrates the wisdom of the arrangements that had been made. It was a joint tenancy.

All the World's a Stage

The new Globe Theatre must have been a sight much remarked upon as it rose on Bankside. To protect the building against the flooding to which the area was prone, the site was raised with earth and buttressed with wooden revetments, the sloping structures placed in banks to absorb the energy of encroaching water. The timbers rescued from The Theatre may have been used for this purpose. Peter Street, who had overseen the purloining of those timbers, was engaged to do the job, so the overall design was probably his. Excavations that took place in 1988 on the small part of the site that was not covered by existing buildings suggested that the edifice was a twenty-sided polygon.

The eighteenth-century antiquarian William Oldys claimed to have seen in a now lost manuscript that the words TOTUS MUNDUS AGIT HISTRIONEM were inscribed over the Globe's entrance. This quote from the Roman Latin author Petronius is the source of the famous line from *As You like It* – 'All the World's a Stage' – although literally, it means 'All the world plays the actor'.

On 16 May 1599, a post-mortem inquisition of the estate of Sir Thomas Brend, father of Sir Nicholas, listed among his properties in Southwark, the Globe playhouse, '*vna domo de novo edificata … in occupacione Willielmi Shakespeare et aliorum*', so the Globe was probably built before that date. If that is the case, then the first play performed at the new theatre was probably *Henry V*. In the prologue to Act V, the Chorus makes the most topical allusion in Shakespeare's works:

> Were now the General of our gracious Empress –
> As in good time he may – from Ireland coming,
> Bringing rebellion broached on his sword;
> How many would the peaceful city quit
> To welcome him!

The reference is to the Earl of Essex's campaign in Ireland in the summer of 1599. The lines may be Shakespeare's, or they could be an interpolation to note the event. On 27 March, Essex's huge army paraded on Tower Hill before marching north to take ship to Dublin. Cheering crowds saw them off. It is likely that the Globe Theatre opened in the spring of 1599 to capitalise on a full season to offset some of the considerable outlay that had been expended. A performance of *Julius Caesar* occurred at the Globe that September. This was late in the season, so unless difficulties associated with the marshy site had delayed the construction, it is unlikely that was the first play presented at the new theatre.

'The Straw-Thatched House'

Around two in the afternoon of 21 September 1599, a Swiss visitor, Thomas Platter, took a boat across the Thames to visit 'the straw-thatched house', a building better known as the Globe Theatre, and 'witnessed an excellent performance of the tragedy of the first Emperor Julius Caesar'. He does not seem to have fully understood it, describing the extraneous detail rather than the performance itself. There were some fifteen actors. 'The playhouses are so constructed that they play on a raised platform, so that everyone has a good view,' whether they were standing below and paid just a penny, or were among those who sat, who paid an extra penny and entered through another door. Those who entered through a third door sat on cushioned seats and paid yet another penny. The theatregoer who did this gained a little cachet. It was a place 'where he not only sees everything well, but can also be seen'. During the performance food and drink were carried around among the audience, 'so that for what one cares to pay, one may also have refreshment'. The actors were 'most expensively and elaborately costumed'. It was customary 'for eminent Lords or Knights' to bequeath their best clothes to their serving men, which it was 'unseemly' for them to wear[3] so they sold them for a small sum to the actors.

Platter enjoyed the finale best. 'When the play was over, they danced very marvellously and gracefully together as is their wont, two dressed as men and two as women.' The same happened at another play he saw, probably at the Curtain Theatre, 'in the suburb of Bishopsgate'. At the end, the actors 'danced very charmingly, in English and Irish fashion'.

The writing of *Julius Caesar* represents a new phase in Shakespeare's career. He had a splendid new theatre as the vehicle for his talents. He had completed his great history cycle. The hugely popular Kempe had been the focus of much of his work since the Lord Chamberlain's Men were founded. He had created a series of parts that are readily identified with him: Costard, Lancelot Gobbo, Touchstone, Sir Toby Belch, Falstaff and Bottom. Now he could give his attention to other issues. With the exception of *King John*, which does not appear to have enjoyed great success, *Julius Caesar* was the first play to be presented by the Company without a part for a clown. It does contain an enduring Shakespearean theme: the fear of the ignorant mob. Cinna the poet is torn to pieces by the mob because he is the namesake of the conspirator. Caesar's downfall – and thus his tragedy – is brought about by his own foibles and arrogance. In Casca's view, he aspires to overthrow the republic established by a forebear of Brutus and make himself King. When Mark Antony offers him the Crown, he pushes it aside three times, 'but to my thinking, he was very loath to lay his fingers off it'. Cassius has already observed that Caesar is trying to exalt himself into the god-like status of a Roman Emperor, although he knows he is a mere man:

> He had a fever when he was in Spain,
> And when the fit was on him, I did mark
> How he did shake. 'Tis true, this god did shake.

This incipient vision of deity leads Caesar to ignore abundant signs of his imminent doom. He mocks the prophecies of the soothsayer – 'He is a dreamer. Let us leave him.' He ignores the premonitions of his wife and the augurers. He treats the warning letter of Artemidorus with contempt – 'What is this fellow mad?' Pride and an inflated sense of divine grandeur bring about his downfall.

In contrast, Brutus is brought down by his sense of duty and his patriotism, but also the flaws represented by his lack of judgement and mistaken faith in his fellow conspirators: points expressed by Mark Antony in his famous valedictory speech:

This was the noblest Roman of them all.
All the conspirators save only he
Did that they did in envy of great Caesar:
He only in a general honest thought
And common good to all made one of them.

'A New House and Stadge for a Plaiehouse'

If the opening of the Globe proclaimed a new era for the Lord Chamberlain's Men, it constituted a severe threat to Philip Henslowe, Edward Alleyn and the Rose Theatre, which had become somewhat rundown. It was decided to make the bold move across the river to Shoreditch, the very area that the Lord Chamberlain's Men had vacated. On 22 December 1599, Alleyn paid £240 for a thirty-year lease of a plot of land in Golding Lane in the parish of St Giles without Cripplegate. The creator of the Globe, Peter Street, was contracted 'ffor the erectinge, building & settinge upp of a new house and Stadge for a Plaiehouse'. This new theatre was called The Fortune, and the contract survives. Street was paid £440, painting and other expenses cost £80. With legal fees and other expenses, total costs came to £1,320. The stage was to be 'in all other proportions contrived and fashioned like unto the stage of the said playhouse called the Globe'. It was to be 43 feet wide and tiled. Alleyn and Henslowe fulfilled the old adage that imitation is the sincerest form of flattery:

> All other contrivations, conveyances, fashions, thing, and things, [were to be] effected, finished and done according to the manner and fashion of the said house called the Globe, saving only that all the principal and main posts ... shall be square and wrought pilasterwise, with carved proportions called satyrs to be placed and set on the top of every of the said posts.'

Satyrs were lustful, drunken woodland gods, presumably forming grotesque carved heads surmounting the supporting pillars and supporting the roof. The whole venture appears to have been funded by Alleyn. He later sold a half-share to Henslowe. It was probably to put the new theatre on the map that he made a comeback to the stage.

The War of the Theatres

Ben Jonson's escape from the gallows did not have a chastening effect. He had lost nothing of his aggression. He quarrelled with John Marston, telling William Drummond that he 'beat him and took his pistol from him ... The beginning of yt,' he continued, 'were that Marston represented him in the stage.' In his lengthy play of 1599, *Histriomastix, or The Player Whipt*, Marston lampooned the entire theatrical profession, Ben is portrayed as 'Christoganus, a Master Pedant'. The play was probably first performed during the 1598/9 Christmas revels at the Middle Temple.[4] The title literally means 'The Scourge of Actors', so it is unlikely it was intended to be performed by professional players. The numbers in the cast also point to an amateur production. The play was published in 1610 without an author's name on the title page.

Why Marston had chosen to attack such a volatile figure as Jonson is a mystery. That both were involved at various times in writing for Henslowe makes the conjunction even less likely, unless it was their very proximity that caused alienation. As well as physical retaliation, Jonson sought a more appropriate revenge. *Every Man out of His Humour*, the sequel to his play of 1598, was produced in the following year. It was apparently less successful, although it was published in three editions during 1600. In historical terms, it is perhaps most notable for its references to other contemporary works, which assists in their dating and indicates Jonson's propensity to scrutinise the activities of other playwrights. He refers to Justice Silence in *Henry IV, Part II* and the famous quote from *Julius Caesar* – 'Et tu Brute' is cited. His subtle attacks on his former colleagues with Henslowe represent a retaliatory shot in what Dekker called the *Poetomachia*, or 'War of the Theatres'. The retrospective problem of such satires is that they are so much contemporary 'in-jokes' that they are virtually unintelligible today to all but erudite scholars. In *Every Man Out*, the character of Fastidious Brisk is clearly a representation of Marston, whose supposedly turgid prose in *Histriomastix* is parodied as 'fustian' by Clove, the clown. Jonson, ever seeking new enemies, seems to have decided to widen his assault. The character Carlo Buffone, 'a public, scurrilous and profane jester' has been variously identified as Dekker, Marston and even an almost forgotten double agent called Charles Chester.

One of the more curious characters in *Every Man out* is Sogliardo, a country bumpkin, new to the City, who has bought himself a coat-of-arms for £30.[5] It is suggested to him that he adopt the motto, 'Not without Mustard'. Is Jonson referring to William Shakespeare, certainly a country boy, but by no means new to the city? In 1596, John Shakespeare was awarded a coat-of-arms, a project in which he was probably encouraged by his now-wealthy son. The motto the newly gentrified family adopted appears defensive – 'Not without Right', probably a response to those who considered that such an award to a mere country glover demeaned the honour.

If the character of Sogliardo was intended as a lampoon of Shakespeare, the man of Avon appears to have got his revenge. The third Parnassus play, which was probably performed during the Christmas Season of 1601/2, features a dialogue between characters representing Richard Burbage and Will Kempe. 'Why here's our fellow Shakespeare putts them all downe,' says Kempe, 'aye, and Ben Jonson too. O that *Ben Ionson* is a pestilent fellow; he brought up *Horace*, giving the poets a pill; but our fellow *Shakespeare* hath given him a purge, that made him betraye his credit.'

What this 'purge' was is a mystery. None of the suggestions that have been put forward is particularly convincing. There is an assumption that the 'put down' was contained in a play, so the works have been scanned in vain, but it could have been a devastating *mot juste*. 'Many were the wit combats between him and Ben Jonson,' wrote Thomas Fuller,

> Which two I behold like a Spanish great galleon and an English man of War; Master Johnson (like the former) was built higher in Learning, Solid, but slow in his performances. Shake-spear with the English man of War, lesser in bulk, but lighter in sailing, could turn with all tides, tack about, and take advantage of all winds, by the quickness of his Wit and Invention.

John Marston was moved to fire another shot in the war. His play *Jack Drum's Entertainment* parodies Ben Jonson as the arrogant and complacent libertine and spendthrift Brabant Senior, who is cuckolded through his own machinations. It was performed by the Children of Paul's during 1600. At this point, the feud may have gone beyond personalities to the nature of the drama itself. In his preface, Marston attacks the 'mouldy fopperies of stale Poetry' and the 'Unpossible drie mustie Fictions' he associates with the popular theatre. Jonson hit back in the play that was published as *Narcissus the Fountain of Self-love*, but became better known as *Cynthia's Revels*, performed at Blackfriars by the Children of the Chapel. Marston's riposte came through the Children of Paul's with his play, *What you Will*. The limited plot concerns the rivalry of two poets: the bitter and antisocial satirist, Lampatho Doria (Jonson) and the kindly bon viveur Quadratus (Marston). This clearly riled Ben. His further riposte came next year with the production of his next play by the Children of the Chapel. He told Drummond that he 'wrote his Poetaster' on Marston, of whom Crispinus, whose lines are overblown and pretentious is clearly a parody, while Dekker is Demetrius Fannius, a plagiarist, 'a very simple honest fellow ... a dresser of plays'. Horace (Jonson) gives them both a pill to make them vomit up their pretentious vocabulary. He gives us an idea of Marston's appearance. Crispinus has red hair and small legs.

That Thomas Dekker was indeed the figure lampooned as Demetrius Fannius is made more likely by his decision to join the war. He hit back with *Satiromastix*, *or The Untrussing of the Humorous Poet*, who is, of course, Ben, personified in the name he gave himself in *The Poetaster* – Horace – who is determined to maintain the high integrity of poetry despite its decline in the hands of inferior 'Poetasters'. He is a pretentious poet, obsessed with his status, who overrates his abilities and denigrates the efforts of others. His writing is tedious and heavy. He is a place-seeker. He dresses scruffily. In Act 4, he refers to Jonson's bricklaying, the unfortunate incident of *The Isle of Dogs* and his reading of the 'Neck Verse'. Other characters clearly represent contemporary figures, although who, it is not clear. The play was successful. After being performed by the Children of the Chapel, it was taken up by the Lord Chamberlain's Men at the Globe, who may have had good reasons to have a pop at Ben.

Satiromastix was the last salvo in the war, but not the last word. William Shakespeare was about to have his say. In *Hamlet* Act 2 Scene 2, he refers to the children's companies. Despite their shrill unbroken voices, their popularity is so great that they've forced the professional companies to tour the provinces in search of audiences:

Rosencrantz: Even those you were wont to take delight in, the tragedians of the city.
Hamlet: How chances it they travel? Their residence, both in reputation and profit, was better both ways.
Rosencrantz: I think their inhibition comes by the means of the late innovation.
Hamlet: Do they hold the same estimation they did when I was in the city? Are they followed?
Rosencrantz: No, indeed they are not.
Hamlet: How comes it? Do they grow rusty?
Rosencrantz: Nay, their endeavor keeps in the wonted pace. But there is, sir, an eyrie of children, little eyases, that cry out on the top of the question and are most tyrannically clapped for 't. These are now the fashion, and so berattle the common stages – so they call them – that many wearing rapiers are afraid of goose quills and dare scarce come thither.

The Children's companies had clearly benefitted from the enactments following the *Isle of Dogs* affair, restricting the number of professional companies permitted to play in the city to two. The satire was clearly hitting home. Unless Shakespeare is deliberately exaggerating the effect, the old adage about the pen ('goose quills') being mightier than the sword ('rapiers') is amply borne out.

The War of the Theatres contributed greatly to the revival of the Children's companies. That it may even have been engineered to do precisely that is indicated by the fact that the apparent enmity did not endure. In 1604, Marston dedicated all three editions of his highly-successful play, *The Malcontent*, to his ELEGANTISSIMO GRAVISSIMO AMICO, Ben Jonson. In the following year, the two collaborated with George Chapman, on the ill-fated production of *Eastward Ho!* It has to be wondered how serious the *Poetomachia* actually was. Did it arise from, as an intense animosity between rival playwrights, or was it, like the verbal savaging of his forthcoming opponents by the boxer, Muhammad Ali, a means of arousing public interest?

The young actors were, of course, choirboys, which provided a further dimension to the visit of Frederic Gershow, secretary to the Duke of Stettin-Pomerania, to the Blackfriars Theatre in 1602.

> For a whole hour before the play begins, one listens to a delightful instrumental concert, as on the present occasion, when a boy *cum voce tremula* sang so charmingly to a base-viol that we have not heard the like of in the whole of our journey.

Hamlet (or Shakespeare) expresses concern, perhaps uniquely, about the welfare of the choristers. 'What, are they children?' Who maintains 'em? How are they escorted? Will they pursue the quality no longer than they can sing?'

'Where be your Jibes Now?

The play of Sir John Oldcastle had been sufficiently popular for it to be published in 1600. Henslowe decided that a sequel would be worthwhile and presumably engaged the same dramatists to create it. On 21 August 1602. he paid 'John Duck and John Thayr to bye a sewt for Owld Castell, and a sewt and a dublet of saffen'. These two actors handled the finances of Worcester's Men. On the same day, he advanced 'John Ducke' the money to pay for 'ij womens gownes mackinge, and fresh water for owld castell'. He was also authorised to pay 'Harry Chettell'. It appears that his team was not delivering as required because, on 7 September, Henslowe 'lent unto John Thore ... to give unto Thomas Dickers [Dekker] for his adicions in owld castell'. The payments towards the second part of 'Oldcastle' coincide with ones he made to Kempe. It appears he intended to launch Kempe in this renewed riposte to the Lord Chamberlain's Men. What a coup it would be if the original Falstaff performed in the play intended to exonerate Oldcastle's reputation! If this second part was ever performed, it is now lost. The career of Will Kempe was over. The parish registers of St

The Plimpton 'Sieve' Portrait of Queen Elizabeth, patron of the Queen's Players, by George Gower (c1540-96). In Roman mythology, Tuccia, a Vestal Virgin, proved her chastity by carrying a sieve full of water from the Tiber to the Temple of Vesta. The Italian motto, 'Tutto Vedo & Multo Mancha' means 'I see everything and much is lacking'. The Globe signifies England's emergence as a Global power. *Folger Shakespeare Library call number ART 246171.*

mes VI and I, patron of the King's Men, his Coronation robes by Paul van Somer 1576-1621). In the background may be seen e Banqueting Hall of Whitehall Palace, signed by Inigo Jones, the scene of many ourt masques during the reigns of James and s successor. *Royal Collection Trust ref RCN)4446.*

Anne of Denmark and a Groom by Paul van Somer. The Queen was an enthusiastic theatregoer and patron of the Queen's Majesty's Servants. *Royal Collections Trust ref RCN 40587.*

Robert Dudley, Earl of Leicester by Steven van der Meulen (1552-88), patron of Leicester's Men, the first theatrical troupe to gain a royal patent. *Yale Center for British Art, access number B1981,25.445.*

Richard Tarlton, the greatest comic actor of his age, renowned for his 'wondrous, plentiful, pleasant, extemporal wit'. (*Author's collection*)

:ichard Burbage, the first performer King Richard III': from *Shakespeare 'ustrated* by Sylvester Harding 745–1809), from the original, putedly a self-portrait, in Dulwich ollege Picture Gallery. (*Folger Imaging epartment 17945*)

'Edward Alleyn, founder of Dulwich College' from *Shakespeare Illustrated* by Sylvester Harding (1745-1809), from the original in Dulwich College Picture Gallery. (*Royal Collections RC1N 650158*)

Kemps nine daies vvonder.

Performed in a daunce from

London to Norwich.

Containing the pleaſure, paines and kinde entertainment of *William Kemp* betweene *London* and that Citty in his late Morrice.

Wherein is ſomewhat ſet downe worth note; to reprooue the ſlaunders ſpred of him: many things merry, nothing hurtfull.

Written by himſelfe to ſatisfie his friends.

LONDON

Printed by *E. A.* for *Nicholas Ling*, and are to be ſolde at his ſhop at the weſt doore of Saint Paules Church 1600.

Woodcut of Will Kempe's 'Nine Daies Wonder', performed in a journey from London to Norwich in 1600 – 'Wherein euery dayes journey is pleasantly set down, to satisfie his friends the truth against all lying ballad-makers; what hee did, how he was welcome, and by whome entertained. Ed. from the original ms. by Edmund Goldsmid, F.R.H.S.' (*Folger Shakespeare Library – ART File K32.2 no 1*)

THE
Hiſtory of the two Maids of More-clacke,
VVith the life and ſimple maner of IOHN
in the Hoſpitall.
Played by the Children of the Kings
Maieſties Reuels.
VVritten by ROBERT ARMIN, ſeruant to the Kings
moſt excellent Maieſtie.

LONDON,
Printed by *N.O.* for *Thomas Archer*, and is to be ſold at his
ſhop in Popes head Pallace, 1609.

ROBERT ARMIN,
was an Actor in Shakespears Plays.
See the list of Actors in the first Folio Edition.
London Pub April 1790 by E Harding No 132 Fleet Street.

Image of Robert Armin on stage from title page of 'The History of the two Maids of More-clacke VVith the life and simple maner of Iohn in the Hospitall / Played by the Children of the Kings Maiesties Reuels. VVritten by Robert Armin, seruant to the Kings most excellent Maiestie. London, Printed by N. O. for Thomas Archer, and is to be sold at his shop in Popes-head Pallace, 1609.' (*Folger Shakespeare Library. Call number STC 773*)

Woodcut of actor John Lowin, 1640, by Thomas Holloway (1748-1827) from original picture in Ashmole Museum, Oxford'. (*Royal Collections Trust RCN 658249*)

Portrait of actor/dramatist Nathan Field (artist unknown), the only contemporary portrait showing an actor in costume, from original picture in the Dulwich Picture Gallery by William Nelson Gardiner (1766-1809). (*Nathaniel Field: published 1 Apr 1790: Royal Collections Trust RCN 654460*)

The interior of the Swan Theatre by Johannes de Witt, 1596, during what appears to be a performance of *Twelfth Night*. (*Author's collection*)

/oodcut showing Robert Greene at work in his grave clothes, from John Dickenson's *Greene in his* *onceipt*, 1598. (Wikimedia)

etail from Nicholaes Visscher's panorama of London, 1616, showing Henslowe's Bear Garden (left) and e Globe Theatre (right). (*Library of Congress*)

The Church of St Gregory by St Paul's by Wenceslaus Hollar (1607-1677): the home of the Children of Paul's acting troupe. The church was built into the walls of the cathedral. (*Thomas Fisher Rare Book Library, University of Toronto, Hollar Collection*)

Bel Savage Inn, Ludgate Hiil, one of four inns in the City licensed for dramatic performances, fro *Old and New London* by Walter Thornbury, Vol 1, 1889.

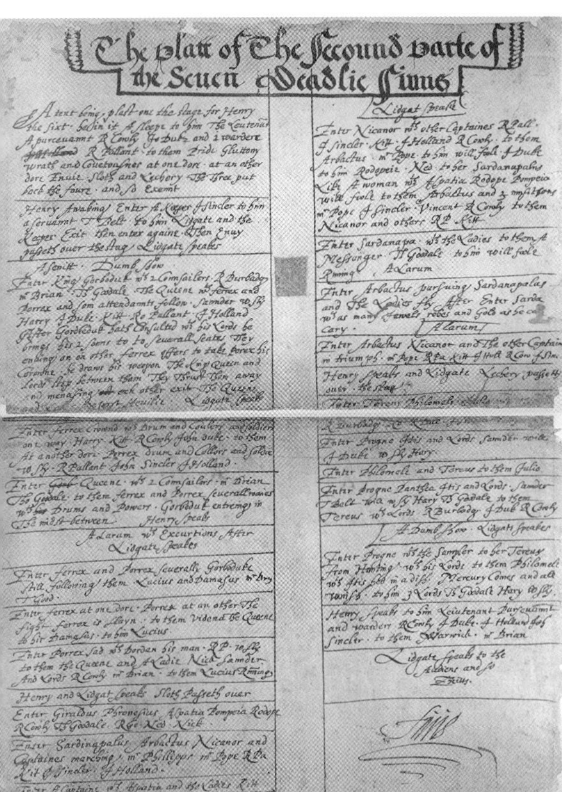

The platt of The Secound parte of the Seven Deadlie Sinns

The 'Platt' of *The Seven Deadly Sins*, a chart that summarised the workings of a play that was hung backstage. It includes the names of a number of actors later associated with Shakespeare's Company, including Richard Burbage. (*Courtesy of the Governors of Dulwich College - MS number XIX*)

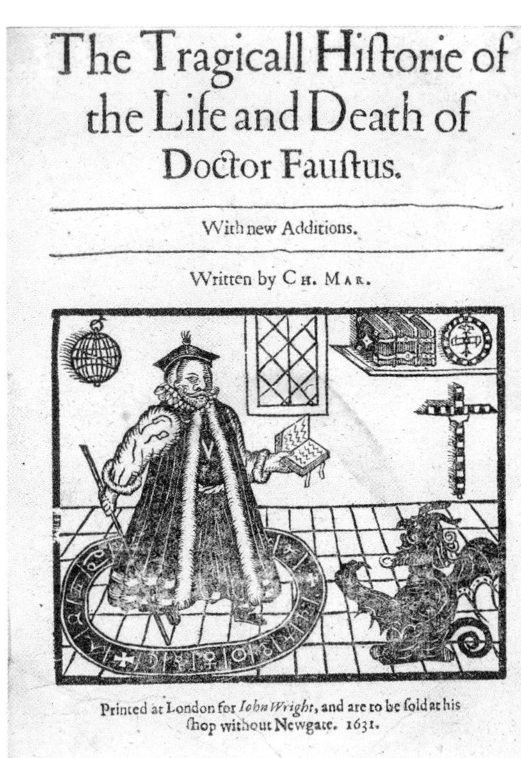

The Tragicall Hiſtorie of the Life and Death of Doctor Fauſtus.

With new Additions.

Written by Ch. Mar.

Printed at London for *Iohn Wright*, and are to be ſold at his ſhop without Newgate. 1631.

Frontispiece of 1620 quarto of *The Tragical History and Death of Dr Faustus*, published by John Wright, showing a demon rising through the stage trapdoor. (*Folger Shakespeare Library STC 17436*)

Title page of Thomas Kyd's *The Spanish Tragedy, or Hieronimo is Mad Again.* This publication in 1615, over 25 years after its first performance, demonstrates the play's continuing popularity. (*Digital version of Early English books 1729:4*)

The Spanish Tragedie:
OR,
Hieronimo is mad againe.

Containing the lamentable end of *Don Horatio*, and *Belimperia*; with the pittifull death of *Hieronimo.*

Newly corrected, amended, and enlarged with new Additions of the *Painters* part, and others, as it hath of late been diuers times acted.

LONDON,
Printed by W. White, for I. White and T. Langley, and are to be sold at their Shop ouer against the Sarazens head without New-gate. 1615.

The Witch of Edmonton
A known true STORY.
Composed into
A TRAGI-COMEDY
By divers well-esteemed Poets;
William Rowley, Thomas Dekker, John Ford, &c
Acted by the Princes Servants, often at the Cock-Pit in *Drury-Lane*, once at Court, with singular Applause.
Never printed till now.

Ho have I found thee Cuding
Sanctabecetur nomen tuum
Mother Sawyer
Help Help I am Drownd
Cuddy Banks

London, *Printed by* J. Cottrel, *for* Edward Blackmore, *at the Angel in* Paul's *Church-yard.* 1658.

Title page of *The Witch of Edmonton*, 1658. 'Enter a Black Dog': 'Now thou art mine own'. (*Houghton Library, Harvard University*)

Title page of *A Game at Chess.* The features of the fat Bishop and the Black Knight are caricatures of the Dean of Windsor and the Spanish Ambassador, both well-known around London. (*Folger Shakespeare Library acc. no. 7043*)

Frontispiece to *The Wits, or Sport upon Sport*, a collection of 27 drolls (the short dramatic pieces permitted during the Commonwealth era) assembled by the early theatre historian, Francis Kirkman, in 1662. The setting may be the Red Bull Theatre, which he visited during that time. The onstage characters are from various drolls and include Falstaff, Mistress Quickly and Clause, the King of the Beggars from *Beggars Bush.* (*Folger Shakespeare Library: call number W328*)

THE
WITS,
OR,
SPORT upon SPORT.
IN
Select Pieces of DROLLERY,
Digested into SCENES by way of
DIALOGUE.
Together with Variety of Humors of several Nations, fitted for the pleasure and content of all Persons, either in Court, City, Countrey, or Camp. The like never before Published.

PART I.

LONDON,
Printed for *Henry Marsh*, at the Sign of the *Princes Arms* in *Chancery-Lane*, 1662.

Mary Frith, aka 'Moll Cutpurse', smoking her pipe, from the 1611 title page of *The Roaring Girl* by Thomas Middleton and Thomas Dekker. The setting appears to show Mary during one of her illegal onstage appearances during performances of the play. (*Boston Public Library Rare Books Department*)

Anonymous portrait, possibly of Christopher Marlowe. The age of the sitter fits the period when he was up at Corpus Christi College, Cambridge, as does his arrogant demeanour. (*Public domain*)

Mr. WILLIAM
SHAKESPEARES
COMEDIES,
HISTORIES, &
TRAGEDIES.
Publiſhed according to the True Originall Copies.
LONDON
Printed by Iſaac Iaggard, and Ed. Blount. 1623.

William Shakespeare, from the title page of the First Folio, 1623. (*Author's collection*)

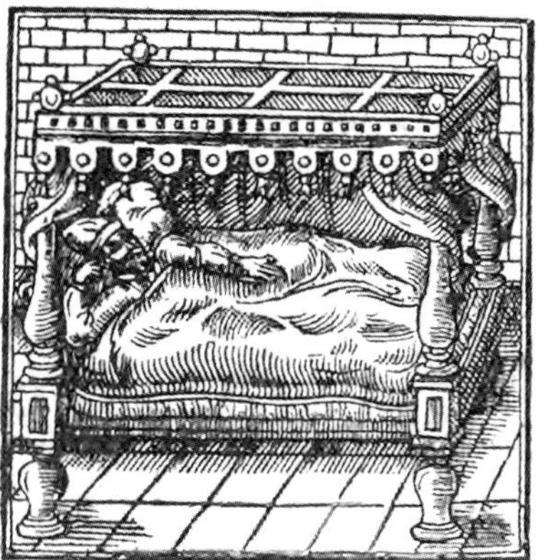
Dekker his Dreame.
In which, beeing rapt with a Poëticall *Enthuſiaſme*, *the great Volumes of Heauen* and Hell to Him were opened, in which he *read many Wonderfull Things.*

Eſt Deus in Nobis, agitante calescimus illo.

LONDON,
Printed by Nicholas Okes. 1620.

homas Dekker lying in bed. Woodcut om the title page of his poem, *Dekker His reame…*, 1620. (*University of Michigan igital Collections*)

Ben Jonson by George Vertue, 1730. (*Library of Congress: 2009617622*)

Thomas Nashe in chains after the production of The Isle of Dogs. In fact, he escaped arrest by fleeing to Norfolk. Richard Lichfield, *The Trimming of Thomas Nashe Gentleman* (London 1597). (*Folger Shakespeare Library – Digital Collections – call number. STC 12906*)

ımes Shirley, engraving by William Henry
'orthington after a drawing by Jo John Thurston.
'he Courtauld, London (*Samuel Courtauld Trust*)
:cession no. nu– G1990 WL. 5872,15)

Title page engraving of William Davenant after a portrait by John Greenhill. The reconstruction of his nose after a bout of syphilis is clearly apparent. From *The Works of Sir William Davenant*, 1673, frontispiece, printed by TN for Henry Herringman, London, 1673. (*Folger Shakespeare Library*)

Portrait of Sir John Suckling holding a copy of Shakespeare's First Folio by Anthony van Dyck (Flemish 1599-1641), Oil on canvas. (*The Frick Collection, New York*)

Noctes atque dies patet atri Ianua Ditis.

Vnto this Island and great Plutoes Court,
none are deny'd that willingly resort,
Charon or'e Phlegeton will set on shoare,
and Cerberus will guard you to the doore:
Where dainty Devils drest in humane shape,
upon your senses soone will make a rape.
They that come freely to this house of sinne,
in Hell as freely may have entrance in.

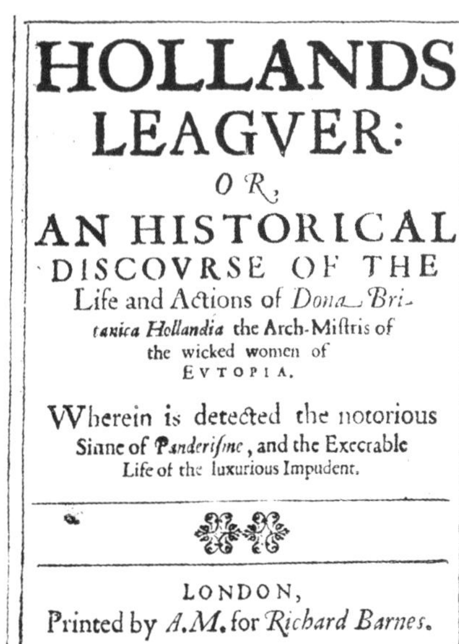

HOLLANDS
LEAGVER:
OR,
AN HISTORICAL
DISCOVRSE OF THE
Life and Actions of *Dona Britanica Hollandia* the Arch-Mistris of
the wicked women of
EVTOPIA.

Wherein is detected the notorious
Sinne of *Panderisme*, and the Execrable
Life of the luxurious Impudent.

LONDON,
Printed by *A.M.* for *Richard Barnes*.
1632.

Title page of *Holland's Leaguer*, a successful play and even more successful brothel. (*Early Modern Litera Studies*)

Somerset House Conference, 1604: peace negotiations between England and Spain. The English delegatic on the right is led by Thomas Sackville, 1sr Earl of Dorset, co-author of *Gorboduc* – nearest the windov To his left is Charles Howard, 1st Earl of Nottingham, Patron of the Admiral's Men. Fourth from tl left is Henry Howard, 1st Earl of Northampton, the 'mortal enemy' of Ben Jonson. (*National Portra Gallery: ref NPG 665*)

Saviour's, Southwark record the death of 'Kempe a man' late in 1603. This was the plague year of which Thomas Dekker wrote. 'THE PESTILENCE, THE SICKNESS hath a Preheminence above all others … none being able to match it for Violence, Strength, Incertainty, Suttlety, Catching, Universality, and Desolation … many who had health in the morning, lay in their Graves at night.' One such may have been Will Kempe. Whether he performed in the early version of *Hamlet* or not, Shakespeare wrote his epitaph in that play. 'Where be your jibes now? Your gambols? Your songs? Your flashes of merriment that were wont to set the table on a roar?'

According to the True and Perfect Coppie

Hamlet represents an enigma, not only in its complexities, but in its stage and publication history. The text of the first quarto is not half as long as that of the second, published in 1604 and there are significant differences between the two. Even the most famous lines that Shakespeare wrote vary drastically:

> To be, or not to be, I there's the point,
> To die, to sleepe, is that all? I all.
> No, to sleepe, to dreame, aye mary, there it goes.

Perhaps we are in the presence of the old play of *Hamlet* that Shakespeare was in the process of revising. A tenable viewpoint, but this ghost does not cry, in the manner of a fishwife, 'Hamlet, revenge!' This thesis is supported, however, by the difference in the names of several characters from the familiar ones. Polonius is Corambis; Reynaldo, Montano; Osric, 'A Braggart Gentleman'; Fransisco, 'A Sentinel', and then there are 'Guildenstone' and 'Ravenscraft'. Yet the first quarto possesses a validity in itself. Its precise stage directions do not appear elsewhere and there is an entire additional scene (usually labelled 4.6). It has been suggested that this is a pirated version, dictated inaccurately to the stationer by an actor who played a minor part. Suspicion falls on he who played Marcellus and doubled as Lucianus, the third player in the play within the play, since his lines accord most closely with subsequent versions.

Another possibility is that the first quarto is a touring version of the play, abridged for a smaller company, is supported by the fact that the script refers to attendants, but gives them no lines, suggesting that they may have been played by the supernumeraries that were recruited locally when productions were on tour. The title page states that it was 'At London printed for N.L. and John Trundell'. Trundell knew the world of theatre. He was a friend of Ben Jonson and published at least one of his plays. He was best known for publishing sensational pamphlets, so pirating plays could have been within his remit. The issue is complicated by the fact that the 'N.L.' of the title page was the stationer, Nicholas Ling. On 26 July 1602, the printer James Roberts had entered 'A booke, The Revenge of Hamlett, prince of Denmarke, as yt was lately acted by the Lord Chamberlayn, his servantes' on the Stationers' Register. Having registered the volume, he must have enlisted Ling's aid as a member of the Stationers Company, in the publication of the second quarto in 1603. That Ling was also the publisher of the first quarto lessens the possibility that it was a pirated version, as do the words on the title page: 'Newly printed and enlarged to almost as much againe as it was, according to the true and perfect coppie.' In other words, this is the complete version. The earlier quarto is not negated, but has been revised from the original manuscript. No other of Shskespeare's plays had so many published variants. Collected together, the result would be a play that takes over four hours to perform, surely too lengthy for 'the two hours traffic of the stage' to which the playgoer was accustomed.

Hamlet represents Shakespeare's return to the tragic muse, but a return with a difference. Rather than Senecan *grand guignol* melodramas, he creates a drama of characters struggling with dilemmas greater than their ability to solve. The tragedy of *Hamlet* is a universal rather than a particular one. The beautiful speech of Marcellus after the cock crows is something more than a pious legend about the spirit of Christmas. It is an invocation of the salvation that Christ will bring to the fallen world represented by the Ghost of Old Hamlet:

> Some say that ever 'gainst that season comes
> Whereon our Saviour's birth is celebrated
> The bird of dawning singeth all night long;
> And then, they say, no spirit durst walk abroad,
> The nights are wholesome, then do no planets strike,
> No fairy takes, nor witch hath power to charm,
> So hallowed and so gracious is that time.

At Hamlet's first encounter with the Ghost, he poses the question that nails the play:

> Be thou a spirit of health or a goblin damn'd?
> Bring with thee airs from heaven or blasts from hell?
> Be thy intents wicked or charitable?
> Thou com'st in such questionable shape
> That I will speak to thee. I'll call thee,
> Hamlet, father, royal Dane.

The answer is that the Ghost is both. In the first scene, Horatio gives him the benefit of being a benevolent spirit:

> If there be any good thing to be done,
> That may to thee do ease and grace to me,
> Speak to me.
> If thou art privy to thy country's fate,
> Which happily foreknowing may avoid,
> O speak.

The Ghost passes in silence. His purpose is not to seek the well-being of his kingdom. It is revenge on his brother and his wife that will tear away the entire edifice of the Danish Court, taking with it innocent and the guilty alike. Hamlet is the first victim of the Ghost's intransigence. Horatio warns him of the potential hazard of following the spectre, 'which might deprive your sovereignty of reason / And draw you into madness.' This is why the Ghost must return to the torments of Purgatory. The evil that he self-confessedly did lives after him. He pursues Hamlet relentlessly towards his nemesis. 'This visitation,' he tells him after the killing of Polonius, 'is but to whet thy almost blunted purpose.' As Horatio has warned, Hamlet's dealings with the Ghost indeed draw him into madness. Every major character apart from the loyal Horatio, comments on his mental condition.

In *Hamlet*, Shakespeare returns to the theme he began to explore in *Julius Caesar* – of the tragic hero brought down by his own foibles. Conscience is a factor in this, bringing a depth of humanity to the characters. It is conscience that makes a 'coward' of Hamlet, as he seeks certainty about the Ghost's account of his father's murder. Even Claudius, who in revenge tragedies might be portrayed as a *grand guignol* villain, is troubled by the terrible act he has committed. Penance is an over-riding theme. Old Hamlet is suffering the torments of Purgatory because he has been murdered without the redemptive grace of Extreme Unction. The saving grace of the Eucharist has been denied him ('unhouseled'). He has not prepared himself for death ('disappointed'). He has not been absolved through the confessional (unanal'd):

> Cut off even in the blossoms of my sin
> Unhouse'led, disappointed, unanel'd;
> No reckoning made, but sent to my account
> With all my imperfections on my head.

Claudius is a genuinely tragic character, who, like the Macbeth to come, realises he has made a temporal gain at the cost of his immortal soul. Expiation is not possible for those who retain the fruits of their sin.

> But, O, what form of prayer
> Can serve my turn? 'Forgive me my foul murder!'
> That cannot be, since I am still possess'd
> Of those effects for which I did the murder –
> My crown, mine own ambition and my queen.

It is Claudius rather than Hamlet who becomes the catalyst for the Ghost's revenge, a point inferred by Horatio in the final scene:

> So shall you hear
> Of carnal, bloody and unnatural acts
> Of accidental judgments, casual slaughter;
> Of deaths put on by cunning and forc'd cause:
> And, in this upshot, purposes mistook
> Falling on th' inventors heads.

With the deaths of Polonius and Ophelia, the play becomes a double-revenge tragedy as Laertes seeks to avenge their deaths on Hamlet, who is still pursuing his mission to destroy Claudius. As Shakespeare has demonstrated in *Richard III*, and will demonstrate again in *Macbeth*, one gross offence against the moral code is not entire to itself. It leads to others. It is Claudius who plots the denouement that leads to the destruction of the Royal House of Denmark. This leaves us with the question as to why we not only sympathise with Hamlet, but identify with him. He is cruel, capricious, revengeful and indecisive. The answer lies in Shakespeare's brilliance as a dramatist. Hamlet is the sole party to the dreadful secret that the Ghost reveals. No one else on the stage can grasp the immensity of the revelation, although the suspicions of Claudius slowly change his attitude from avuncular bonhomie to murderous psychopathy. Yet a collective personality is party to the secret from the start. The audience follows Hamlet's career through his great soliloquies to the final denouement, at every point perceiving the action from his viewpoint and, at the last, witnessing his self-discovery. He is aware that Claudius has designs to kill him but returns to Elsinor to face his destiny. He expresses 'gaingiving' (foreboding) about the forthcoming fencing match with Laertes, but when Horatio urges him not to go through with it, he expresses faith in the divine purpose and indicates that he has overcome his fear of death for which he is now prepared. He rejects the methods of the classical augurers, who predicted the future by observing birds in flight – hence the sparrow. Instead he seeks Christian absolution ('readiness'), quoting Matthew 10:29:

> We defy augury. There is a special providence in the fall of a sparrow. If it be not now, 'tis not to come; if it be not to come, it will be now; yet it will come – the readiness is all.

Another vital part of Hamlet's redemption is his penitence for his treatment of Laertes. At the last, they find mutual forgiveness. Hamlet has gone through a form of shriving. His last words, 'The rest is silence', betoken that he has nominated Horatio to recount on his behalf the drama that has brought him here and who pronounces his benediction: 'Good night, sweet prince, and flights of angels sing thee to thy rest.'

The court of Denmark is purged of mortal sin, but is swept away in the process. The pattern follows that of the centuries. The flamboyant military leader restores order.

Much Applause

It was through the Children's companies that the War of the Theatres was fought. The talents of these boy actors cannot be doubted. It may have been the Thomas Day who was acting with the company in 1601 who became musician to the Princes Henry and Charles and Master of those same Children of the Chapel Royal. The impressive acting skills represented in these troupes is demonstrated in Ben Jonson's eulogy to the boy actor Salamon Pavy, who died in 1602 at the age of just 13. Although Jonson reveals that he was noted for his portrayal of old men, in *Cynthia's Revels* he played one of the three pages who speak the prologue to the play:

> Weep with me; all ye that read
>   This little story;
> And know, for whom a tear you shed,
>   Death's self is sorry.
> 'Twas a child, that so did thrive
>   In grace and feature,
> As heaven and nature seemed to strive
>   Which own'd the creature.
> Years he number'd scarce thirteen
>   When fates turned cruel,

Yet three fill'd zodiacs had he been
The stage's jewel;
And did act (what now we moan)
Old men so duly,
As, sooth, the Parcae[6] thought him onr
He play'd so truly.
So, by error, to his fate
They all consented:
But viewing him since (alas too late)
They have repented;
And have sought (to give new birth)
In baths to steep him;
But being so much too good for earth.
Heaven vows to keep him.

The poem reveals that Salomon had been acting with the Children of the Chapel Royal since he was ten when he had been summarily recruited. Since the Chapel Royal was within the jurisdiction of the Monarch, its Master possessed the power to recruit boys of his choosing, forcibly if necessary, as choristers. Nathaniel Giles, as Master of the Chapel, had allowed Henry Evans to seize such promising boys. One so impressed was Nathan Field, a boy whose background made him an unlikely candidate for a stage career. He was baptised at St Giles, Cripplegate, on 17 October 1587, the seventh child of John Field, the vehement Puritan enemy of the theatre. He died in 1588 when his youngest son was just a year old. This may well have been a blessed release. Nathan became a prominent figure in the theatre his father regarded as the Devil's work. Even more humiliating for a man who had been imprisoned for his attacks on the Anglican Church would have been that another son, Theophilus, became Bishop of Llandaff.

Nathan Field was educated at St Paul's School. He was fortunate in that his headmaster, Richard Mulcaster, introduced English as the language of education. Until then, Latin was the vehicle of learning. He began the standardisation of English spelling, producing a lexicon of 8,000 words. He even started to codify the rules of football to resemble the game as it is today. It's nice to think of young Nathan enjoying a kick-about.

Although the Children of Paul's had ceased to present plays in public from around 1590, they would almost certainly have performed plays as part of their curriculum. They resumed public playing in 1600 under a new Master, Edward Peers. Unlike the Children of the Chapel, they had no theatre of their own, but performed in the church in which they were based, St Gregory by St Paul's, which was built into the walls of the cathedral. At least two plays were performed by the reconstituted troupe. Both *The Maid's Metamorphosis* and *The Wisdom of Doctor Dodypoll* were characteristic pastoral fantasies, heavily influenced by the work of John Lyly and George Peele, if not actually written by them.

The company presented the plays of Marston and Dekker, while the Chapel children performed Ben Jonson's. Animosity between those playwrights may have extended to their children's companies. If so, the temptation to poach a leading boy player from the rival company may have been irresistible to Evans and Giles. They had the powers to do so. Certain it is that around this time, Nathan Field left Paul's to join the Chapel. Although he was impressed into the Company, he may have been a willing victim. The boys were provided with a good education and training, full board and lodging and the distinctive uniform of the royal livery. Since the choir constituted a royal peculiar, it accompanied the Queen on her progresses and visits to her various residences. Young Nathan may have already decided that his ambitions lay on the stage and the Chapel Company was the best place to fulfill them.

Not all were grateful for their kidnapping. On 13 December 1600, one of Giles' henchmen, James Robinson, seized 13-year-old Thomas Clifton on his way to school. He was dragged off 'with great force and violence, to his great terror'. He must have shown some talent in school plays, so he was borne off to follow 'the base trade of a mercenary interlude player'. Giles and his colleagues had miscalculated. When the father, a well-connected Norfolk squire by the name of Henry Clifton, heard what had happened, he stormed round to Blackfriars and demanded his son's release. Robinson refused, saying he had the royal warrant to keep the boy and threatened to whip him unless he learned his lines. He had reckoned without Henry Clifton's friends in high places; Clifton obtained an injunction from Sir John Fortescue, Chancellor of the Exchequer and Privy Councillor, for the boy's release.

He was public-spirited enough to wish to stop the practice of summarily snatching boys and took the issue to the Star Chamber. Although it had the reputation for harsh and arbitrary decisions, determined in camera, it had been originally established to ensure justice against people who were powerful enough to escape the normal consequences of the law. In this case, the powerful person at the end of the line was the Queen, but the court came up with a decision that was judicious in the fullest sense. Giles and Evans had a warrant to forcibly recruit boy choristers, but not boy actors. Indeed, young Tom Clifton was 'noe way able or fitt for singing', nor was he 'by anie the said confederates endeavowed to be taught to sing'. Henry Evans was censured for 'taking up of gentlemen's children against their will and to ymploy them as players'. According to Sir Edward Coke, the Chief Justice, 'Evans for the said offence were grievously punished'. Giles seems to have escaped unscathed. The case revealed the names of seven boys who had been impressed as Chapel children, including Nathan Field and Salomon Pavy, who did not take advantage of this opportunity to leave the Company. They were clearly bent on the base trade of interlude players.

From the Stage to the State

The expedition of Robert Devereux, Earl of Essex, to Ireland, so vaunted by the Chorus in *Henry V*, ended in disaster. Far from broaching rebellion with his sword, he underestimated consistently the strength of the rebels. Eventually realising that he had little hope of success, he agreed a truce with the leading insurgent, Hugh O'Neill, Earl of Tyrone, partitioning the island between royal and rebel lands. Despite the fact that the Queen had forbidden him to leave Ireland without her permission, he sped back to England to plead his case with her. None of the cheering crowds that the Chorus had anticipated were there to greet him. Although the treaty made sense from certain perspectives, the Queen was furious. 'To trust this traitor upon oath is to trust a devil upon religion,' she fulminated against O'NeilI. Essex did not help his cause by forcing his way into her bedchamber at Nonsuch Palace before she was dressed and bewigged. He was relieved of his command which was conferred on Charles Blount, the 8th Baron Mountjoy – father of four children by Essex's sister, Penelope, Lady Rich, the muse of Sidney's sonnets. He was placed under house arrest and subjected to an enquiry into his conduct. He was cleared of treason, but found guilty of gross misconduct, stripped of most of his offices of profit under the Crown – including the lucrative monopoly of the duties on sweet wine – banished from Court and kept under house arrest. The latter was rescinded on 26 August, but he was left embittered. He was bereft of influence at Court, where his enemy, Robert Cecil, was ascendant. Cecil supported a negotiated peace to end the long war with Spain; Essex favoured continued bellicosity. Doubtless his feelings on the issue were exacerbated by the arrival of the emissaries from the Hapsburg Empire to discuss peace terms. The loss of his income was another grievous blow. He was not possessed of vast estates, so he was dependent on Crown perquisites to maintain his status and position.

Devereux inspired great loyalty. 'For his sake I would have hazarded my life,' said the Earl of Southampton, The disaffected attract others of their ilk. Secret meetings were held. At some point, the conversation turned away from the question of how the Earl might reingratiate himself with the Queen into a discussion of the possibility of a coup in which the strategic centres of the City might be seized and Essex installed as Regent. He was active in what was becoming an elaborate plot, contacting such vital potential allies as Mountjoy, about the support he might give to the coup by bringing his army from Ireland;

King James VI of Scotland, about the succession to the throne; and the Sheriff of London, Thomas Smythe, about the possibility of raising the trained bands in his support. Early in 1601, he began to fortify Essex House, his mansion in The Strand, which aroused the suspicions of his enemies that desperate measures were being prepared.

Essex's aggressive preparations must have excited considerable talk and speculation, not least among the Lord Chamberlain's Men. The Earl was a theatre buff, well-known to the Company. They could not have realised that they were about to be drawn into this dangerous business. In a curious move, three of Essex's supporters, Sir Charles and Sir Jocelyn Percy and Lord Monteagle, together with three other conspirators – who probably included Essex's Steward, Sir Gelli Meyrick, and Sir Henry Cuffe, his secretary – spoke with Augustine Phillips and others of the Company. They were specific about what they wanted: a performance of 'the play of the deposying and killing of Rychard the second to be played the Saterday next'. According to Phillips, the actors expressed reluctance, pleading the play was out of their repertoire. The conspirators, however, made an offer they could not refuse. They would pay them £10 over the normal Saturday take. They must have gone into rapid rehearsal. That the play was a favourite of Essex is suggested by the official evidence compiled against him for the enquiry into his conduct: 'the Erle himself being so often at the playing thereof, and with great applause giving countenance and lyking to the same'. The performance may have been commissioned in the hope of precipitating riots among the disaffected populace. Essex would have remembered previous disorders and may have been seeking to provoke another outburst to give him the pretext of intervening with his preassembled force to restore order. If so, this was another miscalculation. Previous uprisings were caused by rising food prices and resentment against immigrants. No such foment was ever caused by the mere production of a play. Indeed the performance may have had the opposite effect to that intended by alerting the authorities that something was afoot.

The conspirators dined together before crossing the Thames to see the play. Next day the Queen, in a spirit of reconciliation and alarmed at the way things were developing, sent four of her senior councillors to attempt to talk Essex out of his rash venture, but their presence escalated tensions. Devereux's supporters surrounded them, shouting 'Kill them! Kill them!' Essex had them locked in the library, whether to protect them or to take them hostage is unclear. The presence of the four statesmen had achieved the opposite of what was intended; the hysteria of his supporters forced Essex into precipitate action. Soon after the Sunday sermon had been preached at St Paul's Cross, he marched his 300 supporters to Smythe's house in Fenchurch Street. 'Where is the Sheriff?' he asked. 'Let him bring muskets and pistols, for I am credibly informed that the Kingdom of England is sold to the Spaniard', a reference to Cecil's peace negotiations. Later, several witnesses claimed they heard Smythe conferring with Essex, suggesting that if he seized Aldgate and Ludgate, he would bring reinforcements. In other words, he would support the coup if it appeared to be succeeding. Essex must have realised that he was not getting the support he expected. The City's seven gates had been shut by forces loyal to the Crown and Cecil had sent out heralds to proclaim him a traitor. Outflanked in every direction, he ordered a retreat to Essex House. One of his followers, Sir Charles Danvers, had previously urged him to flee 'to Wales or other parts beyond the seas rather than trust to the city'. It was sound advice. A force commanded by Charles Howard, Earl of Nottingham, patron of the Admiral's Men, surrounded the house and trained their cannons upon it. In the resulting skirmish, there were casualties on both sides. Just after 10 pm, Essex surrendered, with eighty-five of his adherents.

The Essex rebellion reveals how closely the theatre was connected with the political establishment. Two of the three patrons of the licensed London Companies were involved. As well as the Earl of Nottingham, the Earl of Worcester was one of the four kidnapped emissaries sent to negotiate with Essex. The actors who had participated in the production of *Richard II*, must have felt deep anxiety about the outcome of their inadvertent part in the rebellion. The precedence of *The Isle of Dogs* demonstrated that serious charges could be levelled against those who had merely enacted their parts on stage. As author of the play, William Shakespeare must have shared this anxiety, although he would appear to have had little or no involvement in the affair. Most anxious of all would have been Augustine Phillips who had negotiated the performance with the conspirators. On 18 February, he was examined before the Privy Council together with 'one of hys players'. This was probably the actor who had played Richard, or Bolingbroke. Under cross-examination, he declared that it had been a purely commercial arrangement, with no political intent. In the event, the Privy Council did not pursue the issue with the Company, but Sir Gilly Meyrick and Sir Henry Cuffe were charged with treason. The others involved were indicted and punished according to the parts they were deemed to have played in the rebellion.

The two leading conspirators, Essex and Southampton, were brought to trial for high treason on 19 February. In the dock, they kissed each other's hands and embraced. The trial was hardly objective. Many of the judges and jury were numbered among Essex's enemies. Although the authorities had not pursued the actors on the issue of the commissioning of *Richard II*, it was not forgotten; Sir Edward Coke, who led the case for the Crown, clearly referred to the play when he told Essex of what he considered would have been the Queen's fate had the rebellion succeeded:

> I protest vpon my soul and conscience I doe beleeve she should not have long lived after she had been in your power. Note but the precedents of former ages, how long lived Richard the Second after he was surprised in the same manner? The presence was alike for the removing of certain counsellors, but shortly after cost him his life.

After both Earls were found guilty as charged, the dreadful sentence was passed that they should be 'hanged, bowelled and quartered. Your head and quarters to be disposed of at Her Majesty's pleasure.' Even then Essex had a reply: 'I think it fit my poor quarters that have done her Majesty such true service in divers parts of the world should be sacrificed and disposed at her Majesty's pleasure.' The two men were returned to the Tower to await their fate.

On 24 February, Shrove Tuesday, the day of feasting before the Lenten fast, the Lord Chamberlain's Men performed at court. The circumstances are unknown – not even which play they performed. It was not their business to know that the Earl of Essex was to be executed next morning. The Queen, who had signed the death warrant four days before, may well have pleaded affairs of state and absented herself. Whether she was there or not, the company surely regarded the performance, which must have been arranged before the rebellion, as a token that no blame was attached to them for their inadvertent part in it.

In writing the official account of the rebellion, Sir Francis Bacon used a theatrical analogy in relation to Meyrick's trial:

> So earnest was hee to satisfie his eyes with the sight of that tragedie which hee thought soone after that his lord should bring from the stage to the state, .but that God turned it vpon their own heads.

Whether this is a quotation from the trial or represents Bacon's own verdict is unclear. His knowledge of Shakespeare's histories was certainly vague (particularly for a man that some believe wrote them). He refers to the wrong play of Richard:

> The example was remembered of Richard III, who (though he were king in possession, and the rightful inheritors but infants) could never sleep quiet in his bed till they were made away.

Sir Gilly Meyrick and Sir Henry Cuffe were hanged at Tyburn on 13 March, probably the only men in history to have been executed for commissioning a play (although, perhaps, others should have been). Ten men were condemned to death for their part in the rebellion. One of the four reprieved was the Earl of Southampton. His plea for the Queen's mercy from the dock was heeded. His sentence was deferred and he was incarcerated in the Tower awaiting her pleasure.

On 4 August, the Queen was at Greenwich, examining rolls from previous reigns with William Lambarde, the Keeper of the Records. She picked up a document from the reign of Richard II. 'I am Richard, know ye not that?' she said. 'Such a wicked imagination was determined and attempted by a most unkind Gent, the most adorned creature that ever your Majestie made,' Lambarde replied. 'He that will forget God,' the Queen responded, in a reference to Essex's alleged atheism, 'will also forget his benefactors. This tragedy was played out 40 times in open streets and houses.' The remark is puzzling. Perhaps the Queen was referring to the public playhouses.

'Like a Ripe Apple from a Tree'

In her 68th year, the Queen was sinking into a slow decline. On 21 November 1601, she made her last speech to Parliament. Her magnificent oration has a valedictory quality. There is a Shakespearean perspective in her view of the monarchy. 'To be a King and to wear a crown, is a thing more glorious to them that see it, than to them that bear it.'

The Lord Chamberlain's Men performed before the Queen on St Stephen's Day and St John's Day, but it was a shadow of previous revels. 'There has been such a small Court this Christmas,' wrote Dudley Carleton, 'that the guard were not troubled to keep doors at the plays and pastimes.' The actors appeared before her again on 1 January and on Valentine's Day. Later in the year, she relapsed, complaining of a sore throat and aches and pains. She seemed to have lost the will to live. She lay resignedly on cushions in her private apartments, refused the ministrations of her doctors and could not be persuaded to take to her bed. The Lord Chamberlain's Men played before her for the last time on 2 February 1603. A thoughtful courtier must have engaged them in the hope of stirring her from her deadly lethargy. As her condition deteriorated, she lost the power of speech and could only communicate by gestures. When the Archbishop of Canterbury spoke of her recovery, she made no response, but when he spoke of the joys of heaven, she squeezed his hand. The issue of the succession remained unresolved to the last. Ironically, Essex's rebellion had given Robert Cecil, his principal enemy, the power he craved to be its arbiter. Now he adopted Essex's major project. He was in secret communication with King James VI of Scotland, the Queen's nearest blood relative. His accession would, at a stroke, remove Scotland as England's traditional enemy and further the imperial vision. He claimed that when he mentioned James as her putative heir, the Queen squeezed his hand, so supposedly giving approval to his schemes. The Elizabethan era came to an end in the early hours of 24 March 1602/3. The diarist John Massingham heard that the Queen's passing was 'mildly like a Lambe, easily like a ripe apple from a tree'. She had reigned for forty-five years. Most people had known no other monarch. Within eight hours of her death, Cecil had James proclaimed King.

In the midst of the confusion about what the new reign might bring, the actors at least must have felt optimistic. The new King was a known lover of the theatre. Court masques had been a feature of his reign, an enthusiasm he would bring with him to England. In 1589, Queen Elizabeth had sent a company of players to Scotland to entertain him. Little is known of them except that they were led by Lawrence Fletcher and the former Admiral's Man, Martin Slater. They had probably been recruited at the request of the 23-year-old King, who desired to emulate his southern cousin by having his own troupe of actors. The cost is likely to have been born by Elizabeth, who was already paying subsidies to the Scottish court. They played before the King at a 'sumptious banquet' given by the Earl of Arran at Dirleton Castle when 'divers of the nobility and gentry passed the time right pleasantly with the play of Robin Hood'. Fletcher and Martin were at the Scottish court in 1595. Their presence produced a predictable reaction from the land's dour Calvinists. Sermons were preached against them. There was even a conspiracy theory. The English Ambassador, George Nicholson, reported to Cecil that 'the bellows blowers say that they are sent by England to sow dissension between the King and the Kirk'. The King would not hear of his players being censored and continued to hold them in high regard. They were in Scotland again between October 1599 and December 1601. Despite the hostility of the Kirk, their prestige in other quarters was high. On 22 October 1601, Lawrence Fletcher, 'Comedian to his Majesty', was granted the Freedom of Aberdeen. The theatre companies must have looked forward to the new reign with a sense of anticipation. They were not to be disappointed.

Three days after the death of Queen Elizabeth, James VI of Scotland received the news that he had been proclaimed James I of England. On 5 April, he left Edinburgh for London. His progress was slow so that he would arrive in the capital after the completion of the obsequies of his predecessor. As he entered London, the crowds were so great that 'they covered the beauty of the fields, and so greedy were they to behold the King that they injured and hurt one another'.

The actors' hopes were fulfilled beyond their expectations. The new King instructed 'our trusty and welloved councillor' Robert Cecil, to issue Letters Patent under the Great Seal of England to provide a royal charter for Shakespeare's Company, who were now to be known as the King's Men. The royal warrant was issued on 17 May, just ten days after the King's arrival in London. Two days later, the all-embracing formal patent gave licence to:

> Theise our servauntes, lawrence fletcher William Shakespeare Richard Burbage Augustyne Phillippes John heninges henrie Condell William Sly Robert Armyn Richard Cowley and the rest of theire Associates freely to use and exercise the Arte and facultie of playinge Comedies Tragedies histories Enterludes moralls pastoralles Stage-plaies and suche others like as theie have alreadie studied or hereafter shall use or studie as well for the recreation of our lovinge Subjectes as for our Solace and Pleasure.

It was noted that 'theire nowe usuall howse called the Globe' was their customary base. All justices, mayors, other officers and loving subjects were instructed 'to allowe them such former Curtesies as hath bene given to men of theire place and qualitie and alsoe what favour you shall shewe to these our Servauntes for our sake'. In return for such courtesy, it was promised that 'wee shall take kindlie at your handes'. The Company was now obviated from the necessity to negotiate with difficult officials. The Royal Warrant would have accompanied them on tour to be produced triumphantly to local Dogberries.

The nine sharers in the Company became 'Grooms Extraordinary of the Chamber', with stipends of £52 4*d.* per year. These were normally relatively minor courtiers who performed domestic functions, but in the case of the actors, the position was almost, but not entirely, honorific. Such a position in the royal household gave them valued social standing, which would have been increased considerably by their wearing the royal livery.

The list of actors on the patent is headed by Lawrence Fletcher. James may have expressed a desire to amalgamate members of his own troupe into the new company, or perhaps the canny actors saw the engagement of Fletcher, who had probably come south with James, as a useful adjunct in the new and breathtaking scheme of things. He was a popular addition to the Company. In his will, probated on 13 May 1605, Augustine Phillips left him 20/- in gold.

The former Lord Chamberlain's Men was not the only company to feel happy with the new regime. Henslowe's Company, the Earl of Nottingham's Men, received the patronage of the 9-year-old heir to the throne, Prince Henry. The Earl of Worcester's Men became Queen Anne's Men.

Like Hissing Snakes

With a number of rival candidates for the throne waiting in the wings, King James wished to get himself established as the anointed monarch as soon as possible. The date for his coronation was fixed for 23 July, but, in June, plague was recorded in that same poor parish of St Botolph where it began in 1593. It spread through the city and did not abate until mid-September. To go ahead with the celebrations associated with the coronation would be impossible. The religious ceremony took place as planned; the pomp and circumstance was postponed to a later date.

Despite the plague, it was a busy year for the King's Men. When the theatres reopened in the autumn, William Shakespeare appeared as an actor in Ben Jonson's tragedy, *Sejanus, His Fall.* This is the last specific mention of him as such. John Lowin also appears on the cast list as a hired man. He was to be one of the company's mainstays. He was baptised on 9 December 1576, at St Giles, Cripplegate, the son of a tanner. Like Robert Armin, he was apprenticed to a goldsmith. At some point, he embarked on a stage career. His name appears frequently in Henslowe's account books while he was acting with Worcester's Men at the Rose. A further note places him in a touring company in 1602. Like a number of other actors, he maintained his links with his livery company. In Anthony Munday's 1611 City pageant, he is described as a 'brother' of the Goldsmith's Company.

Jonson must have extolled his work to the company as an example of what a tragedy should be, scrupulously following Aristotle's 'Unities'. Unfortunately, his play – which was co-authored by 'a second pen' (probably George Chapman), described by Jonson as 'so happy a genius' – was hooted off the stage. The more sophisticated members of the audience, versed in the classical tradition, seem to have appreciated it, but it was not to the taste of the groundlings. Given how many enemies Ben had acquired, a claque may have been organised against it. It would be a new experience for Shakespeare, Burbage and the rest of the Company, to 'get the bird' – a term even then. In 1605, one of Jonson's admirers expressed his outrage at the play's treatment in dedicatory lines to the first quarto:

> When in the Globe's fair ring, our world's best stage,
> I saw Sejanus, set with that rich foil,
> I looked the author should have borne the spoil
> Of conquest from the writers of the age;
> But when I viewed the people's beastly rage,
> Bent to confound thy grave and learned toil,
> That cost thee so much sweat, and so much oil,
> My indignation I could hardly 'suage.

The reception of *Sejanus*, indicates a dichotomy between the 'illiterate and rude' groundlings and the more sophisticated 'wits of gentry'. In 1616, the poet, William Fennor wrote:

> sweet Poesy
> Is oft convict, condemned, and judged to die
> Without just trial, by a multitude
> Whose judgments are illiterate, and rude.
> Witness Sejanus, whose approvéd worth,
> Sounds from the calm south, to the freezing north …
> With more than human art it was bedewed,
> Yet to the multitude it nothing showed;
> They screwed their scurvy jaws and looked awry,
> Like hissing snakes adjudging it to die,
> When wits of gentry did applaud the same
> With silver shouts of high loud-sounding fame.

Ben Jomson's capacity to get into deep trouble continued unabated. He was in a fracas with a servant of the highly influential Earl of Northampton. Subsequently the Earl, whom Ben described as his 'mortal enemy' (yet another), had him hauled before the Privy Council on charges of 'Popery and Treason' based on topical references in *Sejanus*. It was an odd business. Jonson was indeed a Papist, but it was a charge that was levelled at Northampton who died a Catholic. There appears little in *Sejanus*, a play set in pre-Christian Rome, to merit such an accusation. Whatever the matter may have been, the offending passages were excised.

Around this time the leading actor of the newly named Prince Henry's Men, Edward Alleyn, made the decision to retire for the second and final time. He invested his huge fortune in buying the vast manor of Dulwich for a staggering £35,000. His mind was turned to philanthropy, precipitated, according to John Aubrey, by an incident entirely appropriate to the creator of the role of Dr Faustus:

> Mr Alleyn, being a tragedian, and one of the original actors in many of the celebrated Shakespeare plays,, in one of which he played a demon, with six others, surprised by an apparition of the devil, which so worked on his fancy that he made a vow, which he performed at this place.

It is unlikely that Alleyn played one of seven devils in a play in which he was the lead. Nor was he the original actor in many of Shakespeare's plays.

The royal household stayed clear of the City for the rest of Coronation year. In the third week of September, James held court at Wilton House in Wiltshire, the seat of William Herbert, 3rd Earl of Pembroke, and some people's choice as the beautiful youth of the sonnets. Late in November, the King's Men were summoned there 'upon the Councell's warrant'. They departed from Augustine Phillips' house at Mortlake, where they may have been undertaking extra rehearsals, such was the importance of this first appearance before their royal patron. In the event, the King was delighted. The Company played at Wilton on 2 December and received the goodly sum of £30 'by way of his majesties reward'.

With the abating of the plague, the royal family felt it safe to move to Hampton Court for the Christmas festivities. The Company's efforts at Wilton ensured that they were much in demand over the season, performing four times before the King and twice for Prince Henry under the Gothic roof of the Great Hall, whose walls were draped – then and now – with tapestries representing the story of Abraham. As early as 1572, a stage had been erected and an adjacent chamber used as a tiring room. The arrival of this new audience from Scotland represented an opportunity to revive old dramas from the repertoire. One of the pieces acted before the Prince was 'a play of Robin Goodfellow', probably *A Midsummer Night's Dream*. Again the players received a handsome reward, departing with £53. They reappeared at Hampton Court at Candlemas. Six days later, Richard Burbage was paid £30 'for the mayntenance and reliefe of himself and the reste of his companie'. Such sums provided a much-needed boost to the finances while the theatres were closed. The virulence of the plague would have diminished during the winter months, but the Privy Council maintained the closure orders 'in or neare London by reason of the great perill that might growe through the extraordinarie concourse and assemblie of people'.

Chapter Seven

'The Whole Course of the Present Time'

The Magnificent Entertainment

The restrictive orders against the plague were lifted by 15 March 1604, when the King made his long-awaited progress through the City. The cost was 'incomparable'. Much of it was picked up by the City livery companies. Three days before the event, the King, Queen and Prince Henry took up residence in the Tower. The royal suite had been lavishly prepared. 'Such glory in the hangings,' eulogised Gilbert Dugdale, 'such majesty in the ornaments of the chamber!' It was felt inappropriate that the prisoners under sentence of death should remain on the premises.

> The Tower was emptye of his prisoners; and I beheld the late Walter Rawly, the late Lord Cobham[1] ... with others, conveyed, some to the Marshalsea, others to the Gatehouse, and others to appointed prisons.

'Late'? Whether Dugdale considered the prisoners as good as dead is unclear. Sir Walter Raleigh was impressively vigorous for a dead man, begetting his son Carew, born in the following year, while in the Tower.

On the evening before the great pageant, a mock sea-battle was fought on the Thames, 'at the cost of ye Sinke-ports', opposite the Tower. Next morning, the royal party embarked on their triumphal route. Unlike his predecessor, who had a high boredom quotient, the King became impatient at lengthy shows, so much of the content was curtailed. Seven great arches had been erected around the City, the handiwork of the joiner Stephen Harrison. 'A stately shew of workmanship and glory as I never saw the like,' enthused Dugdale. The first spectacle was a pageant devised by Ben Jonson: '*Monarchia Britannia*', a celebration of the Union of Crowns. Saints George and Andrew met in combat, but a passing hermit joined their hands and 'so, for ever, hath made them as one heart: to the joy of the King, the delight of the Lords, and the unspeakable comfort of the community'.

The first arch in Fenchurch Street was sponsored by the City. In Thomas Dekker's words, 'the upper roof thereof ... bore up the true moddels of all the notable Houses, Turrets, and Steeples, within the Citie.' Edward Alleyn, 'seruant to the young Prince', returned to public view for this 'Magnificent Entertainment', appearing as 'the Genius of the City', a role performed with 'excellent action and a well tun'd audible voice', with 'one of the children of Her Maiesties Reuals' at his feet, representing the River Thames. Other children represented the six daughters of the City: Veneration, Promptitude, Vigilance, Gladness, Loving Affection and Unanimity.

'Servant to the young Prince' indicates Alleyn's continuing involvement with the company now called Prince Henry's Men. No sooner had the royal party passed on its way, than he rushed through the alleys, pausing to change his costume, before appearing at the fourth triumphal arch in priestly garb. He delivered a speech and presented the King with a pendant bearing the flaming heart of London, a symbol of mercy, love and charity. It was part of *The King's Entertainment*, co-written by Jonson and Dekker, in which a host of classical figures delivered paeans to the royal dynasty. It may have been the only time the King heard Alleyn speak in public.

Another triumphal gate supported a mechanically moving globe. The City's French, Italian and Dutch merchants had commissioned lavish pageants. Orations abounded and the air was full of 'harmonies of drums, trumpets and music of all sorts'. Every conduit between the Tower and Westminster ran with wine with obvious effects, 'as many were shipped to the Isle of Sleep…'.

As members of the Royal Household, each sharer in the Queen's and King's Companies received four and a half yards of scarlet cloth from the Master of the Great Wardrobe. William Shakespeare's name heads the list. Robert Armin gives an indication of what their role might have been. He claimed to have written *Time Triumphant*, the account of the pageant published under Gilbert Dugdale's name. This would explain how the author had seen the decorations in the Tower's royal apartments and the removal of the state prisoners. The sharers, as Grooms of the Chamber, may have been called upon to wait on the King in their scarlet liveries. They could have delivered the orations composed by Jonson and Dekker.

The King's approbation of the actors was as strong as ever. Just twenty days after the great extravaganza he caused the Privy Council to write to the Lord Mayor and the Justices of Middlesex and Surrey requesting them to refrain from interfering with the right of his players to perform at their 'usual home', the Globe. The same privilege was requested for the Queen's Servants at the Fortune and the Prince's at the Curtain.

The Court Masque

Despite his clear support for the theatre and the company bearing his name, the court masque was the King's most favoured form of entertainment. These extravagant productions featured breathtaking special effects and fantastical stage and costume design. The spectacle had been introduced into England from Italy as early as 1512. It was a feature of court entertainment under the Tudors, but it reached its apotheosis under the first two Stuart monarchs. The first masque of the reign, *The Vision of the Twelve Goddesses*, was staged in the Great Hall at Hampton Court on 8 January 1603/4. It was written by the Licenser of the Queen's Revels, Samuel Daniel. It followed the usual pattern of spectacular effects and vacuous plot, but it was different in one respect. Courtiers participated along with professional actors, singers and musicians, Queen Anne and eleven of her ladies danced as classical goddesses. Their sumptuous costumes were created from the the late Queen's vast wardrobe. Despite such economy, it cost over £2,000 to stage. Women appearing in prominent roles reversed the practice of the public stage. The courtier, Sir Dudley Carleton, commented cryptically on the Queen's somewhat daring costume: 'her clothes were not so much below the knee but that we might see a woman had both feet and legs which I never knew before.' It is not recorded who designed the vast sets consisting of a large mountain, Temple of Peace and Cave of Sleep.

The masque celebrated the monarchy's perception of itself, presenting 'the figure of those blessings, with the wish of their increase and continuance, which this mightie Kingdom now enjoyes by the benefit of his most gracious Majestie: by whom we have this glory of peace, with the accession of so great state and power.' Symbolic characters personified chaos and despair until harmony was brought by the Stuart King, but it was a limited means of propaganda for the regime, since it was only seen by a small number of courtiers, the strongest supporters of the status quo.

The royal penchant for this type of extravagant entertainment brought Ben Jonson to his zenith of fortune. He had created a prototype with *The Satyr*, an entertainment commissioned by the politically ambitious Robert Spencer, performed at Althorp in Northamptonshire to welcome Queen Anne and Prince Henry on their progress towards London. The theme was appropriately pastoral, featuring elves, fairies and figures from English folklore. Ben was to perfect the dramatic quality of the masque, such as it was, writing thirty-seven in all. His partner in much of this endeavour was Inigo Jones, the first identifiable English architect of distinction. He introduced the Palladian style of the Italian Renaissance to England, but it was as the designer of the costumes and settings for court masques that he first became noted. Their earliest collaboration was *The Masque of Blackness* in 1605. It was compiled at the request of the Queen, who, contrary to prevailing taste, regarded the Africans of Niger as beautiful. 'That in their black, the perfect beauty grows', says one line. The Queen led the dancing, accompanied by her eleven ladies, Rather than wearing the masks that were the norm for such charades, they were blacked-up with grease paint. Their costumes of blue, silver and pearl were designed by Jones to contrast with their blackness. His raised, mobile stage concealed space for the mechanisms and the crew who worked them to create the opening spectacle in which 'an artificial sea was seen to shoot forth, as if it flowed to the land, raised with waves which seemed to move, and in some places the billows to break, as imitating that orderly disorder which is common in nature'. Oceanus, the God of the Atlantic, and his son, Niger the river God, appeared, seated in a giant seashell. Oceanus declared the poets of the North had told his daughters that they were not as beautiful as once thought. The epitome of African beauty, born of the sun-drenched deserts of Ethiopia, they now cursed the sun that gave them life for making them so dark. Aethiopia, the moon goddess told them that if they could find a land whose name ended in 'tania' they would find an answer to their problem. The conclusion was that the two Kingdoms under the rule of the Stuarts represented the pinnacle of good government and civilised values.

The spectacle of twelve handsome women, blacked-up and in gorgeous costumes, did not charm Sir Dudley. The costumes were 'too light and courtesan like ... Instead of Vizzards, their Faces and Arms up to the Elbows, were painted black, which was a Disguise sufficient, for they were hard to be known ... and you cannot imagine a more ugly sight.'

'In everyone's opinion no other Court could have displayed such pomp and riches', wrote the Venetian ambassador of the Christmas masque of 1604. It is estimated that *The Masque of Blackness* cost the Exchequer around £3,000 and the even vaster sum of £4,000 was spent on *The Masque of Beauty* in 1608: 3 per cent of the annual budget deficit. 'This extreem cost and riches makes us all poore,' wrote John Chamberlain. It was an extravagant strain on the revenues and played its part in the drift towards civil war, although it had its effects on theatre history. Inigo Jones incorporated the proscenium arch and moveable scenery for the first time and women were among the performers.

'Perpetual Peace and Alliance'

From his first accession, the King realised the necessity to end to the war with Spain, which had dragged on for nineteen years. After overtures and diplomatic exchanges, in August 1604 delegations from Spain and the Spanish Netherlands arrived in London. In their capacity as Grooms of the Chamber, the sharers of the King's Men were called upon to wait on the Spanish delegation at Somerset House; a like service was performed at Durham House by Queen Anne's Men for the delegation from Flanders. It says much for the King's respect for the actors that he preferred they attend his distinguished guests rather than his courtly retinue. What they did is uncertain, but they were paid £21 12*s*. 0*d*. for their services. Only Augustine Phillips and John Heminges were named in the Treasurer's accounts, but William Shakespeare must have been among the 'tenne of their ffellowes' in attendance. He who had written so much of history was now present at its making. Juan Fernandez de Velasco y Tovar, Duke of Frias and Constable of Castile, led the delegations. Shakespeare would have been familiar with the members of the English delegation: Lord Robert Cecil; Charles Blount, Earl of Devonshire; the Lord Treasurer, Thomas Sackville, Earl of Dorset, co-author of *Gorbuduc*; Henry Howard, Earl of Northampton, Ben Jonson's 'mortal enemy'; and Charles Howard, Earl of Nottingham, former patron of the Admiral's Men.

With both sides desiring to end the conflict, negotiations were rapidly concluded. The Treaty of Perpetual Peace and Alliance was signed on 19 August by King James and the Constable of Castile in the Chapel at Whitehall Palace. After the signing, those involved in the negotiations, including the Grooms of the Chamber, processed to a grand banquet. The Earls of Southampton and Pembroke acted as stewards. Southampton's rehabilitation was complete. He had become a great favourite of the 28-year-old Queen. The King's continuing delight in his actors was demonstrated when 'the Kings Maiesties plaiers' presented eleven of the seventeen performances at Court between All Souls Day and Shrove Tuesday in 1604/5, of which, seven were by Shakespeare. The first, performed on 'Hallamas Day being the first of November', was 'A Play in the Banketinghouse at Whit Hall Called The Moor of Venis'. This first known performance of *Othello* was recorded by the Clerk to the Master of the Revels under its subsequent subtitle. The source was *Il Capitano Moro*, one of 110 tales by Giavanni Battista Giraldi, published in 1565 as *Gli Ecatommiti*. There was no English translation, Shakespeare accessed the plot by some means – perhaps he understood Italian. He retained the name of the female lead – Desdemona.

Offending the King

Crossing the authorities, advertently or otherwise, was a hazard for contemporary dramatists. Unlike some other playwrights, William Shakespeare was wise to this. When the second quarto of *Hamlet* was published in 1604, derogatory references to the Danish court were expunged – the Queen was Danish – as were the passages critical of the Children's companies. She was their patron.

In contrast, the Children of the Revels, under the direction of Henry Evans, seemed to delight in personal satire, violence and lewdness. Shakespeare at least regarded it as unseemly to use children as a vehicle for such material, although few others seemed troubled The nation holds it no sin to tarre them to controversy,' says Hamlet. In 1604, the Company achieved a great success. John Marston's *The Malcontent* deals skilfully with issues of corruption in high places, using Shakespeare's ploy of distancing the action from the contemporary scene. It is ostensibly about corruption in the Ducal Court of Genoa, but the extent to which this might be regarded as a commentary on the Court of King James is shrouded in ambiguity. Malevole, the malcontent of the title, is an archetypal figure in contemporary drama, a prototype of those who act as a chorus of disillusion ranging from Jacques to Timon. The play's publication in three separate quartos within the year indicates its popularity. The first two reflect the script performed by the Children of the Revels at Blackfriars, but the title page of the third reveals it is now being performed by the King's Men at the Globe. It has been augmented by Marston, with additions by John Webster, who adds an Induction built around a conversation between the actors who are about to perform. Richard Burbage, Henry Condell and John Lowin play themselves, William Sly a young theatregoer who introduces John Sinklo as 'my cousin, Master Doomsday's son, the usurer'. He quotes Osrick's lines from *Hamlet*, so he may have created that part. That Webster was commissioned to revise and expand the script may have been because the original incorporated extended interludes with the boys singing, so it was necessary to fill these gaps; 'To entertain a little more time and to abridge the nor-received custom of musick in our theatre,' says Burbage, who exits to prepare to play Malevole.

'Sir, I would know how you came you by this play,' asks Sly of Condell, who replies that the Revels Children stole a play from the King's Men, so they have taken this one in return. The stolen play was *The Spanish Tragedy*, or one of its sequels. 'Why not Malevole in folio with us, as well as Ieronimo in decimo sexto[2] with them?' 'They taught us a name for our play,' he adds, 'We call it, One for another' (i.e., Tit for Tat).

The authorities continued to keep an eye on Blackfriars. The political sensitivities of the governing class were revealed when Samuel Daniel's *The Tragedy of Philotas* was performed by the Children of the Revels on 3 January 1605. Despite the ostensible theme being the trial and execution of a proud and ambitious Macedonian General, who was accused of participating in a plot to overthrow Alexander the Great, the play was deemed to have parallels with the Essex rebellion. Daniel was hauled before the Privy Council but acquitted himself well, pleading that the first three acts were written before the rebellion occurred and had been passed by the Master of the Revels. He felt obliged, however, to offer an apology for the confusion he had caused when the play was published in 1607, but there were still repercussions, with the Queen withdrawing her patronage from the Revels Children.

Henry Evans appears to have escaped unscathed from the episode, but the capacity of the Revels Children to get into trouble continued unabated. 'The play[er]s do not forbear to represent upon their stage the whole course of the present time, not sparing King, State or Religion in so great absurdity, and with such liberty, that any would be afraid to hear them,' Samuel Calvert remarked on it in a letter to Ralph Winwood on 25 March 1605. These were no passing comments. Winwood was Clerk to the Privy Council. Its judicial tribunal, the court known as the Star Chamber, could find defendants guilty of actions that were not illegal, but that it deemed reprehensible. It could inflict any punishment short of death – the pillory, imprisonment, whipping, swingeing fines, or physical mutilation.

In August the company was in greater trouble. Ben Jonson had written *Eastward Ho!* in collaboration with George Chapman and John Marston, as a riposte to Thomas Dekker and John Webster's satirical comedy, *Westward Ho!* that had been performed by the Children of Paul's in the previous year. The titles echo the calls of the Thames boatmen as they shouted their intended direction. *Eastward Ho!* references such contemporary dramas as *The Spanish Tragedy*, *Tamburlaine* and *Hamlet*. Several characters have Shakespearean names – Touchstone, Gertrude, 'Bettrice', Mistress Ford and Hamlet. There is even a Winifred, the name of Richard Burbage's wife. Why the writers (most likely Jonson) chose to do this is unclear, but the play's most biting piece of satire is completely clear. There are references to the place-seeking Scots who had followed King James southwards. Nor is the royal practice of selling honours overlooked. 'I ken Sir Petrone well,' says the First Gentleman in a clear Scottish accent, 'he is one of my thirty-pound knights.' Captain Seagull wishes a hundred thousand of the Scots were in Virginia, because 'we should find ten times more comfort of them there than we do here'. The King was on a progress to Oxford when the play was first performed and took great offence when informed of it by a Scottish courtier, Sir James Murray (perhaps himself a thirty pound knight), and ordered the arrest of the playwrights. Marston fled, but Jonson and Chapman were, 'without examining, without hearing, or without any proof, hurried to bondage and fetters'. Jonson told William Drummond that 'the report was that they should then had their ears cut and their noses'. The prisoners wrote pleading letters to anyone who might have influence on the matter. Chapman claimed to the King that the offending passages were interpolations. There were 'but two clauses, and both of them not our own'. This plea may have led to their release without charge. Naturally, following the controversy, the play proved hugely popular; four quartos were published within five months, lacking the offending passages. James' noted capacity to forgive slights was evidenced in 1614 when it was performed at Court, with the actors receiving above the usual stipend. A further riposte from Dekker and Webster. *Northwood Ho*, a city comedy presented by the Children of Paul's later in 1605, wisely steered clear of matters relating to the Court.

A legal resource used by those of rank who held themselves offended by scurrilous portrayals was the Statutes of *Scandalum Magnatum* – 'the Scandal of Magnates', which provided that actions for defamation could be determined by the standing of the person offended. Penalties could be severe. In 1579, a Puritan, John Stubbs, published *The Discovery of a Gaping Gap…*, a pamphlet attacking the projected marriage of the Queen with the French Duke of Alençon. Such a 'contrary coupling' was described as an 'immoral union', like 'a cleanly ox with an unseemly ass'. The Queen's advisors were accused of pursuing the interests of the French court, 'where Machiavelli is their new testament and atheism their religion'. He claimed venereal disease was endemic in the ducal family, so such a marriage would expose the Queen to a harrowing death. She was furious and demanded that Stubbs; Hugh Singleton, the printer; and William Page, the distributor, be executed. After a complicated legal process, Stubbs was found to have 'written maliciously of his own imagination … false, seditious and slanderous news, sayings, or tales'. Singleton seems to have been pardoned, perhaps because he was 80 years old, but Stubbs and Page were sentenced to have their right hands severed. This gory deed was accomplished in Westminster market place with a butcher's cleaver and a mallet, with surgeons standing by to prevent the unfortunate pair bleeding to death. After this ordeal, they were imprisoned in the Tower for two years.

In the year *Eastward Ho!* appeared, Lewes Pickering, 'a scholar religiously disposed' (he was a Cambridge undergraduate and a Puritan), was charged with attempting to 'stirre the people to a desire of reformation, which is not tolerable in a monarchie but in a democracie'. He had written a poem entitled *The Lamentation of Dickie for the deathe of his brother Jockie*. 'Dickie' was Richard Bancroft, the Archbishop of Canterbury, and 'Jockie', his predecessor, John Whitgift. It was customary to place valedictory messages on the hearses of the deceased, but in February 1603/4 when Whitgift's 'Corps was carried to Croydon … and there honourably interred in the Parish Church … with a decent solemnity', it was discovered that someone had placed this piece of derogatory doggerel on his coffin. Whether it was Pickering or another is unclear, but it took a year to track him down and bring him before the Star Chamber. His defence that the dead could not be libelled was refuted by Sir Edward Coke, who posited the distinction between libelling 'a private man' and 'a magistrate or public person'. He was fined £1,000, sentenced to a year's imprisonment and compelled to stand in the pillory in London, his home town of Northampton and Croydon. If he failed to openly confess the offence, his ears would be pinned to the pillory.

Even those of standing could run foul of such laws. At the Coronation, Sir Edward Dymoke of Scrivelsby in Lincolnshire, as hereditary Champion of England, had challenged anyone who denied the King's right to reign. He was High Sheriff of Lincolnshire and a Member of Parliament. In 1588, he was named as one of twelve knights of 'great possession' who could support a peerage. Around this time he became involved in a lengthy and acrimonious dispute about land rights with his uncle, Henry Clinton, the litigious, violent and much-loathed Earl of Lincoln, who was generally considered deranged. The quarrel reached the level of a private war, with frequent affrays between adherents of the two parties. In 1610, Dymoke's brother staged a play on the village green at Scrivelsby. After lampooning the Earl, a character dressed as a minister (Clinton was a severe Puritan) climbed into a pulpit erected next to a maypole (an ungodly symbol to Puritans) and 'did most profanely … pronounce vain and scurrilous matter', before nailing a diatribe against the Earl to the maypole for all to see. When an action was brought in the Star Chamber against Dymoke and others 'for contriving and acting a stage play … containing scurrilous and slanderous matter', Coke's precedent was followed. The Earl might be an appalling person, but the dignity of his title must be upheld. The participants in the play were sentenced to be imprisoned, pilloried, fined and whipped. The brother had died soon after the performance, but Sir Edward was imprisoned in the Fleet and fined £1,000.

So why did the Children of the Revels continue to rile authority in the face of such potentially severe sanctions? The King may simply have had too heavy an agenda to bother overmuch about what was happening at Blackfriars, unless it was brought to his attention in such a way that he was obliged to act. Much of his energy was spent elsewhere. 'The Puritans are more than ever troublesome and annoying to the King,' wrote Nicolo Molin, the Venetian Ambassador on 25 March 1605. A month earlier, the Archbishop of Canterbury had summoned Puritan ministers and told them they must recognise bishops as their hierarchical superiors and adhere to the formulae of the Established Church. When the most militant refused, they were deprived of their benefices and ordered into exile; others were suspended from their livings and given twenty days to decide whether to conform. 'This has caused a great turmoil in the City, which is full of people who belong to the Puritan sect,' wrote the Ambassador. 'The King thinks of nothing else but the humbling of the pride and the audacity of this party, but he meets with much opposition.' To James, the Puritans resembled the insolent Presbyterian preachers in Scotland, who told him to his face that unless he supported them, they would overthrow him and appoint their own

Regent. Such insolence was epitomised when Thomas Bywater, a Puritan minister, presented him with a book, *The Errors of the King of Great Britain*, while he was out hunting. It 'spares neither King, Councillor, nor Court, but teaches the King in every point his duty', said Morin. Despite claiming not to have written the offending volume, Bywater was duly committed to the Tower.

The King was also embarrassed by reports that he was sympathetic to Catholics, a belief enhanced by his emissary in Rome, Sir Robert Lindsay, who assured the Pope that James was ripe for conversion. At his accession the penal enactments against Catholics had been relaxed, but, to affirm his conformity to Anglican doctrines, it was determined, in the words of Molin, 'to enforce against Catholics the laws which are of great severity and bitterness, affecting property and life'. Despair about this affliction led to the Gunpowder Plot in the following November.

In the light of such matters, the pinpricks caused by the iconoclasts at Blackfriars may not have seemed a priority. It was a private theatre with audiences drawn from the upper classes. When such productions were presented in the public theatres, with their large plebeian audiences and potential for civic unrest, the reaction was likely to be more severe, as the *Isle of Dogs* affair demonstrated. That the actors at Blackfriars were choirboys made them less responsible for their utterances. The prospect of pursuing children for slander held out the prospect of appearing absurd.

That there may have been another factor in the lack of serious pursuit of the Revels Company was recorded by the French ambassador:

> Consider for pity's sake what must be the state and condition of a prince, whom the preachers publicly from the pulpit assail, whom the comedians of the metropolis bring upon the stage, whose wife attends these representations in order to enjoy the laugh against her husband.

Whether Queen Anne attended performances at Blackfriars is uncertain, but as the first Queen Consort since the reign of Henry VIII she possessed her own court to which she could summon the young players. She had a great enthusiasm for the theatre. When Sir Walter Cope was asked by Robert Cecil to select a play to be performed for the Queen during her brother Ulrick of Holstein's visit to her Court, he wrote that 'Burbage is come and says that there is no new play the Queen has not seen but they have revived an old one called Love's Labour's Lost which for wit and mirth he says will please her exceedingly.'

Although the King and Queen lived apart for much of the time (but still coming together to fulfil the royal duty of begetting children), the Queen possessed considerable influence, often interceding on behalf of those in trouble with the authorities. She could well have done this when the Children of the Revels were in trouble and others of influence could make representations on the Company's behalf at Court, as the *Eastward Ho!* affair demonstrated.

Despite previous furores, the Revels Children continued to bait the royal establishment. Indeed, during 1606, the provocations increased. 'At this time (about 15 February),' wrote the diplomat and courtier, Sir Edward Hoby, 'was much speech of a play in Blackfriars, where in the "Isle of Gulls", from the highest to the lowest, all men's parts were acted of two divers nations.' The play appears to be John Day's first foray into the world of children's theatre. It was based on incidents in one of the most admired works of the age, Sidney's *Arcadia*. The plot has all the complexities of mistaken identities and misunderstandings of the period comedy. Suffice it to state that the 'two diverse nations' mentioned by Hoby – the Arcadians and the Lacedemonians – represented the English and Scots and were played in an exaggerated style by the boy actors as a satire on the King's desire to unite his two kingdoms. The character of Manasses may represent the lampooning of an actual person, or at least of the royal habit of elevating 'base-born' persons into the top echelons – 'My great Grandfather was a Rat-catcher, my Grandsire a Hangman, my Father a Promoter, and my selfe an Informer,' he says. The offence caused by the play may have been anticipated because the prologue specifically denied that 'any great man's life' was represented. This apologia carried little weight. 'As I understand,' wrote Sir Edward, 'several were committed to the Bridewell.' This may well have included some of the Revels boys. The Bridewell, according to John Stow, was 'a workhouse for the poor and idle persons of the city'. John Day was questioned by the Privy Council, but his fate is unknown. Perhaps he joined the children in the Bridewell.

The Red Bull

Another theatre added to the venues for playgoers in 1604 may have given the authorities different kinds of headaches. The Red Bull Inn in Clerkenwell had long housed performances in its courtyard, but, in 1605, the landlord Aaron Holland built a theatre on the site which was at least as large as the Globe. Perhaps because of its function as a drinking establishment, it had a reputation for rowdiness. *Albumazar*, a play commissioned in 1615 from one of its Fellows, Thomas Tomkis, by Trinity College, Cambridge, to entertain the King, cited the Red Bull and Fortune as theatres with raucous audiences, which served up such outmoded fare as *The Spanish Tragedy*.

Nevertheless, the Red Bull seems to have maintained a high standard. Holland and the actor Martin Slater attempted to form a Company under the patronage of Ulrik, Duke of Holstein, but it came to nothing. Perhaps the Queen desired that her own company should play there. It included such well-known names as Christopher Beeston, John Duke and Thomas Heywood, who achieved a status similar to that of William Shakespeare at the Globe, as its resident actor–dramatist. His greatest success was *If You Know Not Me You Know No Bodie: or, The troubles of Queen Elizabeth*, a play in two parts loosely centred around the life and times of the late Queen. The first part was entered onto the Stationers' Register on 5 July 1605, just two years after her death. It deals with the main events of the reign of Queen Mary, including the tribulations of her sister, Elizabeth, and culminates in her accession to the throne. It was hugely popular. The first quarto of 1605 was followed by others in 1606, 1608, 1610, 1611, 1623 and 1639. The first three acts of Part Two revolve around the building of the Royal Exchange by Thomas Gresham, which provide the background for a reversion to city comedy. Gresham binds John, his nephew, to Hobson, a gullible haberdasher, who is having problems with his riotous apprentices. John is equal to any of them when it comes to debauchery. When sent to France on business, he departs with £100 stolen from his uncle. Hobson follows him and finds him in the house of a French courtesan. John tricks him into believing that she is a respectable businesswoman. When her profession is revealed, John threatens to split on the long-suffering Hobson to his wife. In return for his silence, Hobson agrees not to punish him, but insists on bringing him back to London to avoid further escapades. He has been conned by a fraudster into believing that the Queen is asking him for money, but when he approaches her at a royal pageant he is surprised to find that she doesn't know him, hence the play's title. The action moves to such events as Dr Parry's supposed attempt to assassinate the Queen and ends on a triumphal and patriotic note that would have pleased the groundlings with the defeat of the Spanish Armada, with Sir Francis Drake a leading character.

Christopher Beeston had become the prime figure in the company by 1611. In that year, the Red Bull had another great success with the *Tu Quoque*, ot *The City Gallant*, by John Cooke, a playwright of whom little is known.[3] The lead role of Bubbles was played by the Company's clown, Thomas Greene. The script refers to this popular actor and the theatre in the very play in which he was performing.

Geraldine: Why then, we'll go to the Red Bull. They say Greene's a good clown.
Bubble: Greene! Greeene's an ass.
Scattergood: Wherefore do you say so?
Bubble: Indeed I ha' no reason, for they say he is as unlike me as ever he can look.

The play was performed at Court during the Christmas Revels. It was a great success because it was repeated at Candlemas, but not until 18 June, did Greene receive £20 for the two performances on behalf of the Company. The theatre saw the first performance of John Webster's *The White Devil* in 1612, although it was not a success. In his preface to the quarto edition, Webster praised the acting of the Queen's Men. 'In particular I must remember the well-approved industry of my friend Master Perkins, and confess the worth of his action did crown both the beginning and the end.' He was not so complimentary about the audience – 'ignorant asses'. The theatre was 'open and black', which is hardly surprising since the play was performed at 'so dull a time of winter'. Perhaps it was just as well. The plot, loosely based on an actual murder in Padua some thirty years before, could well have been interpreted as a commentary on the political and moral state of England.

'The Scottish Play'

A play certainly not intended to offend the King was *Macbeth*. The weird sisters prophesy that Banquo, the legendary founder of the House of Stuart, will beget kings, but will not reign himself. The kings that Macbeth sees in a vision in Act 4 represent the eight Stuart kings that preceded James (his mother, Mary Queen of Scots, is tactfully forgotten). They carry 'twofold balls and treble sceptres'. The first symbolises James' kingship of Scotland and England, the latter adds Ireland to the equation. The play reflects the King's interest in witchcraft. In 1597, he had published *Daemonologue*, his treatise on the issue. He carried this passion with him when he inherited the English throne, instigating the Witchcraft Act of 1604, which made proven practice of the black arts subject to a mandatory death sentence. In his *Masque of Queens*, presented before the Court on 2 February 1609, Ben Jonson presented a dance for a dozen women in 'the habit of hags or witches ... the opposites of good Fame', in 'a spectacle of strangeness'. If *Macbeth* was indeed Shakespeare's attempt to compliment the King and demonstrate his legitimacy, it could have misfired. James was relieved to be out of Scotland, with its feuding nobility, fierce sectarianism and dark history. When he left Edinburgh for London in 1603, he promised to make a speedy return. It took him seventeen years to do so. There are indications that he viewed with some embarrassment his involvement in the Scottish witch trials. He regarded England as an infinitely more sophisticated place than Scotland. *Macbeth* may have epitomised the more primitive society he was seeking to put behind him. There is no record of a performance at Court, or indeed anywhere, until the astrologer Simon Forman saw the play at the Globe on 20 April 1610. Interestingly, he notes that Macbeth and Banquo rode onto the stage on horseback. He recalls the scene graphically in which Macbeth toasts the absent Banquo at a banquet. The ghost of the murdered thane has occupied his chair and is revealed when he turns it round to be seated. This staging clearly made a huge impression. Francis Beaumont, in his *Knight of the Burning Pestle* in 1607, gives an indication of how it was performed:

> When thou art at thy table with thy friends,
> Merry in heart, and filled with swelling wine,
> I'll come in midst of all thy pride and mirth,
> Invisible to all men but thyself,
> And whisper such a sad tale in thine ear
> Shall make thee let the cup fall from thy hand,
> And stand as mute and pale as death itself.

There are also apparent references in the Porter's comic soliloquy in Act 2, Scene 3, to the trial of the Jesuit, Henry Garnett, in April 1606. One of Garnett's alias was 'Farmer' and the Porter refers to 'a farmer that hath hanged himself on th' expectation of plenty', although the allusion to a farmer who had anticipated a rich harvest and committed suicide when it failed hardly equates. More likely is 'an equivocator that could swear in both the scales against either scale, who committed treason enough for God's sake, but could not equivocate to heaven'. Garnett had written *A Treatise on Equivocation* in 1598 and he was vehemently accused of equivocation at his trial. The word in this context means a statement that is not untrue but which is intended to mislead. It was particularly used by Catholics when interrogated about whether they had harboured priests. Whether these lines were written by Shakespeare or are interpolations by the comedian who played the part, cannot be determined, but they contain their own ambiguity. The Porter's equivocator has indeed committed treason, but it has been 'for God's sake'. Yet equivocation is undoubtedly a theme of the play. It features in the Porter's famous lines on the effect of drinking on sexual potency – 'increaseth the desire but taketh away the performance'. Even more so are the three prophecies that the weird sisters make to Macbeth, which appear to make him invincible, but which are unravelled one by one.

The only extant text of *Macbeth* is that in the First Folio of 1623. A lack of continuity underlines Shakespeare's customary haste in writing. In Act I, Lady Macbeth familiarly declares, 'I have given suck'. In Act III, Macbeth bewails the fact that his heirs will not inherit the throne, but in Act IV, Macduff declares that Macbeth has no children. 'How many children had Lady Macbeth?' indeed! By the time of its first publication, the play contained interpolations. Anomalous scenes involve the goddess Hecate, and two songs were taken from Thomas

Middleton's *The Witch*. As it stands, *Macbeth* is by far the shortest of Shakespeare's tragedies. Yet, despite its textual shortcomings, it is one of his great works. The theme of the seizure of power by a single criminal act further evokes Chapter 8 of *The Prince* that Shakespeare had invoked in *Richard III* – 'Concerning those who have obtained a Principality by Wickedness'. The argument underlies the very course on which Claudius and Macbeth are to embark:

> In seizing a state, the usurper ought to examine closely all those injuries that is necessary for him to inflict , and to do them all at one stroke so as not to have to repeat them daily; and thus by not unsettling men he will be able to reassure them, and win them to himself by benefits.

In a sense, *Macbeth* is *Hamlet* written from the perspective of Claudius: an intense psychological study of the effect that conscience can have on the human psyche. 'Conscience makes cowards of us all,' says Hamlet. Macbeth must overcome huge scruples to do the deed the witches tell him is preordained. Like that of Claudius, his is a crime against the natural order. It is not only an outrage against the fealties of kinship and kingship, it is one against hospitality. 'He's here in double right,' he says of Duncan.

> First, as I am his kinsman and his subject –
> Strong both against the deed; then as his host,
> Who should against the murderer shut the door,
> Not bear the knife myself.

Macbeth powerfully evokes Machiavelli's argument:

> If it were done when 'tis done, then 'twere well
> It were done quickly: if the assassination
> Could trammel up the consequence, and catch
> With his surcease success; that but this blow
> Might be the be-all and end-all here.

Macbeth and Claudius fall short of the injunction to deal with 'all at one stroke' and are led into further crimes, as Machiavelli warned:

> He who does otherwise, either from timidity or evil advice, is always compelled to keep the knife in his hand; neither can he rely on his subjects, nor can they attach themselves to him, owing to their continued and repeated wrongs; For injuries ought to be done all at one time, so that, being tasted less, they offend less.

While Macbeth is inhibited by conscience, it is Lady Macbeth who appears the strong one. 'Screw your courage to the sticking place,' she urges him. Yet, there are indications of frailty within. 'Had he not resembled my father as he slept, I had done 't,' she says of Duncan's murder. It is she who is brought down by guilt, not Macbeth.

Macbeth's crime against nature and his failure to excise the consequences in one swift blow, leads him to further crimes, beginning with the murder of Duncan's guards and ending with the massacre of Macduff's household. Like Claudius, he gains the terrible self-knowledge that the game has not been worth the reckoning. His closing soliloquies are contemplations on the Christ-like theme of 'What shall it profit a man if he gain the whole world yet lose his own soul?' His crimes have placed him beyond a state of salvation and made life meaningless, without divine or human comfort:

> Out, out, brief candle!
> Life's but a walking shadow, a poor player
> That struts and frets his hour upon the stage
> And then is heard no more: it is a tale
> Told by an idiot, full of sound and fury,
> signifying nothing.

Wherefore to Dover

In September 1604, the King's Men departed on their annual tour into Kent. William Shakespeare was probably with them. On 4 October, they played at Dover. The great chalk cliffs were fresh in his memory when he wrote the play he may even then have been contemplating. His description of the cliff that now bears his name has the feel of an eyewitness account:

> How fearful
> And dizzy 'tis, to cast one's eyes so low!
> The crows and choughs that wing the midway air
> Show scarce so gross as beetles; half way down
> Hangs one that gathers samphire, dreadful trade!
> Methinks he seems no bigger than his head:
> The fishermen, that walk upon the beach,
> Appear like mice; and yond tall anchoring bark,
> Diminished to her cock; her cock, a buoy
> Almost too small for sight: the murmuring surge,
> That on the unmolested idle pebbles chafes,

Cannot be heard so high. I'll look no more;
Lest my brain turn, and the deficient sight
Topple down headlong.

In 1606, Richard Burbage was 38. It was some five years since he had created the part of the undergraduate, Hamlet, who was conveniently aged 30; a little elderly, perhaps, for a student. Such was the faith of William Shakespeare in his leading actor that he now determined he should play an old man. He was about to perform the greatest part ever written. The first recorded performance of *King Lear* was at Court: at the Whitehall Palace on St Stephen's Day in 1606. What the royal party made of this, the most socially radical of Shakespeare's works, can only be surmised.

Take physic, pomp;
Expose thyself to what wretches feel,
That thou may shake the superflux to them,
And show the heavens more just.

Act 3.4.,33–36.

So distribution should undo excess,
And each man have enough.

Act 4.1.70–71

The play was not one of Shakespeare's most popular. The royal performance is the only one recorded as occurring during his lifetime, although 'kind Lear' was one of Burbage's outstanding roles, according to his anonymous elegist in 1619. It seems to have been revised a great deal in performance. The quartos of 1608 and 1619 and the First Folio text of 1623 show considerable variations. It is based on one of Shakespeare's favourite sources, Holinshed's *Chronicles*.... The Gloucester sub-plot is taken from a passage in Sidney's *Arcadia*. It is set in a period of ancient British history. Shakespeare follows his usual pattern of placing it in context. The invocations are to the gods, rather than the one God. There are no directly Christian references – not even anachronistically. Yet the play is the apotheosis of his concept of Christian tragedy. If a text is to be taken to epitomise its themes, it must surely come from St Paul's First Epistle to the Corinthians.

Do not deceive yourselves. If any of you think that he is wise by the standards of this age, he should become a 'Fool' so that he may become wise. For the wisdom of this world is foolishness in God's eyes.

It is the Fool who sees the foolishness of Lear's actions, providing a Chorus of sanity in a world run insane. Presumably the part was played by Robert Armin, who probably exercised his noted capacity to extemporise, so how much of the part is his creation and how much Shakespeare's is a matter of speculation. After the storm scenes, the Fool fades from view. We never discover his fate. He is no longer required. In his madness Lear has become his own fool and has learnt the wisdom of the foolish. At the terrible nadir of existence, man finds the truth about himself. Until this moment, his view of the world has been influenced by material circumstance. The lines when he realises that the Bedlam beggar epitomises mankind as it is, without pretentions, nail the play. 'Is man no more than this?'

> Consider him well. Thou owest the worm no silk, the beast no hide, the sheep no wool, the cat no perfume. Ha! Here's three on 's are sophisticated! Thou art the thing itself: unaccommodated man is no more but such a poor bare, forked animal as thou art. Off, off, you lendings! Come unbutton here.

In his madness, Lear finds empathy with man's basic condition. Similarly, Gloucester begins to see reality once he is blinded. 'I stumbled when I saw.' The universe appears as disordered as the forces that control it. 'As flies to wanton boys are we to the gods / They kill us for their sport.'

The process by which the protagonists gather upon the stormy heath is not morally neutral. Actions have consequences. Lear's downfall is the product of his desire for flattery, which Goneril and Regan are prepared to provide. Like Isabella in *Measure for Measure*, Cordelia will not abandon principle for expediency. She cannot bestow on her father the love that duty demands she owes her future husband. There is irony in Gloucester's claim that the gods kill men for their sport. 'There was good sport at his making', is as far as he goes in acknowledging his paternal duty to his illegitimate son, Edmund. It is the very product of this 'good sport' who engineers the downfall that leads to his enlightenment. Shakespeare suggests that sexual acts cannot be morally neutral. Edgar answers his father's impassioned cry against the gods when he tells the stricken Edmund:

> The gods are just and of our pleasant vices
> Make instruments to plague us:
> The dark and vicious place where thee he got
> Cost him his eyes.

Mankind is no longer 'star-crossed', as Edmund had posited, but is responsible for its own destiny. Lear's journey through madness enables him to view the universe as a place governed by man's hypocrisy and pretentions. He underlines Gloucester's newfound sense of reality since his blinding. 'A man may see how this world goes with no eyes.' This vision, born of his suffering, goes beyond the self-knowledge gained by Shakespeare's other tragic heroes. He gains a terrifying universal knowledge of man's innate corruptibility, born of the Fall. 'Thou hast seen a farmer's dog bark at a beggar?' he asks Gloucester:

> And the creature run from the cur? There thou
> Might behold the great image of authority: a dog's
> Obeyed in office.
> Thou rascal beadle, hold thy bloody hand!
> Why dost thou lash that whore? Strip thine own back;
> Thou hotly lusts to use her in that kind
> For which thou whip'st her. The usurer hangs the cozener.
> Through tatter'd clothes small vices do appear;
> Robes and furr'd gowns hold all. Plate sin with gold,
> And the strong lance of justice hurtles breaks:
> Arm it in rags, a pigmy's straw doth pierce it.

Nowhere else does Shakespeare speak with such a radical voice.

It seems odd to go from Shakespeare's greatest play to what was probably his greatest flop. *Timon of Athens* only appears in the First Folio. It may never have seen the light of a public stage. It is difficult to put a date on it, but its theme of total disillusion with corruptible mankind places it in the era of *King Lear*. The play incorporates a number of such bizarre scenes as the one where Timon seeks revenge on the Athenians by paying whores to spread the pox among them.

Another play whose provenance is unclear appeared around this time. Many scholars regard *Pericles* as the product of Shakespeare's collaboration with George Wilkins, who kept an unruly tavern on Cow Gate, Clerkenwell. The host appears to have been as unruly as his tavern. He was arrested several times for punching prostitutes, harbouring pickpockets and assaulting the constabulary. There is no direct evidence that he kept a brothel, as has been suggested. His court appearances suggest nothing more than that the goings-on at the Eastcheap Tavern were not atypical. Yet he was a man of some education who had literary aspirations and connections. Around 1607, he collaborated with William Rowley and John Day in *The Travels of Three English Brothers*, a dramatisation of the recent adventures in Persia of the three Shirley brothers. Around the same time, he wrote *The Miseries of Enforced Marriage*.

Quick Comedy Refined

Ben Jonson had something of a schizophrenic approach towards his art. It is curious that this favourite of the royal court, much-lauded for his masques, should be associated with the most virulent critics of the royal establishment. His Catholicism was a disturbing issue for the authorities. A month before the discovery of the Gunpowder Plot, he supped with the chief conspirator, Robert Catesby, and a number of his fellows. He was brought in for questioning in the immediate aftermath. Since we are in the murky world of plot and counter-plot, what occurred is not clear, but it appears that he agreed to assist the authorities in tracking down a Catholic priest they wished to interview. Needless to say, the quest was not a success. It was not a moment for a priest to raise his head, but Jonson seems to have made his peace with the authorities as far as it could be made. No sooner was this resolved, however, than more trouble appeared. In January, he and his wife Anne were summoned before the Consistory Court, the tribunal that examined offences against ecclesiastical law. It was alleged they had absented themselves from Holy Communion. It was part of a national crackdown on Catholics following the 'Great Treason'. William Shakespeare's daughter, Susanna, was arraigned before such a court for failing to attend the communion service on Easter Sunday in Stratford. The main purpose of such courts was reform, so their censures could be relatively light, although the ultimate penalty of excommunication could mean virtual social exclusion. Jonson's situation was rendered potentially more severe by the observation on the charge sheet that 'he is a poet and by fame a seducer of youth to the Popish religion'. At the hearing on 26 April, he claimed he and Anne had regularly attended their parish church, St Ann Blackfriars, for the previous six months. After a number of further appearances, the authorities seem to have given up on the case, but not entirely. It is marked 'stayed at seal': final judgement had been suspended.

During these latest troubles, Ben was working on his most successful play, In his Prologue, he reveals how rapidly he wrote *Volpone*.

> 'Tis known, five weeks fully penn'd it,
> From his own hand, without a co-adjutor,
> Novice, journey-man, or tutor.

Nor can he resist glorying in its adhesion to the Aristotelian unities:

> And so presents quick comedy refined,
> As best critics have designed;
> The laws of time, place, persons he observeth,
> From no needful rule he swerveth.

In *Volpone*, Ben Jonson imitates a technique of the *Commedia del Arte* in which masks were used to indicate the nature of the characters, but, rather than masks, he used Italian animal names. The play is set in Venice, a city notorious for the avarice, double-dealing and venality represented by Volpone (the Fox). His worship of his wealth is manifested in the first line – 'Good morning to the day; and next, my gold. Open the shrine,' he instructs his servant, Mosca (the Fly), 'that I may see my Saint.'

MOSCA WITHDRAWS THE CURTAIN, AND DISCOVERS PILES OF GOLD, PLATE, JEWELS, ETC.

Volpone continues his adoration of his riches:

Hail the world's soul, and mine! more glad than is
The teeming earth to see the long'd-for sun
Peep through the horns of the celestial Ram,
Am I, to view thy splendour darkening his;
That lying here, amongst my other hoards,
Shew'st like a flame by night; or like the day
Struck out of chaos, when all darkness fled
Unto the centre.

The devotional images are drawn from Jonson's Catholicism. They emphasise the idolatrous nature of this worship of Mammon. So why is this miserly and grasping individual not completely repulsive? Because he is seeking to dupe three characters even more obnoxious than himself. Voltore (the Vulture), a corrupt lawyer; Corbaccio (the Raven), an avaricious old miser; and Corvino (the Carrion Crow), a greedy merchant, are attempting to ingratiate themselves with him in order to inherit his wealth. Volpone's naked deceit of them is abetted by the devious Mosca.

Volpone was first performed early in 1606. That it was hugely popular is recorded by Jasper Mayne in his eulogy *To the Memory of Ben Jonson*. 'So when thy FOXE had ten times acted been / Each day was first, but that was cheaper seen.' It was normal to reduce charges after the opening performance, as attendances fell off, but even after a run of ten days, *Volpone* was still packing in the audiences. The quarto informs us that the play was performed at the universities of Oxford and Cambridge 'to great applause'. Indeed, he dedicates the play 'to the most noble and most equal sisters, the two famous universities, for their love and acceptance shewn to his poem' [i.e. *Volpone*].

The preface cannot have endeared Ben Jonson to those he calls 'the writers of these days'.

> Not only their manners, but their natures are inverted, and nothing remaining with them of the dignity of poet, but the abused name, which every scribe usurps; that now, especially in dramatic, or, as they term it, stage-poetry, nothing but ribaldry, profanation, blasphemy, all license of offence to God and man is practised.

The only dramatist who escapes censure is Ben himself:

> For my particular, I can, and from a most clear conscience, affirm, that I have ever trembled to think toward the least profaneness: have loathed the use of such foul and unwashed bawdry, as is now made the food of the scene.

Jonson exhibits breathtaking gall when he claims that nothing in his works has ever caused upset. 'What nation, or general order or state have I provoked? What public person? Whether I have not in all these preserved their dignity, as mine own person, safe?' He distances himself from previous controversies by implying his co-authors were responsible. 'My works are read, allowed (I speak of those that are entirely mine)', although Thomas Nashe claimed to have written only the introduction and first act of *The Isle of Dogs*, imputing that Jonson had written the rest.

It would be four years before Ben's next play, *Epicene, or The Silent Woman*, was presented by The Children of the Queen's Revels at Whitefriars around December 1609. It was not a success. In his conversation with William Drummond, Ben hinted that the play was aptly named since the audience had remained silent at the close. The reason that Ben ceased to work with the King's Men might have had little to do with the offence his preface to *Volpone* may have caused. He might have concentrated on the more lucrative production of masques, creating six between the productions of *Volpone* and *Epicene*. He returned to the King's Men in 1610, with another sparkling comedy, *The Alchemist*. There are indications it was intended for performance at Blackfriars, but another bout of plague drove it to the provinces and it was first acted in Oxford. There is an air of topicality in the opening with an upper-crust gentleman, Lovewit, quitting his London home for fear of plague, leaving Jeremy, his butler, in sole charge. No sooner has he left than the trusted servant assumes the alias of Captain Face and turns the house into a criminal den, with the aid of Subtle, a fellow conman, the alchemist of the title, and Doll Common, a prostitute. Complex but hilarious scenes follow as the venality of society is exposed in such characters as the aptly named pharmacist, Abel Drugger, and the libertine, Sir Epicure Mammon.

In 1611 Ben returned to the tragic muse with *Catiline His Conspiracy*, a play set in the era of Julius Caesar, an important character in the play, which includes the Senecan necessities of a ghost and chorus. Despite Ben's ambitions to bring the splendours of the classical unities to the public, it had an even worse reception than *Sejanus*. The poet Leonard Digges describes it as 'tedious (though well-laboured)'. Nahum Tate, while admiring the work, acknowledged its lack of success: 'How few are there that this fine work approve.' Characteristically, did not ascribe the failure to his own shortcomings. 'Nothing is more dangerous than a foolish praise,' he wrote in his preface to the published edition, citing audiences who 'commend out of affection, self-tickling, an easiness, or imitation'. He justifies himself further in the dedication to the Earl of Pembroke:

> Posterity may pay your benefit the honour and thanks, when it shall know that you dare, in these jig-given times, to countenance a legitimate poem. I must call it so, against all noise of opinion, from whose crude and airy reports I appeal to that great and singular faculty of judgement in Your Lordship, able to vindicate truth from error.

Ben's view that his work would get the approbation it deserved was partly justified. It was performed frequently at the Restoration, but since then it has faded again into the obscurity to which its earliest audiences consigned it.

After the failure of *Catiline*, Ben Jonson gave up, sensibly, but probably resentfully, the writing of Senecan tragedy. In 1616, his position as official Court poet was recognised by the award of an annual pension of 100 marks and an annual butt of sack. He may be regarded as the first Poet Laureate.

The Vogue of France

George Chapman had become a sharer at Blackfriars, acquiring a 'full sixte parte' of the 'Lease, goodes and profitts'. His fascination with contemporary French politics and history is encapsulated in a series of plays he wrote on the theme. *Bussy D'Ambois*, was performed by the Children of Paul's around 1603/4. A quarto of 1641 associates Nathan Field with the lead role. It follows events in the life of Louis de Clermont, Seigneur de Bussy d'Amboise, except that the actual Bussy came from the upper ranks of the aristocracy, whereas Chapman's hero is humbler born and the supernatural elements incorporated in the play may not have featured in the Seigneur's life. This is widely regarded as Chapman's finest play, even his masterpiece, but that word pales when it is compared to the finest works of the era. It lacks immediate dramatic quality. It opens with a long and tortuous soliloquy. Chapman maintains the *grand guignol* vogue of earlier times, presaging the decadence to come. Bussy embarks on a licentious affair with Tamyra, wife of the powerful and corrupt Count Mountsurry, who, to get her to confess it, tortures her on the rack. He forces her to write to Bussy, in her own blood, to arrange an assignation. A friar, who has passed messages between the lovers, dies of shock at her torture. Mountsurry dons his robes to deliver the message. The melodrama increases when the Friar's ghost warns Bussy of impending disaster. In the subsequent confrontation, he is gunned down in an early use of firearms on stage. The play has had few revivals since the era of its first performance. Yet it has received considerable acclaim. The poet Swinburne admired its 'force and vehemence of imagination'. The skilfully drawn character of Bussy redeems it. He lives in a society in which ingratiation with the great is the key to temporal success. It is a world in which, in the words of the opening soliloquy, 'Fortune, not Reason, rules the state of things, Reward goes backward, Honour on his head:' He attempts to reconcile himself to this actuality, even accepting a huge bribe, but he cannot curb his turbulent nature. Like Shakespeare's tragic heroes, his foibles bring him down. The play incorporates the Shakespearean theme of sexual degeneracy reflecting a decayed society. Yet, as Shakespeare realised, strict adhesion to the Senecan model was not the route to posterity. While not entirely concurring with John Dryden's vitriolic verdict on the play, it may be seen as a flawed work:

> I have sometimes wondered, in the reading, what has become of those glaring colours which annoyed me in *Bussy D'Ambois*, but when I had taken up what I supposed a fallen star, I found I had been cozened with a jelly; nothing but a cold dull mass, which glittered no longer than it was shooting; a dwarfish thought, dressed up in gigantic words, repetition in abundance, looseness of expression, and gross hyperboles; the sense of one line expanded prodigiously into ten; and, to sum up all, uncorrect English, and a hideous mingle of false poetry and true nonsense; or, at best, a scantling of wit, which lay gasping for life, and groaning beneath a heap of rubbish.

That *Bussy D'Ambois* was a popular success is demonstrated by the appearance of a sequel. *The Revenge of Bussy D'Ambois* was entered onto the Stationers' Register on 17 April 1612 and probably performed by the Children of the Chapel. Its dramatic effect is hardly enhanced by many important developments occurring off-stage as subjects of reportage. Even Chapman, in his preface, acknowledged that 'in the scaenicall presentation it might meet with some maligners'.

Bussy gives an inkling of the nature of the audience at Blackfriars. The host of classical allusions indicates that Chapman intended to flatter an audience that considered itself more sophisticated than that in the public theatres. It was also an audience that had come to expect the iconoclastic attacks on the political establishment that were the Children of the Revels' stock-in-trade. Plays without such a provenance were likely to fail, as was the case with Francis Beaumont's *The Knight of the Burning Pestle*, in 1607. Although the play was a satire and arguably the first example of a parody in the English drama, it is a satire on the merchant classes rather than being pointedly directed at the authorities. The subtleties of this satire of city comedy masquerading as a satire of courtly romances such as *Don Quixote* eluded the audience. Its failure was the subject of a letter from its publisher, Walter Burre, to 'HIS MANY WAIES ENDEERED FRIEND Master Robert Keysar', who had taken over the management of the Revels Children:

> SIR, this vnfortunate child … was by his parents (perhaps because hee was so vnlike his brethren) exposed to the wide world, who for want of iudgment, or not vnderstanding the priuy marke of Ironie about it (which shewed it was no ofspriong of any vulgar braine) vtterly reiected it: so that for want of acceptance it was euen ready to give up the Ghost, and was in danger to have bene smothered in perpetuall oblivion, if you (out of your direct ANTIPATHY to ingratitude) had not bene moved both to relieve and cherish it.

The implication is that the fantastical plot and extraordinary setting, with members of the audience unsure what they were watching was exonerated by Keysar's realisation of the quality of the piece, a view which, in the longer term, proved justified.

After a seemly pause in their capacity to create controversy, the Children of Blackfriars (as the Children of the Chapel had become) upset a royal house in 1608 – but that of Bourbon, rather than Stuart. Whereas previously, living grandees had been referenced on stage by thinly-veiled satire and innuendo, now actual names and incidents were invoked. The double play, *The conspiracie and Tragedy of Charles, Duke of Byron, Marshall of France* was performed soon after the publication in 1607 of Chapman's main source *A General Inventory of the History of France* by Edward Grimeston. Byron was another contemporary figure. Charles de Gontaut, duc de Biron, was executed for treason in 1602 for plotting to overthrow the King and divide the kingdom into its constituent parts. He too is brought down by overweening pride, comparing himself to Hercules, Alexander and other classical heroes, but it was a scene in *The tragedie* in which the French Queen slapped the face of the King's mistress that caused offence. It was made even more sensitive by reflecting a real situation. It was sufficiently common for those in the upper echelons of society to take mistresses for it almost to be regarded as normal. Marriage was for dynastic purposes; sexual satisfaction was to be found elsewhere, but it was expected that appropriate proprieties be observed. Reigning monarchs bore such titles as 'Most Christian King' and 'Defender of the Faith', added to which, humbler transgressors against strict sexual codes faced censure, so it ill-behoved those in high places to flaunt their peccadilloes. An exception to this unwritten rule was King Henry IV of France, a womaniser on the grand scale. His promise to marry his *maitresse en titre*, Gabrielle d'Estrées, who had borne him three children, was somewhat inhibited by the fact that he was already married to his second cousin, Margaret of Valois. That marriage was childless and Henry sought an annulment, possibly to enable a match with Gabrielle, whose fecundity was not in doubt. The marriage was indeed annulled, but Gabrielle died in childbirth that month. Her replacement Henriette d'Entragues, Marquise de Verneuil, not only aspired to marriage, but possessed a note from the King, promising such. Material considerations triumphed over emotion. Henry had borrowed heavily from Europe's banker, Francisco de' Medici, Grand Duke of Tuscany. An obvious way to negate this debt was to turn it into a dowry, so, on 9 December 1600, he married Medici's daughter, Marie. The circumstance of the marriage did not escape the rejected mistress, Henriette dubbing the new Queen '*La Grosse Banquière*'.

Queen Marie fulfilled amply the unspoken codicil of the marriage contract by delivering a Dauphin within a year and going on to have five more children, but apart from necessary sexual encounters, the couple had effectively separated by 1603. The Queen took exception to her husband's conspicuous promiscuity and his flaunting of his mistress at Court as if she were his unofficial wife. The Queen's dissatisfaction was underlined by the King's parsimony with her regal allowance, preventing her from establishing the courtly establishment befitting her station. Indeed, the mistress appears to have exercised a greater influence over events than the Queen, swaying the King's conversion to Catholicism as a means towards national unity. This influence must have been galling for the Queen, whose coronation Henry persisted in postponing. There may have been reasons for this. He may have had little faith in her judgement or abilities. If she were crowned, with the Dauphin a minor, she would become Regent in the event of his death.[4]

Word of the tensions between Queen and mistress reached London, the ears of George Chapman and those of the sophisticated audience at Blackfriars. The face-slapping scene in *The tragedie* referenced current gossip, so its inclusion was irresistible. Another scene in the play caused offence for different reasons. The Duc de Biron had been sent by Henry IV as an emissary in 1601 to thank Queen Elizabeth for her support against the Spanish. His lack of tact infuriated her when he lamented the death of the Earl of Essex. Although the topic was from the previous reign, anything that imputed that an uprising against a divinely-anointed monarch was legitimate was *outré* and James' reign had not been without such suspected conspiracies as the Main and Bye plots from the outset.

There seems to have been considerable awareness in informed circles in both England and France as to what was occurring in the other's capital. During 1603, the English Ambassador, Sir Ralph Winwood, complained to the Assistant Secretary of State, the Seigneur de Villeroy, that 'certain base Comedians' had put on such plays as the 'Tragedy of the late Queen of Scottes'. This had an effect; Winwood informed Lord Salisbury that he had obtained an injunction against the presentation of such plays and that three of the performers had been imprisoned. This caused some upset. 'Some standers by' commented that 'the death of the Duke of Guise hath ben plaied at London [and] by some others that the Massacre of St Bartholomew hath ben publickly acted, and this King represented upon the stage'.[5] Winwood's reference was to *L'Ecossaise, ou Le Désastre* by Antoine de Montchrestien, an author as bellicose as many of his English fellows. He fought a number of duels, narrowly escaping death in one in 1603. Within two years he had killed his opponent in another. Potentially facing a capital charge, he fled to England. He had had the wit to dedicate the 1st edition of *L'Ecossaise* to James I, who apparently had no objections to this play about his mother and appears to have assisted Montchrestien's return to France without charge.

The French Ambassador in London. Antoine Lefèvre de la Boderie was a trusted associate of King Henry and a jealous guardian of the royal reputation. He must have visited the Blackfriars Theatre because he complained to the King's chief minister, Lord Salisbury, about the comedians who had dared to represent the French Queen on the public stage in an angry altercation with the King's mistress, culminating in her giving her a slap (*un soufflet*). The company had completely disregarded the prohibitions placed on the play by Sir George Buck, the Master of the Revels. Salisbury must have referred the matter to King James, who would not have welcomed a diplomatic clash with France. The twin plays were duly suppressed but, in an astonishing piece of audacity, revived when the Court left London that summer. The King was predictably furious and swift action was taken. All dramatic performances were suppressed and the Company ejected from Blackfriars. Nor were the Children exempt from the regal wrath. Three were imprisoned in the Bridewell. The intention appears to have been to break up the company. Chapman again followed precedent and fled, seeking refuge with the influential Duke of Lennox and writing to Buc disclaiming any part in the presentation.

There was to be an even greater cause for the King's ire. A play – not surprisingly now lost – called *The Silver Mine* was presented at Blackfriars, The matter is revealed in a letter to his Assistant Secretary of State from the French Ambassador on 8 April 1608. 'A day or two before,' he reported, 'they had slandered their King, his mine in Scotland and all his favourites in a most pointed fashion.' The reference was to the discovery of a bed of silver ore near Linlithgow in 1606. The find caused great excitement and the King commandeered a lease on the resultant mine, probably hoping the expected riches would assuage his financial difficulties. It proved a false hope. The lack of consistency in the quality of the ore made it a less than commercial proposition. More enigmatic is de la Boderie's statement that the character playing the King railed 'against heaven over the flight of a bird and had a gentleman beaten for calling off his dogs'. This may be based on actual incidents. James regarded hunting as part of his divinely ordained prerogative. Rather than restrict his pursuit of game to Crown lands as had his predecessors, he claimed the right to ride where he pleased, over crops newly planted and those ripe for harvesting, seizing farm labourers as huntsmen and imposing himself and his entourage on the hospitality of landowners. A burlesque hunting scene would hit a chord. The issue was mentioned in a report on 24 March by the Florentine agent in London, Ottaviano Lotti:

> A comedy has been acted here by the public players which has given a good deal of displeasure, because it made fun of the new fashion found in Scotland. One expects to see the players banned, and the author of the play has run off in fear of losing his life, probably because he mingled ideas that were too wicked, in which so much was concealed.

'Ideas that were too wicked' probably alluded to the King's liking for the company of attractive young men, with obvious innuendos. Although there is no absolute evidence for James' bisexuality, it was probably the case,[6] although in *Basilikon Doron*, his treatise on kingship, he had listed sodomy among the crimes 'ye are bound in conscience never to forgive'. Such slurs against the royal person amounted to treason, so it is little wonder that the anonymous author of the play fled in fear of losing his life. So who was he? The finger points at Marston. Not only was he a dramatist associated with the company, he had a reputation as the creator of pointed political satire. He had escaped imprisonment with Chapman and Jonson after *Eastward Ho!* by fleeing until the furore had subsided. It appears he did the same again. This time he was not so fortunate. A man called John Marston recorded as incarcerated in Newgate Prison on 8 June was probably the playwright. Newgate was the severest prison in the land, reserved for the most serious offenders. It may have been intended to charge him with seditious libel, an offence that could lead to the bodily maiming inflicted on Stubbs and Page, or even with treason, for which the penalty was death. Marston's involvement as a sharer in the Blackfriars could have made him a marked man. His best-known play, *The Malcontent*, could be interpreted as a satire on King James' Court. His *Parasitaster, or The Fawn*, presented by the Children around 1605 depicted the Court of Gonzago, a stupid and pompous Italian Duke, whose courtiers are lecherous place-seekers. The parallels with the Court of King James were evident, but, as with all skilful satire, the authorities were rendered powerless to act because, in so doing, they would acknowledge the accuracy of the parallel.

Once again, when things had calmed down, the King's ire abated. His love of the theatre was too great for him to exclude himself from it for too long, but there was another factor that was probably even stronger for the cash-strapped monarch. In his letter to de Sillery, de la Boderie stated that to persuade the King to end the prohibition on their acting, 'four other companies which are still there are already offering a hundred thousand francs, which could well restore permission to them'. If such a bribe was what was required, it seems to have been paid off, for the theatres were soon back in business – but that is not to say that things returned to the previous *status quo*. 'At the very least,' de la Boderie adds, 'this will be on condition that they should no longer perform any modern histories nor speak of contemporary affairs.' That the authorities took the issue extremely seriously is encapsulated in the threatening words 'on pain of death'.

Chapter Eight

We are Such Stuff as Dreams are Made On

Oblivium Sacrem

John Marston's play, *The Dutch Courtesan*, was among the entertainments presented at Court in the summer of 1607 for the visit of the Queen's brother, the King of Denmark. The sub-plot is a satire on the Puritan sect the Family of Love, which James had described in *Basilikon Doron* as an *infamen baptistarum*, so it would have gone down well, as would the portrayal of the major character, Malheureux as a hypocritical Puritan who, like Angelo in *Measure for Measure*, cannot resist his carnal desires. The play's major theme that the sanctity of the marriage bed is always preferable to tawdry carnality made it an obvious choice for performance during the celebrations of the marriage of the King's daughter, Princess Elizabeth.

Yet Marston's rehabilitation signified little for he had resolved to take holy orders, perhaps as a result of spiritual reflection during his incarceration. After a period of study, he was ordained deacon on 24 September 1609 and priest three months later. His rapid transformation from playwright to clergyman caused comment. Yet it cannot entirely have been a surprise. His works are permeated with the kind of moral dilemmas that may have generated a process of conversion, a point of which his father – an eminent lawyer in the Middle Temple, who had been deeply disappointed at his son's failure to follow him into that profession – appeared aware. In the first draft of his will, he referred to 'my wilfull disobedient sonne' and prayed that 'god blesse hym and give hym trewe knowledge of himself and to forgoe his playes, vayne studdyes and fooleries'. He later wrote 'Man purposeth and god disposeth his will to be donne and send my son his grace to feare and serve him.' Marston's father-in-law was Dr William Wilkes, a Chaplain to the King. Ben Jonson told William Drummond that 'Marston wrott his Father jn Lawes preachings & his Father jn Law his Commedies.' This enigmatic remark perhaps expresses Ben's mischievous view that Marston possessed greater piety than Dr Wilkes, but the chaplain had a better sense of humour. In 1610, the newly ordained priest became 'clerk' (curate) at Barford St Martin in Wiltshire. In 1616, he was appointed Rector of Christchurch in Hampshire. He wrote nothing more in any genre, at least not for publication, spending the rest of his life shunning the publicity he had once so effortlessly garnered. His name was even removed from the edition of his works, published in 1633. Such self-effacement was long his declared intent, in paradoxical contrast with the furores his writings provoked. The epitaph on his grave in the Temple Church reads *Oblivium Sacrem* – 'Sacred to oblivion', a sentiment he had expressed in his dedicatory address to *The Scourge of Villainy* some forty years before.

> Let others pray
> Forever their fair poems flourish may,
> But as for me, hungry Oblivion,
> Devour me quick. Accept my orison,
> My earnest prayer, which do importune thee,
> With gloomy shade of thy still empery
> To veil both me and my rude poesy.

A Wonderful Consimility

Not all the dramatic offerings at Blackfriars were contentious. *The Knight of the Burning Pestle* was a notable exception. A similar fate awaited *The Faithful Shepherdess*, possibly the debut solo drama of John Fletcher, which received a lukewarm reception in 1608. It was published in quarto in 1609 with commendatory verses by Ben Jonson, George Chapman, Francis Beaumont and Nathan Field. In his 'Address to the Reader', Fletcher explained that the failure was due to the audience's mistaken expectation that the play would feature dancing, singing and shepherds wearing 'gray cloaks with curtailed dogs in strings'. This led him to give his noted definition of tragicomedy, the genre into which he considered the play fell:

> A tragicomedy is not so called in respect of mirth and killing, but in respect it wants deaths, which is enough to make it no tragedy, yet brings some near it, which is enough to make it no comedy.

The first product of his collaboration with Francis Beaumont, *The Woman Hater*, was published in 1607, with the information that it had been acted by the Children of Paul's, who'd ceased to perform in the summer of 1606, but with no indication as to its authorship. A second quarto of 1649 attributes it to the playwrights as co-authors. The play is notable for its first recorded usage of a number of words, including 'earshot' and 'prostitute'.

'There was a wonderful consimility [mutual similarity] between him and Mr John Fletcher,' wrote Aubrey of Francis Beaumont, 'which caused that dearness of friendship between them.' Aubrey, who had a penchant for scurrilous and not-always-accurate gossip, hints that the relationship may have gone beyond the professional. He heard that they 'lived together on the Bankside, not far from the playhouse, both bachelors; lay together ... had ... the same clothes and cloak, etc. ... They ... had one wench in the house between them, which they did admire,' he adds enigmatically. Their background is another indication of the rising social status of the theatre. Beaumont's father was a Justice of the Common Pleas, his grandfather Master of the Rolls. He, too, appeared bound for a legal career, entering the Inner Temple in 1600 at the age of 16, but he lacked enthusiasm for the law, becoming a member of the group centred on the *Mermaid Tavern* on Cheapside that he extolled in a verse letter to Ben Jonson:

> What things have we seen
> Done at the Mermaid! heard words that have been
> So nimble and so full of subtle flame,
>
> As if that everyone from whence they came
> Had meant to put his whole wit in a jest,
> And had resolved to live a fool the rest
> Of his dull life.

John Fletcher was born in 1573 in Rye where his father, a future Bishop, was vicar. His son also appeared destined for the church, becoming a Bible Clerk[1] at his Cambridge College. He too became part of the Mermaid set. In 1607, he wrote verses prefacing the quarto edition of *Volpone*.

Perhaps the most successful product of the collaboration was *The Scornful Lady*, first performed by the Children of the Revels, probably in 1609. It is one of a number of plays in which a lady urges her loved one to kill his closest friend, of which *Much Ado About Nothing* is the best-known. It was revived by the King's Men in 1624.

A play by Fletcher that enjoyed considerable, and occasionally controversial, success was *The Woman's Prize, or The Tamer Tamed*, which is noteworthy as the only sequel to a Shakespeare play written in his lifetime by another playwright. Kate, 'the Shrew' of the original title, has died and Petruchio has married Maria, who he attempts to 'tame' like Kate. In scenes drawn from Aristophanes' *Lysistrata*, she refuses to consummate the marriage until he changes his attitudes and persuades other women to do the same. The tricks they pull on each other reflect Shakespeare's play, except that Maria always comes out best. When Petruchio feigns illness to gain his wife's sympathy, she has him walled up as a plague victim. In desperation, he feigns death and is borne onstage in a coffin.

Maria weeps, but not from grief, but in apparent fury at his 'unmanly, foolish life. How far below a man, how far from reason.' This volley of abuse causes Petruchio to sit up in his coffin and confess his misery at the situation. The tamer has been tamed and Maria is prepared to normalise marital relations. 'I have tamed ye, / And now I am your servant.'

The epilogue has a vision of marriage that would be more familiar to later audiences:

> The Tamer's tamed, but so, as nor the men
> Can find one just cause to complain of, when
> They fitly do consider in their lives,
> They should not reign as Tyrants o'er their wives.
> Nor can the women from this precedent
> Insult, or triumph: it being aptly meant
> To teach both Sexes due equality.
> And as they stand bound, to love mutually.
> If this effect, arising from a cause
> Well laid, and grounded, may deserve applause,
> We something more than hope, our honest ends
> Will keep the men, and women too, our friends.

It would appear that the play was revised considerably in the course of production. Like *The Taming of the Shrew*, the original setting was probably Italy, but, as it has come down to us, the setting is London, although the names are still Italianate. A 1633 revival provoked Sir Henry Herbert, Master of the Revels, to issue a warrant to the King's Men prohibiting 'the acting of your play called *The Tamer Tamed* or *The Taming of the Tamer*, this afternoon, or any more till you have leave from me – and this is at your peril'. He had received complaints that the play contained 'foul and offensive material'. The Company complied with the prohibition, reviving *The Scornful Lady*, a play that became standard in the repertoire after the Restoration. Samuel Pepys saw it six times.

The precise nature of the collaboration is difficult to determine. The quartos of their works sometimes attribute authorship to one alone, sometimes to both. The First Folio of 1647 and the second, of 1679, add to the confusion, incorporating plays that are indubitably the work of others and omitting ones clearly theirs. Although the Second Folio includes fifty-three plays, it is generally thought the collaboration represents no more than fifteen. The tortuous plots and obscure allusions have consigned many of the works into oblivion, belying their contemporary estimation.

The Children of the Chapel never returned to Blackfriars, probably as a result of official sanction. In 1609, Richard Burbage achieved his long-unfulfilled desire to open an indoor theatre. That there was no public protest from the local residents probably reflects an unofficial royal decree. These were, after all, Grooms of the King's Bedchamber. The Company did not occupy the space vacated by the Children, but the *Dorter* of the old monastery. Galleries were erected to increase capacity, which may have been as many as a thousand. The Burbage brothers still owned the freehold, so the Company agreed a twenty-one-year lease with them at a rental of £40 per year. As with the Globe, it was necessary to bring in other sharers to spread the load. Each paid £5 14*s*. 4*d*. towards the annual rental. Richard Burbage, William Shakespeare, Henry Condell, John Hemminges, Will Sly and Cuthbert Burbage are familiar names. The seventh sharer was Thomas Evans, a cousin of Henry Evans. His use of a proxy was probably because two previous sharers were engaged in a legal action against him. He probably thought it politic to conceal his assets. He is listed as the sharer in later actions. That the same plays were performed at the Globe in summer and at Blackfriars in winter is indicated by the first quarto of *The Duchess of Malfi*, published in 1623. It was 'presented privately, at the Black-friars, and publiquely at the Globe'. The concept of 'privately' is curious. Was the Blackfriars Theatre a kind of theatrical club, or was attendance selective? There is no such doubt about the Globe's status as a popular playhouse.

The Children of the Chapel maintained their connection with the old monastic system by moving to the former Whitefriars Monastery. This had been established as a theatre in 1608 on a seven-year lease by the poet/playwright Michael Drayton, Thomas Woodford (nephew of Thomas Lodge) and the actor, Martin Slater. The company was re-formed as The Children of the Queen's Revels, although the precise identity of the companies performing at the Whitefriars is confused. Plays such as *The Scornful Lady*, *Epicene*, Nathan Field's *A Woman in a Weathercock*, and Robert Daborne's *A Christian turn'd Turk* were presented, but the venture was not a success. Another bout of plague closing the theatres for several months must have contributed. After little more than a year, the lease was taken over by the Court lutenist, Philip Rosseter, Robert Keysar, a goldsmith, Martin Slater, who retained his interest and the dramatist (and future pirate!) Lording Barry, who was in the process of suing six of the sharers in the Blackfriars Theatre. Curiously, the seventh sharer, William Shakespeare, was not included in the action. Keysar had bought John Marston's shares in the Blackfriars Theatre for £100. He claimed that Richard Burbage and the others had promised not to defraud him of any part of the profits, which he put 'at the leaste of fifteene hundred pounds', a sum which indicates the returns investment in the theatre could bring.[2] Through another onset of the plague, the Blackfriars Theatre was closed between July and December in 1608 and, in a renewed outbreak, between July and December in 1609, so those profits were amassed in just six months. Keysar's suit was made more urgent by his claim that he had laid out £500 to maintain the company's boys in expectation of the renewal of 'playes in the said howse upon the ceasing of the general sicknes'.

The pandemic could not curtail the King's love of the drama. Despite the closure, the King's Men frequently appeared at Court during the Christmas Revels. On 5 April 1609, John Hemminges collected payment for twelve performances. Three weeks later he collected a further £40, 'his Majesty's reward for their private practice in time of infection'. This was royal recognition of the need to keep the company solvent in troubled times. A year later, Hemminges collected another £30 payment for the King's Men, 'being restrained from public playing within the City of London in the time of infection for the space of six weeks in which time they performed privately for his Majesty's service'.

On 27 April 1611, a new company, Lady Elizabeth's Men, under the patronage of the King's daughter, received the royal patent to play in London. It drew on former boy actors, including Nathan Field and Joseph Taylor. Initially, it toured the provinces, but next year it returned to London, playing four times at Court. Possibly the need for a permanent location caused it to join forces with the King's Revels Children at the Whitefriars, performing Middleton's *A Chaste Maid in Cheapside*. Their tenure was brief. The lease expired in 1614 and was not renewed. The theatre staggered along, probably as a venue for itinerant companies until 1621 when he owner, Sir Anthony Ashley, 'turned out the players'.

In the early years of James' reign, many of the original members of the King's Men were fading away. An obvious source for replacements was the children's companies, those 'little eyases' evoked in *Hamlet*. 'In processe of time,' declared Cuthbert Burbage in the 1630s, 'the boyes growing up to bee men, which were Underwood, Field, Ostler and were taken up to strengthen the Kings service.'

John Underwood had played with the Children of the Chapel in *Cynthia's Revels* in 1600, together with Salamon Pavy, Nathan Field and in *The Poetaster* in 1601, together with Field and Ostler. He joined the King's Men at around the same time as Ostler and appeared in the 1610 production of *The Alchemist*, as well as *Cataline* in 1611, as Bonario in a subsequent production of *Volpone* and in the revival of *The Duchess of Malfi* in 1621. He is listed in eighteen of the cast lists in the Beaumont and Fletcher Second Folio.

William Ostler enjoyed a successful, albeit brief, career with the Company. Having joined it around 1608, he appeared in the 1610 production of *The Alchemist*, as well as in Fletcher's historical fantasy, *Bonduca*, his tragedy, *Valentinian* and the somewhat bizarre Beaumont and Fletcher play, *The Captain*.

Sir John Davies, described him as 'the Roscius of these times' and 'Sole king of actors'. In 1611 he married John Heminges' daughter Thomasine, becoming a sharer in both the Blackfriars and Globe theatres. On 18 May 1612, Beaumont Ostler was baptised. The playwright was probably his godfather. Ostler played Antonio in *The Duchess of Malfi* at Blackfriars in 1613, which later transferred to the Globe. His death in December 1614 must have been sudden and unexpected, for he died intestate. Under Common Law, his estate should have passed to his wife, but her father seized the shares that were her due. That all was not well in the family was demonstrated when Thomasine sued her father for their return. The outcome is uncertain, but it would appear he retained them, perhaps by buying off his daughter. He was probably seeking to prevent them passing beyond the control of the other sharers, which could be the outcome were his daughter to marry again. A parallel case four years later demonstrates the concern. In 1608, Anne, widow of Augustine Phillips, married John Witter of Mortlake; a clause in her late husband's will stipulated that should she remarry, the executorship of his estate should pass to his overseers, John Heminges, Richard Burbage, William Sly and Timothy Whitehorn, who was probably his lawyer. It would appear that the executers allowed the dividends of the shareholding to continue, which would have devolved to Witter as the husband. Anne died in January 1618. In the following year, Witter sued Heminges and Condell in the Court of Requests for the return on interest forfeited while the Globe was being rebuilt. The proceedings revealed that Witter had deserted his wife after receiving considerable sums in respect of the shares and Heminges 'out of charitie was at the charges of the buryeing of her'. The defence case was based on Witter's ineligibility to benefit under the terms of Phillips' will. He appears to have realised his cause was hopeless and did not proceed. On 29 November, the Court delivered its judgement in favour of the defendants.

The King's Men moved rapidly to replace Ostler, recruiting Robert Benfield, a leading member of Lady Elizabeth's Men. In 1613 he had appeared in Fletcher's *The Coxcomb* and in Fletcher, Field and Massinger's *The Honest Man's Fortune*. He appears in eighteen of the twenty-five cast-lists added to the Beaumont and Fletcher Second Folio.

John Sinklo fades from view after his appearance in the Induction to *The Malcontent*. That the skinny-man roles appear to have been taken over by John Shank is revealed by his casting in the 'lean-clown' role of Hilano in the 1629 production of Massinger's *The Picture*. He had begun his career in the closing years of Elizabeth's reign with Pembroke's Men, working subsequently with Queen Elizabeth's Men. In 1610 he was with Prince Henry's Men, with which he was a sharer in 1613. He was a popular draw, who was a sharer with the King's Men by 1619. He played the Curate in its revival of *The Scornful Lady* in 1624.

He had an important role in training its boy actors, including John Honyman, Thomas Holcomb, Thomas Pollard, Nicholas Burt and John Thompson. Walter Clun and Charles Hart were apprenticed to Richard Robinson. In *Historia Histrionica*, James Wright stated that Hart, who was baptised on 11 December 1625, played the Duchess in James Shirley's *The Cardinal*, 'the first play that gave him reputation'. Nicholas Burt was apprenticed to John Shank with the King's Men before joining Queen Henrietta's Men and playing Clariana in Shirley's *Love's Cruelty*. Other notable boy actors included John Lacy and Robert Shatterell.

William Shakespeare was entering the final phase of his literary career. Although he never seems to have been involved in the production of the masques beloved at court – he remained a man of the public theatre, his instincts as a dramatist caused him to bring a flavour of these entertainments into the popular arena. In these closing years of his dramatic output, he embarked upon a series of fantasies incorporating such elements. *Cymbeline* was probably written around 1609. Together with *The Winter's Tale* and *The Tempest*, it might have been written specifically for performance at Blackfriars, with its intimate atmosphere and potential lighting effects, but this is not the case. During May 1611, Simon Forman saw performances of *Cymbeline* and *The Winter's Tale* at the Globe. He seems, literally, to have lost the plot with *Cymbeline* for he concludes his summary of the play with the words, 'And how she was found by Lucius, etc.'. Shakespeare achieved his masque-like effect in Act V, Scene 4, when apparitions of his family appear before the condemned Posthumous Leonatus. The stage direction is on a grand scale. 'Jupiter descends in thunder and lightening; sitting upon an eagle, he throws a thunderbolt.' Forman makes no mention of this amazing scene. Had he seen it, he surely would have referred to it. Perhaps it just featured in one of some forty unnamed plays performed before the King around 1610. With its somewhat unusual setting in Milford Haven, it may have formed part of the celebrations for the investiture of Prince Henry as Prince of Wales that year.

The Winter's Tale contains Shakespeare's best-known stage direction: 'Exit, pursued by bear.' Frustratingly, Forman makes no mention of this scene and how it was played. It is tempting to suggest that the famous Sackerson, or his colleague Harry Hunks, might have been hired in from the nearby Bear Garden, but this is highly unlikely. These fearsome animals were capable of killing anyone who strayed into their path. It would have been madness to have introduced them into a public theatre. The play was performed before the King on 5 November 1611 and again as part of the festivities surrounding the marriage of Princess Elizabeth. It may have been for this occasion that the play acquired elements of the court masque. The dance of the twelve satyrs in Act IV appears to have been lifted from Ben Jonson's *Masque of Oberon*, which had been performed at Whitehall on 1 January. The spectacle is announced with the words 'one three of them, by their own report, hath danced before the king'.

The last of Shakespeare's fantasy trilogy is *The Tempest*. Although set in a magical world, it was rooted in widely credited travellers' tales. It reflects the growing interest in the world beyond that led to England's great trading empire. The popular imagination was caught by the remarkable voyage of Admiral George Somers in 1609. A celebrated figure who had sailed with Drake and been instrumental in founding the Virginia colony, while conveying stores and settlers to Jamestown, his ship, the *Sea Venture*, was driven ashore on Bermuda in a storm. The Admiral and his crew remained on the island for ten months, sustained by an abundance of flora and fauna. Most disturbing were the mysterious sounds that permeated the air at nights, probably the calls of native birds, but Somers and his men concluded they were made by spirits and demons. 'The isle is full of noises,' says Caliban in Act 3 of *The Tempest*. Eventually they escaped the island in two boats they had constructed. When they reached Jamestown, they found that the colony had all but perished. Somers returned to Bermuda to get supplies, but died there in November 1610. It had been assumed that the *Sea Venture* was lost with all hands. The first news of her crew's survival came in a letter from the voyager William Strachey. He was a theatre buff; a member of the *Mermaid Tavern*'s Friday Street Club, the writer of a sonnet to Jonson's *Sejanus* and a sharer in the Children of the Revels and the Blackfriars Theatre.

Although Shakespeare set *The Tempest* on an Italian island rather than Bermuda, it was on his mind when he wrote Ariel's recall of the site of the shipwreck 'in the deep nook, where once thou call'dst me up at midnight to fetch dew / From the still-vex'd Bermoothes, there she's hid'.

In an inspired stroke, Ariel becomes the St Elmo's Fire Strachey described as hovering around the doomed ship like 'a little round light, like a faint star, trembling and streaming along with a sparkling blaze half the height upon the mainmast'.

The Tempest is a play about magic. The magic of Prospero has brought the wrecked ship to the island. Yet this magic is a mere catalyst for the action, a means of creating a fantasy world. Prospero's powers are forces for good. By contrast, Caliban is the opposite of Rousseau's 'natural man'. There is little that is noble about this savage. Prospero claims to have treated him well until he attempted to rape Miranda, an outrage for which he shows no remorse:

> O ho, O ho! wouldst had been done!
> Thou didst prevent me; I had peopled
> This isle with Calibans.

Caliban is the son of the witch Sycorax, who was banished from the Barbary city of Argier (Algiers) to the island. There she enslaved the spirits, including Ariel, who she imprisoned in torment in a split pine. Caliban claims that Prospero has usurped his sovereignty over the island following his mother's death.

The play echoes the account of the peoples of Patagonia written by the Venetian explorer, Pigafetta, and translated into English by Richard Eden in his *History of Travel* in 1577. It tells of a race of grotesque giants inhabiting the hinterland. Shakespeare had already used such travellers' tales in Othello's account of his travels.

And of the Cannibals that do each other eat,
The Anthropophagi and men whose heads
Do grow beneath their shoulders.

Sir Walter Raleigh, in his *Discoverie of Guiana* of 1596, mentions on hearsay a deformed race inhabiting that region of South America, but Caliban seems to have had Bermudian roots. A passage in Strachey's narrative combines human and bovine imagery in a description of a sea turtle. Shakespeare joined these elements together in creating his wild man, giving him arms like turtle fins and the nickname 'mooncalf' – a term meaning a deformed child, but one evoking cattle.

In *The Tempest*, Shakespeare fulfilled Ben Jonson's highest aspiration and observed the supposed classical unities of time, place and action. Not that Ben gave him credit for it. In the Induction to *Bartholomew Fair*, he refers scathingly to a 'servant monster' and to 'Tales, Tempests and such like drolleries'.

Shakespeare writes some of his finest lyrical poetry in his three fantasy plays. In *Cymbeline*, the language and syntax can be as convoluted and tortured as the plot, but the heights are reached with the exquisite dirge:

Fear no more the heat o' the sun,
Nor the furious winter's rages;
Thou the wordly task hath done,
Home art gone, and ta'en thy wages;
Golden lads and girls all must,
Like chimney-sweepers, come to dust.

In *The Winter's Tale*, the lightening of the tone in the speeches of Autolycus and Perdita presages the happy conclusion of another convoluted plot. The flowers of spring anticipate a new beginning with 'daffodils that come before the swallow dares, and take the winds of March with beauty'. The two beautiful songs in

The Tempest, 'Where the bee sucks' and 'Full fathom five' were set to music by the distinguished lutenist, Richard Johnson. Even the man-beast Caliban has his share of beautiful lyrics, as he tells the crew of the wonders of the island he regards as his own:

> Be not afeard. The isle is full of noises,
> Sounds, and sweet airs, that give delight, and hurt not.
> Sometimes a thousand twanging instruments
> Will hum about mine ears; and sometimes voices;

The fantasy world of *The Tempest* represents the fantasy world of the theatre itself, a place for the purveying of dreams. At the end of time, all will dissolve:

> These our actors,
> As I foretold you, are all spirits and
> Are melted into air: thin air:
> And like the baseless fabric of this vision,
> The cloud-capp'd towers, the gorgeous palaces;
> The solemn temples, the great globe itself,
> Ye all which it inherit, shall dissolve
> And like this insubstantial pageant faded,
> Leave not a rack behind. We are such stuff
> As dreams are made on, and our little life
> Is rounded with a sleep.

The poet Thomas Campbell first suggested, in 1838, that Shakespeare modelled the character of Prospero upon himself. The graves that at his command 'have wak'd their sleepers' are the galaxy of characters he has exhumed from history:

> But this rough magic
> I have abjured, and, when I have requir'd
> Some heavenly music – which even now I do –
> To work mine end upon their senses that
> This airy charm is for, I'll break my staff
> Bury it certain fathoms in the earth,
> And, deeper than did ever plummet sound,
> I'll drown my book.

Is Shakespeare taking his leave? It is an appealing thought and fits the context. The only snag is that the play was not his last for the company, but there are indications that he had been contemplating his exit from the stage. When he appeared as a witness on 11 May 1612 in the case between Stephen Belott and his father-in-law, Shakespeare's former landlord, Christopher Mountjoy, he is described as 'of Stratford-vpon-Avon', so he had already made his move, just a year or so after *The Tempest* first appeared. Let us suppose that he announced his intention to take his leave of the stage. Consternation follows. The King's Men are about to lose the greatest name in theatrical history. He is persuaded to maintain his relationship with the company. He remains a sharer and agrees to collaborate with the rising dramatist, John Fletcher. The company will have a continuing association with his name. Fletcher's partnership with Francis Beaumont had ceased after Beaumont suffered a stroke in 1613.

The collaboration was not a great success, at least in comparison with Shakespeare's previous career. Two plays ensued from the partnership – and perhaps a third. *The Two Noble Kinsmen* was based on Chaucer's *Knight's Tale* of Palemon and Arcite. Although the 1634 quarto claimed that it had been received with 'great applause' when 'presented at the Blackfriars Theatre by the King's Majesties Servants', it was rarely revived, although there was probably a performance at Court in 1619. There is a reference to a play of 'Palamon' in *Bartholomew Fair*, which was first performed in October 1614, so it was in the public mind at that date.

The other certain product of this collaboration enjoyed even less success and its provenance is vague. Although there is no record of a public performance, *Cardenio* was acted at court by the King's Men on 20 May 1613 during the celebrations for the royal marriage and again on 8 June before the Ambassador of the Duchy of Savoy. The play's title indicates that it was based on the adventures of the lovelorn Cardenio from the first part of *Don Quixote*. No move was made to publish it until 1653 when Humphrey Moseley, a London stationer, obtained a licence for the publication of *The History of Cardenio* by Fletcher and Shakespeare. It never appeared. Moseley probably decided that a play that had achieved little success on the stage was unlikely to do better in print. No more is heard of it until 1727 when the Drury Lane Theatre staged a play called *Double Falsehood* or *The Distrest Lover*. It was described as 'written originally by W. Shakespeare and now revised and adapted by Mr Theobald'.

Lewis Theobald recognised that the play's reappearance stretched credulity, but claimed he possessed a copy which had been transcribed by John Downes, whose *Roscius Anglicanus* is the seminal history of contemporary theatre. This would take the narrative almost back to Moseley's aborted attempt to publish it.

The third play cited as the product of the collaboration is the *Famous History of the Life of King Henry VIII*, or *All is True*. Unlike the other two, Fletcher's name was not associated with it until the author James Spedding suggested that he had a hand in it in 1850. This is now accepted by most scholarly opinion. Part of the argument against co-authorship is the play's inclusion in the Shakespeare First Folio. Heminges and Condell excluded both *Pericles* and *The Two Noble Kinsmen* from the volume, presumably because they were collaborations. Nor does the play appear in the Folio of Fletcher's works that included all his known collaborations.

It is likely that Shakespeare was in London for the most spectacular series of courtly occasions to involve the King's Men. On 14 February 1613, Princess Elizabeth, the King's only surviving daughter, married Friedrich V, the Elector Palatine, at the Chapel Royal. Both bride and groom were 16. The Palatinate was the notional principal power in the Union of Protestant Princes, with which James I desired an alliance. Lavish celebrations followed: plays, pageants, processions and pyrotechnics. The King's Men performed twenty plays, eight by their leading playwright. It is possible that a ninth was requested by royal command. Two days after the wedding, hundreds of people queued to see a play that was cancelled in favour of the 'greater pleasure' of a court masque. This unperformed play may have been *King Henry VIII*. It has all the elements expected from a work written for such an occasion, including a masque and two lavish processions. Sir Henry Wotton noted the 'many extraordinary circumstances of pomp and majesty…; the Knights of the Order with their Georges[3] and garters, the Guards with their embroidered coats and the like: sufficient in truth to make greatness very familiar.' The fulsome royal tributes also indicate a command performance.[4] Cranmer greets the newborn Princess Elizabeth with a prophecy:

> This royal infant – heaven still move about her!
> Though in her cradle, yet now promises
> Upon this land a thousand thousand blessings,
> Which time shall bring to ripeness.

Not surprisingly, England's good fortune extended into the next reign when 'Another heir' would succeed 'as great in admiration':

> Wherever the bright sun of heaven shall shine'
> His honour and the brightness of his name
> Shall be, and make new nations.

Despite such extravagant praise of the King, it may have been that the royal party, surfeited with the celebrations, decided to forego the play and just see the masque within it. It must have been decided to share the spectacle with the public. Sir Henry Wooton was impressed that even the matting on the stage when the play was presented at the Globe had been painted to resemble the rich carpets adorning the royal chamber. All the effects from the putative royal performance were presented. It was a recipe for disaster. The play was staged several times before nemesis struck on 20 June 1613, when this particular 'insubstantial pageant' caused the destruction of the 'great Globe itself'. Sir Henry recounted the sad tale in a letter to his nephew:

> King Henry making a masque at Cardinal Wolsey's house and certain chambers [cannons] being shot off at his entry, some of the papers, or other stuff, wherewith one of them was stopped, did light on the thatch, where being thought at first but an idle smoke, and their eyes attentive to the show, it kindled inwardly, and ran round like a train, consuming within an hour
> the whole house to the very ground.
>
> This was the fatal period of that virtuous fabric, wherein nothing did perish but wood and straw; and a few forsaken cloaks; only one man had his breeches set on fire, that would perhaps have broiled him, if he had not by the benefit of a provident wit put it out with bottle ale.

It may be presumed that Shakespeare was not present during this catastrophe. Had he been there, the anonymous author of a piece of mournful doggerel would surely have mentioned him. 'All is true,' he assures the reader, in a reference to the play's sub-title:

> Out ran the knights, out ran the lords,
> And there was great ado,
> Some lose their hats and some their swords,
> Then out run Burbage too;
> The reprobates, though drunk as Monday,
> Prayed for the fool and Henry Condye.
> Oh sorrow, pitiful sorrow, and yet, all this is true.

It is unlikely that the King's Men pursued the balladeer's suggestion that, to rebuild the Globe, they should seek 'A license for to beg for it, / In churches, sans churchwardens checks / In Surrey and Middlesex.'

Within a year, a new and even more splendid theatre rose from the ashes, with a tiled roof to prevent a repetition of the disaster. It was built on the footprint of its predecessor, but was grander in scale. To foot the bill, each sharer contributed £50 or £60. William Shakespeare's name was not among them. England's greatest man of the theatre had made his exit. He was still only 49. None of his colleagues quit so early, although the great actor Edward Alleyn had long since adjourned to his Manor of Dulwich. It is sufficient and satisfactory to say that his objective was to resume his life in Stratford with an elevated social status, having overcome the financial problems that dogged his father. Yet there may be more to it. The spirit of the age was swinging away from his natural metier, the popular theatre, in which his greatest triumphs had been achieved. *The Tempest* was an undoubted triumph, but his collaborations with Fletcher were, at best, moderately received. If Shakespeare indeed wrote *Henry VIII* in its entirety (or, at least the last scene), it's almost too obvious to suggest that the epilogue was the last thing he wrote for the stage:

> 'Tis ten to one this play can never please
> All that are here: some come to take their ease
> And sleep an act or two; but those, we fear,
> We have frighted with our trumpets; so, 'tis clear,
> They'll say 'tis naught: others, to hear the city
> Abused extremely; and to cry "That's witty!"

If Shakespeare wrote such doggerel, he may have realised that his literary powers were fading. If he wrote anything further in the short time he had left, it is lost to posterity.

'Such as are your Stage-players'

Despite the royal approbation for the theatre, the Puritan assault was as virulent as ever. In 1612, the actor and prolific dramatist Thomas Heywood made a response in *An Apology for Actors*. In the first of his 'three briefe treatises', he emulated the Puritan custom of citing scripture, or, rather, in this case, the lack of such citation.

> In the full and perfect time our Sauiour soiurned on the earth, euen in those happy peacefull dayes the spacious Theaters were in the greatest opinion amongst the Romans; yet, neither Christ himselfe, nor any of his sanctified Apostles, in any of their Sermons, Acts, or Documents, so much as named them, or vpon any abusiue occasion touched them.

Heywood quoted the important part theatre had played in Greek and Roman life. He acknowledged that there had been abuses within the contemporary theatre, but cleverly turned the argument back against those who cited them:

> Shall we condemne a generallity for any one particular misconstruction? giue me then leaue to argue thus: Amongst Kings haue there not beene some tyrants? Ye the office of a King is the image of the Maiesty of God. Amongst true subiects haue there not crept in some false traitors? euen amongst the twelue there was one *Judas*, but shall we for his fault, censure worse of the eleuen? God forbid: art thou Prince or Peasant? art thou of the Nobility, or Commonalty? Art thou merchant or Souldier? of the Citty or Country? Art thou Preacher or Auditor? Art thou Tutor or Pupill? There haue beene of thy function bad and good, prophane and holy. I induce these instances to confirme this common argument, that the vse of any generall thing is not for any one particular abuse to be condemned: for if that assertion stood firme, wee should run into many notable inconueniences.

He also made what may be the first reference to its contribution to tourism:

> Playing is an ornament to the Citty, which strangers of all Nations, repairing hither, report of in their Countries, beholding them here with some admiration: for what variety of entertainment can there be in any Citty of Christendome, more then in *London*?

Nor can he resist extolling the contribution the theatre has made to the new-found beauty of the English language:

> Our *English* tongue, which hath ben the most harsh, vneuen, and broken language of the world, part *Dutch*, part *Irish*, *Saxon*, *Scotch*, *Welsh*, and indeed a gallimaffry of many, but perfect in none, is now by this secondary meanes of playing, continually refined, euery writer striuing in himselfe to adde a new florish vnto it; so that in processe, from the most rude and vnpolisht tongue, it is growne to a most perfect and composed language, and many excellent workers, and elaborate Poems writ in the same, that many Nations grow inamored of our tongue (before despised.).

There were less subtle ways to attack the Puritans. Lucy Hutchinson, widow of the Puritan parliamentarian and New Model Army Commander Colonel John Hutchinson, described the mockery levelled at them during the reign of James I:

> Every stage, every table and every puppet play belched forth profane scoffs upon them, the drunkards made their songs and all fiddlers and mimics learned to abuse them, as finding it the most gameful way of fooling.

As the contemporary drama has come down to us, few plays satirise Puritans. Perhaps Mistress Hutchinson was referring to the ribald ad libs of the clowns. Malvolio in *Twelfth Night* is described as 'a kind of Puritan', but it is his 'self-love' that engenders his downfall, not his religious adhesion. *The Puritan*, published in 1608 and attributed to Thomas Middleton, is a more direct assault on Puritan hypocrisy and venality. The most abrasive assault of all was made by Ben Jonson, whose residual Catholicism would make him particularly virulent towards those popish-loathing sects. Like all skilful satirists, he knows his target. He lampoons the Puritan custom of naming their children after moral qualities, or literally translated Hebraic biblical names. such as Ananias and his Pastor, Tribulation Wholesome, Dame Purecraft and Win-the-Fight Littlewit. In *Bartholomew Fair*, Zeal-of-the-Land Busy claims that a puppet show is a manifestation of the devil worship of a Babylonian fertility god. Jonson's clever parody of a Puritan preacher is well-observed and captures the rhythm and style of their denunciations of the theatre:

Busy: Down with *Dagon*: down with *Dagon*. 'Tis I, will no longer endure your profanations.

Lantern: What mean you, Sir?

Busy. I will remove *Dagon* there, I say, that *Idol*, that heathenish *Idol*, that remains (as I may say) a Beam, a very Beam, not a Beam of the *Sun*, nor a Beam of the *Moon*, nor a Beam of a Ballance, neither a House-Beam, nor a Weavers Beam, but a Beam in the Eye, in the Eye of the Brethren; a very great Beam, an exceeding great Beam; such as are your *Stage-players*, *Rimers*, and *Morrise-dancers*, who have walked hand in hand, in contempt of the *Brethren*, and the *Cause*, and been born out by Instruments of no mean Countenance.

Yet the very bitterness of Jonson's satire indicates the growing power of the Puritans. Their day would come.

The play is the essence of city comedy. The supposed classical tradition of the action taking place over one day enables Jonson to create a stunning kaleidoscope of the fair with a host of characters as a backdrop, including pickpockets, stallholders, prostitutes, gentry, Puritans and justices. The King must have been desperately keen to see it, for it was performed at Court next day. The Revels accounts reveal that the leading actor, Nathan Field, was paid the huge sum of £10 for his performance. He was a power on the stage, challenging existing ascendency, as the line in Act 5 tells us: 'Your best actor, your Field.'

'Complaint and Grievance'

The creation of a grander Globe represented a clear challenge to Henslowe and he responded characteristically, going into partnership with Jacob Meade, a waterman, who, presumably, provided funding. On 29 August 1613 they contracted Gilbert Katherens, a master carpenter, for a fee of £360, to demolish the Bear Garden and build the Hope Theatre in its stead. He was reluctant to give up his lucrative animal-baiting business. The contract stipulated a 'Plaiehouse fitt & convenient in all thinges, bothe for players to playe in, and for the game of Beares and Bulls to be bayted in the same', so the stage could 'be carryed and taken avaie and to stande vppon tressels',

That it was to be built in the manner of the Swan Theatre implies it was conceived on an even grander scale than the new Globe. Its construction took over a year. In March 1613, Henslowe made an agreement with Lady Elizabeth's Men to perform at the Hope. Through his lawyer, Edward Griffin, he agreed to loan the company £80. The theatre was open by 31 October 1614, when the company first performed *Bartholomew Fair*. Ben Jonson expressed severe dissatisfaction with it. When the stage was 'carryed and taken awaie', it became an arena for animal baiting, with the inevitable result. He compared the pong with that reeking around London's main meat market, 'as dirty as Smithfield and stinking every whit'.

Uniquely, the three-year contract Henslowe entered into on 7 April 1614 with the actor, Robert Dawes survives; it is probably typical of its ilk. If Dawes was late for a rehearsal, he could be fined twelve pence; if he missed it altogether, the fine doubled. If he was late for a performance, it rose to three shillings. If, in the opinion of four members of the company, he was drunk at the start of a performance, it was ten shillings. Most swingeing of all was the fine of £40 if he was found to have sequestered the costumes or any other of the company's properties. There was some irony in this, since, in 1615, members of Lady Elizabeth's Men composed articles of 'complaint and grievance' against 'Mr Hinslowe', whom they accused of selling the company's apparel and playbooks, retaining more than his share of the profits and underpaying them for performances lost when the Hope was used for bear-baiting. They claimed he had contracted hired men 'in his owne name whose wages though wee have truly paid yet att his pleasure hee hath taken them a waye and turned then over to others to the breakinge of companie'. The huge returns from a theatrical enterprise are again revealed. On every breach of the contract with the company, Henslowe took out 'more bondes for his stocke, and our securitie for playimge with him, soe that he hath in his hands, bondes of ours to the value of 5,000li [£5,000]'. He had seized control of the 'stocke which he denies to deliver'. The complainants had a sharp final flourish. 'Also within 3 yeares hee hath broken and dissmemnbered five companies.' The complaint was signed by the leading players Nathan Field, Robert Pallant, Robert Dawes, William Ecclestone and Joseph Taylor; Philip Rosseter, the manager and Robert Daborne, the playwright.

Henslowe had counter-complaints against the company. They had failed to repay the £80 owed him, Daborne had failed to deliver a play and was threatening to take another to the rival company at the Globe.

At some point Field, Daborne and the playwright Philip Massinger were jailed for what Field described as an 'vnfortunate extremitie'. He asked Henslowe for a loan of £6 to enable them to obtain bail, arguing that it was in his interest to do so. His imprisonment meant he was unable to 'play any more till this be dispatch'd, it will loose you xxl [£20] ere the end of the next weeke'. If they remained in jail they could not complete the play on which they were working. 'Pray, sir, consider our cases with humanitie, and now give us cause to acknowledge that you our true freind in time of neede.' Daborne suggested the loan should be 'abated out of the mony remayns for the play of mr ffletcher and owrs', so a noted additional dramatist was employed in Henslowe's characteristic style of multi-authorship.

On Henslowe's death on 6 January 1615/16, his considerable estate passed to his wife, Agnes; on her death, a year later, to her daughter, Joan, and her husband, Edward Alleyn. The legacy included Henslowe's share in the Hope Theatre, which was then leased to Meade, giving him control of the whole business. That Henslowe's grievances may have had some validity is revealed in Articles of Agreement in which nine named members of the company acknowledged 'standing indebted to Phillipp Henchlowe esq' and Jacob Meade for the sum upwards of £400 for loans and 'playinge apparell'. Alleyn agreed to accept £200 in lieu of the debt, the money to be taken from their wages. Once it was cleared, the Company could have to its use 'all such stock of apparell'. It was decreed that the actors 'shall and will playe at the said howse called the hope, or elsewhere with the likinge of the said Edward and Jacob'. Alleyn's generous offer did not settle matters. On 15 March 1617, accompanied by a vast entourage, King James embarked on a long journey north, finally fulfilling his promise, made on his accession to the English throne, to return to Scotland; Lady Elizabeth's Men went with him. On 16 July, a payment of £30 was recorded to the Company's John Townsend and Joseph Moore, 'Stageplayers ... for acting three severall playes before his Maste in his iorney towards Scotlande.' The performances would have take place in the great noble houses that accommodated the King and his retinue. The company appeared at the Moot Hall in Carlisle in 1620, where the Chamberlain's Accounts recorded a payment of 26 8*d.* 'geauen to me Ladye Elibethe players'.

Exit Burbage

On 25 March 1616, William Shakespeare signed a revised draft of his last Will and Testament. It is a lawyer's document, containing no religious formulae, or expressions of familial affection. The only reference to the theatre is of great significance. 'My ffellowes John Hemmynges, Richard Burbage and Henry Cundell' were each left 26 8*d*. 'to buy them Ringes'. A ring is the symbol of a pledge. That year, Ben Jonson became the first author to supervise the publication of a folio of his complete works. Perhaps Shakespeare cracked a few jests at his expense while planning to follow suit, discussing the project with the three major sharers in his old company, which owned the scripts. Obviously they were stored in some other place than the gutted Globe, or had been rescued from the flames. When he knew he was dying, did he ask them to continue the task and leave them rings in token of their pledge? If such was the case, Burbage did not live to complete it. His death on 13 March 1619 caused an outpouring of grief that threatened to eclipse the official mourning for Queen Anne, who had died ten days before. 'The deaths of men who act our Queens and Kings,' wrote one homespun poet, 'Are now more mourn'd than are the real things.' William Herbert, 3rd Earl of Pembroke, could not face going to a play 'so soon after the loss of my acquaintance Burbage'. He was buried in St Leonard's Church six days after his death. It was claimed that the lost epitaph on his tombstone simply read 'Exit Burbage'. He was the greatest actor of all time, if only because of what he created. An anonymous poet's *Funerall Elegye* summed it up.[5]

He's gone and with him what a world are dead.
To be reviv'd, to be revived so
No more young Hamlet, old Hieronimo,
Kind Lear, the grieved Moor, and more beside,
That liv'd in him have now forever died.
Oft I have seen him leap into a grave
Suiting the person, which he seem'd to have,
Of a sad lover, with so true an eye
That there (I would have sworn) he meant to die.

Burbage created virtually all Shakespeare's leading male roles and must have influenced their creation. The parts aged with him from the 18-year-old Romeo, to the 30-year-old Hamlet to aged Lear and mature Prospero. Something of his acting skills were recalled by Richard Flecknoe in his *Short Discourse of the English Stage*, in 1664:

> He had all the parts of an excellent actor, animating all his words with speaking, and speech with action; his auditors being never more delighted than when he spoke, nor more sorry than when he held his peace. Yet even then, he was an excellent actor still, never failing in his part when he had done speaking, but with his looks and gesture maintaining it still unto the height …

As was their practice, the King's Men moved quickly to find a replacement. Joseph Taylor, the Prince Charles' Company's leading man, joined the company just a month after Burbage's death. He was around 30, the ideal age to revive some of the great parts. His casting as Mosca ('the Fly') may indicate that he shared Burbage's shortness of stature. According to James Wright's *Historia Hjistrionica*, he acted Hamlet 'incomparably well', and was noted for his Iago. Other revived parts included Face in *The Alchemist* and Truewit in *Epicene.* He played Ferdinand in a revival of *The Duchess of Malfi* in the year he joined the Company. The play was consistently in the repertoire. In 1618, Orazio Busino, Chaplain to the Venetian Ambassador, attended a performance and was appalled by the portrayal of the Cardinal, a Prince of his Church, as cruel, treacherous and lascivious. He was particularly offended by the scene in which the Cardinal is initiated as a soldier at the Shrine of Loreto, which he regarded as a 'condemnation of the grandeur of the Church, which they despise and which in this kingdom they hate to death'.

On 13 May 1619, the statesman Johan van Oldenbarnevelt was executed in The Hague, having been found guilty of the 'subversion' of the religion and politics of the United Provinces. This would have been an international sensation. He was regarded as second only to William the Silent as the founder of the independent Netherlands. He had masterminded the Dutch revolt and was architect of the Triple Alliance against Spain. Dramas dealing with the events of the day were great attractions in the contemporary theatre, whether as allegories or plays purporting to recount actual history. John Fletcher and Philip Massinger began an immediate collaboration to bring this extraordinary event to the stage at the Globe. They had completed their work by 14 August, when Sir Dudley Carleton, English Ambassador at The Hague, wrote that 'the players heere were bringing of Barnavelt upon the stage, and had bestowed a great deal of money to prepare all things for this purpose, but at the instant were prohibited by my Lo. Of London'.[6] John King, Bishop of London, had indeed intervened. A factor in van Oldenbarnevelt's impeachment was his adhesion to the more liberal doctrines of Arminianism in contrast to the prevailing severity of Calvinism. Both sects were alien to the beliefs of an Anglican Bishop, although the play was far from espousing any particular theology. It found favour with the

Master of the Revels, Sir George Buck, because it followed the official line on van Oldenbarnevelt's trial and execution. Prince Maurice of Orange, who was the main architect of his downfall, was a close ally of James I, so he is portrayed as a just, wise and merciful ruler, who only moves against van Oldenbarnevelt to prevent the disastrous consequences that would follow his undermining of the state, although Buck took exception to a scene in which the Prince is forcibly excluded from a meeting of the Lords of the State, presumably because such treatment of a ruling royal by his noblemen might provide a dangerous precedent to the disaffected in England. 'I like not this', he scrawled, before excising the scene. Nevertheless, it was brought to the stage. 'Our players have found the meanea,' wrote a playgoer on 27 August, 'to goe through with the play of Barnavelt and it hath had many spectators and received applause.'

The play drew factual detail from a recently-published pamphlet entitled *Newes from Holland*, but there is no equivocation in the verdict on its titular character. He is portrayed as brought down by his jealous pride and overweening ambition. In a completely unhistorical scene, he engages Leidenberch, his co-conspirator, to persuade English soldiers to join his sedition. Some attempt was made at balance by giving van Oldenbarnevelt the customary speech in his defence at his trial, but Buck was having none of such equity and struck it through with his quill.

The authors could not resist such occasional diversions from the main plot as a confrontation between an English gentlewoman and four 'Duch-woemen' who were adherents of the Arminian sect, who attempt unsuccessfully to convince her of the merits of a society in which their sex has a greater say in political matters: an early discussion of the role of women:

> Your owne Cuntry breedes ye hansom, maintains ye brave
> But with a stubborn hand, the husbands awe ye.
> You speake but what they please, looke where they point ye,
> And though ye have some liberty, 'tis lymited.

The Englishwoman's reply is redolent of Kate's 'Thy husband is thy lord' in *The Taming of the Shrew*:

> Our Cuntry brings us up to faire obedience.
> To know our husbands for our Governors.
> So yo obey and seve 'em: two heads make monsters.
> Nor dare we think of what is above us.

In a grotesque scene, the public executioners of Haarlem, Leyden and Utrecht cast lots to decide who is to have the privilege of executing van Oldenbarnevelt. Utrecht wins. He tells the others that he will fake a few tears on the scaffold in order to persuade the condemned man to give him money. While he is praying, he will lop off his head.

The execution is preceded by the gibbeting of Leidenberch's corpse on the scaffold. The executioner complains that 'he stincks like a hung pole cat'. The intention of the authors was clearly to appeal to the instincts that made people flock to public executions. Barneveld's final prayer is literally cut off when the executioner fulfils his pledge:

> Honour, and world, I fling ye thus behind me,
> And thus a naked poore-man, kneele to heaven:
> Be gratious to me, heare me, strengthen me,
> I come, I come: ô gratious heaven: now: now:
> Now I present — [*Head struck off*]

This leaves the question of how this sensational effect was achieved. The answer lies in *The Rebellion of Naples*, a play by 'T.B.', published in 1649. When the revolutionary Massenello is executed, the stage direction reads: 'He thrusts out his head, and they cut off a false head made of a bladder, filled with blood.' The manoeuvre must have taken a high degree of skill on the part of the 'Executioner'. A mishandled sword could do severe damage to the unfortunate actor. This is probably why, as Margaret E. Owens notes, there are only three other known plays with an on-stage beheading, Marston's *The Insatiable Countess*, Dekker and Massinger's *The Virgin Martyr* and Markham and Sampson's *Herod and Antipater*.[7] This play went beyond those. 'You have struck his fingers too,' roars an aghast spectator, 'but we forgive your haste.'

The manuscript of the play carries the names of some of the actors who played the minor parts, including 'G. Lowen', who played Barnevelt's daughter. This could be a son of John Lowin, who may well have performed the lead. Whoever the lad was, he was not destined for stardom. This brief mention is the sole extant record of his stage career.

The unchallenged role of the King's Men as the premier theatre company was compounded by a disaster occurring to their main rivals. The Company originally known as Lord Howard's Men had become successively the Admiral's Men, Nottingham's Men, Prince Henry's Men and, finally, the Elector Palatinate's or Palsgrave's Men, as the titles of its noble patrons changed. On 9 December 1621, their base at the Fortune Theatre was destroyed by fire. This had happened to the first Globe Theatre and the King's Men had recovered, but for Palatine's

Men the loss was more severe. They not only lost their theatre, their scripts[8] and costumes also perished. Edward Alleyn, the owner, rebuilt the theatre in brick in 1623, but the reconstituted company struggled.

Around this time another rising playwright became associated with the King's Men. John Ford was born in 1586. He was another example of higher social status becoming involved in the theatre. He came from a family of minor gentry in Devon. He became a junior member of the Middle Temple in his late teens, but was expelled in 1606 due to financial problems. His earliest published works were attempts to engender patronage and appear to have succeeded, for by June 1608, he was readmitted to the Middle Temple. *Fame's Memorial* is a lengthy elegy on the death of Charles Blount, 1st Earl of Devonshire, while *Honour Triumphant* is a pamphlet celebrating the jousts planned for the visit of the King of Denmark in the summer of 1606. He did not start writing for the stage until around 1620 at the comparatively late age of 34. It appears that he collaborated with the established dramatist Philip Massinger on *The Laws of Candy*, which was first published in the 1647 Beaumont and Fletcher Folio. If Massinger was the co-author, it may have been his reputation that secured its place on the stage at the Globe, but it may not have been a great success. The plot is as complicated as anything devised by John Fletcher and the work is turgid. Further collaboration followed. The lost play, *Keep the Widow Waking*, was licensed by the Master of the Revels who credited the authorship to 'Forde and Webster'. A subsequent legal action added the names of Dekker and Rowley. How large a contribution was required for a playwright to be so accredited is uncertain.

John Fletcher had settled into the role of the King's Men's chief dramatist. *The Island Princess*, which the company acted at Court in 1621, reflects the growing national consciousness of world-wide maritime perspectives. Portugal's virtual monopoly over the sea-bound eastern trade was being increasingly challenged by the English and Dutch. The East India Company was founded in 1600. Fletcher's linguistic abilities are revealed by his use of two original sources. *Conquista de las islas Malucas*, by the Spanish poet, priest and historian Bartolomé Leonardo de Argensola, was published in 1609; *L'histoire de Ruis Dias, et de Quizaire, Princess des Moloques*, by Le Seigneur de Bellam, in 1615. The latter provides the main storyline, a characteristic Fletcher narrative of great intricacy, as unlikely as any of his others. It is set in the rival island sultanates of Tidore and Ternate in the Moluccas. That Fletcher was taking the audience into a world of which they know as little as himself is demonstrated by his ignorance of Islam, the supposed religion of the islanders. The play's heroine, Quisara, the Island Princess of the title, states beliefs that are far from Islamic. 'The Sun and Moon we worship,' she says, 'those are heavenly / And their bright influences we believe.' She vows to pledge her troth to the man who will free her brother, the King, who has been captured by his rival of Ternate. When the play's hero, Armusia, does so, she agrees to become his wife if he converts to her religion. He tells her that even winning her hand cannot compensate for the loss of his divine faith. He reveals her religion includes human sacrifice:

> I adore the Maker of that Sun and Moon,
> That gives those bodies light and influence;
> That pointed out their paths, and taught their motions;
> They are not so great as we, they are our servants,
> Plac'd there to teach us time, to give us knowledge
> Of when and how the swellings of the main are,
> And their returns agen; they are but our Stewards
> To make the earth fat, with their influence
> That she may bring forth her increase, and feed us.
> Shall I fall from this faith to please a woman?
> For her embraces bring my soul to ruin?
> I look'd you should have said, make me a *Christian*,
> Work that great cure ....,
> I look'd ye should have wept and kneel'd to beg it,
> Washt off your mist of ignorance, with water,
> Pure and repentant, from those eyes; I look'd.
> You should have brought me your chief god ye worship.
> He that you offer humane bloud and life to
> And make a sacrifice of him to memory,
> Beat down his Altars, ruin'd his false Temples.

The Governor of Ternate, disguised as a religious seer, seeks revenge on Armusia and persuades the restored King to throw him into prison. He will face torture unless he apostatises from his Christian faith. This he refuses to do, whatever the cost. Quisara, who has been won over by his courtesy and grace, is overwhelmed by his steadfast beliefs. Rather than demanding he embrace her faith, she will embrace his.

> Your Faith, and your Religion must be like ye,
> They that can shew you these, must be pure mirrors,
> When the streams flow clear and fair, what are the fountains?
> I do embrace your faith, Sir, and your fortune;
> Go on, I will assist ye, I feel a sparkle here,
> A lively spark that kindles my affection,

And tells me it will rise to flames of glory:
Let 'em put on their angers, suffer nobly,
Shew me the way, and when I faint, instruct me.

The audience must have realised that as a Portuguese, Armusia would have been a Roman Catholic. His choice of martyrdom rather than apostasy may have struck at least some as a parallel with Catholics in England who made the same choice.

The Island Princess was part of a fashion for plays with Iberian themes, despite the delicate political situation with that region. Fletcher returned to Spanish sources for his *Women Pleased*, based on *Grisel y Mirabella* by Juan de Flores. He collaborated on several plays with Philip Massinger, although it is difficult to determine who wrote what and by whom it was performed. *The Prophetess* was licensed for performance on 14 May 1622. Its characteristically bizarre plot has echoes of *The Tempest*. The next collaboration, *The Sea Voyage*, licensed by the Master of the Revels on 22 June 1622, has even more echoes of that play. The similarity is hardly surprising since both were drawn from the accounts of the adventurer and theatre buff, William Strachey. It opens with a storm, a shipwreck, and a party of castaways marooned on a remote and exotic island. That isle too is 'full of noises', but they are from a tribe of Amazons, who have developed a strongly anti-male ideology, but, after many complications, love triumphs and the leading characters paired off appropriately.

Further plays from the collaboration followed. *The Little French Lawyer*, was based on *Il Novellino*, a collection of stories by Masuccio di Salerno. *The Spanish Curate*, licensed for performance on 24 October 1622 and performed at Court on St Stephen's Day, was based on the translation by Leonard Digges[9] of Gonzalo de Céspedes' *Gerardo, the unfortunate Spaniard*. In its turn, it is based on *Los Trabajos de Persiles y Sigismunda* by Cervantes. *The Spanish Gypsy*, performed by Lady Elizabeth's Men at the Cockpit in 1622 and attributed to Middleton and Rowley, is also based on the novellas of Miguel de Cervantes. Its plot is as complicated as the fashion of the period decrees.

The creative combination of Fletcher and Massinger found favour at Court that year, for, on 'St John's Day at night', the Company performed *The Beggars Bush*. It takes up the themes of the exiled ruler of *As You Like It* and of the disguised aristocrat rising to the fore among those on the fringes of society of Munday's Robin Hood plays. After a fictional war between Flanders and Brabant, Clause's natural authority ensures that he is elected King of the Beggars. In the final scene he is revealed as Gerrard, the deposed Earl of Flanders and his domain is restored. The theme that the beggar is as content as the King must have reassured the royal party after the indulgences of the Revels season:

This is the beggars' holiday:
At the crowning of our king,
Thus we ever dance and sing,
In the world look out and see,
Where so happy a prince as he?
Where the nation live so free,
And so merry as do we?
Be it peace, or be it war,
Here at liberty we are.

The Wild Goose Chase, a comedy presented in the following year, was another huge success. *The Pilgrim*, a comedy based on an English translation of *El Perigrino en su Patria*, a prose romance by Lope de Vega, was among three of Fletcher's plays acted at Court during that year's Christmas Revels.

Perhaps the most bizarre of Fletcher's many bizarre scenarios was *A Wife for a Month* of 1624, with its wacky sexual nuances in which chastity triumphs against the odds. Chastity is represented by Evanthe, a beautiful lady-in-waiting to the Queen of Naples. The lustful eye of King Frederick lights upon her and he offers her riches to become his mistress. Her wicked brother, Sorano, is party to this, seeing the chance of advancement. When she refuses, the King commands her to marry the gallant Valerio. She is content to do this, regarding marriage as a sacred calling, but the King decrees that her husband be killed after a month of marriage. She is then to marry another suitor, who will suffer the same fate – and so on. Evanthe and Valerio fall in love and plan to consummate the marriage, but the King, a thorough-going spoilsport, gets Sorano to warn Valerio that if they do, she will face immediate death. She will face the same fate if he tells her of it, so, on the wedding night, he feigns impotence to his eager bride. Frederick hopes sheer frustration will drive her into his arms. In a desperate attempt to achieve his wicked goal, he even proposes a wife-swap to Valerio, but the lovers remain constant. Like Iago, Frederick delights in evil for evil's sake. 'I must torture him a little further,' he gloats, 'And make myself sport with his miseries.' In his riposte, Valerio reminds Frederick that his immortal soul is imperilled:

You are growne a tyrant
To deny these rights the Lord has given me,
The holy law, and make her life the pennance,
In such a studied and unheard of malice,
No heart that is not hyred from Hell dare think of
Is there not heaven above you that sees all?

As in *Measure for Measure*, there is a clash between an absolute morality and 'situational ethics' – that morality can be adjusted according to circumstance. 'A little evil may well be suffered for the general good,' Evanthe's maid, Cassandra, tells her.

After the decreed month, Frederick orders that Valerio be executed. In another parallel with *Measure for Measure*, he supposes that this has been done and the body thrown into the sea, but he is saved by upright courtiers. The King orders that Evanthe be married to another for a month. In a scene reminiscent of *The Merchant of Venice*, various suitors – not surprisingly – withdraw when they hear of the alarming terms of the nuptials. Valerio returns, disguised as 'Prince Urbino' and agrees to the match, knowing he will die. Frederick's misrule causes him to be overthrown. Valerio reveals his true identity. The new and rightful king, Alphonso, banishes Frederick and Sorano to a monastic life of prayer, fasting and penitence.

In the same period Fletcher wrote *The Maid in the Mill* in collaboration with William Rowley, which was licensed for performance at the Globe on 29 August 1623. Rowley was a comic actor who wrote plays in collaboration and such solo works as *A Shoemaker a Gentleman*, of around 1608 and *All's Lost by Lust* of 1619. Three lost plays, *Hymen's Holidays* (1612), *A Knave in Print* and *The Fool without Book* (both of 1613) may also be his works. When he wrote plays with others, his main contribution was a fat clown part for himself. In *A Maid in the Mill* he plays Bustopha, the son of Franio, the old miller, a 'gross compound' with abundant flesh about him'. Nothing is known of his early life. He was one of the seven founders of the Duke of York's Men, in 1608. This became Prince Charles' Men after the death of Prince Henry in 1612. It was based in several theatres, including the Curtain, Hope and Red Bull. Rowley appears to have handled its finances, receiving payments for its appearances at Court between 1610 and 1615.

Another of the Company's stalwarts died in 1623. The last identifiable parts played by Nicholas Tooley were the dual roles of Forobosco and a madman in *The Duchess of Malfi* revival of 1619. At the time of his death, he was still living in Cuthbert Burbage's house in the parish of St Giles, Cripplegate. He is listed in the second Beaumont and Fletcher Folio as acting in *A Wife for a Month*, which was not performed until a year after his death. This may have been a simple error. More likely, it indicates that playwrights wrote parts for specific actors. In his will made on 3 June, with the frequent contemporary perspicacity of those whose demise was near – he was buried two days later – he left £10 to the Burbage's daughter, Elizabeth, describing one Moxy as her 'pretended husband'. The money was to be paid 'into her own hands', presumably to prevent it getting into Moxy's. The extent of his wealth is revealed in his huge bequest of £80 to the poor of St Leonard's parish, another indication that the church constituted something of a chaplaincy to the Company. Among other bequests was one to Sara Burbage of £29 13*s*. 0*d*., owed him by Richard Robinson. The debt is large and it may have been a dividend to a sharer in the Company. Robinson had been a sharer since 1619 and probably handled the Company's finances. In that year, he married Winifred, his old master's widow. The difference in their ages was significant. As a boy actor with the Company in 1611, the groom played the Lady in Thomas Middleton's *The Lady's Tragedy*, so he was probably aged around 25 at the time of the marriage, certainly not more than 30.

Winifred Burbage seems to have had some responsibility for managing the Company after her husband's death. On 4 July 1620, four trustees were appointed to oversee her estate – her husband left her 'better than £300 in land'. These included her trusted friends and neighbours, Henry Hodge, 'citizen and brewer' who had strong associations with her parish church of St Leonard, and John Milton, scrivener, probably the father of the poet.

Little is known of Winifred's background except her maiden name. On 6 August 1622, she was granted letters of administration for the estate of her father, Edmund Turner, who died intestate. He too was of the parish of St Leonard's, so he may have been living with his daughter. The name 'Winfret burbidg' appears in the casebook of the astrologer Simon Forman on 7 October 1601. The first-recorded baptism of one of her children was on 2 January 1602–3. This may have been her second child. There is no extant record of the baptism of her son Richard, who died in 1607. Thus the latest date for Winifred's birth is 1587 and this assumes that she married in 1601 at the age of 14, which is possible but unlikely. If it were the case, she would have been at least 36 at the time of her second marriage, probably older. Given the age difference and Robinson's possible sexuality, it may have been an alliance with a trusted associate to protect her widow's holdings and position in the Company. That he fulfilled this role in protecting the Company's interests is demonstrated in a complaint concerning the renewal of the lease on the Globe Theatre he filed in the Court of Requests on 28 January 1632, together with Winifred, Cuthbert Burbage, John Heminges, Joseph Taylor and John Lowin.

In *The Devil is an Ass* of 1616, Ben Jonson reveals that Robinson's cross-dressing was not restricted to the stage. The character Meercraft expresses a wish to see 'a witty boy' impersonate a lady. In what appears to be recall of an actual incident, another character, Engine, suggests:

There's Dick Robinson,

A very pretty fellow. And comes often
To a gentleman's chamber, a friend of mine.
        We had
The merriest supper there, one night,
The gentleman's landlady invited him
T' a gossip's feast: now he, sir, brought Dick
        Robinson,
Drest like a lawyer's wife, amongst 'em all;
(I lent him clothes) but to see him behave it,
And lay the law, and carve and drink unto 'em,
And then talk bawdy, and send frolicks! O!
It would have burst your buttons, or not left
A seam.

'They say he's an ingenious youth,' says Meercraft. 'Oh sir!' comes the reply. 'And dresses himself the best! Beyond forty of your ladies.'

That Robinson was another former boy player who became a cult actor is revealed in Abraham Cowley's lines in the dedication of his comedy *Love's Riddle*, to Sir Kenelm Digby. 'Nor has it a part for Robinson, whom they / At school account essential to a play.'

Chapter Nine

Our Revels Now are Ended

For All Time

It took John Heminges and Henry Condell seven years to complete the epic task of editing Shakespeare's plays for publication. In the prefatory epistle they regretted the loss of his role in the preparations. 'It had been a thing, we confess, worthy to have wished that the author himself had liv'd to have set forth his own writings.' Despite their confessed shortcomings, their achievement was remarkable. Without their efforts, no less than eighteen plays would have been lost, including *Twelfth Night*, *Measure for Measure*, *Macbeth* and *The Tempest*. The texts of others would have been flawed. Shakespeare's massive reputation would have been the less without the dedicated work of his colleagues.

Scholarly scrutiny shows that that the volume was compiled from a variety of sources, which the editors must have been assiduous in locating. The best manuscripts were those annotated by the scrivener, Ralph Crane, and include the texts of *The Tempest*, *The Two Gentlemen of Verona*, *The Merry Wives of Windsor* and *Measure for Measure*. Others were typeset from the various quartos. For some texts it appears that the editors recoursed to Shakespeare's 'foul papers' – the working drafts in his own hand. *The Comedy of Errors* may be one such. Other texts, like that of *A Midsummer Night's Dream*, may have come from the Company's prompt books. It seems extraordinary that once these documents had been transcribed and printed, it was not considered worthwhile to preserve them for posterity. Once published, there would have seemed no reason to retain them.

The editors asked several of Shakespeare's associates to append valedictory verses. Ben Jonson overcame his scruples about his friend's lack of classical learning to append what was probably the most eloquent and generous tribute ever paid by one poet to another. Its wonder and perspicacity may be summarised in a single line – 'He was not for an age, but for all time.'

The Folio was dedicated to William Herbert, the 3rd Earl of Pembroke and his brother Philip, the Earl of Montgomery. This is the William Herbert who was too distressed to go to the theatre after the death of his friend Richard Burbage.

Printing the work was assigned to William Jaggard. This seems a surprising choice since he had caused upset in literary circles by publishing, in 1599, *The*

Passionate Pilgrim, which attributed poems to William Shakespeare that were the work of others. In 1619, he had published ten quartos of Shakespeare's plays to which he did not possess the rights, with false dates and title pages. His selection may have been because the stationer, John Smethwick, had been a business partner of his brother, John. In 1607, he had acquired the publication rights of *Love's Labours Lost*, *Romeo and Juliet* and *Hamlet*, producing the latter two in quarto in 1611. The other stationer who had to be included as a partner in the project was William Aspley, who entered *Henry IV* and *Much Ado About Nothing* onto the Stationers' Register in 1600 and so owned the copyrights. A further factor may have been that Jaggard's was the only print shop capable of fulfilling the task. A large amount of the rag paper required had to be imported from France and Jaggard – or rather his son Isaac, for he was infirm and blind by this time and died a month before the Folio was published – was in a position to do this.

The first recorded purchase of the Folio came on 5 December 1623, when Sir Edward Deering, the antiquarian, bought two copies for £3. The cost is brought into perspective by the fact that, in the same account, he paid one John Barton £3 15*s*. 0*d*. for six months' wages.

The Folio usefully lists 'The Names of the Principall Actors in these Playes'. There are twenty-six in all, arranged in what may have been considered an order of eminence. Naturally, William Shakespeare's name heads the list and the name of Richard Burbage follows. Heminges and Condell rate themselves at third and eighth respectively. The list is brought up-to-date by the inclusion of Joseph Taylor, who never acted with the Company in Shakespeare's time. Those who had long departed the fellowship were not forgotten. Will Kempe is in fifth place, one behind Augustine Phillips. The list has its enigmas. 'Samuel Crosse' is listed fourteenth. There is no other reference to his association with the Company, but, in *Apology for Actors*, Thomas Heywood, who arrived in London around 1594, named 'Crosse' as a famous actor before his time. The theatres were closed by plague during 1593 and 1594, so he must have performed in Shakespeare's earliest plays. Perhaps he was the original Titus Andronicus. Clearly his impact was such that his memory lingered long after his acting career was over. Samuel Gilburne is another whose presence on the list rescues his name for posterity. The only other known mention of his name is as Augustine Phillips' 'late apprentice' in his will in 1605.[1]

John Rice is the final name. He was apprenticed to Heminges as a boy actor. He recited at a banquet given on 7 July 1607 by the Merchant Taylors' Company before 'the King's most excellent Majste with our gracious Queene and the noble Prince and Honble Lordes … on the day of the Election of the Master and Wardens'. He was described as 'a very proper child, well spoken, being clothed like an angell of gladness with a Taper of Frankinsense burning in his hand'. He delivered a speech 'contayning eighteen verses, devised by Mr Ben Johnson [sic], the Poet, which pleased his Majste marvelously well'. The Company accounts[2] show that Mr Hemmyngs' was paid forty shillings 'for his direction of his boy that made the speech given to his Maj.'. The boy got rather less, five shillings, but since the average weekly remuneration for a boy actor in the Admiral's Men was three shillings, he was probably well pleased. Ben Jonson was paid an astonishing £20, 'for inventing the speech to his Maj. and making the songs, and his directions to others in that business'. That the average annual wage of a farm labourer at the time was around five guineas puts this huge fee into perspective. Three years later, on 11 May 1610, the exquisite boy featured with Richard Burbage in the Thames pageant celebrating the creation of Prince Henry as Prince of Wales, appearing as 'Corinea, a very fayre and beautifull Nimphe ... suited in her waterie habit, yet riche and costly, with a Coronet of Pearles and Cockle Shells on her head.' His apprenticeship over, he joined Lady Elizabeth's Men under Henslowe, but soon returned to the King's Men. He played a Captain in *Sir John van Olden Barnevelt* and the Marquis of Pescara in *The Duchess of Malfi*. He signed the apology for playing *The Spanish Viceroy* without a licence on 7 April 1611, and is listed in the cast of Fletcher and Massimger's play of 1619, *The False One*. He was a recipient of mourning cloth for the King's funeral on 7 May 1625, but left the company soon after. He did not journey far. In a Chancery disputation on 16 October 1626, he described himself as clerk of St Saviour's Southwark, the parish in which the Globe Theatre stood, although whether this signified that he had been ordained or was simply a parish functionary is unclear. He was living with an 'uxor ... near the playhouse' in 1619. He was a trusted friend of John Heminges, who bequeathed him £12 as 'a remembrance of my love'. He oversaw his will and may even have conducted his funeral.

The Cockpit

Prince Charles' Men probably shared Ben's distaste for the pongs permeating the Hope, for, in 1622, they decamped to the Cockpit Theatre. As the name suggests, it had been built as an arena for cockfighting as long ago as the reign of Henry VIII. The lease was acquired in August 1616 by Christopher Beeston, who converted it into an indoor theatre. His plan was probably similar to that of the King's Men in taking over Blackfriars – to perform in summer in the Red Bull and in winter in the Cockpit. If so, the scheme misfired. On the following Shrove Tuesday – 4 March – the place was stormed by a mob of apprentices, who cut up the costumes and set the building alight. They were infuriated that plays they had paid a penny to see at the Red Bull were now presented at the Cockpit for the inflated price of sixpence. They did not escape unscathed. The actors shot at them, killing three. Doubtless the usual plea of self-defence was entered. A new and larger indoor theatre, which Beeston named The Phoenix, although it was still popularly known as The Cockpit, rapidly arose from the ashes. It may have been designed by Inigo Jones. Queen Anne's Men performed there until 1619, when, on the death of their patron, they returned to the Red Bull, renaming themselves the Revels Company. The period of reshuffling of companies which follows makes their precise histories difficult to follow, although the Cockpit saw some great successes. *The Witch of Edmonton*, 'a known true story', was first performed there by Prince Charles' Men in 1621. The title page of the edition of 1658 attributes the play to the 'divers well-esteemed Poets, William Rowley, Thomas Dekker, John Ford, &c.' The '&c' was probably John Webster, who was working at the time with the others on a now-lost play, *Keep the Widow Waking.*

The play tells the tragic story of Elizabeth Sawyer who was hanged at Tyburn the previous April, under the Witchcraft Act which had come onto the Statute Book that month. She fulfilled the prototype: malformed with just one eye and she collected brushwood to make broomsticks. Although she had long been considered a witch in her local community of Edmonton, it was a minor incident that brought about her downfall; an altercation with a neighbour, Agnes Radcliffe, who hit her sow with a stick after claiming it was eating her soap. Four days later, she was struck by a mystery illness, for which, on her deathbed, she blamed Elizabeth Sawyer's witchcraft. As a result, her antagonist was arrested and accused of causing the deaths of many women and children. She was strip-searched by women looking for the mark that showed she had fed the Devil with her blood. At her trial, the jury disagreed on her guilt. The judge was sceptical about the whole business and she was declared innocent. All seemed well, but it emerged that in Newgate Prison she had made a full confession to the Chaplain, delineating her encounters with the Devil and his familiars. It would seem she believed in her own dark powers. Her fate was sealed. Hers is not the play's central narrative. It may have been added to an existing script because of its topicality. She does not appear until the second act. Thomas Dekker is the most likely author of the scenes involving her. He has an intuitive sympathy with her. Her predetermined status as a witch, he suggests, makes it more likely that she will seek to be one:

> And why on me? why should the envious world
> Throw all their scandalous malice upon me?
> 'Cause I am poor, deformed, and ignorant,

And like a bow buckled and bent together
By some more strong in mischiefs than myself,
Must I for that be made a common sink
For all the filth and rubbish of men's tongues
To fall and run into? Some call me witch,
And being ignorant of myself, they go
About to teach me how to be one; urging
That my bad tongue — by their bad usage made so —
Forspeaks their cattle, doth bewitch their corn,
Themselves, their servants, and their babes at nurse.
This they enforce upon me, and in part
Make me to credit it; and here comes one
Of my chief adversaries.

Mother Sawyer's chief adversary is Old Banks who pours invective on her and strikes her. Dekker gives her further motivation for her witchcraft. 'I have heard old beldams,' she says,

Talk of familiars in the shape of mice,
Rats, weasels, ferrets and I know not what,
That have appeared and sucked, some say, their blood;
But by what means they came acquainted with them
I am now ignorant. Would some power, good or bad,
Instruct me which way I might be revenged
Upon this churl.

Dekker perceptively returns to the theme that Mother Sawyer is inexorably driven to her fate by the hostility of her antagonists:

'Tis all one
To be a witch as to be counted one:
Vengeance, shame, ruin light upon that canker!

She gets her wish. 'Enter a Black Dog', the stage direction reads. The Devil has arrived. 'Ho! Have I found thee cursing? Now thou art mine own.' 'Thine!' exclaims Mother Sawyer, who expresses no surprise at meeting a talking dog, 'What art thou?' 'He thou hast so often importuned to appear to thee, the devil,' comes the reply. Mother Sawyer is not a jot phased as she takes this astonishing revelation in her stride. 'Bless me! the devil?' is all she can exclaim. Her pact with him, sealed in her blood, is made on terms reminiscent of Dr Faustus. 'See!

Now I dare call thee mine,' says the Devil. 'For proof, command me; instantly I'll run / To any mischief; goodness can I none.' She goes for the obvious, but the Devil is powerless to strike Old Banks down:

> Though we have power, know it is circumscribed
> And tied in limits: though he be curst to thee,
> Yet of himself he's loving to the world,
> And charitable to the poor: now men that,
> As he, love goodness, though in smallest measure,
> Live without compass of our reach.

Dog reappears in the comic sub-plot. The yokel, Cuddy Banks – son of Old Banks – probably written and played by William Rowley, is a member of a Morris-dance. The scenes involving the troupe represent something of an almanac of contemporary dance. Even Dog is involved, playing the fiddle.

Dog is the unifying factor in the three strands of the play. He is an apparent catalyst to the titular plot. The choice of title may indicate where its appeal was thought most likely to lie. Significantly, the illustration on the title page of the edition of 1658 features Mother Sawyer, the Dog and the comical Cuddy, but does not refer to the main plot, attributed to John Ford, in which farmer's son Frank Thorney is forced by his father into a bigamous marriage with Susan Carter, whose father is suitably wealthy. His actual wife, Winnifride, is a former maidservant in the household of Sir Arthur Clarington, who has coerced her into a sexual relationship. She is pregnant by him, but Frank thinks the child is his. He flees with her but Susan follows. Rather bizarrely he accuses her of adultery, based on her inadvertent bigamous marriage, and stabs her to death – a fate she freely accepts.

> Die? O, 'twas time!
> How many years might I have slept in sin,
> The sin of my most hatred, too, adultery!

The good-hearted Cuddy has fallen in love with Kate, Susan's sister, and asks Mother Sawyer to invoke her powers to see off a rival – Warbeck, a stuffy scholar. The result is the farce that was Rowley's forte, as the bumpkin is deposited in a pond through the machinations of Dog, who has turned practical joker.

Within the confused compass of the play, caused at least in part by the varied inputs of its co-authors, serious moral issues are presented, such as the extent to which people are influenced by external forces. Mother Sawyer sells herself to the Devil to gain revenge on those who have abused her, so they may be deemed to have precipitated the series of disasters. Does the presence of Dog at such tragic events as Frank's murder of Susan mean that people are bound by forces beyond their control, so that their moral cupidity is less – or are they driven by their own flaws of character such as Frank's weakness? The play makes clear that human beings need no demonic intervention to achieve moral downfall. 'No. there's a dog already biting – his conscience,' responds Dog when Mother Sawyer demands he 'pluck out' the throat of Sir Arthur Clarington. At the last, it is the universal malaise of mankind that stands condemned. 'A witch!' exclaims Mother Sawyer. 'Who is not?

> Hold not that universal name in scorn, then.
> What are your painted things in princes' courts,
> Upon whose eyelids lust sits, blowing fires
> To burn men's souls in sensual hot desires,
> Upon whose naked paps a lecher's thought
> Acts sin in fouler shapes than can be wrought?

'But those work not as you do?' the Justice interrupts – 'No, but far worse,' she retorts:

> These by enchantments can whole lordships change
> To trunks of rich attire, turn ploughs and teams
> To Flanders mares and coaches, and huge trains
> Of servitors to a French butterfly.
> Have you not city-witches who can turn
> Their husband's wares, whole standing shops of wares,
> To sumptuous tables, gardens of stolen sin;
> In one year wasting what scarce twenty win?
> Are not these witches?

She was not the only witch around!

Lady Elizabeth's Men returned to The Cockpit in 1622. As sole sharer, Beeston exercised the total control Henslowe once had. *The Changeling*, co-authored by Middleton and Rowley, was licensed to the company on 7 May. The quarto of 1652, describes it as having been 'Acted (with great applause) at the Private house in Drury's Lane and at *Salisbury Court*'.[3] The latter reference demonstrates that the play was still pulling in audiences, seven years after it was first produced. Salisbury Court Theatre did not open until 1629.

'Principall Actors'

Given the decline of the drama from its heyday, it is no surprise that many plays of the previous generation retained their popularity. A poem by Leonard Digges some time before 1635 reveals that Shakespeare was still best box-office. 'But oh! What praise more powerfull can give / The dead, than by him the King Men live?' The drawing power of the favourite characters has not diminished:

> ...when let but Falstaffe come,
> *Hall*, Poines, the you scarce shall have a roome
> All is so pester'd: let but *Beatreice* ,
> And *Beneficke* be seene, loe in a trice
> The Cockpit Gallerioes, Boxes, all are full
> To have *Malvoglio*, that crosse garter's gull.

With Taylor's arrival, the King's Men underwent a period of great stability. In *Historia Histrionica*, his account of the seventeenth-century stage, James Wright states that of the 'Old Black-friers Men of the time before the [Civil] wars', John Lowin acted Falstaff, Morose in *The Silent Woman*, and Melantius in *The Maid's Tragedy*, 'with mighty applause', Joseph Taylor played the protagonists in Massinger's *The Picture* and Arthur Wilson's *The Swisser*. He inherited the part of Bussy D'Ambois after Nathan Field's death in 1620. When he grew too 'grey' to play the young firebrand, it passed to Eliard Swanson, who continued to play Othello. Beaumont and Fletcher's *The Maid's Tragedy* enjoyed frequent revivals, with Swanson succeeding Lowin and, in his turn, by the acting prodigy, Stephen Hammerton, in playing Amintor.

The original 'Band of Brothers' was diminishing. Robert Gough was buried at St Saviour's, Southwark on 19 February 1624. He had been with the Company and its predecessors for over thirty years, having appeared in *Seven Deadly Sins* as a boy actor. The troop lost a further 'Principall Actor' next year. John Underwood was another who demonstrated that perspicacity of his impending end so frequent among the Elizabethans. He made his will on 4 October 1624 and had died before the 11th. He left his property in trust for his five children, all of whom were minors. His third child was baptised Burbage, either after the actor or the family. His will reveals he was a sharer in the Globe, Blackfriars and Curtain Theatres. This mention of the Curtain shows it was still in business, but like the Fortune, it was struggling in the 1620s. There is no mention of it after 1627. Bankside was more propitious place for a theatre than Shoreditch.

To replace Underwood or Robert Gough, the King's Players followed their practice of poaching a leading actor from another company. Eliard Swanston cannot have been much more than a youth. His acting career seems to have started with Prince Charles' Men around 1620, but he had married in 1619 and was to father ten children. By the time he joined the King's Men, he had progressed to Lady Elizabeth's Men. In 1631, he could still play the young lover, Alcidonus, in *The Swisser*.

This is the last generation of the King's Men. Most of the Company would remain with it until the theatres closed in 1642. Clues of its make-up and the way it worked were revealed when the first quarto of *The Duchess of Malfi* was published in 1623, the first printed play to list virtually the entire cast – not only for the first production of around 1612–13, but for the revival of 1619. It shows that actors pretty well made a part their own. John Lowin maintained his role as Bosola. John Underwood continued as Delio through the two runs. Richard Sharpe created the role of the Duchess and, six years on, repeated it, but his performance as a youth of around 19 must have been rather different from that of the boy of 12 or 13. The same transition was made by John Thompson, who played Julia, the Cardinal's mistress. He appears to have undertaken the role near the beginning of his seven-year apprenticeship to John Shank. In a legal action in 1636, Shank claimed to have spent the huge sum of £40 in acquiring his indenture. The Cardinal was played in the first run by Henry Condell; on his retirement, the part was taken by Richard Robinson. After the death of William Ostler, the part of Antonio was taken by Robert Benfield. Another former boy actor, Robert Pallant, continued to play a succession of small parts, including Cariola. The cast list reveals that eleven actors filled sixteen speaking parts and there were walk-on roles as ladies, children, pilgrims, officials and attendants.

In August 1624, the Company enjoyed its greatest commercial success – and its most sensational production. In *A Game at Chess*, Thomas Middleton reverted to the old style of characters representing abstract personae and even, in the final act, incorporated elements of the mystery plays. John Webster was probably the co-author.

The play is set against a backdrop of contemporary events. Building an amicable relationship with the Catholic powers, while retaining his realm's Protestant identity was the cornerstone of James I's foreign policy. He was determined to avoid becoming embroiled in the growing tensions between Protestant and Catholic nations. To this end it was proposed that the Heir Apparent, Prince Henry, marry Philip III of Spain's daughter, the Infanta Maria Ana. With Henry's death in 1613, the task fell to the new Heir Apparent, Prince Charles. The project was made infinitely more attractive when the Spanish Ambassador, the Count of Gondamar, offered an enormous dowry of £500,000, later increased to £600,000. Such a windfall would mean the King no longer had to plead, not at least for a while, with Parliament for subsidies.

Although the projected 'Spanish Match' suited the King well, many in the country regarded Spain as England's natural enemy and memories of the long war between the two countries were still strong. The situation was exacerbated by the events of 1618, when the Bohemian Estates overthrew the Holy Roman Emperor Matthias. To the alarm of James I, the crown of Bohemia was accepted by his son-in-law Frederick V, the Elector Palatine. A popular revolt ensued. Spanish and Bavarian forces invaded Bohemia and the Palatinate. Frederick's ill-considered actions lost him both realms and precipitated the very situation James was striving to avoid – the division of Europe on sectarian lines, leading to what became known as 'The Thirty Years War'.

Frederick was well-known to the King's Men. They had participated in performances during the festivities to celebrate his marriage to the King's daughter. Following the death of Prince Henry, he had assumed the patronage of his acting company, which became the Elector Palatine or Palsgrave's Men.[4] It was unlikely that this deposed monarch from afar was a very active patron, but his name would have impressed local officials. Despite these huge setbacks to his policy of attempting to build diplomatic relations that transcended sectarian divides, the King persisted in his efforts to bring about the Spanish match, but war fever was growing. Gondomar, who was pivotal in the execution of the popular hero Sir Walter Raleigh, was hissed in street, but that not all despised him is shown in a letter sent by John Chamberlain to Sir Dudley Carleton on Saturday, 21 July 1621:

> The Spanish Ambassador … is growne so affable and familiar, that on Monday with his whole traine he went to a common play at the Fortune in Golding-Lane, and the players (not to be overcome with curtesie) made him a banket when the play was don in the garden adjoining.[5]

Palsgrave's Men seem to have made a habit of wining and dining visitors, although whether this was a general practice is unclear. 'I have beene at Bess Turnups,' declares a character in Nathan Field's *Amends for Ladies*, 'and she swears all the Gentlewomen went to see a play at the Fortune, and are not come in yet, and she believes they sup with the Players.'

On 18 December 1621, the House of Commons tabled a Protestation to the King that Prince Charles should be 'married to one of our own religion'. James was furious, considering royal marriages a royal matter. He adjourned the sitting of Parliament, tore the Proclamation from the Commons Journal and ordered the imprisonment of Sir Edward Coke, the former Chief Justice, its principal author. Several other members were arrested, including a future architect of the English revolution, John Pym. This outraged the members, who regarded free speech as an 'ancient and undoubted right received from our ancestors'.[6] It is not difficult to discern the outset of the tensions between King and Parliament that ultimately brought down the monarchy.

A widely-circulated, virulently anti-Catholic and anti-Spanish pamphlet entitled *Vox Populi – News from Spain* did much to stir popular outrage against the Spanish Match. Its author was Thomas Scott, a radical Puritan preacher. It consisted of the entirely fictional tale of Gondomar's return to Madrid and his account of his schemes for the subversion of the English and their religion.

James persisted in attempting to rearrange the diplomatic map of Europe. He realised that a Spanish alliance was the only hope of restoring Frederick to his throne. In an extraordinary development, Prince Charles took the initiative, journeying to Spain incognito with his father's favourite, George Villiers, Duke of Buckingham, to woo the Infanta for himself. He fell deeply in love with her and agreed to most of the Spanish terms for the marriage, including the repeal of the anti-Catholic penal laws. Even the dying Pope apparently endorsed the arrangement. It was not to be. While the devout 17-year-old Maria Ana would have been content to surrender her virginity in the Hapsburg cause, she was not keen on a Protestant match, particularly if the products of such a union were to be raised as Protestants. She appears to have developed a distaste for Charles, echoing Shakespeare in declaring that she would rather enter a nunnery than marry him – the one destiny that the Most Catholic King could not deny. With the outbreak of war in Central Europe, the death of Philip III and the fall from grace of Gondomar, Spanish enthusiasm for the accord lessened. The Infanta's reluctance provided an opportunity to call it off. Charles returned home humiliated, reversing his previous stance by calling for war with Spain. The failure of the negotiations was met with rejoicing. Ben Jonson celebrated Charles' return with a masque, *Neptune's Triumph for the Return of Albion*. War fever grew.

This is the background to *A Game at Chess*. The initiative for its creation could have been to create a vehicle for William Rowley, who had joined the King's Men in the previous year. Several of Middleton's previous plays had been performed by the King's Men: *Anything for a Quiet Life* was staged around 1621 at Blackfriars. He had also gained the lucrative commission of writing and orchestrating the spectacle at the annual Lord Mayor's Show, for a handsome annual salary of £10.

The play is a satire on the negotiations around the Spanish Match. As the title implies, it is set around a symbolic chess match. The white pieces represent England, the black, Spain, so there is an implicit conflict between good and bad. Individual characters are portrayed. The Black Knight is Count Gondomar. He is easily identified: It was well-known that he suffered from an anal fistula and had to use 'a chair of ease'. If further assistance was required, the King's Men bought items from his wardrobe as costumes for the role.[7]

Rowley probably wrote and played the part of the Fat Bishop. It was based on the character of Marco Antonio de Dominis, the renegade Archbishop of Spalatro, who after siding with the Venetian Republic against the Pope had sought refuge in England where he became an Anglican, was created Dean of Windsor and received a generous pension from the King. On 16 January 1622, he announced his intention to return to Rome. Despite his ample allowance, he was discontented with his financial lot. It was widely believed that Gondomar had worked on his pride and avarice, promising him an annual pension of 12,000 crowns. Once out of England, his attacks on his former place of refuge were as violent as those he had previously made against Rome. The audience would surely have recognised the Black Knight's description of him as 'Yond greasy, turncoat, gormandising prelate'.

The characters move and act according to the rules of the play's title. There is even a genuine chess opening – the Queen's Gambit Declined. The action concerns the attempts of the black set to subvert the white. Middleton incorporated material from *Vox Populi* to set the play's anti-Catholic, anti-Spanish tone. It was licensed by the Master of the Revels on 12 June 1624. Realising the potential success of this highly topical play, the Company dispensed with its usual repertory system and played it on a straight run. It opened on 6 August and became the 'must see' event. On 16 August, the authorities closed it down after a record run of nine performances following a complaint to the King by the Spanish Ambassador – Gondomar's successor, Don Carlos Coloma. That he regarded the play as an intense provocation is shown by a lengthy letter he wrote to the Chief Minister, the Count-Duke of Olivarese. It is worth quoting at length as an indication of the outrage the play provoked among the Spanish and for the insight it gives into the workings of the contemporary theatre:

> The actors whom they call here 'the King's Men' have recently acted and are still acting, in London, a play that so many people come to see that were more than 3,000 on the day that the audience was the smallest. There was such merriment, hubbub and applause that even I had been many leagues away it would not have been possible for me not have taken notice of it.
>
> The subject of the play is a game of chess, with white squares and black squares, then kings and other pieces, acted by the players, and the king of the blacks has easily been taken for our lord the King, because of his youth, dress and other details. The first act, or rather game was played by their ministers, impersonated by the white pieces, and the Jesuits, by the black ones. Here there were remarkable acts of sacrilege and among other

> abominations, a minister summoned St Ignatius from hell, and when he found himself again in the world, the first thing he did was to rape one of his female penitents; in all this, these accursed and abominable men revealed the depths of their heresy by their lewd and obscene actions.
>
> The second act was directed against the Archbishop of Spalatro, at that time a white piece, but afterwards won over to the black side by the Count of Gondomar, who was brought onto the stage in his litter almost to the life, and seated in his chair with a hole in it (they said). He confessed all the treacherous actions with which he had deceived and soothed the king of the whites, and, when he discussed the matter of confession with the Jesuits, the actor disguised as the count took out a book in which were rated all the prices for which hence-forth sins were to be forgiven.
>
> The last act ended with long, obstinate struggle between all the whites and the blacks, and in it he who acted the Prince of Wales heartily beat and kicked the Count of Gondomar into Hell, which consisted of a great hole and hideous figures and the white king [drove] the black king and even his queen [there] almost as offensively.
>
> It cannot be pleaded that those who repeat and hear these insults are merely rogues because during these last four days more than 12,000 persons have all heard the play of *A Game at Chess*, for so they call it, including all the nobility still in London. All these people come out of the theatre so inflamed against Spain that, as a few Catholics have told me secretly, that, if I went to the play, my person would not be safe in the streets; others have advised me to keep to my house with a good guard and this is being done.

The outrage felt by the Ambassador must have reached the ears of the ailing King James, who was still determined to keep his kingdoms out of war with Spain. The play was banned; not because of its offensiveness, but because it was illegal to represent a living head of state on the public stage, as the King's Men must have known. In *A Game at Chess* two were so portrayed. The Privy Council could not ignore such flouting of its rules and took out a prosecution against the actors and playwright on 18 August. The Globe Theatre was closed during the hearing. The Company probably escaped severe censure because it could claim it had gone through the appropriate channels. The question as to why Master of the Revels passed it remains. He was probably influenced by the pro-war party, which saw it as a golden opportunity to whip up popular fervour against Spain and Catholicism.

No such fortune attended Thomas Middleton. If the Privy Council needed a scapegoat to appease the Spanish Ambassador, he was the obvious choice. He did the usual thing and disappeared. His 20-year-old son, Edward, was brought before the Privy Council, presumably to be questioned about his whereabouts. He was soon found. It appears he addressed a flippant verse petition to the King which revealed that he was confined 'in the Fleet'. He seems to assume that His Majesty had a sense of humour. Hopefully, he was correct:

> A harmless game coyned only for delight,
> Was play'd betwixt the black and the white:
> The white house won. Yet still the black doth brag;
> Use your royal hand, 'twill set me free.
> 'Tis but the removing of a man. That's ME.

The description of the play as 'A harmless game coyned only for delight', was hardly the Spanish view, but for the management of the Globe Theatre it must have initially have produced the euphoria of success. On 11 August, Sir Francis Nethersole told Sir Dudley Carleton that it was taking '100 a night'. Whether or no in response to his supposed verse petition, Middleton appears to have been released soon after, but the episode seems to have sent him into severe decline. He wrote nothing more for the stage. He may have been forbidden to do so. His relationship with the City fathers was also in trouble. On 1 February 1626, the Common Council resolved to end his annual salary, 'unless he give this court satisfaction according as what was intended he should do when the said pension was first granted him'. In the event, the Drapers' Company commissioned Middleton and his 'artificer', (designer) Garrett Christmas, to stage the pageant, *The Triumphs of Health and Prosperity* for the Lord Mayor's Show. That year's Lord Mayor, Sir Cuthbert Hackett, was a draper. On 31 December, the two men complained to the Court of Assistants that they had not been paid. The Drapers' Company replied that payment had been 'putt of ill performance of the pageant'. They were paid eventually, but it was less than they had received previously. Middleton was ailing and had lost the style and panache that had characterised much of his work. On 4 July 1627 he was buried at his parish church, St Mary's, Newington Butts. He left his widow in a state of penury. In February 1627/8, she applied to the City authorities for assistance. Her husband's past services struck a chord, for she was granted a sum of 20 marks.

A Game at Chess represents a serious phase in the decline of the theatre. Some two decades after *Hamlet* had graced the stage of the Globe, Shakespeare's Company was putting on a crude parody with an aggressive political message full of tasteless pornography, geared to the lowest possible popular prejudice. If the object of the production was to prepare public opinion for war with Spain, it succeeded. James I, still attempting to arbitrate for peace, refused to declare war. It was left to his successor, probably still smarting from the failure of the Spanish Match, to do so. It was a disaster. An expedition intended to emulate Drake's storming of Cadiz was a fiasco. England found herself allied with the French Crown in its civil war against the Huguenots, which stirred the ire of the Puritans. The eventual peace was a humiliation. The cost of the war and the incompetence of its prosecution caused severe rifts between the Monarchy and Parliament: another stage in the process that would lead to Civil War and see the fulfilment of the Puritan ambition to abolish the theatre, which had assisted its own downfall.

The Fatal Vespers

A disaster on 26 October 1623 must have had considerable impact on the King's Men, if only because of its proximity to the Blackfriars Theatre. The only Catholic masses permitted were those held in foreign embassies. Following the death of the 2nd Lord Hunsdon without a male heir in 1603, his property in Blackfriars was acquired by the French ambassador, the Comte de Tillières. Although the authorities discouraged local attendance at masses in foreign embassies, the faithful ignored such strictures. When people climbed the great staircase at the former Priory, they could attend a play by turning right or a liturgy by turning left. Blackfriars had returned to its origins by becoming London's the most important mass centre.

On that Sunday afternoon, 300 worshippers were listening to a sermon by a young Jesuit, Fr. Robert Drury. Those keen to hear him crowded round the pulpit. The weight of numbers caused the floor to collapse, precipitating them to the floor below. A contemporary chronicler described the dreadful scene:

> Here some buried, some dismembered, some only parts of men, here some wounded and weltering in their own and others blood, others pulling forth their failing hands and crying out for help. Here some gasping and panting for breath; others stifled for want of air.

The people in the less-crowded areas, where the floor had held, found themselves marooned. To escape they cut their way through the plaster wall. News of the catastrophe spread rapidly. The Lord Mayor ordered the Priory gates shut to keep out crowds of the curious and guards were placed on all the passages. The French Ambassador and his family were evacuated. Ninety-five people perished, including Fr. Drury. Naturally the Puritans ascribed the disaster to God's anger at idolatry. The Coroner's inquest took a more sanguine view, denoting it caused by the collapse of an unsound beam.

What became known as the 'fatal vespers' not only occurred in the part of the old friary that was adjacent to the Blackfriars Theatre, but members of the King's Men are likely to have been in the congregation. 'Most of our present English actors,' wrote William Prynne, in 1633, '(as I am credibly informed) [are] professed Papists.' While there may have been a tendency for Puritans to confuse Anglicanism with Catholicism, there was some truth in this. A number of those associated with the Company were known to be 'popishly affected'. Ben Jonson was a Catholic for many years. The dramatist Thomas Lodge went into exile when his conversion to Rome became known in 1603, but returned in 1610 and died a Catholic in 1625. James Shirley was another convert. Years after his death, William Shakespeare was recorded by a senior member of the Anglican hierarchy as having 'died a papist'.

'Wee have Offended'

The box-office success of *A Game at Chess* may have persuaded the Company to present another play with an anti-Spanish theme. The first performance of *The Spanish Viceroy* by Philip Massinger in December 1624 was likely at Blackfriars. Given the past consequences it seems extraordinary that the King's Men should perform a play for which they had not obtained a licence from the Master of the Revels. Possibly they were persuaded by members of the war party at Court that the issue would be overlooked. Sir Henry Herbert took a different view. On 20 December, the principal actors in the production wrote him a grovelling letter of apology. He did not copy it into his record book until October 1633, nearly nine years after the offence. ''Tis entered here in remembrance of their disorders,' he wrote. It appears another company may have transgressed in a similar way and he was recording the precedent:

> Whereas not long since we acted a play called the Spanish Viceroy, not being licensed under your lordships hande, nor allowed of: wee doe confess and herby acknowledge that wee have offended, and that it is in your powere to punish this offense, and are very sorry for it, and doe likewise promise herby that we will not act any play without your hand or substituts hereafter; nor doe any thinge that may prejudice the authority of your office: So hoping that this humble submission of ours may bee accepted, wee have thereunto sett our hands.
>
> This twentiethe of Decem. 1624.
>
> Joseph Taylor John Lowen.
> Richard Robinson. John Shancke.

Elyard Swanston.	John Rice.
Thomas Pollard	Will Rowley.
Robert Benfeilde.	Richard Sharpe.
George Burght.	

The Spanish Viceroy represents something of a mystery. It was not until 1653 that a play was entered on the Stationers' Register under the title, 'The Spanish Viceroy or the honor of women by Phill Massinger'. A play with the latter name was presented by the Company in 1628, so it is possible that, with the Spanish war over and with less interest in portraying that country in a negative way, Massinger simply rewrote the earlier play and gave it a different title. On the other hand, the stationer, Humphrey Moseley, was in the habit of registering two plays as if they were one as a cost-saving exercise so there could have been two different plays. The issue is academic because neither has survived. The manuscript of *The Honour of Women* came into the possession of the eighteenth century bibliophile, John Warburton. It was one of over fifty scripts destroyed by Betsy Baker, his cook; thinking they were scrap paper, she used them to light the fire.

The controversies in which the King's Men were embroiled over their productions of *A Game at Chess* and *The Spanish Viceroy* do not seem to have affected their standing at Court. As they were officially royal servants, members of the company were immune from arrest warrants for travelling abroad in time of plague. Nor could they be 'pressed for soldiers'. On 27 December 1624, just a week after the apology to Sir Henry, these privileges were extended to twenty-one 'musicians and other necessary attendants'. The name of Edward Knight, the prompter, tops the list, such was his importance as compiler of the Company's scripts. Another vital functionary was John Rhodes, wardrobe master at Blackfriars. The list was issued in the name of Sir Henry Herbert, so clearly he bore no resentment at the disregard of his position.

The King's Men's royal patron was growing increasingly infirm. Early in 1625, he suffered severe attacks of arthritis, gout and fainting fits. He fell seriously ill in March with a tertian ague and suffered a stroke. He died at the royal residence of Theobald's House near Cheshunt on 27 March. The requisite period of mourning meant places of public entertainment were closed for several weeks. Those members of the Company who were Gentlemen of the Chamber followed the royal coffin to Westminster Abbey on 7 May. Each was given four yards of black cloth to create mourning dress. In his sermon, delivered over two hours, the Bishop of Lincoln compared James to King Solomon. The magnificent hearse was designed by Inigo Jones. An onlooker commented that it was the 'fairest and best fashioned that hath ben seen'.

It may have been some consolation to the players that the theatres would have had to close anyway. That month the River Thames went into full flood from the highest tide ever recorded. Westminster Hall was under 3 feet of water. A more virulent reason for closure occurred in the week of 15 April. The plague followed its usual pattern by first appearing in St Botolph's Ward. The theatres were closed for the whole season. James' reign had ended as it had begun – with the plague. Among the many victims, there was one whose loss represented a severe blow for the King's Men. John Aubrey wrote an account of his death:

> John Fletcher, invited to goe with a Knight into Norfolke or Suffolke in the Plague-time of 1625, stayd but to make himselfe a suite of Cloathes, and while it was makeing, fell sick of the Plague and dyed.
>
> This I had (1668) from his Tayler, who is now a very old man, and Clarke of St Mary Overy's in Southwark. Mr Fletcher had an Issue in his arm … The Clarke (who was wont to bring him Ivy-leaves to dresse it) when he came, found the Spotts upon him. Death stopped his Journey and laid him low here.

He was buried on 29 August, at the minster church of St Mary Overie, close to the Globe Theatre he had served. He wrote, or collaborated in, over fifty plays, more than one for each of the forty-five years of his life.

The new King, Charles Stuart, was noted for his love of theatricals. He was to possess a copy of the Second Folio of Shakespeare's Works, published in one 1632, which he annotated with the names of the leading characters. In his reign, the court masque assumed new levels of extravagance. Members of the King's Men took speaking roles, but the main parts were reserved for the Royal Family and its courtiers.

The plague may have taken two other prominent men of the theatre in the following February. On the 11th, William Rowley was buried at St James', Clerkenwell. The soldier/author, Cyril Tourneur, had embarked on the disastrous expedition against Cadiz. On the homeward voyage, he was put ashore at Kinsale with other sick men and died on 28 February. His best-known work is *The Atheist's Tragedy or The Honest Man's Revenge*, which was entered onto the Stationer's Register on 14 September 1611. In a scenario which appears prophetic of later secular ages, the protagonist of the title, D'Amville, exchanges the religious concept of eternal life for that of genetic inheritance and reason as the prevailing sentiment for a life well-lived:

Here are my sons …
There's my eternity. My life in them
And their succession shall for ever live,
And in my reason dwells the *providence*
To add to life as much of happiness.

Yet, his atheism ensures he lacks a moral compass:

Let all men lose, so I increase my gain.
I have no feeling of another's pain.

This was an understatement. D'Amville is a Machiavellian character who murders Montferrers, his brother plots the ruin of his nephew and attempts to rape the heroine. His excesses lead to his derangement and suicide. Moral order is restored by the ghost of Montferrers, who, in contrast to Hamlet's father, counsels the abjuration of revenge and reliance on the divine providence that D'Amville has rejected.

John Fletcher was active till the last. On 22 January 1626, the Master of the Revels recorded his authorship of a play called *The Fair Maid of the Inn*. Despite this singular attribution, it appears to have been a collaboration, or perhaps another hand completed it after Fletcher's death. It was included in Beaumont and Fletcher's First Folio of 1647. Whoever the author of the Prologue may have been, he understood the essence of Fletcher's work:

Plays have their fates, not as in their true sense.
They're understood, but as the influence
Of idle custom, madly works upon
The dross of many tongu'd opinion.

'The dross of many tongu'd opinion' might have been regarded by some as epitomising the growing news industry. 'If any read nowadays, it is a play-booke, or pamphlete of newes,' declared Robert Burton in the *Anatomie of Melancholy*. Pamphlets had been published on events of interest, but they appeared irregularly. Chief architect of a media revolution was the stationer Nathaniel Butter, who published from his 'shop at the sign of the Pied Bull', the first quarto of *King Lear* in 1608, plays by Thomas Heywood, Samuel Rowley, Thomas Dekker and Fulke Greville and the two books of Chapman's *Homer*. In 1620, he published a pamphlet with the lengthy and provocative title, *A Plain Demonstration of the Unlawful Succession of Ferdinand II, Because of the Incestuous Marriage of His Parents*: an attack on the Holy Roman Emperor who had succeeded in the previous year.

King James was desperate to keep his domains out of the religious war raging in Europe, so swift action was taken. Butter and William Stansby, the printer, were jailed before successfully petitioning for release, Butter on behalf of himself, his pregnant wife, and their three children. Stansby blamed the whole affair on Butter.

On his release, Butter went into a new venture. In 1621, a licence was granted to 'N.B.' to disseminate a style of news bulletin called a coranto[8] that had been developed in Amsterdam, printed in English and distributed in London. On 22 May 1622, he published the first edition of what may be considered the first English newspaper; the first news sheet to be published at regular intervals in numbered editions. Unlike the pamphlets that had dealt with single topics like the Calverley murders, the corantos covered a variety of issues. The significant exception is realised in the full title of Butter's broadsheet: *Weekly News from Italy, Germany, Hungaria, Bohemia, the Palatinate, France and the Low Countries.* Reporting events in England was not popular with the authorities.

The new venture was not entirely well-received. *The Fair Maid of the Inn* contains satirical references to 'the ghost of some lying Stationer, a spirit that shall look as if butter would not melt in his mouth'. Such scorn was as nothing compared with that evoked when Ben Jonson's first work for the stage for a decade was premiered at Blackfriars in February 1626. *The Staple of News* invokes his familiar theme of women running out of control, but it also assails the contemporary financial system. Pennyboy Junior is a spendthrift, his uncle, Pennyboy Senior, a miser. Lady Aurelia Clara Percunia's nurse is even called Mortgage, and one of her maids, Statute. The scene is set in the Prologue when four 'Gossips', aptly named Mirth, Tattle, Expectation and Censure, insist on sitting on the stage. 'We are persons of quality, I assure you,' says Mirth, 'and women of fashion; and come to see, and to be seen.' They reappear to give a cryptic commentary on the action at the end of each act. The satiric intent is declared in the first scene. 'What newes?' Thomas Barber is asked. 'Oh, sir, a Staple of News!' he replies. 'What's that?' asks Pennyboy Junior. 'An *Office*, Sir, a brave young *Office* set up: I had forgot to tell your worship.' 'For what?' 'To enter all the *News*, sir, o' the time.' 'And vent it as occasion serves! A Place / Of huge commerce it will be.' 'What is it, an Office?' asks Fashioner. The reply could be a description of the offices of a modern Fleet Street newspaper.

Newly erected
Here in the house, almost on the same floor,
Where all the news of all sorts shall be brought,
And there be examined, and then register'd,
And so be issued under the seal of an office,
As Staple News; no other news be current.

'The Governour o' the Staple, Master Cymball', is a caricature of Butter. Preposterous stories flow into his office. 'The King of Spain is chosen Pope'. The famous Spanish General, Don Spinola, has been appointed Vicar General of the Jesuits.

Ben brings his favourite tippling place and its host into the action. Pennyboy Senior announces his intention to 'dine in the Apollo with Percunia at brave Duke Wadloe's'. Pennyboy Junior replies 'Our meal shall be brought thither, Simon the King will bid us welcome.' Simon Wadloe kept the ancient hostelry, *The Devil and St Dunstan*, which stood near the Temple Bar in Fleet Street. Here Ben presided over a group of his admirers who met in the room called the Apollo, after the God of Poetry whose bust was mounted above the door. The membership of the confraternity was defined by Jonson in a set of rules in Latin engraved over the mantelpiece. A contemporary translation records:

> Let none but guests or clubbers hither come;
> Let dunces, fools, sad sordid men keep home …

There would be no talk of religion or politics:

> Let none of us be mute or talk too much;
> On serious things or sacred let's not touch.

Anyone of a literary and convivial bent was welcome, but likely participants may be identified among the groups known variously as the 'Sons' or 'Tribe' of Ben, who professed admiration for the Laureate and claimed to model their works on his. Although they may have constituted two different names for the same thing: the 'Sons' appears to have been an epithet bestowed by Ben himself. He had no surviving children, so, if not heirs to his body, they were heirs to his genius. They included playwrights Richard Brome, Thomas Nabbes, Thomas Killigrew, Shackerley Marmion, William Randolph and Walter Montagu. The 'Tribe of Ben' was a self-description by a group later described as Cavalier poets. They included Richard Lovelace, Sir John Suckling and Thomas Carew.

That Ben's conviviality was not restricted to gatherings at *The Mermaid* and *The Devil* is revealed in lines by his devotee, Robert Herrick:

> Ah Ben!
> Say how, or when
> Shall we thy guests
> Meet at those lyric feasts
> Made at the Sun,
> The Dog, the Triple Tun?
> Where we such clusters had,
> As made us nobly wild, not mad;

Under fain'd names on the stage

The new King was the patron of Prince Charles' Men, and the thought must have occurred that they would become King Charles' Men and the royal patronage of the King's Men withdrawn, but Charles was hardly likely to abandon the most prestigious company in the land, so the 'King's Men' remained that. Without royal patronage, Prince Charles' Men rapidly dissolved. Thomas Hobbs, William Penn and Anthony Smith joined the King's Men as hired men. Others may have gone to Christopher Beeston's new company, Queen Henrietta's Men, aka 'The Queen's Comedians', formed under the patronage of the new Queen. Many leading playwrights would work with it, including Philip Massinger, John Ford and Thomas Heywood. The chief in-house dramatist, however, was James Shirley. A prolific author, he had been 'a minister of God's word in or near St Alban's', but resigned his living after his conversion to Catholicism. His first play, *Love Tricks* was performed by Lady Elizabeth's Men at the Cockpit Theatre just before the plague closed the theatres. His next play, *The Maid's Revenge* was licensed on 9 February 1626 was also performed there, the first production by Queen Henrietta's Men.

The new Company did to the King's Men what it had done unto others. Richard Perkins had joined the Company as recently as 1623, but does not seem to have achieved any great distinction with them. This may have been what induced him to throw in his lot with the new company. He made the right move, achieving great prominence with them. He was noted for his performance as Barabbas in the 1633 revival of *The Jew of Malta*. In his prologue to the Cockpit performance, Thomas Heywood praised Perkins' for living up to 'the best of actors', Edward Alleyn.

William Robbins had also performed with Queen Anne's Men as their leading comic actor. Most of the others in the new company had been with the previous resident company at the Cockpit, the Lady Elizabeth's Men, now the Queen of Bohemia's Men. One such was Anthony Turner. Nothing is known of his early years, but by 1622 he was playing leading roles. Although he seemed to specialise in the playing of older men, he appeared as a kitchen maid in a revival of the first part of Thomas Heywood's *The Fair Maid of the West*.

The new Company inherited its predecessor's portfolio of plays, so it possessed works of authors of the calibre of Chapman, Massinger and Heywood. Over the next decade, it performed sixty-six times at Court, for which they were paid a total of £900. Only the King's Men gave more royal performances in the period.

On 21 November 1626, there died the other great actor of the Elizabethan theatre. 'Others speak, but only thou dost act,' Ben Jonson wrote of Edward Alleyn. At the time of his death, he had not trodden the boards for over twenty years, but he did not forsake the drama altogether, coaching the boys at the College of God's Gift in the dramatic arts. On 6 January 1622, during the Christmas season, 'the boyes play'd a play'. The documents he bequeathed to the college he founded would prove an invaluable resource for future scholars.

Just two years after the death of Robert Gough, his son Alexander joined the King's Men as a boy actor. He was just 12 years old. He probably made his debut in Philip Massinger's *The Roman Actor*, playing the part of Caenis at Blackfriars. Another boy actor, John Honyman, probably also made his debut in this production. The cast list in the 1629 quarto demonstrates a virtual complete turnaround from the company of Shakespeare and Burbage. Of the old-stagers, only John Lowin and Robert Robinson played significant roles. Joseph Taylor played Paris, the title character; Eliard Swanson, Aretinus Clemems, Caesar's spy; and Robert Benfield, Junius Rusticus. The play, with its emphasis on the contrast between public and private morality, was regarded by Massinger as his finest. It strikes a contemporary note, perhaps reflecting the anxieties felt as to whether the new King would renew the Company's Royal Patronage, opening with a conversation between Paris and two actors in his company, Latinus and Aesopus (played by Robert Robinson) about the dismal prospects facing the stage. 'The times are dull,' he says, 'and all that wee receue, / Will hardlie satisfie the dayes Expenc.' Is it to gain a cheer or a laugh that he ascribes the plight to the moral degeneracy of the contemporary audience?

> Pleasures of worse nature
> Are gladly entertayn'd, and they that shun vs,
> Practise in priuate sports the *Stewes* would blush at.

The only hope is for the return from campaigning of the tyrannous Emperor, who esteems Paris and may bestow his patronage upon him.

Messengers arrive to summon Paris to appear before the Senate: 'there to answer what shall be urged against you'. Arctimus defines the charges:

> In thee, as being the chiefe of thy profession,
> I doe accuse the qualitie of treason,
> As libellers against the state and *Caesa*r.

'Meere accusations are not proofes, my Lord,' Paris replies. 'In what are we delinquents?'

The indictment pronounced by Arctimus would sound familiar to those connected with the theatre, which had indeed searched into 'the secrets o' the time'. 'Under fain'd names' is redolent of one of the Puritan objections to the theatre:

You are they
That search into the secrets o' the time,
And vnder fain'd names on the Stage present
Actions not to be toucht at; and traduce
Persons of rancke, and qualitie of both Sexes,
And with Satiricall. and bitter iests
Make euen the Senators ridiculous
To the Plebeans.

In his spirited riposte, Paris seeks the moral high ground. The theatre is a place where vice, corruption and wrong-doing are exposed and a proper pattern of behaviour is set. Knowing the Emperor will support him, he invokes his name before the Senate. He is,

So confident in the iustice of our cause,
That I could wish *Caesar*, in whose great name
All Kings are comprehended sate as iudge,
To heare our Plea ...[9]

The hearing comes to no conclusion. It is suspended until the return of the Emperor Domitianus. On his return, his lascivious eye of the Emperor Domitianus falls on Domitia, the beautiful wife of a Senator, Aelius Lamia. Under duress, he is persuaded to divorce her. There follow scenes of characters being wiped out one by one by the Emperor. The climax comes when he stabs Paris, who has been engaged in a romance with Domitia, during a performance of a play within a play. In an ending as bizarre as any of the period, Domitianus is told of the hour of his death by an astrologer, who pays with his life for his pains. To prevent such a happening, the Emperor surrounds himself with bodyguards, but is deceived by Parthenius, a freed slave, into thinking the hour has passed. After the guard is dismissed, he is stabbed to death by most of his surviving antagonists, including Domitia. ''Tis done, 'tis done basely' are the Emperor's last words in terms redolent of Macbeth.

The golden age of the theatre was drawing to a close. Plots were becoming increasingly involved and absurd, theatrical companies more and more diffuse. It becomes more difficult to discern the authorship of plays and the date of their first production. Even the King's Players who had tended to favour plays by individual playwrights began to promote more of the group productions that

Henslowe had favoured. John Ford's *The Lover's Melancholy*, was licensed for performance on 24 November 1628 and acted at the Globe and Blackfriars. In his dedicatory epistle to the edition published in 1629, he declares it his first dramatic piece 'that ever courted reader'. The plot and sub-plot are of such complexity that it is difficult to conceive how the audience could have followed them. The Senecan style of gratuitous violence was on the increase. *The Broken Heart*, Ford's play of indeterminate date, performed by the King's Men at the Blackfriars, features a number of bizarre deaths. His best-known play, *'Tis Pity She's a Whore*, plunges further into decadence. It was first performed by Queen Henrietta's Men at the Cockpit some time before 1633, when it was first published. It incorporates many of the sensational scenes that featured in the contemporary drama in a single work, including a poisoned sword and chalice (*Hamlet*), a corrupt cardinal (*Duchess of Malfi*), the blinding of a woman (*Titus Andronicus*) and a final bloodbath (too frequent to specify). It opens in a confessional setting with a discussion between the central character, Giovanni, and Bonaventura, a Friar, of the moral issues surrounding incest. At first, the Friar assumes that Giovanni is attempting to intellectualise an untenable argument in the manner of the medieval schoolmen and warns him of the spiritual hazards of such speculation:

> Dispute no more in this; for know, young man,
> These are no school-points; nice philosophy
> May tolerate unlikely arguments,
> But heaven admits no jests; wits that presum'd
> On wit too much – by striving how to prove
> There was no God; – with foolish grounds of art
> Discovered first the nearest way to hell.
> And filled the world with devilish atheism.

But this is no intellectual exercise. Giovanni has developed an incestuous passion for his sister, Annabella, and considers the injunctions against such relations to be based on mere custom:

> Shall a peevish sound,
> A customary form, from man to man,
> Of brother and of sister, be a bar
> Twixt my perpetual happiness and me?
> Say that we had one father, say one womb,
> (Curse to my joys) gave both us life, and birth;
> Are we not therefore each to other bound

So much the more by Nature; by the the links
Of blood, of reason; Nay if you will have 't,
Even of Religion, to be ever one,
One soul, one flesh, one love, one heart, one *All*?

The Friar tries to divert Giovanni from the path to damnation – 'Have done, unhappy youth, for thou art lost.' He speaks in vain. Annabella succumbs to her brother's passion and surrenders the virginity that is much sought by suitors she does not care for. 'No more sister now, but love, a name more gracious,' he tells her. Inevitable and sensational nemesis follows.

Squeamishly Beheld and Censored

Ben Jonson's career had faltered during the 1620s. While John Dryden's description of his later comedies as 'dotages' may overlook aspects of their quality, they were not the sparkling triumphs of his earlier works. *The Staple of News* was not a popular success. Indeed the third act, with its concentration on the news medium of the title so confused audiences that, in the printed edition of 1631, he added an address 'To the Readers', somewhat unusually, within the play itself. 'The allegory and purpose of the Author' was 'wholly mistaken'. Perhaps the relative obscurity of the subject might have contributed to its lack of success. Many in the audience might have been unfamiliar with Butter's *Weekly News*.

If *The Staple of News* was not entirely a success, Ben's next production can only be described as catastrophic. *The New Inn, or The Light Heart* was licensed for performance on 19 January 1629 and performed later that year by the King's Men at Blackfriars. The plot is bizarrely complicated and must have puzzled the audience. Of course the resultant flop was nothing to do with Ben, according to Ben. In the 1631 edition of the play, he blamed both actors and audience. 'As it was never Acted, but most negligently Play'd by some, the KING'S SERVENTS and more squeamishly Beheld and Censured by others, the KING'S SUBJECTS.'

In his *Ode to Himself*, written that year, he vented further scorn on the audience:

Say that thou pour'st 'em wheat,
   And they would acorns eat;
'Twere simple fury, still thyself to waste
   On such as have no taste;
To offer them a surfeit of pure bread,
   Whose appetites are dead;

No, give them grains their fill,
Husks, draff to drink, and swill;
If they love lees, and leave the lusty wine,
Envy them not, their palate's with the swine.[10]

Ben was not in good physical or mental shape. 'The maker is sick and sad,' he confesses in his epilogue to the Blackfriars production. His situation is reflected in the words of Lovell, a character in the play – 'poverty, restraint, captivity, bereavement, loss of children, long disease'. His bile appears to have been further exacerbated by the success of a now-lost play, *The Love-sick Maid*, which was performed at Blackfriars shortly after the failure of *The New Inn*. It was followed in the same year by *The Northern Lass*, by the same author, which was acted at the Globe and Blackfriars 'with good applause'. The unkindest cut of all was that the playwright, Richard Brome, had been Ben's servant. He is first recorded in The Induction to *Bartholomew Fair* where he is described as 'Master Brome, behind the Arras'. Perhaps he was employed as the prompter. By 1628, he was a member of the Queen of Bohemia's Men. His success as a playwright produced a bitter attack from Ben, which dwelt on his previous menial career:

Brome's sweepings do as well
There, as his master's meal,
For who the relish of these guests will fit
Needs set them but the almshouses of wit.[11]

Not surprisingly, Jonson's vitriolic attacks provoked responses. Thomas Carew was cryptic about the decline of his dramatic powers:

And yet 'tis true
Thy comic muse from the exalted line
Touch'd by thy *Alchemist* doth since decline
From that her zenith ….

And this from one of the Tribe of Ben!

The anonymous author of *The Country's Censure on Ben Jonson's New Inn* was rather more personal, implying that drink had sodden the poet's 'poor crackbrain':

Listen (decaying Ben) and counsel hear.
Wits have their date, and strength of brains may wear.
Age, steeped in sack, hath quenched thy Enthean fire;
We pity now, whom once we did admire.

Ben's disputes with Inigo Jones had reached the level of a feud. Ostensibly, they had much in common, as disciples of the classical forms in their respective arts, but as they were collaborating on prestigious courtly productions, rivalry in terms of royal appreciation was always likely, particularly given Ben's volatility and touchiness about his achievements. Jones' spectacular sets and costumes won gasps of admiration and fuelled his resentment. Intimations of mutual disenchantment came as early as 1619, when he told Drummond of Hawthornden that 'when he wanted words to express the greatest villain in the world, he would call him an Inigo'.

'Hissed, Hooted and Pippin-pelted'

In 1629, the Blackfriars Theatre was the setting for a revolutionary development: the first appearance of actresses on an English stage. It did not go down well. 'Glad I am to saye,' a member of audience wrote to William Laud, Bishop of London, 'that they were "hissed, hooted and pippin-pelted from the stage".' The ladies were members of a French acting troupe. Their appearance would have been of no consequence in their native land. The letter-writer, Thomas Brande, 'did not think they would soon be ready to try the same again'. He was wrong. They reappeared at both the Red Bull and Fortune Theatres, but with so little success that the good-hearted Master of the Revels, Sir Henry Herbert, returned part of their licence fee 'in respect of their ill luck'.

The French troupe may have been invited to London by Queen Henrietta Maria. French actors played before her at Somerset House on 15 February 1635. They may have been *Les Comêdiens du Roy*, the Company under the patronage of her brother, the King of France. Obviously they impressed for she 'commended' them to the King and two days later they performed the comedy of *Mélise* before him at Whitehall. He was delighted and ordered Sir Henry Herbert to instruct Christopher Beeston to allow them to perform at the Cockpit Theatre on 'Sermon days' during Lent. Naturally, he 'obeyd readily'.[11] Native-born ladies would have to wait a while longer to take the stage, but their hour would come.

Chapter Ten

As it was Lately Acted

The late 1620s saw the rise of another new phenomenon: courtiers writing plays. The earliest example may be *The Deserving Favourite*, which was published in 1629. The author, Lodowick Carlell, was born in 1602, the son of Sir Herbert Carlell of Dumfriesshire. He probably obtained a position at Court through the influence of his namesake and probable godfather, Lodowick Stewart, Duke of Lennox, one of the Scottish noblemen who had come south with the King. At some point, he was appointed Gentleman of the Bows and a Groom of the Chamber. Later he became the Keeper of the Great Forest at Richmond Park, accompanying the King out hunting.

To the modern eye, *The Deserving Favourite* might seem another example of the examining of sexual themes previously regarded as unsuited for the public stage. It centres round a love triangle. Lysander (played by Richard Sharpe) and Clarinda (John Honyman) are in love, but the King's cousin, the Duke – the deserving favourite of the title (Joseph Taylor), also loves Clarinda and seeks her hand in marriage. The suitors fight a duel and both are severely wounded. Princess Cleonarda, the King's sister, finds them while out hunting. She falls in love with Lysander and has him taken to her hunting lodge to nurse him back to health. She assumes the other man is dead, but when her men go back to find him, he has disappeared. He has been rescued by a Hermit (Richard Robinson) who tends him until his wounds heal. It is rumoured that Lysander has killed him and the King offers a reward for his capture. When Cleonarda learns of Lysander's love for Clarinda, she calls her to his side, despite her own love for him. She is rescued from the vagaries of the villainous servant Iacomo (John Lowin), by a man that she doesn't recognise as the Duke. She is reunited with Lysander, but Iacomo has reported his whereabouts to the King. He is arrested and sentenced to death. Cleonarda pleads for him in vain, but the Duke reappears and he is reprieved. He is about to marry Clarinda when the Hermit appears to reveal that he is not the son of Count Orsino, his supposed father, but Clarinda's brother, stolen in infancy. The opportunity to stage a sequel to *'Tis Pity* is wisely ignored, although it was a close-run thing. Lysander praises Clarinda for her wisdom in ensuring that he has not 'inioyed the sweets of love'. Instead the obvious solution is found. 'It does not grieve me that you are my

Brother,' says Clarinda. 'And for my part,' replies Lysander, 'I did ever love you as a sister rather than as a Mistris.' Clarinda switches allegiance to the Duke with equal ease:

> ... the large testimony you have given
> Both of your worth and affection to me,
> Have turn'd that great affection in an instant,
> That I bare Lysander, as you could wish it,
> Vpon you; nay, to say truth, I ever lov'd you,
> Though not as well as hee, and I held your worth
> As great.

Now is the opportunity for Cleonarda's love for Lysander to be fulfilled, but, despite his upmarket origins, he doesn't match up to a royal princess. 'What is it, sir, in your opinion,' she asks, 'makes Lysander unworthy of me?' 'His blood compared to yours is base,' but the King capitulates when they threaten mutual suicide.

The dialogue on the first encounter between Clarinda and Cleonarda appears to verge on the homoerotic. 'The Princess is the fairest creature,' says Clarinda, 'That mine eyes ever beheld.'

> Why does she look
> So steadfastly upon me? Gracious Madame,
> What see you in this worthless frame,
> That so attracts your eyes?

'By my life,' Cleonarda responds, 'I take delight to look on thee.'

Later, Lysander tells Clarinda that after his execution, 'You and the Princess may make a kind of marriage', but the apparent overtones are quite the reverse. They reflect the cult of Platonism prevailing at the Court under the Queen's influence. The love of Clarinda and Cleonarda represents a view that true relationships achieve a purity beyond the carnal that are applicable to same-sex relationships. The same sentiment exists in a superior literary form in the sonnet tradition, Milton's *Lycidas* and Tennyson's *In Memoriam*. Many marriages in the upper reaches of society were based on dynastic and material considerations. The ideal of such a marriage was personified by the King and Queen, whose devotion was based on mutual duty and respect. The upper classes did not generally enjoy what poorer people took for granted: to marry where they chose. In the final act, Mariana tells Clarinda that her newly revealed brother 'will take that pains for you', in finding her a husband, but she insists on her own freedom of choice:

He shall have leave to name me one;
But if I doe not thinke him worthy of me,
I'le break that kingly custome, of marrying
For the good of the State, since it makes Princes
More miserable than beggars, for Beggards marry
Only those they love.

'As it was lately Acted,' states the title page, 'first before the Kings Maiestie, and since publikely at the BLACK-FRIERS By his MAIESTIES Seruants.' The order of playing is a departure.

Productions seen at Court normally received their first airing in the public theatre, as preparation for any later prestigious and lucrative Court staging.

Another play by a courtier, Sir John Suckling's[1] *Aglaura*, was presented by the King's Men at Blackfriars in 1637. It was produced at Suckling's expense at lavish cost – the cuffs and ruffs of the costumes were of real silver and gold. It was presented at Court in April 1638. In anticipation of the Restoration stage, the elaborate sets that Inigo Jones created for *Luminalia*, that year's Queen's masque, were utilised. Suckling changed the play's genre for this royal performance, perhaps, like the Mechanicals in *The Dream*, in order not to frighten the ladies. As the printed edition of 1646 expresses it: 'First, a bloody tragedy, then by the said Sir IOHN turn'd to a *COMEDY*'. Either way, the play can only be described as mediocre, although it contains Suckling's best-known lyric:

Why so pale and wan, fond lover?
    Prithee why so pale?
Will, when looking well can't move her,
    Looking ill prevail?

The play was published in 1638 by the stationer Thomas Walkley, with a subsidy from Suckling in what would be known as 'vanity publishing'. The King's Men were probably also taking subsidies for performing courtiers' plays. Another play by Suckling, *The Goblins*, received its licence on 17 November 1638 and was performed at Court by the King's Men three days later. The gap in appreciation between courtiers who understood the ideal of courtly love and the common man who knew nothing of such things is expressed in the preface to *The Platonick Lovers*, 'a Tragicomedy' by Sir William Davenant, 'Servant to her Majestie':

    ... the Title needs must cause
From the indulgent Court, a kind applause,
Since there hee learn't it first, and had command
T' interpret what hee scarce doth understand.

Yet Davenant cannot resist satirising the convention. Theander and Eurithea, the lovers of the title, are 'Lovers of a pure Coelestiall kind, such as some stile Platonicall'. By contrast, her brother Phylomont, and his sister Ariola, 'affect ... such a way as Libertines call Lust' and long for the 'Game and Pleasure' of marriage. Circumstances change when the blood of Theander and Eurithea is heated by the doctor, Buonateste, arousing their desires. They realise that the norm is physical love within the marriage bond with the wife subservient to her husband. The 'bounty' of platonic love 'had been excellent', Theander tells Eurithea, 'but now,

> Your charter's out of date, and mine
> Begins to rule: the Priest attends below
> To celebrate our Nuptiall rites, which is
> The happy houre that doth advance
> The husband's government; come, to the Chappell, Love.

In fact, the Queen was fully cognisant of the fact that 'the world must be peopled', bearing her husband nine children. This did not negate her attachment to the ideal of platonic love. In fact, the play was one of her favourites. It enjoyed considerable success in the public arena undergoing frequent revival, after the Restoration.

Davenant claimed the best possible literary connection. William Shakespeare was his godfather. His mother Jane (or Jennet) Sheppard, daughter of a minor court official, was baptised at St Margaret's, Westminster, in 1568. John Aubrey heard she was 'of a very good witt and of conversation extremely agreeable'. In 1593 she married John Davenant, a widower and vintner with premises on the Thames at Queenhithe, on the opposite bank to the Globe.

Jennet suffered several miscarriages during the 1590s as well as bearing two daughters. Around 1600, the family moved to Oxford when Davenant became tenant of the Salutation Tavern in the Cornmarket. According to the antiquary Anthony Wood, Shakespeare 'frequented his house in his journies between Warwickshire and London'. He was a great favourite. William Davenant's, younger brother Robert, told John Aubrey that 'Mr W. Shakespeare had given him a hundred kisses'. He had probably known the family from its London days. Wood adds that Davenant was 'an admirer of plays and play-makers, especially Shakespeare'.

The change of air improved Jennet's gynaecological prospects. She gave birth to another eight children. William, her sixth surviving child, was baptised at St Martin's Church in Oxford on 3 March 1606. Unless represented by a proxy, William Shakespeare may have been there that day and, in the words of the

Oxford antiquary Thomas Hearne, 'gave him his name' (the baby was named after him). As he stood by the font, it may have been with some embarrassment, if later gossip is credited. Hearne recounts the story of young William once running home, when an elderly gentleman asked him why he was rushing. 'To see my godfather Shakespeare,' replied the lad. 'That's a good boy,' admonished the old fellow, 'but have a care you don't take *God's* name in vain.' Certainly, whatever the connection may have been, Davenant gloried in it, writing an Ode to Shakespeare at the age of 12. According to Aubrey, 'Sir William would sometimes, when he was pleasant over a glasse of wine with his most intimate friends ... say that it seemed to him that he wrote with the very spirit that was Shakespeare and seemed contented enough to be thought his son.' 'In which way,' he adds, 'his mother had a very light report.' Doubtless, Davenant desired to claim the genetic inheritance of Shakespeare's genius, but the story, although it freely circulated around Oxford in the seventeenth century, is unlikely. Women do not usually embark on extra-marital affairs to achieve their twelfth pregnancy, although the gossip could reflect a memory of an earlier relationship between poet and landlady.

The Davenants were a devoted couple. After Jennet died in 1621, her husband, by then Oxford's Mayor, desired to be buried 'as nere my wife as the place will give leave where she lyeth'. He achieved his desire just eighteen days later. In his will, dated 19 April 1622, he stated that William, who had quit Lincoln College without a degree, should be 'put to prentice to some good merchant or other tradesman', but such a potentially lucrative, respectable but rather dull career was not for him. He became a page to the exotic, well-connected and eccentric Frances, Duchess of Lennox and Richmond. Both her grandfathers were dukes. At the age of 13 she married the son of a City Alderman who left her a wealthy widow of 20. A year later she became the third wife of Edward Seymour, Lord Hertford, who was forty years her senior. She became a lady-in-waiting and close friend to Queen Anne and was widowed again after twenty years of marriage. Two months later she married the Duke of Lennox, the King's cousin. A year before his death, in 1624, he was created Duke of Richmond. As her page, Davenant would have become conversant with courtly ways and manners, a knowledge enhanced when he joined the service of the polymath, Fulke Greville, Lord Brooke, whose career is summarised in the epitaph he wrote himself – 'Servant to Queen Elizabeth, Councillour to King James, and Friend to Sir Philip Sidney'. A poet who wrote a sonnet sequence, a courtier who held the office of Chancellor of the Exchequer and a political philosopher, he wrote three 'closet dramas' – plays intended for private reading, *Alaham* and *Mustapha* were Senecan tragedies. In 1601, the intriguingly named *Antony and Cleopatra* was 'sacrificed to the fire, the executioner, the author himself', because it was 'apt enough to be construed or strained to a personating of vices in the present governors or government'. Davenant was in Greville's service in 1628 when he was murdered by Ralph Haywood, a servant aggrieved at being omitted from his master's will. In the words of the DNB, he 'became a hanger about court, and betook himself to writing plays and poetry, which obtained him the friendship of … many … persons of influence'. His first play, *The Tragedy of Albovine, King of the Lombards*, was probably never staged. It was printed in 1629 but not entered onto the Stationers' Register. Yet it enjoyed some success. On 27 July 1639, the Stationers' Company gave John Benson leave to print the significant number of 1,500 copies of the play, which, because it had never been entered, was at its disposal. The next year saw the production by the King's Men at Blackfriars of *The Cruel Brother*, a tragedy, and *The Just Italian*, a tragi-comedy. What was probably his most successful play, *The Witts*, was largely based on *Wit at Several Weapons*, a play attributed to Beaumont and Fletcher in their First Folio. It did not initially survive the rigorous quill of Sir Henry Herbert, who took exception to its strong and blasphemous language. Davenant considered a dimension had been lost and approached his friend, Endymion Porter, who, according to Anthony Wood, was beloved of Charles I for 'his general bearing, brave style, sweet temper, great experience, travels and modern languages'. Herbert recorded the King's response to Porter's lobbying:

> This morning, being the 9th Jan. 1633, the Kinge was pleased to call mee into his withdrawinge chamber, to the windowe, wher he went over all that I had croste in Davenant's play-booke, and allowing of faith and slight to be asseverations only, and no oaths, market them to stande, and some other few things, but in the greater part allowed of my reformations.

A number of words remained expurgated, but Herbert was unhappy with what had been restored, although how 'faith' and 'slight' gave offence is puzzling. Next day, he 'returned unto Mr Davenant his play-booke of The Witts, corrected by the Kinge'. It was performed before the King and Queen on 28 January, to a mixed reception. 'The Kinge commended the language,' wrote Herbert, 'but dislikt the plott and characters.' When it was presented over a year later, at Blackfriars, it had 'a various fate'. Nevertheless, Davenant had achieved sufficient success at Court to be Inigo Jones' choice to replace the irascible Ben Jonson. *The Temple of Love*, a masque, was 'presented by the QVEENES Majesty, and her Ladies, at *White-hall* on Shrove-Tuesday, 1634'. Her Majesty herself commissioned the work and took the role of Indamora, the Indian Queen, who personifies platonic love, although Davenant appeared unconvinced by such 'strange doctrines':

> *Indamora*, the delight of Destiny!
> Shee, and the beauties of her Traine: who sure
> Though they discover Summer in their lookes,
> Still carry frozen Winter in their blood.
> They raise strange doctrines, and new sects of Love:
> Which must not wooe or court the Person, but
> The Mind; and practise generation not
> Of Bodies but of Soules.

The apparent frigidity of the ladies in the Queen's train who 'carry frozen winter in their blood' is perceived as another virtue. Davenant possessed a physical reminder that he had not always pursued such a path. In 1630, in Aubrey's words, 'he got a terrible clap of a black handsome wench that lay in Axe Yard, Westminster … Which lost him his nose'. It was destroyed by the disease or the mercury used to treat it. As his godson put it in *Timon of Athens*, 'down with the nose … take the bridge quite away'. This explains the gap of some three years between the production of *The Just Italian* and *The Witts*. Davenant must have been deeply embarrassed by his condition and taken cover. It appears that he went to live with relatives in Essex. While there, he had an unfortunate encounter with a tapster, Thomas Warren of Braintree, who perhaps made ribald remarks about his singular facial appearance. Davenant attacked him with his rapier. He died a few days later. Charged with murder, Davenant fled to Holland. He returned after the prosecution was dropped after another intervention by Endymion Porter. He was pardoned by the King in 1638.

Davenant was treated for his dose by Sir Thomas Cadyman, physician to the Queen. This skilful practitioner rebuilt his nose, at least partially, by skin grafts. John Greenhill's engraving on the title page of Davenant's collected works shows his remoulded snub nose. The restructured organ achieved something approaching national fame. 'You're like Cheapside without a cross,' the poetess, Lady Hester Pulter, told him.[2]

It may be wondered that a Queen of such sexual rectitude should tolerate one whose very appearance demonstrated past licentiousness. The answer is probably that, like her father-in-law, her love of the theatre caused her to overlook such scruples. She subsidised the company that bore her name when the theatres were closed by plague. She appointed the playwright, James Shirley, a Valet of her Chamber. She may have been the first senior royal to attend a performance in a public theatre. On 13 May 1634 she saw a play by Philip Massinger at Blackfriars. In 1635 she saw the second part of Lodovick Carlel's tragicomedy, *Arviragus and Philicia* and visited again in May 1636.

A Newe Fair Play-house

This is the last generation of the boy actors who had graced the theatre since its inception. They fretted and strutted their hour upon the stage until the last. In 1629 'a newe fair Play-house', the only theatre created in Charles I's reign, opened in Salisbury Court, from which it took its name. Just to the west of the City Walls between Fleet Street and the River Thames, it was the London residence of the Bishops of Salisbury until bought by Sir Richard Sackville, the Chancellor of the Exchequer, in 1564. His son Thomas, the co-author of *Gorboduc*, was created Earl of Dorset in 1604. He converted a barn or granary in the grounds into a theatre. Like the Cockpit and the Blackfriars, it was a private house, catering to a select audience. 'If you had seen the Cockpit Theatre, then you had seen the other two in effect,' Trueman tells Lovewit in *Historia Histrionica*, 'for they were all build almost exactly alike for form and bigness.'

The prime movers behind the project were the old Palsgrave's man and playwright, Richard Gunnell, and William Blagrave, who, as Deputy Master of the Revels, might be regarded as having a conflict of interest. Their purpose was to revive the theatrical form of the Children's Company. It was a gamble worth taking. The boys' companies of the previous era were a huge success and were far less costly to run than those employing adult actors: another reason for its formation was revealed in a lawsuit brought by an investor, Christopher Babham, who stated that Gunnell and Blagrave 'did join together to train and bring up certain boys in the quality of playing … with intent to be a supply of able actors to his Majesty's servants at the Black Friars'.

The previous boy's companies were based on such institutions as choir schools which provided a flow of young actors. Now Gunnell and Blagrave actively recruited the lads needed for the 'King's Revels Children'. The potential of Stephen Hammerton must have been considered huge because Blagrave bought out the remaining nine years of his apprenticeship to William Waverley, a merchant tailor in The Strand, in October 1629. It was not the best of times. The plague had closed the theatres so Gurnell and Blagrave found themselves supporting fourteen boys without prospect of any return. According to one report, the boys had just seven shirts between them and one died of neglect.[3]

The theatre opened late in 1630 with a performance of *The Muses Looking Glasse (or, the Stage review'd)* by Thomas Randolph, a young man-about-town and protêgê of Ben Jonson. The 'play' is hardly worthy of the name, being more of a pageant. Two Puritans, hostile to the theatre, are accosted by the famous Roman actor, Roscius. Dialogues ensue between characters representing various vices and virtues. The leading Puritan foe of the theatre, William Prynne, took great exception to this mild critique and the theatre staging it. In *Histrio Mastrix*, which bore the telling sub-title of *the Players Scourge or Actors Tragedie*, published in 1632, he describes the 'first Play that was acted in the New-erected Playhouse' as 'a fit consecration sermon for that Divil's Chappell'. In his diatribe he castigated women actors as 'impudent, shameful, unwomanish and gracelesse' and 'notorious whores'. This was ill-judged. On 9 January 1633, some ten weeks after its publication, 'at Somerset House before the King', Queen Henrietta Maria participated in *The Shepheard's Paradise*, a masque by Walter Montagu.[4] It was the first time she had spoken in such a production. Prynne's violent polemic was regarded as insulting to her. Lord Cottington, the Chancellor of the Exchequer, denounced the book's 'strangeness and heinousness' and ordered it 'burnt, in the most public manner that can be'. It was immolated before Prynne by the public hangman. Since it contained 1,000 pages, he was nigh-suffocated by the smoke. The Attorney-General began proceedings against him in the Star Chamber. He lay imprisoned in the Tower for a year. His eventual sentence on 17 February 1634 was comprehensive and severe: life imprisonment, a fine of £5,000, expulsion from Lincoln's Inn, deprival of his Oxford University degree and the amputation of his ears in the pillory, Prynne had dedicated his hysterical attack to the very Inns of Court from which he was expelled. There is some irony that his supposed attack on the Queen's participation in a court masque led to the commissioning of the most spectacular of all masques. To assuage the embarrassment caused by his dedication, the four Inns commissioned James Shirley to write *The Triumph of Peace*, with sets and costumes by Inigo Jones and musical settings by William Lawes and Simon Ives. According to Bulstrode Whitelocke, who managed the event, 882 participants departed from Ely House, off Holborn, on the evening of 3 February 1634. The King's Marshal and his men led the way, followed by twenty-five members from each Inn, dressed in gold and silver lace. Then came two chariots: the first containing eight lutenists dressed as priests and Sybils, with three flambeau bearers on each side. In the second, singers 'struck picturesque poses in costumes representing the celestial bodies in harmonious motion'. The boys in an 'anti-masque', who performed comic or grotesque dances between the acts of the 'Grand Masque' were dressed as birds. The principal masquers rode in four chariots, each with two 'flaming huge flambeaux' on its sides drawn by four horses decked in silver and crimson cloths and white and red feathers, 'After these an hundred Gentlemen, gloriously furnished and gallantly mounted, riding two and two a breast, every Gentleman having his two Pages richly attired, and a groome to attend him.'

The great cavalcade passed down Chancery Lane into The Strand and on to Banqueting House, where the King and Queen awaited. The King was so impressed that he bade it turn around and go past them again. The great hall was fitted with raked seating on three sides, with a stage at the end. A team of sixteen Grand Masquers portraying virtues and vocations represented the 'most handsome, youthful and graceful members of the inns'. In Inigo Jones' spectacular effect, the moon set and 'Amphiluche', the harbinger of morning, rose in its place. The Spirits of Peace, Law and Justice descended to honour the King and Queen. The House of Stuart had brought all three to a fortunate nation. All who saw it were delighted. Whitelocke calculated that the event cost the enormous sum of £21,000.[5] The Queen was so impressed that she requested the wonderful show be repeated in the City, which occurred on 13 February in the Great Hall of the Merchant Taylor's Company.

Despite the outrages against his pocket and person, Prynne's campaign against the Anglican establishment continued relentlessly. A stream of letters and tracts poured forth from his cell in the Tower. With an anonymous attack on the Bishop of Norwich in 1637, he went too far. Its source discovered, on 14 June he was returned before the Star Chamber and sentenced to another fine of £5,000 (where was he supposed to find that kind of money?), a further life sentence and the loss of what remained of his ears. An additional cruel punishment was that he should have the initials 'SL' – for 'Seditious Libeller' – branded on his cheeks. He even managed to turn this to his advantage, claiming that the initials represented '*Stigmata Laudit*' – 'Sign of Praise'.

Despite his extreme hostility to the theatre, Prynne had an obsessive's awareness of its day-to-day detail. He described Stephen Hammerton as 'a most noted and beautiful woman-actor', so, he must have seen him in person. At the time Prynne wrote his diatribe, this rising young actor had decamped to, or been lured to join, the King's Men. As a result, William Beeston joined with William Blagrove in a suit in the Court of Requests in November 1632 for his return to Prince Charles' Men, a company with which his father was associated. The action was lost, possibly because the company's *raison d'etre*, as cited by Christopher Badham, was to supply 'able actors to His Majesty's Servants at the Black Friars'. In his new career, young Hammerton appeared as Oriana in the revival of Fletcher's *Wild Goose Chase*, in which the part of Mirabel was 'incomparably acted by Mr Joseph Taylor', that of Belieur 'most naturally acted by Mr John Lowin', and Pinac 'admirably acted by Mr Thomas Pollard'.

Realism

While courtiers enjoyed their lavish masques, popular drama continued to flourish in the public theatres. The early 1630s saw a vogue for plays related to specific localities, a genre that became known as 'place-realism'. The publication of *Bartholomew Fair* in 1631 may have started the trend. Richard Brome's *The Weeding of Covent Garden, or The Middlesex Justice of the Peace* deals with urban development – then a less familiar topic than in modern times. In the early seventeenth century, there was still open space between the cities of London and Westminster, epitomised in the name of the church situated between the two, St Martin-in-the-Fields. Inevitable pressure of population led to a gradual expansion of the City of London, fuelled partly by the desire of the wealthy to escape its confines. The area known as Covent Garden, from the convent that once stood there, was an obvious area for development, but there was a problem. A proclamation by the King in the early years of his reign had prohibited the building of new houses except on old foundations. It was largely ignored, but a proposed development of forty-eight acres could hardly escape notice. The solution was simple. The King had dissolved Parliament to inaugurate eleven years of personal rule in 1629. It was Parliament that voted the monarch's annual allowance. It was its failure to do this, at least on the levels the King deemed adequate, that had led to the dissolution. The King was desperate for cash and had to find other means to obtain it. In January 1630/1, his financial pressures were temporarily eased when he sold a waiver of the legal restraints on new building to the owner of the Covent Garden estate, Francis Russell, 4th Earl of Bedford, for the princely sum of £2,000. Russell engaged two architects for a development to be built around London's first planned square, designed by Inigo Jones in the style of an Italian piazza. The French architect, Isaac de Caus, designed the houses to the north and east of the square and oversaw the entire scheme, which included the first church, St Paul's, built in London since the Reformation. The grand project was draining Bedford's resources, so he instructed Inigo to build 'nothing more than a barn'. Covent Garden remains a much-loved spot in the cityscape, but this is not how Richard Brome saw it. He satirises the developers' greed rather than the quality of their creations. In the Prologue, although not surprisingly he claims there are no allusions to actual people, Jones is clearly represented by two characters: Rooksbill, a builder – which, at a basic level, he was – and Cockbraybe, a Justice of the Peace (Jones served as such for Westminster and Middlesex). These two aspects of his worldly persona meet in the first scene and discuss the profits the venture will bring. 'I have pil'd up a Leash of thousand pounds in walls and windows there,' says Rooksbill. 'It will all come again with large en-crease,' advises the alter ego, Cockbrayne.

The play must have delighted Ben Jonson, with its swipes against his great antagonist. As befits a drama of place realism, it is nothing if not topical. In June 1632, the King issued a proclamation, 'commanding the Gentry to keepe their Residence at their Mansions in the Countreye' and forbidding them to make their 'Habitations in London, and places adjoyning'. This extraordinary edict was based on practicalities. By moving to London, the gentry abandoned their rural duties and caused pressure on the City's infrastructure. That this was seen as an act against liberty was a point made in the play by Will Crossewill. a cantankerous squire, who has determined to come to London after 'the Proclamation of restraint spur'd him up'. Brome also followed his former master in satirising Puritans. Gabriel Crossewill, Will's son, embodies the lasciviousness and hypocrisy that sect was deemed to possess. 'He has hang'd the head … ever since Holiday sports were cried up in the country', refers to James I's Declaration of Sports of 1618, which defined the pastimes permitted on the Sabbath. Animal-baiting was banned, as were 'interludes' (not good news for actors) and, curiously, the sedate pursuit of bowls; a number of activities endorsed were anathema to Puritans: May-games, Whitsun Ales, Morris-dancing, and the setting up of maypoles. The unpopularity of a Government-sponsored monopoly in the manufacture of soap is also referenced. 'The women begin to grumble against that slippery project and, ''tis feard, will mutinie shortly'. Brome follows Ben's achievement in *Bartholomew Fair*, creating a skimpy plot filled with a galaxy of characters, including Damaris, a supposed Venetian courtesan dressed in scarlet who is actually Dorcas, a maid who has been abandoned by the 'slippery Trojan', Nicholas Rooksbill. Much of the action is devoted to a bunch of tavern-going hooligans, both male and female, called – in obvious sexual allusion – 'the Brothers of the Blade and the Sisters of the Scabbard'. Their expulsion from the area gives the play its title.

Brome's penchant for topicality and place is evident in his collaboration with Thomas Heywood in *The Late Lancashire Witches*. A search for spectacular effects had been a constant factor throughout Heywood's career. He was currently engaged in creating the public pageants that marked the inauguration of a new Lord Mayor and this play would include many amazing stunts. Plays such as *Macbeth* and *The Witch of Edmonton* reflected a widespread belief that witchcraft was a real manifestation of unearthly powers, a view shared by many of those accused. The play concerned an unfolding event. Lancashire was a county much associated with witchcraft. The Pendle Witch Trials of 1612 had produced one of the greatest sensations of the era. Nine people were hanged 'at the common place of execution near Lancaster' after somewhat fragile convictions, even if the original basis of their prosecution were accepted. On 10 February 1633, another witch trial aroused great interest when alleged witches were prosecuted at Lancaster on the testimony of Edmund Robinson, a 10-year-old miller's son. While out picking 'bulloes' (wild plums), he claimed two greyhounds appeared, one black, one grey, which he initially thought were coursing hares. They turned into a woman, who he recognised as Frances Dickonson, and a boy, who she turned into a white horse upon which she set Edmund. It carried him to a house called Hoarstones. Some sixty other witches arrived on horseback and went into a barn. Six knelt down and tugged on ropes hanging from the roof, from which smoking flesh, lumps of butter and milk fell into basins. When Edmund took fright and ran off, some witches chased him, led by a woman he knew as 'Loynd's wife', to a place called Boggard Hole, where they gave up the chase after running into two men on horseback. As well as Dickonson's wife, he identified another witch as Jennet Davies, both neighbours of his family. His father seems to have bought the tale. Thus encouraged, the boy said he'd seen Loynd's wife sitting in their chimney and claimed to have wrestled with a boy with cloven feet he met in the fields. The miller claimed to have investigated the issue, questioning around the locality until he had names to refer to the authorities, As a result, twenty people were brought to trial. One of them, Margaret Johnson, although not mentioned in Edmund's allegations, did the expected thing and acknowledged her witchcraft in a long rambling confession. Mary Spencer was accused of making her pail come to her by witchcraft, but stated that when, as a young girl, she went to the well for water, she would roll the collock [pail] downhill and run after it, sometimes overtaking it, 'and then she might call it to come to her, but utterly denies that she could ever make it come to her by any witchcraft'. The jury found them guilty, but the judge had his doubts. Rather than sentencing them to death as was mandatory, he placed them on remand and consulted the Bishop of Chester, the Rt. Rev. John Bridgeman, who examined the prisoners and concluded that, apart from the demented testimony of Margaret Johnson, there was no supporting evidence.

Frances Dickonson revealed a possible financial motive behind the accusations. Robinson had tried to buy a cow off her husband, but he wouldn't release it until the money was paid. His inability to do so resulted in animosity. There was corroborated evidence that he had offered to drop his allegations if the Dickonsons paid him 40 shillings, which they refused to do. The Bishop's report determined the view of the authorities. The miller and his son were confined in Newgate Prison, but the alleged witches were lodged at the Ship Tavern in Greenwich. They were examined by a team led by the eminent physician, William Harvey.[6] No supposed marks of communion with the Devil were found upon them.

The play was staged by the King's Men in August 1634. The judicial investigation was still ongoing, so any concept of *sub judice* was flouted. The plot was partly based on the ongoing hearings and partly fictional. 'Although, the ripeness of time, has not yet reveal'd' the outcome', the guilt of the accused was assumed; the crudely comic antics of witches made better popular theatre than serious examination of the issues. Nevertheless, it was hoped that 'great mercy' might give the accused their lives. One of the fullest contemporary accounts of a play is contained in a letter sent by Nathaniel Tomkyns to his friend, Sir

Robert Phelips on 16 August. He had been to see 'a new comedy at the Globe called The Witches of Lancashire'. Such was the demand to see it that it was 'acted by reason of the great concourse of people three days together'. He was surprised to find 'a greater appearance of fine folk, gentlemen and gentlewomen, than I thought had been in town in the vacation'. Unlike the play itself, he kept an open mind on the issue. 'The subject was of the sleights and passages done *or* supposed to be done by these witches.' These included the discredited allegation of 'walking of pails of milk by themselves'. People were posted 'to and from places far distant in an incredible short time'. Another scene involved 'the conveying away of the good cheer and bringing in a mock feast of bones and stones instead thereof'. Appropriately for a play about witchcraft, there was a strong sexual element; 'the representing of wrong and putative fathers in the shape of mean persons to gentlemen by way of derision', and 'the tying of a knot at a marriage (after the French manner) to "cassate" masculine ability'. Effects included 'transforming men and women into the shapes of several creatures, especially horses, by putting an enchanted bridle into their mouths, 'the cutting off of a witch-gentlewoman's hand in the form of a cat, by a soldier turned miller, known to her husband by a ring thereon (the only tragical part of the story)', and 'the filling of pies with living birds and young cats, etc.'. Tomkyns recognised the play's shortcomings: 'There be not in it (to my understanding) any poetical genius, or art, or language, or judgment to state or tenet of witches (which I expected), or application to virtue', but he enjoyed hugely its ribaldry, topicality and fantastical effects:

> In respect of the newness of the subject (the witches being still visible and in prison here) and in regard it consisteth from the beginning to the end of odd passages and fopperies to provoke laughter, and is mixed with divers songs and dances, it passeth for a merry and excellent new play.

According to the Epilogue, the witches were still awaiting 'their due / By lawful justice'. Fortunately for them, this was not decided by Brome, Heywood, or the audience at the Globe. On 10 July, Edmund Robinson broke down under close questioning before the Privy Council and confessed that 'he had framed the tale out of his own invention'. Faced with the collapse of the case, the father also confessed and was confined in the Gatehouse Jail. Brome and Heywood chose to ignore this. The King pardoning all the accused was not as good box office as the slapstick of witches' pranks.

Another play more than fulfilling the requirements of place realism was *Holland's Leaguer* by the 'Son of Ben', Shackerley Marmion. It referenced the most sensational event occurring in London in 1632. The Holland's Leaguer of the title was the best-appointed brothel in town, which bore the name of its Madame, Elizabeth 'Bess' Holland. A 'leaguer', in its original meaning, was an army encampment, perhaps in recognition of its original ownership by the Military Order of St John, but, as a colloquialism, it had come to mean a brothel. It was located in a charming fortified manor house. Clients crossed a drawbridge over a moat before entering through a portcullis. A contemporary illustration shows a pikeman on duty outside the gate, presumably to repel over-enthusiastic punters. A couple liaise in the exquisite formal garden. This sumptuous establishment was costly. According to Thomas Nashe, supper cost £20, which presumably did not include available extras. It was situated in the Liberty of the Clink, an area beyond the remit of Surrey's judicial authorities, within the jurisdiction of the Bishop of Winchester, whose London palace was nearby. Successive Bishops tended to overlook the empire of vice flourishing on their doorstep. Indeed this highly irregular trade greatly benefitted the Episcopal coffers. Shakespeare was aware of this. 'Thou that givest indulgences to whores to sin,' Gloucester accuses the Bishop in *Henry VI. Part One*. 'Winchester goose' is used as a term for a prostitute in *Troilus and Cressida*.

From the upper windows of Holland's Leaguer, it was possible to see Bankside's three theatres – the Globe, Hope and Francis Langley's old theatre, which, having closed its doors in 1621, had 'fallen into decay and like a dying Swanne, hanging down her head, seemed to sing her own dirge'. The Globe and Holland's Leaguer had connections beyond proximity. With Henry VIII's sequestration of monastic properties, the house passed to the Crown. In 1578, it was sold to Lord Hunsdon, the future patron of the Lord Chamberlain's Men. On his death in 1596, it passed to his son, Sir George Carey. Around 1602, he leased the property that became London's priciest stew to Bess Holland. Perhaps he was a favoured client. He died on 8 September 1603, of a combination of syphilis and the toxic effects of the mercury used to treat it. Doubtless there was a full complement of the company at its patron's funeral in Westminster Abbey. 'We have many pocky cases nowadays,' says the Sexton in *Hamlet*, 'that will scarce survive the lying in.'

Whenever the scandal of the nest of vice over the river became too blatant to ignore, the authorities were moved to action. In 1546, Henry VIII ordered the closure of all brothels. James I approved numerous raids on the stews. On a single day in August 1620, nineteen women were indicted for running brothels. Yet the major threat to the industry was not from the authorities, as noted in a letter from John Chamberlain to Sir Dudley Carleton in 1617:

> On Shrove Tueasday, the 'prentices, or rather the unruly people of the suburbs, played their parts in various places, as Finsbury Fields, about

> Wapping by St Catherine's, and in Lincoln's Inn Fields ... in pulling down of houses, and beating the guards that were set to keep rule.

Shrove Tuesday was traditionally a time to indulge in whatever was being renounced in Lent. Yet some indulgences were mortal sins, so the forcible closure of houses of ill-repute was a popular cause; an opportunity for the riotous behaviour for which the 'ragged regiments' described by 'the Water Poet' John Taylor, as 'youth armed with cudgels, stones, rules, trowels and handsaws [who] put playhouses to the sack, and bawdy-houses to the spoil' were notorious. It was the riot described by Chamberlain that swept away the Cockpit Theatre. Between 1606 and 1641, twenty-four Shrove Tuesday riots were recorded. When King Charles ordered the closure of Holland's Leaguer in December 1631, it may have been intended to forestall any attempts to storm the building. If so, it failed. When the party sent to implement the order crossed the drawbridge, Bess Holland ordered it raised and the posse tumbled into the moat. Further humiliation ensued when the ladies emptied the contents of their chamber pots over them. A siege ensued that lasted – embarrassingly – for a month. Despite receiving two summonses from the ecclesiastical Court of High Commission, which dealt with public morality, Bess slipped away to set up in business elsewhere, at 'Cocke Lane, Finsbury' it was said ... or are we in the presence of a current joke? There can be no doubt about the mirth around the City at the routing of the royal force by a band of whores. A pamphlet appeared even during the siege, describing the hilarious events; a popular ballad, *The Jolly Broom Man*, claimed to tell the tale of a soldier who had fought around the world, but, at Holland's Leaguer, 'the service provd too hot'.

Enterprisingly, the management of the 'private house' in Salisbury Court sought to take advantage of the interest in the affair. *Holland's Leaguer* was entered onto the Stationers' Register on 1 January 1632 and published soon after as 'An excellent comedy as it hath bin lately and often acted with great applause by the high and mighty Prince Charles his servants.' 'The high and mighty Prince' in question, the future Charles II, was just 18 months old. In essence, this was a reconstituted Palsgrave's Men that included the Company's leading comedian, Andrew Cane, who, characteristic of his calling, was famed for his solo jig and exchanges with the audience. It was said his tongue 'could out-strip facetious MERCURY'. Also joining as a sharer was the leading actor from the Red Bull Company, Ellis Worth. The reconstituted company provides further evidence of the links between the stage and the livery companies. Like Armin, Lowin and the theatre manager, Robert Keyser, Cane was a freeman of the Goldsmiths' Company. The 15-year-old John Wright was apprenticed to him in 1629 as was the 14-year-old Arthur Savill in 1631, but it is unclear whether it was as goldsmiths, actors, or both. The play had certainly 'bin lately and often acted with great applause', since it ran for six consecutive performances: only *A Game at Chess* did more. To meet the need for topicality, a play by Marmion already set for production was probably rapidly adapted. The somewhat involved main plot included the familiar ploy of an averted incestuous romance. Holland's Leaguer is the scene in Act IV when four gulls break the siege and gain entrance. If anyone in the audience was still unaware of the place's function, a Pander announces that 'there are lockt a score of *Danees* wenches of delight within this Castle', and makes the obvious pun, that the place was 'wholly given to the deeds of fructation'. 'It is reported that we study physicke,' says a whore. 'Why so?' asks the Bawd. 'Because we know the severall constitutions of men's bodies.' Much bellicose talk about the siege ensues, suitably couched in pseudo-Shakespearean language. Trimalchio, 'a humorous gallant' played by Cane, describes the ordeal the four suffer at the hands of the Leaguers:

> And whilst some stroue to hold my hands,
> The other div'd into my pockets. I am sure,
> There was a fellow with a tand face, whose breath
> Was growne sulphurous with oathes and tobacco,
> Put terror on my face, I shal never bee
> Mine owne man againe

After being forcibly ejected, the gulls are taken into custody by Agurtes and Auttolycus, masquerading as the watch. In reference to Mistress Holland's failure to answer her summonses, they are presented before a mock Court of High Commission, over which Agurtes presides. 'Now set me in my chaire,' he instructs his henchmen, 'That I may looke like a Cathedall Justice.' As expected, the play ends with everyone paired off appropriately. Of the fate of the whores, history, as usual, is silent, but they cannot have expected a quiet life. 'Good sir,' says Trimalchio, resentful at his treatment in the brothel, 'Let's think on some revenge, call up / The gentleman 'prentices; and make a Shrove Tuesday.'

Despite eleven of its members being appointed as Grooms of the Chamber on 10 May 1632, and a number of appearances at Court, Prince Charles' Men struggled. The theatrical world had become extremely litigious and they were involved a number of wearisome and costly legal actions. Recurrences of the plague threatened their very survival. It says much for their resilience that survive they did until forces beyond their control ensured their demise.

Brome's next play, *The Sparagus Garden*, also proved hugely popular, It was played by the King's Revels Men at Salisbury Court in 1635 and was reckoned to have taken the huge sum of £1,000. The garden of the title was a strip of land running up from the Thames towards where Waterloo Station now stands. It was a fashionable place to be seen and, as such places do, drew its share of rogues and conmen. Although it lacks the pungent social satire of *The Weeding of Covent Garden*, it has a similar galaxy of characters, plots and sub-plots, whose complexity reveals the amazing capacity of contemporary audiences to grasp intricacies. The Sparagus Garden was not only a fashionable resort, but a place for sexual liaisons. Booths could be hired by the hour 'to eat asparagus', which Sir Hugh Moneylacks, a down-at heel gent who survives through dodgy deals, regards as an aphrodisiac. 'Of all the plants, herbs, roots, or fruits that grow, it is the most provocative, operative, and effective.' Samuel Touchwood is turned away when he attempts to book a booth with two male friends, but no females. The play references contemporary London life, as well as the activities for which the Garden was noted: the first appearance of sedan chairs and the dromedary rides across the frozen Thames during the Frost Fairs.

As a result of this success, Brome became a hot property, signing a contract with Richard Heton of Salisbury Court to write three plays annually for a salary of 15 shillings a week and the profits of one performance from each play. It appears that Heton considered the outbreak of another pandemic closing the theatre absolved him of the obligation to pay. Desperate for money, Brome turned to Christopher Beeston, who paid him £6 to write a play. Heton, alarmed by the prospect of losing his star writer, offered Brome £10 to write a play for him. Brome accepted this, but after Heton again fell behind with the fee, turned again to Beeston. Heton appealed to Sir Henry Herbert to arbitrate the issue. The Master of the Revels decreed that Brome should be paid a six shillings a week retainer and £5 for each new play. The payments were to continue even when the theatres were closed. Unfortunately the plays were not forthcoming, so Heton again suspended payment. These were tough times. Between 10 May 1636 and 2 October 1637, the playhouses were almost continuously closed. Most likely it was over money that some members of Queen Henrietta's Men fell out with Beeston, and decamped to Salisbury Court. They included the leading actors, Richard Perkins and Anthony Turner, but the resultant troupe was probably too depleted and insolvent to become an effective force. They were rescued by Sir Henry Herbert, who had an interest in the Salisbury Street Theatre.

O Rare Ben Jonson

On 5 August 1637 there died the last great figure of the Elizabethan stage. Ben Jonson's last years were not easy, as he declared himself in 1631:

Disease, the enemy, and his engineers,
Want, with the rest of his concealed compeers,
Have cast a trench about me, now, five years,

He had been 'strucken with the palsy' in 1628. In addition to the infirmities wrought by his paralytic stroke, impecuniousness took its toll. A list of actions in the Lord Chamberlain's office reveals that he owed six people a total of over £200, including a hefty £120 to the noted schoolmaster and scholar, Thomas Farnaby. Yet he was not without resource. He retained the pension[7] awarded him by King James. On the death of Thomas Middleton, he had secured his position as Chronologer to the City of London, which brought him 100 nobles (£33 6*s*. 8*d*.) a year. He had scorned those like Anthony Munday, who took such emoluments, but his need for cash overcame his scruples, His initial instinct was right. The job wasn't for him. On 10 November 1631, the City authorities ordered that 'Mr Chamberlain shall forbear to pay any more fee or wages unto Benjamim Jonson the City's Chronologer until he shall have presented unto this court some fruits of his labours.'

In addition there were the earnings from his writings and hoped-for largesse from the well-connected patrons whose poetic praises he sang, so his indebtedness must have been the product of an irregular lifestyle. His love of conviviality persisted. On 5 April 1635, his friend, the Welsh writer and historian, James Howell, went to a 'solemn supper' at his lodgings. 'There was good company, excellent cheer, choice wines, and jovial welcome!' The 'choice wines' came from the finest source. In 1630, the King tripled Ben's pension to 100 pounds rather than marks and threw in an annual tierce of canary wine from the royal cellars. This was 42 gallons so he was on for well nigh a bottle a day. A letter from Isaak Walton to John Aubrey reveals that Ben lived in lodgings near Westminster Abbey, tended by 'a woman that governed him … and that neither he nor she took much care for next week; and would be sure not to want wine of which he usually took too much before he went to bed, if not oftener and sooner.'

Age did little to curb his acerbity. At the supper party attended by James Howell, 'one thing intervened that almost spoiled the relish of the rest, that B. began to engross all the discourses to vapour extremely of himself, and by vilifying others, to magnify his own muse.'

In fact, Ben overcame his antipathy to Inigo to work with him in the first court masque of the reign, delayed by plague and war. It may have been the King, recalling the elaborate productions relished by his mother, who persuaded them to collaborate. *Love's Triumph through Callipolis* was presented at the Banqueting Hall on Twelfth Night in 1631. The King participated, the first time a reigning monarch had done so. Sensitive to royal taste, the masque picked up the theme of platonic love. The Callipolis (fair city) of the title is a place of love, virtue and beauty, but its peace and harmony are threatened by twelve depraved lovers. The place is purified and proper and ordered love, represented by the King and Queen, restored. The Queen was delighted with this endorsement of her ideal and requested a sequel. She danced with her ladies on Shrove Tuesday, in *Chloridia*, a masque in which Inigo's spectacular effects included participants appearing to float on clouds.

The uneasy truce dissolved when *Callipolis* was published. In what might be thought a conciliatory gesture, Ben included Inigo's name on the title page, but after his own, which Inigo regarded as an insult. Accordingly, when *Chloridia* was published, Ben omitted Inigo's name altogether and attacked him in a series of widely-circulated satirical verses. The most comprehensive of these, *Expostulation with Inigo Jones*, ran to 104 lines. Its main theme is his old one of the superiority of poetry over architecture, but this did not preclude some vicious personal swipes at the 'mountebank', even down to the size of his ears. These diatribes received a mixed reception, Ben was never asked to participate in a court production again (perhaps he hadn't expected to). 'I know you have a commanding [pen],' James Howell, advised, 'but you must not let it tyrannise in that manner.'

Inigo Jones had his own way to respond to Ben's provocations. Desperate for money, the old playwright had picked up his quill and returned to the drama. *The Magnetic Lady, or Humours Reconciled* was licensed on 12 October 1632. The play is typical of Ben's style; the characters Probee and Darnplay have the action explained to them. The host of characters possess ingenious names: Parson Palate, Doctor Rut, Practice the lawyer, Sir Diaphonous Silkwarm, Sir Moth Interest, and Compass, the faithful steward and his friend, Captain Ironside. The familiar theme of avarice is revisited. Women out of control are represented by the governess, Mistress Polish; Mother Chair, the midwife; and Mistress Keep, the nurse. The action finally turns around the issue of babies switched at birth. Of course, matters are set right and appropriate pairings achieved. Given Jonson's remarks about the actors in *The New Inn*, there may have been some doubt as to whether the King's Men would be prepared to stage it, but staged it was, to the delight of Ben's enemies, who were lying in wait. The claque was led by Jones, supported by Nat Butter – still smarting from *The Staple of News*, and Alexander Gil, who considered Ben had insulted his father and namesake, the distinguished philologist and High Master of St Paul's School. Ironically, they were not jeering the play Ben had written. The actors, anticipating a hostile reception, had added oaths, obscenities and blasphemies to hype up the script. As a result, Ben was summoned before the Court of High Commission, but on this occasion he could demonstrate his innocence. After another hearing,

William Laud, the Archbishop of Canterbury, 'laid the whole fault of this play upon the players'.[8]

Ben's enemies were not satisfied with creating another critical disaster for him. Derogatory verse poured at him, Gil reviving the old jibe – 'But to advise thee, Ben, in this strict age. / A brickkiln's better than a stage.' Most telling was Inigo Jones' description of him as 'the best of poets, the worst of men'.

Never one to let his enemies have the last word, Ben returned to the fray. *A Tale of a Tub* was intended as a further riposte, but Inigo anticipated it and got Sir Henry's ear. The play was licensed on 7 May 1633, but the passages ridiculing Inigo as 'Vitruvious Hoop' were excised. It was licensed 'for the Black Friars', but actually performed by Queen Henrietta's Men at the Cockpit. Perhaps Ben's disillusion with the King's Men was mutual. In the Prologue, with rare modesty, he describes it as a 'ridiculous play', but despite its typical convoluted plot, he recovers some of his comic flair and style.

It would appear Ben had been thoroughly routed, but circumstance was turning in his favour. Even while he was working on what was to be his last completed play, King Charles had determined to be crowned King of Scotland in the style of his forebears. In the late spring of 1633, he embarked upon his slow progress towards Edinburgh. En route, important aristocrats would have the privilege of entertaining him and his retinue. William Cavendish, Marquis (later Duke) of Newcastle, a noted literary patron, desired to put on the best possible entertainment for the King. What could be better than to commission his friend Ben to create a masque in the royal honour. *The King's Entertainment at Welbeck* was a lavish affair, setting back the Marquis, according to the Countess, around £4,000 to £5,000. It concluded, as expected, with elaborate tributes to the royal virtues. The King was delighted and intimated that, as he was resolved to make a Northern progress with the Queen next year, a 'like entertainment' would go down well. The Marquis was desirous to show off his newly completed mansion, Bolsover Castle, to the King, so it was agreed that 'Ben Jonson be employed in fitting such scenes and speeches as he could best devise'. *Love's Welcome at Bolsover* was more of the same, with the expected excessive eulogies to the royal couple, but it was different in one respect. Ben incorporated the passages lampooning Inigo that had been excised from *A Tale of a Tub*.

Whether Ben was at peace with himself in the time left to him is unlikely, but the world found its peace with him. His funeral was attended by 'all or the greatest part of the nobility then in town'. Idiosyncratic to the last, he requested to be buried upright to save on funeral expenses. His gravestone measured just two feet square and was left blank until 'Jack Young (afterwards knighted'), feeling that there should be some token of the great figure within it, 'gave the fellow eighteen pence to cut it'. The resultant words passed to posterity as Ben's epithet. O RARE BEN JONSON.

From the Albion Shore

John Ogilny, a Scotsman in the service of Viscount Wentworth, Lord Deputy of Ireland, was, like his patron, a lover of the theatre. He was a professional dancer until an accident while performing in Ben Jonson's masque *The Gypsies Metamorphosed* curtailed his career. Wentworth, with the authority of a Viceroy, appointed him his Master of the Revels and must have encouraged him, at some point in the middle 1630s to open Ireland's first custom-built playhouse, in St Werburgh Street, near Dublin Castle. John Aubrey heard it was 'a pretty little theatre'. How James Shirley was lured to Dublin to run it is not recorded. Most likely Wentworth viewed his status as that of other grand patrons and regarded himself as worthy of his own theatrical troupe. Actors were not unknown in Ireland. In a rare adventure, the Queen's Players had toured there as long ago as 1589.

No actor's name from the company Shirley recruited has passed to posterity. On the opening night on 1 January 1638, excited local notables crowded into the theatre. A member of the audience was so delighted that he wrote an ode *Upon Mr James Shirley His Comedy...*

> And when my Shirley from the Albion shore
> Comes laden with the Muses, all their store
> Transfers to Dublin, full Parnassus brings,
> And all the riches of Castilian springs,

Shirley wrote *The Gentleman of Venice, The Politician* and *Rosiana* for the theatre. Other plays presented included *The Alchemist*, Middleton's *No Wit, No Help like a Woman's* and two unnamed plays by Webster. Even the founder, who had literary pretentions, put a play upon the boards. John Aubrey noted that John Ogilby 'wrot a play at Dublin called the Merchant of Dublin, never printed'.

To Shirley goes the honour of writing the first surviving play with an Irish theme. *St Patrick for Ireland* was presented at the theatre in 1639. The Prologue indicates that Shirley was beginning to have doubts about his Irish project, even accusing members of the audience of having a preconceived bias against his play:

> For some have their opinions so displeas'd,
> They come not with a purpose to be pleas'd.

He had researched the legends associated with the saint and employed many theatrical tricks to impress his audience. 'I choose to leap into these fires,' shouts the greedy enslaver, Milcho to Patrick, 'Rather than hear thee preach thy cursed faith.'The evil magician, Archimagus, plots against those who challenge the Irish Gods. He sinks into Hell amid another spectacular effect. A highly decorated altar had 'two Idolls upon it, Archimagus and priests, lights and incense'. Yet the play may not have gone down well with many of the audience, certainly not the Catholics of English origin who tended to regard themselves as more Irish than the Irish. The play portrays the Irish as uncivilised scoundrels, until converted to better things by St Patrick, a Brit. It may have been as a reaction against such a condescending work that *Landgartha* was performed on St Patrick's Day, 'as it was presented in the new theater in Dublin, with good applause, being an ancient story'. Henry Burnell, the author, came from a prominent landed family in the Pale. It is the first surviving play by an Irishman to be performed in Ireland. The prologue, 'delivered by an Amazon armed with a battle-axe', reveals that a previous effort had not gone down well. 'The present author (having not forgot, How in 's first Play, he met with too much spite'). This lost play may have been *The Irish Gent* for which James Shirley wrote a Prologue. If this was so, it confirms Burnell's view of its doleful reception:

> That wit, and soule-enriching Poesie,
> Transported hither must like Serpents dye
> Unkinde to both alike, shall the faire Traine
> Of Virgin Muses onely here be slaine?

The source of Burnel's 'ancient story' is the vast *Gesta Danorum* ('Deeds of the Danes') of the twelfth-century chronicler Saxo Gramatticus, which tells of the Norwegian heroine. Lagertha, the Landgartha of the title, an Amazonian warrior who enlists the aid of the Danish King Reyner to free her country from the tyranny of the Swedish King Trolio, whom she kills in single combat. Reyner falls in love with her. She has vowed 'chastity unto the Gods', but agrees to marry him, but he betrays her by returning to Denmark and taking up with a mistress, Uraca. Nevertheless, Landgartha rescues him from foreign invasion and defeats his rival, Harald. Reyner is suitably repentant and Landgartha brokers a succession. She will return to him, but conjugal rights are withdrawn:

> Norway shall be preserved for your young sonne;
> And as for me (though yours) I'll end my life,
> An honest widdowe, or forsaken wife.

Given the play was written by an Irishman for performance in Ireland, not surprisingly critics have sought allegorical meanings. The three Scandinavian kingdoms may be seen to represent Charles I's kingdoms of England, Scotland

and Ireland, but it is difficult to push the analogy further. They were certainly on the verge of conflict brought about by Civil War. The opening stages of what became known as the Bishops' War, caused by the King's inept attempt to impose the Book of Common Prayer on the Church of Scotland occurred on 21 March 1639, when Covenanters, sworn to oppose the measure, seized Edinburgh Castle. This was just four days after the performance of *Landgartha* at Werburgh Street, so parallels cannot be drawn. Wentworth was recalled by the King to raise an army to fight the Scots. In his absence, his powers passed to the Lords Justices of Ireland. Resentment grew. A General Assembly at Kilkenny on 24 October 1642, established an independent Irish Parliament. A prominent member was Henry Burnell, the playwright now turned insurrectionist. Ireland was dissolving into chaos. In October, the Lords Justices prohibited further playing at Werburgh Street because of the state of the country. It never reopened. James Shirley realised the hopelessness of the situation and returned to London, where he found that Queen Henrietta's Men, desperate for ready cash, had sold off some dozen of his plays.

Nor were the tensions pulling Scotland and Ireland apart unique to those kingdoms. In England, the King, desperate for money in the absence of Parliament, resorted to other means to raise funds. He claimed it his prerogative to raise 'forced loans'. Those refusing to pay were imprisoned. Soldiers were forcibly billeted on households. What was effectively Martial Law was imposed. Under the guidance of the distinguished jurist Sir Edward Coke, Parliament presented the King with the 'Petition of Right', reaffirming its traditional liberties. Till then, the King had been able to play off the Lords against the Commons, but with both houses united in support of the petition, he had little choice but to accept it. Nevertheless, he pursued a course of attempting to undermine what he had agreed, which raised animosity. The *coup de grâce* came with his imposition of 'Ship Money' in 1634. Till then, the costs of maritime defence had fallen on the coastal regions, now Charles sought to transfer this financial burden to his Kingdom as a whole. Not surprisingly, this was highly unpopular. The leading Parliamentarian, John Hampden, refused to pay, claiming taxes could only be imposed with the consent of Parliament. Following the disaster of the Bishops' War, financial necessity compelled Charles to summon Parliament again. Realising his nation was falling apart, he sought a characteristic solution. He commissioned William Davenant and Inigo Jones to stage *Salmaceda Spolia*, a masque, which was performed at the Whitehall Palace on 21 January 1640. He participated as Philogenes ('Lover of the People'), a wise but misunderstood ruler. After a severe tempest featuring the sprit of Discord, an era of peace and plenty ensues. In order to create a spirit of concord, the King invited some of his aristocratic critics to participate. The royal couple enjoyed this spectacular event so much that it was presented again on Shrove Tuesday, but things had deteriorated too far to be placated by a mere show. A performance more likely to reflect the public mood occurred at the Cockpit Theatre on 4 May 1640. *The Court Beggar* by Richard Brome was presented by the King and Queen's Young Company, a troupe formed in 1637 by Christopher Beeston – hence their popular name of 'Beeston's Boys'. On Beeston's death in October 1638, his son William inherited his theatrical enterprise. The play was probably the last of the era to draw the ire of the Master of the Revels. It satirised the financial machinations around the royal court and the Queen's circle of favourites, including William Davenant and Sir John Suckling, who is represented as the ne'er-do-well, mad, compulsive gambler, Sir Ferdinando, the Court Beggar of the title. As a result, Beeston was imprisoned in the Marshalsea and control of the company surrendered to William Davenant, who proved too busy to take it on, so Beeston resumed control. His time back in charge was brief.

On 2 August 1641, Sir Henry Herbert read a play by Thomas Jordan whose career had begun as a boy actor at Salisbury Court under Gunnell and Blagrave. 'This Comedy,' he wrote, 'called the Walks of Islington and Hogsden, with the Humours of Wood-street Comptor, may be Acted.' It was the last play to receive his approval for nineteen years. It was a great success when performed at the Red Bull. According to the printer's blurb of 1657, 'it was publikely acted nineteen days together with extraordinary Applause.'

Stephen Hammerton had become what might be described as a 'matinee idol' – perhaps the first in theatre history. In the mid-1630s he made the transition from women's roles to men's. He acted at Court with the King's Men in Suckling's *The Goblins* on 17 November 1638. Suckling wrote of him in the Epilogue:

> The women – Oh if Stephen should be killed,
> Or miss the lady, how the play is spoiled.

'If Stephen misses the wench,' says Thomas Killigrew at the end of *The Parson's Wedding*, 'that alone is enough to spoil the play. He appeared in a revival of *The Maid's Tragedy* and James Shirley's *The Doubtful Heir* at the Globe in 1641, a revised version of *Rosania*, which he had written for the Werburgh Street Theatre. In the Prologue, he remarks on the vastmess of the Globe's stage compared to the Dublin one. On 22 January 1641, Stephen Hammerton was appointed a Groom of the Chamber, together with ten others of the King's Men. It was a privilege they were not long to enjoy.

On 1 December, what became known as the Grand Remonstrance was presented by the recalled Parliament to the King. It summed up its grievances against the royal policies – foreign, financial and legal, but it was the religious factor that divided the parties. The Puritan faction in Parliament was deeply disturbed by what it regarded as Romanising tendencies in the Church of England under William Laud, who the King had appointed Archbishop of Canterbury in 1633. It called for his indictment for treason and he was arrested and imprisoned in the Tower. The same faction targeted Thomas Wentworth, who the King had created Earl of Strafford. One of the first acts of the recalled Parliament was to impeach him on a charge of high treason. After this failed, through his skilful defence, a Bill of Attainder passed by the Commons imposed the death sentence upon him. As a mob bayed outside the palace gates, the King signed the death warrant of his loyal supporter. He may not have realised he was signing his own. Realising that power was slipping away from the King's hands, his supporters, including William Davenant and Sir John Suckling, attempted to seize power and spring Strafford from the Tower. After it fizzled out, they fled to France where Suckling, according to Aubrey, committed suicide. Strafford was beheaded by the public hangman on Tower Hill on 12 May 1641 before a vast crowd.

The very existence of the plot served to convince Parliament and King that a rapprochement was impossible. The two sides moved to raise forces and secure strategic points. The King mobilised his levies, while Parliament raised the City trained bands. On 12 August 1642, Charles I declared the nation to be in a state of rebellion and raised his standard at Nottingham, initiating the first Civil War. 'Here ended my allowance of plaies,' Sir Henry Herbert wrote, 'for the war began in Aug. 1642.' Its outbreak gave the Puritans in Parliament the opportunity to realise their long-cherished aim, staled by long waiting. On 2 September, just three weeks after the King's declaration, 'an order for stage plays to cease' was issued. It appears no different from previous closure orders issued in time of plague or civil disturbance, referring to the 'times of humiliation' and the 'sad and pious solemnity' that the nation was enduring, but there was a more serious threat in the phrase that 'public stage plays' were a source of 'lascivious Mirth and Levity'. Yet it may not have been with a complete lack of hope that the flag over the Globe Theatre was hauled down. Parliament was not entirely dominated by the Puritans. There were those who would work to rescind the ban and, of course, if the King's cause triumphed, the problem would be over. It must have slowly dawned that such hopes were illusory. It must have been in a mood approaching despair that 'The Actors remonstrance or complaint for the silencing of their profession, and banishment from their severall play-houses' was presented to Parliament on 24 January 1643. Not only had the actors' working lives been curtailed, they were excluded from the places they exercised their profession. Not that they hadn't attempted to address the Puritans' grievances. 'Wee have purged our stages of all obscene and scurrilous jests,' the petition pleads. It was of no avail. It would be nearly two decades before the doors reopened.

Notes

Chapter One: The Sumptious Theatre Houses

1. Stow: *Annals*, London, 1615, p.697.
2. cited by E.K. Chambers: *The Elizabethan Stage*: Vol. 2: pp.34–35
3. Richard Flecknoe: *A Short Treatise of the English Stage*: London: 1664.
4. The modern Shoreditch High Street.
5. From: 'The Augustinian Priory of St John the Baptist, Holywell', Survey of London: volume 8: Shoreditch (1922), pp.153–187.
6. Acts of the Privy Council, Vol. 9: 1575–7, p.388.
7. from William Vaughan's *Golden Fleece*: London, 1626.
8. Stow: *Annals*, p.692.
9. Quoted by Julian Bowsher in *Shakespeare's London Theatreland.*
10. This is why it was permitted to publish plays during the Commonwealth era, but not to perform them.
11. Ian Frederick Moulton, '"A Monster Great Deforme": The Unruly Masculinity of Richard III': *Shakespeare Quarterly*, Vol. 47, No. 3: Autumn 1996: pp.251.
12. Charles Wallace, *The First London Theatre..*, 1913: p.14.
13. Lansdown MS 41.
14. Landsdown Ms xx 10.

Chapter Two: All Our Pageants of Delight

1. David Kathman: 'Henry Condell and his London Relatives', *Shakespeare Quarterly*: Vol. 63, No. 1, John Hopkins University Press, 2012, pp.108–115.
2. A term coined by George Sainsbury in *Elizabethan Literature* in 1886.
3. Coney-catching was theft by trickery. A coney was a rabbit bred for the table and therefore easy to catch.
4. Faustus is quoting John 1:8.
5. John Quincy Adams, jr: 'Captaine Thomas Stukeley': Journal of English and Germanic Philology, Vol. 15, No. 1. Jan., 1916. pp.107–129.
6. 'Ur' is a prefix in High German meaning 'original' or 'earliest'.
7. Mark Eccles: *Shakespeare in Warwickshire*: University of Wisconsin Press, 1961.
8. An anonymous prequel to Kyd's play, *The First Part of Hieronimo* was printed in 1604.
9. Richard Flecknoe: *A Short Treatise of the English Stage*: London, 1664.
10. The same Fleetwood who did not enforce an injunction against the acting companies in 1584.

Chapter Three: Where the Infectious Pestilence did Reign

1. A 'Separatist' sect, which believed that the church should be self-governing rather than subservient to the state. It took its name from a Puritan Divine, Robert Brown. Shakespeare refers to it in *Twelfth Night*. 'I had as lief be a Brownist as a politician.'

2. J. Robertson and D.J. Gordon (eds): *A Calendar of Dramatic Records in the Book of the Livery Companies of London*: Collections, Vol. 3, Malone Society: 1954.
3. The name generally given the genre is 'domestic tragedy', but this does not express sufficiently its range.
4. *Queenship and Political Discourse in Elizabethan Realms*: Natalie Mears, (C.U.P., 2005) pp.146–156.
5. Masks.
6. Much-loved boy.
7. A gesture of deference.
8. A popular country dance performed as a round.
9. According to *Tarlton's Jests*, Tarlton and his wife kept a tavern in Gracechurch Street.
10. Article in *Comparative Drama*. Vol. 47: No. 4: pp.419–49.

Chapter Four: 'According to their Habilities'

1. Jennifer Roberts-Smith: The Red Lion and White Horse Inn Used by Patronized Performers in Norwich, 1583–1634: Early Theatre, 10:1, pp.110, 111;(2007)
2. The weight of scholarly opinion now credits Fletcher as having a hand in the play. In no contemporary document is he given this accreditation.
3. S.P. Cerasano: 'Henslowe's Curious Diary'. Medieval and Renaissance Drama in England, 17 (2005). pp 72–85.
4. 'Huckle' is an archaic word for the hip: 'duckle' may just be a rhyming word.
5. A harlot.
6. The receiver of a penis?
7. A horse, with the obvious implication that the woman was to be mounted.
8. cf Doll Tearsheet, Shakespeare's prostitute in Henry IV, Part II.
9. Obviously 'bollocks': the woman can shake up a man's testicles while other men are sleeping.
10. Roast crab apples.
11. Part 2 was written no later than 1602 because it refers to Queen Elizabeth as yet living. It states the play had been written in the previous year, so 1601 is the likely date.

Chapter Five: Great Inconveniences and Misrule

1. It was not abolished until 1827
2. James M. Gibson: 'An Early Seventeenth Century Playhouse in Tonbridge, Kent': *Medieval and Renaissance Drama in England*, vol. 20, Associated University Presses, New Jersey, 2007.
3. A fairy who is enamoured of a mortal.
4. It has been suggested that this was the actor who played the Host of the Garter Inn.

Chapter Six: These our Servauntes

1. In fact, Twelfth Night falls on 5 January.
2. An Execration upon Vulcan
3. Strict regulations determined the wearing apparel appropriate to each class of person. Stage performances were exempt from this.
4. George L Geckle, *John Marston's Drama, Themes, Images, Sources*: Rutherford, NJ: Farleigh Dickinson University Press, p.34.
5. The sum at which the King was alleged to be selling knighthoods.
6. The Fates – the three female personifications of Destiny.

Chapter Seven: The Whole Course of the Present Time

1. The son of the 10th Lord Cobham who, as Lord Chamberlain, had briefly made life difficult for the actors. He and Raleigh were imprisoned for their alleged part in the Main Plot intended to place Lady Arabella Stuart on the throne.
2. A sheet of paper folded four times to create a top-face one-sixteenth of its size, perhaps referring to the diminutive size of the children.
3. Mary Bly has demonstrated that John Cooke's previous association with the Whitefriars' Company. Notes & Queries. Vol. 5: issue 3: OUP.
4. Marie was crowned Queen on 13 May 1610. Her husband was assassinated next day, so she duly became Regent. She was eventually ousted by Cardinal Richelieu.
5. The references are to Marlowe's play, *The Massacre at Paris* subtitled *With the Death of the Duke of Guise*. Lord Strange's Men performed a play entitled *The Tragedy of the Guise*, probably a version of Marlowe's drama, on 26 January 1593. It features Charles IX of France and two future Kings, his brother, who became Henri III and the King of Navarre, who became Henri IV.
6. For a discussion of James I's sexuality, see *Gay History and Literature: Essays by Rictor Norton*: http//rictornorton.co.uk/james1htm

Chapter Eight: We are Such Stuff as Dreams are Made on

1. An acolyte who reads from the Bible during the liturgy or at mealtimes.
2. £1,500 in 1610 would be worth around £172,000 in 2024, so the share of the profits Keysar claimed was worth around £29,000.
3. The cross and image of St George on the badge of the Order of the Garter.
4. A stylistic study undertaken by Prof. Cyril Foy in 1962, suggested that these and other passages were written by Fletcher.
5. Quoted by E.K. Chambers, attr. 'Jo ffletcher': *The Elizabethan Stage*, Vol. 2. P.309, Clarendon Prees, Oxford, 1923.
6. Domestic State Papers: James 1: vol CX: No 18.
7. Margaret E. Owens: 'Stages of Dismemberment: the fragmented Body in late Medieval and Early Modern Literature': University of Delaware Press, 2005.
8. A reason why comparatively few of the plays performed at the Fortune survived, compared with those performed at the Globe.
9. Digges contributed a eulogistic verse to Shakespeare's First Folio in the following year.

Chapter Nine: Our Revels now are Ended

1. The signature 'Sam Gill' in a copy of the First Folio in the Folger Shakespeare Library is thought to be Samuel Gilburne's.
2. *Memorials of the Guild of Merchant Taylors of the Fraternity of St John Baptist in the City of London*. Harrison, London, 1875.
3. The 'Private House' would have been the Cockpit Theatre.
4. 'Palsgrave' was the English rendering of the German *Pfalzgraf*.
5. Letters of John Chamberlain, edited Norman Egbert McClure, vol. ii, p.391: American Philosophical Society, Philadelphia, 1939.
6. *The History of Parliament: the House of Commons 1604–1629*, [ed.] Andrew Thrush and John P. Ferris, CUP, Cambridge, 2010
7. Cited by José A Pérez Díez, *Gondomar and the Stage: Diego Sarmiento de Acuña and the Lost Theatrical Connection, The Review of English Studies*, Vol. 73, Issue 309, April 2022, pp.264–88, Oxford Academic.

8. The word comes from the French *courant* – 'running'.
9. A number of actors have performed this speech as a 'short dramatic show-piece'. The first was John Philip Kemble in 1781.
10. Ben Jonson, *Songs and Poems*, 14.
11. N.W, Bawcutt, *The Control and Censorship of Caroline Drama, 1623–73*. OUP, 1996, p.191.

Chapter Ten: As it was Lately Acted

1. A compulsive gambler, Suckling is credited by Aubrey with inventing the game of cribbage.
2. 'To Sir William Davenant: Upon the Unspeakable loss of the Most Conspicuous and Chief Ornament of his Frontispiece.'
3. G.E. Bentley: *The Salisbury Court Theater and Its Boy Players*, Huntington Library Quarterly, Vol. 40, No. 2, February 1977, pp.129–49.
4. Second son of the 1st Duke of Manchester, In 1624, he participated in the mission leading to the marriage of Prince Charles to Princess Henrietta Maria of France. On his conversion to Catholicism in 1636, the King requested he absent himself from Court. He fled to France after being employed by the Queen to raise funds during the Bishop's War. He was ordained in the Benedictine Order, becoming Abbot of Nanteuil. He returned to England during the Commonwealth and was imprisoned in the Tower, but Oliver Cromwell had no desire to upset his ally and he was released and returned to France and became Chaplain to the exiled Queen Henrietta Maria.
5. Nearly £4 million at today's prices.
6. The discoverer of the circulation of the blood.
7. A mark was worth 13*s.* 4*d.* – two-thirds of a pound.
8. The play was not performed again until 1987 when it was presented on BBC Radio 3 to mark the 350th anniversary of Ben's death. In 2010, it was staged by the White Bear Theatre as part of its lost classics project.

Bibliography

Books

Aaron, Melissa B., *Global Economics: A History of the Lord Chamberlain's Men/King's Men and their Plays, 1599-1642*: *p.*120: University of Delaware Press, 2003

Aubrey, John, *Brief Lives*: (ed) Oliver Lawson Dick: Secker & Warburg, London, 1949.

Bentley, G.E., *The Jacobean and Caroline Stage*: 7 Vols, OUP, 1941.

Butler, Martin, *The Stuart Court Masque and Political Culture*, Cambridge University Press, 2008.

Byrne, Joseph P., *Daily Life during the Black Death*: Bloomsbury, London, 2006.

Chambers, E.K., *Notes on the Revels Office under the Tudors*: A.H. Bullen, London, 1906.

Chambers, E.K., *The Elizabethan Stage*, 4 vols: Clarendon Press, Oxford, 1923.

Chambers, E.K., *William Shakespeare, a Study of Facts and Problems*; 2 vols, OUP, 1930.

Cooper, Tanya, *Searching for Shakespeare*, National Portrait Gallery, London, 2007.

Dobson, Michael and Wells, Stanley (eds): *The Oxford Companion to Shakespeare*: Oxford University Press, 2001.

Fogg, Nicholas, *Hidden Shakespeare*, Amberley Publishing, Stroud, 2003.

Foulkes, R.A. (ed), *The Henslowe Papers* (2 vols): Scolar Press, London, 1977.

Gurr, Andrew, *The Shakespearean Playing Companies*: Clarendon Press, 1996.

Gurr, Andrew and Karim-Cooper, Farah (ed), '*A Ruinous Monastery': The Second Blackfriars Playhouse as a Place of Nostalgia, Moving Shakespeare Indoors*: Cambridge University Press, 2014.

Hammer. Paul E.J., *The Polarisation of Elizabethan Politics: The Political Career of Robert Devereux, 2nd Earl of Essex, 1585-97*: Cambridge University Press, 1999.

Heinemaqnn, Margot, *Puritanism and the Theatre*, CUP, 1980.

Honan, Park, *Christopher Marlowe, Poet and Spy*; Oxford University Press, 2005.

Miles, Rosalind, *Ben Jonson, his Life and Work*, Routledge & Keegan Paul, London, 1996.

Nicholl, Alistair, *English Drama, a Modern Viewpoint*, Chambers. London, 1968.

Nungezer, Ewin, *A Dictionary of Actors and other persons associated with the public representation of plays in England before 1642*. Cornell University Press, Ithaca, 1929.

Pollard, Tanya (ed), *Shakespeare's Theatre: A Sourcebook*, Bkackwell, Oxford, 2004.

Rowe, Nicholas, *Some Account of the Life of William Shakespeare*, Jacob Tomson, London, 1709.

Schoenbaum, Samuel, *William Shakespeare, a Documentary Life*, Clarendon Press, Oxford, 1976.

Sohmur, Steve, *The Opening Day at Shakespeare's Globe*, Manchester University Press, 1999.

Wells, Stanley, *Shakespeare and Co...* Penguin Books, London, 2007.

Theses

Boyle, Nicola: *The Documentary History and Repertory of the Lady Elizabeth's Men*. De Montfort University: 2017

Williams, Justine Isabella: *The Irish Plays of James Shirley, 1636-1640*. University of Warwick, 2010.

Articles and Papers

Bentley, G.E., *The Salisbury Court Theatre and its Boy Players*, Huntington Library Quarterly, Vol.40, No 2< February 1977.

Charlotte A Coffin: *Theatre and/as Witchcraft: A Reading of 'The Late Lancashire Witches.* Early Theatre. 16.2.2013: pp.91–109

Egan, Gabriel: *The Closure of the Theatres*: Yearbook of English Studies 44, De Montfort University, Leicester, 2004.

Munro, Lucy, *Plays and Performances in the Indoor Playhouses, 1625–42: Boy Players*, Leading Men and the Caroline Ensemble. Yearbook of English Studies 44, 2014

Munro, Lucy: *The Queen and the Cockpit: Henrietta Maria's Theatrical Patronage Revisited*: Shakespeare Bulletin, Johns Hopkins University, 2019.

Poolle, Kirsten, *Saints Alive! Falstaff, Martin Marprelate and the Staging of Puritanisn*, Shakespeare Quarterly, Vol. 46. Spring 1995, OUP.

Rickard, Jane: *'A Divided Jonson?: Art and Truth in* The Staple of News', *English Literary Renaissance*, 42 (2012), 294–316

Index

INDEX OF PEOPLE

[abbreviations AP = Augustine Phillips: RB = Richard Burbage: BHT = Boar's Head Theatre: BJ = Ben Jonson: BT = Blackfriars Theatre: CM = Christopher Marlowe: DM = Derby's Men: EA = Edward Alleyn: FT = Fortune Theatre: HT = Hope Theatre: JF = John Fletcher: LCM = Lord Chamberlain's Men: FF= First Folio: GT = Globe Theatre: PH = Philip Henslowe: KM = King's Men: LEM = Lady Elizabeth's Men: MoR = Master of Revels: OM = Oxford's Men: PC = Privy Council: PCM = Prince Charles' Men: QM = Queen's Men: QHM = Queen Henrietta's Men: RBT = Red Bull Theatre: RR = Richard Robinson: JS = John Shank: RS = Rose Theatre: TT = The Theatre: WD = William Davenant: WS = William Shakespeare: WT = Whitefriars Theatre: WM = Worcester's Men

Actors (see also individual names) Adams, John, joins QM, 16, 17: Alleyn, John, at TT 31: Benfield, Robert , with LEM 205, joins KM 205: parts played 237, 251: apology to MoR 245: Betterton, Thomas, anecdote of WS 87: Birch, George, apology to MoR 245: Browne, Robert, with DM 88: runs BHT 88: death 88: Burt, Nicholas, apprenticed to JS 206, joins QM 206, part played 206: Bryan, George, 34: performs before rulers of Denmark and Saxony 79: Cane, Andrew, comedian and goldsmith, noted for jig and repartee 273, part played 273: Clun, Walter, apprenticed to RR 206: Cooke, Alexander, in AP's will 87: Cowley, Richard, 79, 166: Crosse, Samuel, mentioned in WS FF 230: Dawes, Robert, contract with PH 216: complainant against PH 217: 210: Duke, John, 35, 106, 181: Dutton, John and Lawrence (fl 1580), join OM 11: join QM 17: Ecclestone, William (fl 1610–23) complainant against PH 217: Fletcher, Lawrence, 166: at Court of James VI 165: granted Freedom of Aberdeen 165: Gilburne, Samuel , apprenticed to AP 87, 230, mentioned in WS FF 230: Gough, Alexander, part played 251: Gough, Robert, 'principal actor,'35, 36, 87, apprentice to RB 36: creates part of Juliet 94: death 236, 251: Greene, Thomas, performs in *Tu Quoque* 181, 182: Hart, Charles, apprenticed to RR 206:: Hobbs, Thomas, joins KM from PCM 250: Holcomb, Thomas, apprenticed to JS 206: Holland, John, in *Seven Deadly Sins* 36: Honyman, John, 251, apprenticed to JS 206: part played 257: Johnson, William, joins QM 16: guardian of Philip Tarlton 54: Juby, Edward, consulted by Sir George Buck 99: Lacy, John, 206: Laneham, John, joins QM 16: Pallant, Robert, 106: sureties of peace sought against 106: complainant against PH 217: player of small parts 237: Pavy, Salamon, 204, noted for playing old men 157: impressed into Chapel Children 169: BJ's eulogy to 157, 158: Penn, William, joins KM from PCM 250: Pollard, Thomas, apprenticed to JS 206: apology to MoR 245: part played 266 Robbins, William, comedian with QHM 250: Sands, Janes, theatrical apprentice, in AP's will 87: Savage, Jerome, opens Newington Butts Theatre 9: Savill, Arthur, boy actor, apprenticed to Andrew Cane 272: Singer, John, joins QM 17: incident with spectator at Norwich 90: Sinkler or Sinklo, John, plays 'skinny man' parts 34, 205: plays Osrick 175: in Induction to *The Malcontent* 205: Sly, William, 166, 175, 203, 205: Smith, Anthony, joins KM from PCM 250: Tallant, Robert, in *Seven Deadly Sins* 36: Thompson, John, apprenticed to JS 206, 237, part played 237: Tooley, Nicholas, background 35: roles played 226: death 226: will of, 226, 227: Towne, John, kills William Kmell in brawl, 48, 108: Turner, Anthony, 274, parts played 250: Underwood, John, with Children of the Chapel 204: joins KM 204, part played 204, 237: death 236: Worth, Ellis, joins PCM 273: Wright, John (fl 1628) boy actor, apprenticed to Andrew Cane 272, 273

Adams, Robert, Queen's Surveyor, guardian of Philip Tarlton 54

Aelius Galenus (Galen), Greek physician, develops physiological theory of humours 121, 122
Allen, Giles, signs lease with James Burbage 6, 7, inherits Holywell Priory 13, 14: disputes with Burbages over lease of The Theatre 14, 15, 82, 132, 142: reaction to removal of timbers of TT 142, 143: declared vexatious litigant, 143
Alleyn, Edward, actor 46, 52, 250: early 'superstar' 17, 31: association with PH 32, 81: background 32, 131: with Worcester's Men 32: known as 'Ned' 36: roles 37s, 39, 97: marries Joan Woodward 39; entrepreneurship 39: funds FT 148: retirement from stage 126, 168: buys manor of Dulwich 168, 213: at Royal Pageant 170, 171: inherits PH's estate together with wife 217: rebuilds FT 222: BJ on 250: death 250
Alleyn, Joan, informs husband of death of Robert Browne 88: inherits PH's estate together with husband 217
Anne of Denmark, Queen, 170, 172, 174, 199, 230, 261: voyage from Denmark, 42: patron of theatre company 169: performs in court masques 172, 173: enthusiasm for theatre 179, 180: death 218, 232
Armin, Robert, clown, 34, 166, 167, 171, 273, background 79: Tarlton's nominated successor 79, 80: writer of ballads 80: noted as singer 80: extemporising ability 80: possible roles, Feste 143: Fool in *King Lear* 187: tract, *A Brief Resolution of the Right Religion* 80, play *Seven Deadly Sins* 33–36
Ashley, Sir Anthony, Clerk to PC, closes WT 204
Aubrey, John, biographer, 275, 278, 282, on WS 48, 49, 260, 261: on BJ 120, on EA 168: on Beaumont and Fletcher 200, 201, 246: on Davenants 260, 261, 263
Authors (see also individual names) Aristio, Ludovoco, Italian poet, *Orlando Furioso* 37: Aristotle, philosopher, Classical Unities 50, 51, 56, 167: *Poetics* 50, 51: Aristophanes, Greek playwright, *Lysistrata* 201: Bale, John, playwright and polemicist, . 3, 136: *Kynge Johan* 62: Barry, Lording, playwright, takes on lease of Whirefriars Theatre 203: Bright, Timothy, physician, *A Treatise on Melancholy* 114: Burton, Robert, scholar, *The Anatomie of Melancholy*, on growing news industry 247: Camden, William, antiquarian, on death of Ferdinando Stanley 82: at Westminster School 120: Campbell, Thomas, poet, suggests that WS is taking leave of stage in *The Tempest* 209: Carew, Thomas, poet and dramatist, ;Tribe of Ben' 249, 255: on BJ 255: Castovetro, Lodovico, Italian neo-classicist 50: Cervantes, Miguel de, Spanish writer, *Don Quixote* source for *Cardenio* 210: novellas of 224: Chaucer, Geoffrey, poet, *The Knight's Tale* source of *The Two Noble Kinsmen* 210: Constable, Henry, poet 102: Cooke, John, playwright, author of *Tu Quoque* 181, 182: Cornish, Richard, composer and playwright, 4: *The Story of Troylus and Pando*, 4: Cowley, Abraham, poet, *Love's Riddle* 227: Dennis, John, on Queen's delight in Falstaff 139, *The Comical Gallant* 139: Downes, John (d 1712) historian, possible transcriber of *Cardenio* 210, *Roscius Anglicanus* 210: Drummond, William, poet, conversations with BJ 126, 148–150, 176, 256: Dryden, John, poet, on *Bussy D'Ambois* 193: on BJ 254: Dugdale, Gilbert, account of James I's progress through City 170, 171, *Time Triumphant* 171: Eden, Richard, writer and translator, *History of Travel*, a source of *The Tempest* 208: Fennor, William, on theatre audiences 167: Flecknoe, Richard, dramatist, 4: on RB 53, 218: Gainsford, Thomas, writer, *The Rich Cabinet* 52: Giraldo, Giovanni Battista, Italian author, *Il Capitano Moro* 174: Goddard, William, satirist, 21: Gulpin, Edward, satirist 142: Gunnell, Richard, actor and playwright, founds King's Revels Children 264: Hall, Edward, historian, *Chronicle* 63, as major source for WS 63: Harrington, Sir John, courtier, *The Metamorphosis of Ajax*, 11: *Orlando Furioso* 37: Hartley, LP, novelist 50: Hathwaye, Richard, playwright, Francis Meres on, 108: *King Arthur* 108: *Sir John Oldcastle* 137, 152: Hearne, Thomas, antiquarian, anecdote of WD 261 Herrick, Robert, poet, *An Ode to Ben Jonson* 249: Holinshed, Raphael, historian, *Chronicles* 63, major source for WS 63, 86 and Marlowe 64: Howell, James, historian, on BJ 275–6: Hutchinson, Lucy, author, on mockery of Puritans in theatre 213, 214: Jordan, Thomas, dramatist, *The Walks of Islington and Hogsdon*, last play to pass censor before Civil War 281: Killigrew, Thomas, dramatist, 'Son of Ben' 249: on Stephen Hammerton 281, *The Parson's Wedding* 281: Lambarde, William, antiquarian 164: Lodge, Thomas, playwright 102, 203: Catholicism of 244: *Wit's Misery and the World's Madness* 47: Lovelace, Richard, poet and dramatist, ;Tribe of Ben' 249: Markham, Gervase (c1588–1637) author, BJ on 108: *Herod and Antipater* 211: Marmion, Shackerley, dramatist, 'Son of Ben' 249, 270: *Holland's Leaguer* 270–3, has second-longest run 273: Martin, Dorcas, translator of Calvinistic works 18: Mayne, Jasper, poet, *To the Memory of Ben Jonson* 190: Melton, Sir John,

statesman, *Astrologaster* 41, 42: Milton, John, poet, *Lycidas* 258: Montagu, Walter, dramatist, 'Son of Ben' 249: masque, *The Shepherd's Paradise* 265: Nabbes, Thomas, dramatist, 'Son of Ben' 249: Norton, Thomas, courtier and playwright, *Gorbuduc*, 4, 63, introduces blank verse into drama, 4: Oldys, William, on GT 143: Overbury, Sir Thomas, writer 20: on acting 53: on Richard Burbage 53: *New Eligies* 20, 53: Pepys, Samuel, diarist 202: Persons, Robert, Jesuit, on Sir John Oldcastle controversy 138, *A Treatise of Three Conversions of England* 138: Plautus, Latin dramatist, 4, 121, 123: **Plays:** *Amphitruo* 50, *Menaechmi* 50: Porter, Henry, playwright, killed by John Day 108: *The Two Angry Women of Abingdon* 108: Pulter. Lady Hester, poet, ode on WD's loss of his nose 263: Randolph, Thomas, dramatist, 'Son of Ben' 249, 274, *The Muses Looking Glasses* 264: Rowe, Nicholas, biographer, anecdotes of WS 86, 87, 125: on Oldcastle controversy 139: Rowlands, Samuel, satirist, 21: Sampson, William, dramatist, *Herod and Antipater* 211: Scott, Thomas, Puritan, *Vox Populi* 239, 240: Seneca, Latin tragedian, 49, 192, 193, 252, 261: Sharpham, Edward, writer, BJ on, 108: Shute, Anthony, poet, *Beauty Dishonoured* 55: Sidney, Sir Philip. poet, 4, 261, adhesion to Classical Unities 51, 52, 79: on clowns 80, *Arcadia* 180, 186: Skelton, John, author, *Magnificence* 62, 63: Smith, Wentworth, playwright and scrivener, significance of initials 109, *Thomas, Lord Cromwell* 97, 109: Spedding, James, writer, suggests that Fletcher and WS collaborated on *King Henry VIII* 210, 211: Speed, John, cartographer: on Sir John Oldcastle controversy 138: *The History of Great Britain* 138: Spenser, Edmond, poet, 23, 46, 102: Stephens, John, lawyer, on actors 52: *Essayes and Characters* 52: Stubbes, Philip, Puritan, 21, 23: :opposition to theatre 19: *Anatomie of Abuses* 16, 19 Swinburne, Algernon, poet, on *Bussy D'Ambois* 193: Tate, Nahum, poet, on *Catiline, His Conspiracy* 192: Taylor, John, water poet 141, on Shrove Tuesday riots 272: Tennyson, Alfred, Lord, poet, *In Memoriam* 258: Terence Latin dramatist, 4, 50, 123: Theobald, Lewis, writer, creates *Double Falsehood* claimed to be version of *Cardenio* 210: Tomkis, Thomas, playwright, *Albumazar* 180: Udall, Nicholas, schoolmaster and playwright, *Ralph Roister Doister*, 3, 4: Vega, Lope de, Spanisf author, *El Peregrino en su Patria* 225: Walton, Izaak, writer 275: Warner, William, poet, translator of Plautus 50, *Amphitruo* 50: Watson, Thomas, poet, 102: stabs William Bradley to death 43: tried for murder snd discharged 43: Wilson, Arthur, dramatist, *The Swisser* 236, 237: Winstanley, William, author, on Thomas Heywood 108: Wood, Anthony, antiquarian 260, 262: Wright, James, historian, *Historia Histrionica* 206, .219, 236, 264

Bacon, Francis, lawyer, on Martin Marprelate controversy 58: at Meyrick trial. 162: lack of knowledge of WS's works 163

Bancroft, Richard, Archbishop of Canterbury, Martin Marprelate controversy 57: censor of *Scourge of Villanie* 103: subject of scurrilous poem 177: relations with Puritans 178, 179

Beaumont, Francis, playwright, 20, background 201: indicates how a scene in *Macbeth* was performed 183: suffers stroke 210: **Works:** FF 202, 204, 246, 262: Second Folio 204, 205, 226: *The Captain* 204: *The Knight of the Burning Pestle* 183, 200, early example of literary parody 194: audience fails to grasp 194: *The Maid's Tragedy* 236, frequently revived 236, 281: *The Woman Hater*, first collaboration with JF 200: *The Scornful Lady* 201–203, 205: *Wit at Several Weapons* 262: difficulty to determine extent of collaboration 202:

Beeston, Christopher, actor-manager 35, 126, 181, 256, 266, 274: in AP's will 87: sureties of the peace sought against 106: alleged rape of Margaret White, 106, 107: abuse of her in court 106: sureties of peace sought against 106: converts Cockpit into indoor theatre 231: founds QHM 250: founds King and Queen's Young Company (Beeston's Boys) 281,

Beeston, William, actor-manager, sues for return of Stephen Hammerton 266: runs Beeston's Boys 281: imprisoned in Marshalsea 281

Bentley, John, actor and poet, joins QM 17, Thomas Dekker on 17: early 'superstar' 17: kills spectator in Norwich 90

Berkeley, Busby, film director 111

Bishop, Nicholas, soap maker, in fracas with Burbages 30, 31

Blagrave, William, Deputy MoR, founds King's Revels Children 264: sues for return of Stephen Hammerton 266

Blount, Charles, 8th Lord Mountjoy, soldier, at Garter ceremony 140: commander in Ireland 160: member of peace delegation 174: elegy to 222

Boderie, Antoine Lefèvre de la, French Ambassador, complains to Lord Salisbury about play at BT 196: reports about *The Silver Mine* 197: mentions companies' payments to King for agreeing to reopen the theatres 198
Boleyn, Anne, Queen, Henry Carey ward of 26: execution 26
Boleyn, Mary, courtier 26: mistress of Henry VIII 26: wife of Sir William Carey and mother of Henry Casrey, 26
Bradley, William, stabbed to death by Thomas Watson 43
Brande, Thomas , writes to Bishop about French actresses in London 256
Brayne, Ellen, née Burbage and son, Ralph, 3, 7: in fracas with Burbages 30, 31
Brayne, John, grocer 3, 6: builds Red Lion Theatre, first built in England since Romans, 3: wealth of, 3, 7: obsession with theatre project 7 8: charged with unlawful assembly, 12; rift with James Burbage, 12, 13: partnership with Robert Myles 13: killed by Robert Myles 15
Brett, Robert, master bricklayer, stepfather of BJ 127, 131
Bridgenan, Rt Revd John, Bishop of Chester, doubts about guilt of Lancashire witches 269
Brome, Richard, dramatist, 'Son of Ben' 249, BJ's servant 255: with Queen of Bohemia's Men 255: contracted for output 274 **Plays** *The Court Beggar* 281, satirises Royal Court, probably last play of era to be censored by MoR 281: great success of *The Love-sick Maid* (now lost) and *The Lovesick Maid* 255: *The Sparagus Garden*, 273–4, huge receipts 273: *The Weeding of Covent Garden* 266–8, 274, lampoons Inigo Jones and Puritans 267: *The Late Lancashire Witches*. 268–270
Brooke, Revd George, Prebendary of York, conspirator 135
Brooke, Henry, 11th Baron Cobham, 135, and *A Yorkshire Tragedy* 74: prisoner in Tower 170
Brooke, William, 10th Lord Cobham, appointed Lord Chancellor 134, 139: indifference to theatre 134: possible grievance against WS 135: death of 135, 139
Buck, Sir George, MoR, consults WS and Edward Juby 99: prohibits play about incident at French Court 196: approves *The Tragedy of Sir John Oldenbarnevelt* 219, 220
Bull, Eleanor , owner of 'safe house' 71
Burbage, Cuthbert, theatre manager, 9, 15, 26, 36, 203, 226: financial acumen 16: in fracas with Robert Myles, etc 30, 31: dispute with Giles Allen over lease of TT142: takes away materials from TT 142, 143: leaseholder of GT 143
Burbage, Elizabeth. carer of Nicholas Tooley 36
Burbage, James, artisan and actor, 1 6, 9, 10, 24, 26, 27, 83, 105: signs lease with Giles Allen 6, 7: building of TT 8: charged with unlawful assembly 12: rift with John Brayne 12, 13: under threat of dispossession at TT 14: disputes with Giles Allen over lease of TT 14, 15, 82, 132: fracas with Robert Myles, etc 30, 31: purchases lease of Blackfriars Priory 132, 133: conversion to theatre opposed by neighbours 133: ownership of timbers of TT 142: death 134
Burbage, Richard, actor, 26, 32, 33, 46, 52, 78, 79, 89, 91, 131, 150, 166, 169, 179, 203, 205, 212, 230: stage debut 15: in fracas with Robert Myles, etc. 30, 31: Thomas Overbury on, 53: Richard Flecknoe on 53: leases BT to Henry Evans 134: shortness of stature 219: roles played 126, Hamlet 186, 218, Hieronimo 218: King Lear 186, 218: Malevole 175: Othello 218: Proteus 53: Richard III 68, Romeo 94: leaseholder of GT 143: opens 2nd BT 203 bequest from WS 218: public grief at death 218, 229: epitaph 218
Burbage, Winifred, marriage and children 176, 227: consults Simon Forman 227: legacy from husband 227: marries RR 227: administrative role in company 227
Burnell, Henry, dramatist, supports Irish Confederacy 280: writes *Landgartha*, first play by an Irishman to be performed in Ireland 279–80, source 278: possibly also wrote *The Irish Gent* 279
Busini, Orazio, chaplain, disturbed by performance of *The Duchess of Malfi* 219
Butter, Nathaniel, stationer, publishes 1st Quarto of *King Lear*, works by Heywood, Rowley. Dekker and Fulke Greville and Chapman's *Homer* 246: jailed for publishing scurrilous work 247, 248: publishes first English newspaper 248, 254: satirised by John Fletcher and BJ 248, 249, 276
Cadyman, Sir Thomasm physician to Queen, rebuild's WD's nose 263
Calvert, Samuel, administrator, complains of Revels Children 176
Carey, George, 2nd Lord Blunsdon, 137, opposes conversion of Blackfriars Priory to theatre 133: succeeds as patron of theatre company 133, 134: owner of Holland's Leaguer 271: Lord Chancellor 139, 140: Knight of Garter 140: contracts syphilis 271; death and funeral 243, 271

Carey, Henry, 1st Lord Blunsdon, 6, 134: patron of acting troupe 26: background 26: ward of Mary Boleyn 26: trust of Queen Elizabeth in 26, 27: opposes pulling down of theatres 27: suppression of Northern Rebellion 70: as patron of LCM 82, 83, 91: intercedes for company 84, 85: owner of Holland's Leaguer 271: death of 133, 134

Carey, William, courtier: marries Mary Boleyn 26: father of Henry Carey 26

Carlell, Lodovick, playwright, background 257, *Arviragus and Philicea* 263: *The Deserving Favourite* 257, 258, reflects cult of Platonism 258

Carleton, Sir Dudley, diplomat, 123, 125, 164, 238, 271: on court masque 172, 173: on *The Tragedy of Sir John Oldenbarnevelt* 219

Caus, Isaac de, architect, oversees Covent Garden scheme 267

Cecil, Robert, 1st Earl of Salisbury, 166, 179:, 180, 196: Chief Minister, enemy of Robert Devereux 160: seeks peace with Hapsburg Empire 162, 174: proclaims Essex traitor 162: and succession 164, 165

Cecil, William, 1st Lord Burghley, Chief Minister 12, 15, 58, 135

Chamberlain, John, theatregoer, 123, 124, 238: on Mary Frith 132: on cost of court masques 172: on Gondamar 238: om Shrove Tuesday riots 271–2

Chapman, George, translator, playwright and poet 200, 259: background 109: imprisoned for *Eastward Ho!* 176: interest in contemporary French culture 192, 193: seeks refuge from arrest with Ludovic Stewart 197: **Works:** translation, Homer's *Iliad* 109, 110, 247: plays, *All Fools* 123, *An Humorous Day's Mirth* 123, 124: *Eastward Ho!* 152, 176, 180, 197: *The Blind Beggar of Alexandria* 122, 123, earliest 'humours' comedy 122: *Bussy D'Ambois* 192, 193, popular success of 193: *Sejanus, His Fall* 167, 168: *The conspiracie and Tragedy of Charles, Duke of Byron* 194, offends French 195–197, banned by Master of Revels 196, 197: *The Revenge of Bussy D'Ambois* 193, 194: poem *Hero and Leander* 109

Charles I, King, 56, 258, 265, 266, becomes heir to throne 237: proposed match with Spanish Infanta 237, 239: travels to Spain to woo her 239: humiliated, calls for war with Spain 239: inherits throne 242: embarks on disastrous war with Spain 243: love of theatre and masques 246, 263: annotates copy of 2nd Folio 246: as patron of company 250: French actors perform before 256: 'corrects' WD's *The Wits* 262: dissolves Parliament for eleven years 267: orders closure of Holland's Leaguer 272: participates in court masque 275–6: crowned King of Scotland 277: Northern Progress 277: increasing conflict 280: signs Strafford's death warrant 282: raises standard to begin Civil War 282

Chettle, Henry, writer 46, 108, 110: publishes *Greene's Groatsworth of Witte* 59: riposte with *Kind Harte's Dream* 61: apology to WS 61; alleged author of interpolations to *Groatsworth* 61: as debtor 61: hand in *Sir Thomas More* 95: called in to 'mend' Robin Hood play 101: reputation 107: appearance 107

Christian IV, King of Denmark, attends court performance of *The Dutch Courtesan* 199: jousting tournament for visit 222

Clifton, Henry, squire, rescues son Thomas from impressment by James Robinson 159: takes case to Star Chamber 159

Clinton, Henry, 2nd Earl of Lincoln 178, feud with Sir Edward Dymoke 178: lampoon of him brought to Star Chamber 178

Coke, Sir Edward (1532–1634) Chief Justice, on Thomas Clifton affair 159: Essex and Southampton trial, 162, 163: defines libel 177, 178: conflict with King 238, 280

Coloma, Don Carlos, Spanish Ambassador, complains to King about *A Game at Chess* 240: writes report to Chief Minister about play 240

Condell, Henry, actor, 126, 166, 175, 203, 212: background 34, 88, 131: and FF 141, 211, 218, 229, compilation of 229: publication of 229, 230: bequest from WS 218: part played 237, retirement 237

Cope, Sir Walter, Gentleman Usher 15, 179

Cottington, Francis, Chancellor of the Exchequer, orders *Histrio Mastix* to be burnt by public hangman 265

Crane, Ralph, scrivener, copyist of WS's plays 229

Cuffe, Sir Henry, conspirator, commissions LCM to perform Richard II 161: trial and execution 162, 163

Daborne, Robert, playwright, complainant against PH 217: failure to deliver play 217: in jail 217: appeals to PH for loan to obtain bail 217: *A Christian Turn'd Turk* 203
Daniel, Samuel, poet 102: brought before PC 175: *The Vision of the Twelve Goddesses*, 171, *The Tragedy of Philotas* 175
Danter, John, printer: publishes *Titus Andronicus*, first WS play to be printed 83, 103: printing books without authority 103: presses seized 104
Davenant, Jennet, née Sheppard, wife and mother 260: marriage and childbirth 260: moves to Oxford 260: rumoured affair with WS 261: death 261
Davenant, John, licensed victualler, marriage 260: moves to Oxford 260: admirer of WS 260: Mayor of Oxford 261: death 261: will 261
Davenant, Sir William. dramatist, WS's godson, 87, 260, 261, 281, rumoured son of WS 261: anecdote of WS 86, 87: early life 261: loses nose after contracting syphilis 263: charged with murder 263: flees to Holland 263: pardoned 263: nose rebuilt 263: part of attempted coup 282 **Works:** masques *Salmaceda Spolia*, 280–1: *The Temple of Love* 262, 263: plays: *The Platonick Lovers*, satirises cult of Platonism 259, 260, 262: *Tragedy of Albovine* 262: *The Cruel Brother* 262: *The Just Italian* 262, 263. *The Wits* 262, 263
Davies, Sir John, poet and lawyer 102: on theatre audience 22: rebukes Thomas Nashe 39: admires William Ostler 205
Day, John, dramatist: 111: background 108: expelled from Cambridge 108: charged with murder of Henry Porter 108: pleads self-defence 108: BJ on 108: laments his poverty 109: questioned by PC 180: **works:** plays, *The Isle of Gulls* 180: *The Travails of Three English Brothers* 106: pamphlet *The Mad Merry Pranks of Merry Moll of the Bankside* 131: poem *The Parliament of Bees* 108: tract, *Peregrinato Scholastica, or Learning's Pilgrimage* 109
Deering, Sir Edward, antiquarian, first known purchaser of WS's FF 230
de Vere, John, 15th Earl of Oxford, realises potential of drama as means of indoctrination 3: commissions John Bale 3
Dekker, Thomas, playwright, 21, 46, 159, 247: :on John Bentley, 17: devises pageants for Lord Mayor's Show 18: hand in *Sir Thomas More* 95: imprisoned for debt 102, 107, 108: possible Dutch background 107: prolific output 107, 108: BJ on 108: War of the Theatres 149–151: on plague 153: on Royal Pageant 170: **Works:** pageant *The King's Entertainment* 170, 171: plays: *Keep the Widow Waking* (now lost) 222: *Knight's Conjuring* 107, *SatirMastrxi* 47, 120, 121, 151: *Shoemakers' Holiday* 104, 129–131: *The Roaring Girl* 131: commissioned to write sequel to *Sir John Oldcastle* 152: *The Virgin Martyr*, onstage beheading in 221: *Westward Ho!* 176: *The Witch of Edmonton* 232–5, 268
Devereux, Robert, 2nd Earl of Essex, 'Essex Circle' 62: charges Dr Lopus with attempted poisoning 118: expedition to Ireland 144: ends in disaster 160: signs treaty with Hugh O'Neill 160: fury of Queen 160: rebellion 160–162, 175: tried for treason 162, 163: execution 163, 196
De Witt, Johannes, Dutch visitor, account of London theatres 111, 112: description and drawing of Swan Theatre 112
Digges, Leonard, poet, on *Catiline, His Conspiracy* 192: on WS's continuing popularity 236: translation of *Gerardo the Unfortunate Spaniard* 224
Dowland, John, composer 103, cult of melancholy, 115, *Semper Dowland, Semper Dolens* 115
Drayton, Michael (1563–1631) poet and playwright 102: income 109: cofounder of WT 203, *Sir John Oldcastle* 137, 152
Dudley, Robert, 1st Earl of Leicester, (1532–88) 1, 2, 118: entertains Queen, 2, 3: death of 33: death of wife 76: expedition to Netherlands 79, 120
Dymoke, Sir Edward, King's Champion, background 178: feud with Earl of Lincoln 178: lampoon of Earl brought to Star Chamber 178: sentenced for scurrilous libel 178
Eccles, Prof Mark, scholar, on death of William Knell 48
Edward I, King, expels Jews from England 118
Edwards, Rebecca, marries William Knell 17: marries John Heminges 88
Elizabeth, Queen, 2, 4, 6, 8, 9, 31, 44, 58, 59, 71, 91, 128, 133, 140, 143, 159: Richard Tarlton favourite of, 11: sends troupe of actors to James VI: projected marriage 177: Oldcastle controversy 139: requests play of Falstaff in love 139: fury with Essex 160: and Essex rebellion 161–164, 196: decline and death 164, 165: wardrobe of 171

Elizabeth Stuart, Princess, patron of LEM 204: marriage to Elector Palatine 199, 206, 210, 211

Entragues, Henriette d', royal mistress, promised marriage by King 195, influences King's conversion to Catholicism 195, face slapped by Queen 194–197

Estrées, Gabrielle d', royal mistress, bears children to Henri IV 195, King seeks to marry her 185, death in childbirth 195

Evans, Henry, scrivener, 203: obtains sublease of BT 8, 31: obtains lease in partnership with Nathaniel Giles 134: permitted by Giles to summarily recruit boys of his choosing 157: censured by Star Chamber 159: and Revels Children's clashes with authorities 174

Farnaby, Thomas, schoolmaster, owed huge debt by BJ 275

Farrant, Richard, appointed choirmaster of St, George's Chapel 8: leases part of Blackfriars Priory to convert as theatre 8

Fastolf, Sir John, soldier, original of Sir John Falstaff 136–139

Fernandez de Velasco, Juan. Constable of Castille, leads Spanish peace delegation 174: signs peace treaty with England 174

Field, Revd. John, Puritan, family 157: on disaster at Bear Garden 19: imprisonment 157; death 157, *A Godly Exhortation...* 19

Field, Nathan. actor and playwright, 200, 204, summarily recruited to Children of Pauls by Henry Evans 157: impressed into Chapel Children 159, 160: plays Bussy D'Ambois 192, 236: reputation as actor 215: complainant against PH 217: in jail 217: appeals to PH for loan to obtain bail 217 death 236: *Amends for Ladies* 131, 132. *The Honest Man's Fortine* 205: *A Woman is a Weathercock* 203

Field, Richard, printer: prints WS's narrative poems 133: opposes conversion of Blackfriars Priory to theatre 133

Fleetwood, William, Recorder, attempts to enforce injunction to close theatres 27: Richard Tarlton presented before 54, 55

Fletcher, John, dramatist, difficulty to determine extent of collaboration with Beaumont, 202: collaboration with WS 210: Principal dramatist of KM 222: linguistic abilities 222: ignorance of Islam 222: collaboration with Massinger 224, 225: will of 231: death of plague 246 **Works** FF 202, 204, 222, 246 :Second Folio 204, 205, 211, 226: *Bonduca* 204: *The Beggar's Bush* 224, 225: *The Captain* 204: *Cardenio* 210: *The Coxcomb* 205, *The Fair Maid of the Inn* 247, satirises Nathaniel Butter 248: *The False One* 231: *The Faithful* Shepherdess, probable his first play, not a success 200: definition of tragicomedy 200: *The Island Princess* 222–224, sources 222: *The Little French Lawyer,* source 224: *The Maid's Tragedy* 236, frequently revived 236, 281: *The Prophetess* 224, echoes of *The Tempest* in 224: *The Pilgrim*, source 224: The *Woman Hater,* first collaboration with Francis Beaumont 200, 210: *The Scornful Lady* 201, 202: possible collaboration with Shakespeare on *King Henry the Eighth* 97, 210, 211: *The Honest Man's Fortune* 205: *The Maid in the Mill* 226: *The Scornful Lady* 201–203, 205: *The Sea Voyage*, based on William Strachey's account of his voyage 224: *The Spanish Curate,* source 224: *The Two Noble Kinsmen* 210, 211: *A Wife for a Month* 225, 226: *The Wild Goose Chase,* source 225: *The Woman's Prize or The Tamer Tamed* 201. only sequel to a WS play written in his lifetime 201, 202, banned by Master of the Revels 202: *The Tragedy of Sir John Oldenbarnevelt* 219–221: *Valentinian* 204: *The Wikd Goose Chase* 266: *Wit at Several Weapons* 262: *Women Pleased*, source 224

Ford, John, dramatist 250: background 222: decadence of themes 253 **Works:** elegy, *Fame's Memorial* 222: pamphlet *Honour Triumphant* 222: plays: *The Broken Heart* 252: *Keep the Widow Waking* (now lost) 222, 232: *The Laws of Candy* 222: *The Lover's Melancholy* 252: *'Tis Pity She's a Whore* 253, 254, 257: *The Witch of Edmonton* 232–5, 268

Forman, Simon. astrologer, sees performances at GT, of *Macbeth* 182, 183. *Cymberline* 206, *The Tempest* 206

Fortescue, Sir John, Privy Councillor, signs warrant for release of Thomas Clifton 159

François, Duke of Alencon, suitor to Queen Elizabeth 177

Frederick II, King of Denmark, English actors play before 79

Frederick V of Palatine, marriage to Princess Elizabeth 199, 206, 210, 211, 238: accepts crown of Bohemia 238: deposed of both his realms 238: patron of Palsgrave's Men 238

Frith, Mary, aka 'Moll Cutpurse', criminal and cross-dresser: subject of *The Roaring Girl* 131: appears on stage during performances 132: sentenced to pay public penance 132: appeared drunk 132
Frizer, Ingram, agent, kills CM in brawl 71: verdict of 'self-defence 71
Fuller, Thomas, historian, on Richard Tarlton, 11: on Oldcastle controversy 138, 139: *History of the Worthies of England* 139
Gardiner, William, money-lender and JP, legal actions against WS. Langley and others 113: dubious character 113
Gershow, Frederic, German visitor, describes boy's beautiful singing before a performance at the BT152
Gil, Alexander, schoolmaster, joins claque against BJ 276–7
Giles, Nathaniel, Master of the Children of the Chapel Royal, leases BT with Henry Evans 134: permits Evans to summarily recruit boys 157, 159
Gondamar, Diego de Acunña, 1st Count, Spanish Ambassador, offers huge dowry for marriage of Prince Charles 237: role in execution of Sir Walter Raleigh 238: visits FT 238: fall from grace 239: satirised in *A Game at Chess* 239–241
Gontaut, Charles de, duc de Biron, offends Queen Elizabeth 196: executed for treason, 194: model for Chapman's character 194
Gosson, Stephen, author, 2, 6, 99:: sees plays at the Bel Savage and Bull Theatres 6: on theatre 16: turns against theatre 22: **Works:** plays: *Captain Mario,* 2, *Cateline's Conspiracies,* 2, *Praise at Parting,* 2: tracts, *The Schoole of Abus,* 2, 22, *Plays Confuted in Five Actions* 16, 22, 23
Greene, 'Doll', wife of Robert Greene, 36, 37: asked to pay his debts 37
Greene, Robert, author, 33, 54: background 36: prolific author 36: Interest in low life 36, 37: death of 37, 59, 61, 86: :criticism of CM 39, 40: supposed attack on WS, CM and Nashe 49, 59, 60: and Marprelate controversy 57, 58: continuing admiration for works 61: **Works:** pamphlets, *In Defence of Conny Catching* 36: *Perimedes thr Blacksmith* 39, 40: plays, *Friar Bacon and Friar Bungay* 36: *The History of Orlando Furioso* 37: 36, 37: *The Scottish Historie of James IV* 36, 62: *A Pleasant Concyted Comdie of George a Green* (attributed) 98, 99: prose romances *Menaphon* 47, *Pandosto* 62: tract, *Greene's Groatsworth of Witte* 59, 60, 107:
Greville, Fulke, poet and statesman 247: employs WD 261, 262: epitaph 261, murder of 262: **Closet Dramas:** *Alaham* 261, *Mustapha* 261 *Antony and Cleopatra* 261, 262
Grimeston, Edward, translator, *A General Inventory of the History of France*, source of *The conspiracie and Tragedy of Charles, Duke of Byron* 194
Griffin, Edward, lawyer, draws up contract for PH with LEM 216
Griggs, John, carpenter 9
Hall, Rt Revd Joseph, Bishop of Norwich, satirist 103, rebukes Thomas Nashe 39: works burnt by public hangman 103
Hammerton, Stephen (fl 1629–47) actor, joins King's Revels Children as boy actor 264: parts played 236, 266, 281: admired by William Prynne 266: joins KM 266: becomes 'matinee idol' 281
Harrison, Stephen, joiner, builds Arches of Triumph for Royal Pageant 170
Haughton, William, playwright, imprisoned for debt 108, **plays,** *Englishmen for my Money* 108, 128, 129: *Grim, the Collier of Croydon* 108, xenophobia in plays of, 116, 117, 128, 129
Harvie, Edward, fencer, performs at TT 25
Harvey, Gabriel, author, 26, 80: on death of Robert Greene 37: criticism of CM 40: *A New Letter of Notable Conceits* 40
Heminges, John, actor, 126, 166, 203–205, 227: background 88: and Grocers' Company 88: sea coal meter 88, 143: marriage 88: churchwarden 88: and FF 141, 211, 218, 229, compilation of 229: publication of 229, 230: leaseholder of GT 143: financial role in company 174 seizes shares due to daughter 205, sued by daughter 205: bequest from WS 218
Henri IV. King of France, womanising 195, seeks annulment of marriage 195, in debt to Francisco de Medici 195, marries Marie de Medici 195, conversion to Catholicism 195: patron of *Les Comediens du Roi* 256
Henrietta Maria, Queen, 56: patron of theatre company 250: and French actors in London 256: and cult of Platonism 258, 262, 263: participant in court masques 262–5, 276: love of theatre 263
Henry VIII, King, 4, 13, 26, 33, 44, 95, 97, 231, 271, orders closure of brothels 271

Henry, King of Portugal. 45
Henry Frederick Prince. 166, 170, 172, 230, patron of theatre company169, investiture as Prince of Wales 206, 231: proposal to marry Spanish Infanta 237: death 226, 237, 238
Henslowe, Philip, 39, 45, 46, 55, 60, 81, 82, 84, 108:, 110, 111, 147, 231, 235, 252: impresario, 33: and RT 32, 37, 39, 97, 106, 123, 167: background 32: 'loans to playwrights 107–109, 120, 121, 124: commissions play of Sir John Oldcastle 137, 152: commissions sequel 152 relocates RT to Shoreditch as FT 148: partnership with Jacob Meade to build HT 216: contract with Robert Dawes 216; complaint against by LEM 216, 217: counter-complaint 217: death 217
Hentzner, Paul, German lawyer, account of London theatres 114
Herbert, Sir Henry, MoR, 274, 277, 281 bans *The Tamer Tamed* 202; receives apology from actors for presenting *The Spanish Curate* without license 245: generous attitude towards French acting troupe 256: censors Davenant's *The Wits* 262: notes end of role with start of Civil War 282
Herbert, Philip. 1st Earl of Montgomery, dedicatee of WS FF 229
Herbert, William. 3rd Earl of Pembroke, 192, beautiful youth of WS's sonnets? 169: steward at celebration of peace treaty 174: grief at death of RB 218, 229: dedicatee of WS's FF 229
Hesketh, Richard, conspirator. 82
Heton, Richard. manager, Salisbury Court Theatre 274
Heywood. Thomas, author, 108, 109, 247, 250: on William Knell 17: obscure background 108: as actor 108, 110: prolific output 108, 109: actor-dramatist at RBT 181: defence of theatre 17, 213, 214: on Richard Perkins: liking for spectacular effects 268 **Works** hand in *Sir Thomas More* 95, 96: tract, *Apology for Actors* 17, 213, 214, 230: plays, *Edward IV* 110, 111: *The English Yraveller* 109, *If You Know Not Me You Know No Bodie* 181, popularity of 181, *The Fair Maid of the West* 250: *The Four Prentices of London* 84, 85, *The Late Lancashire Witches*. 268–270: *A Woman Killed with Kindness* 107
Hide, John. mortgagee of TT 13, 15
Hill, John, arbiter in Brayne/Burbage dispute 13
Hippocrates, Greek physician, develops theory of humours 121
Hoby, Sir Edward, diplomat, comments on *The Isle of Gulls* 180
Holland, Aaron, builds RBT 180: attempt to form company with Martin Slatter 180
Holland, Elizabeth "Bess", brothel madame 271, routs force sent to close Holland's Leaguer 272
Hotson, Leslie, scholar, on *Twelfth Night* 143
Howard, Henry. 1st Earl of Northampton, enmity towards BJ 168, 174: member of peace delegation 174
Howard, Lord Charles of Effingham, 6: marriage 6: patron of theatre company, 6, 162: appointed Lord High Admiral, 6 : suppresses Essex rebellion 162: member of peace delegation 174
Howard, Lord Thomas, Vice Admiral, at Garter ceremony 140
Humphrey, Christopher (d 1586), merchant, 35
Ives, Simon, composer, *The Triumph of Peace* 265
Jaggard, William, stationer, printer of WS FF 229, 230, surprising choice as 229, 230: publishes pirated works 229, 230.only printer capable of fulfilling task 230, illness and death 230
James I, King: 168, 230, 231, as James VI of Scotland, voyage to Denmark 42: and witchcraft 42, 182: enthusiast for theatre 165, 171, 198, 204: successor to English throne 161, 164, 165: proclaimed James I of England 165: progress to London 165–166: awards Royal Charter to LCM, now to be known as KM 165, 166: coronation of 155, 167, 178: Royal Progress through City 170, 171: desire for peace with Spain 173: signs peace treaty with Spain 174: lampooned in *Westward Ho!* 176: orders arrest of playwrights 176: battles with Puritans 178, 179, 215: bans plays to avoid confrontation with France 196: possible bisexuality 197: closes theatre over silver mine affair 197: reopens them after payments from companies 198: seeks Protestant alliance 211, 237: royal progress to Scotland 217: Declaration of Sports 267: foreign policy 237–243 Spanish Match 238–242:infirmity, illness and death 245: funeral 245, 246: *Basikikon Doron* 197: *Daemonoologue* 182
James, Dr Richard, antiquary, and Oldcastle controversy 135–137: *The Legend and Defence of ye noble Knight and Martyr Sir John Oldcastle* 135
Jones, Inigo, architect, 232: introduces Palladian style to England 172, as designer of masques 172: possibly designer of Cockpit Theatre 232: feud with BJ 256, 262, 267, 276–7:: designs London's

first planned square 267 **Masques:** *of Blackness* 172, 173: *Chlorida* 276: *Love's Triumph through Callipolis* 275–6: *Luminalia* 259: *Salmaceda Spolia* 280–1: *The Temple of Love* 262: *The Triumph of Peace* 265

Jonson, Ben, background 120: actor and writer, 102, 200, 253: as bricklayer 127: criticism of CM 40: as actor 47, 120, 121: classical learning of 120, 131: adhesion to Classical Unities 51, 121, 167, 189, 182, 256: criticism of WS 51: jibes against as bricklayer 103, 120, 127, 151, 277: comments on John Day, Thomas Dekker, Edward Sharpham, Thomas Middleton and Gervase Markham 108: on John Marsdon199: as soldier in Netherlands 120: defines 'humours' 122: satirises Anthony Munday 124, 275: arrested after *Isle of Dogs* affair 125: in prison 126: kills Gabriel Spencer in duel 126, 127: charged with murder 126, 127: pleads 'Benefit of Clergy' 127, 151: converts to Catholicism 127, 189, 190, 244: on the GT 143: quarrel with John Marsden 148, 149: conversations with William Drummond 126, 148, 148–150, 176, 191, 199, 256:'put down' by WS 149, 150: War of the Theatre 148–152, 159: imprisoned for *Eastward Ho!* 176: dines with Gunpowder plotters, including Robert Catesby (1572–1605) 189: before Consistory Court 189: attacks other writers 191, 192: first Poet Laureate 192, 231, 275: on *The Tempest* 210: lampoons Puritans 215: distaste for unsavoury smell of HT 216: first writer to publish complete works 218: 'Sons' and 'Tribes' of Ben 249: conviviality of 249: on EA 250: poor state of health 255: on Richard Brome 255: feud with Inigo Jones 256, 262, 267, 275–7: debts 275: : City's Chronologer 275: accused of blasphemy 276: illness and death 274, 275: epitaph 277 **Works:** essay *Timber, or Discoveries* 40: **masques,** *of Beauty* 182: *of Blackness* 172, 173: *The Gypsies Metamorphosed* 278: *The King's Entertainment at Welbeck* 277, cost of 277: *Love's Triumph through Callipolis* 275–6: *Love's Welcome at Bolsover* 277: *Neptune's Triumph for the Return of Albion* 239: *of Oberon* 207: *of Queens* 182: *The Satyr* 172: pageant *The King's Entertainment* 170, 171.:: plays: FF of 1616 103, 126, 218: *The Alchemist* 127, 191, 192, 204, 219, 278: *Bartholomew Fair* 47, 48, 50, 209, 210, 215, 255, 266, 268: *The Case is Altered* 104, 121: *Catiline, His Conspiracy* 192, 204, poorly received 192: *Cynthia's Revels* 150, 157, 204: *The Devil is an Ass* 227, 228: *Eastward Ho!* 152, 176, 177, 180, 197, as satire on King James 176: *Epicene, or The Silent Woman* 191, 219, 236, lack of success 191: *Every Man in His Humour* 77, 104, 122, 126 recommended for performance by Shakespeare 125 cast list, 126: *Every Man out of His Humour* 149, satirises Marston and possibly Dekker and WS 149: *Isle of Dogs* 103, 124, 125, 126: official outrage caused by 124, 125, 162, 191: *The Magnetic Lady* 276: *The New Inn* 254, 276, complete flop 254, blames actors and audience 254: *Poetaster* 151, 204: *The Sad Shepherd* 102: *Sejanus, His Fall* 167, 168, 192: *Staple of News* 48, satire of Nathaniel Butter 248, 249, 276, not a success 254: *A Tale of a Tub* 277: *Volpone*, 189–191, 201, 219, rapidity of writing 189, popularity of 190: **poetry** *The Ballad of Salamon Pavy* 157, 158: *Expostulation with Inigo Jones* 276: *Ode to Himself* 254, 255: valedictory verse to WS 229

Katherens, Gilbert, master carpenter, demolishes Bear Garden and builds HT 216

Kathman, David, scholar 34

Kempe, Will, clown. 36, 78, 79, 91, 104, 105, 126, 150m230: Morris Dance to Norwich 21, 22: jester to Earl of Leicester 79: performs before rulers of Denmark and Saxony 79: parts played 79, 104, 105, 138, 143: appointed sharer, 87: extemporisation 98: leaseholder of GT 143: sells share 143: proposed dance over the Alps 106: joins WM 106: intended to play Sir John Oldcastle 152, 153: death 152: *Kempes Nine Daies Wonder,* 21, 22, 90, 105, 106

Keysar, Robert, financier, 273, takes over Revels Children 194, 203: buys Marston's shares in BT 203

Kiechel, Samuel, German traveller, describes playhouses 10

King, Rt. Revd. John, Bishop of London, prohibits *The Tragedy of Sir John Oldenbarnevelt* 219

Knell, William, actor, 52: joins QM 17: plays King Henry in *The Famous Victories…*: early 'superstar' 17: marries Rebecca Edwards 17, 88: killed in brawl 48, 54, 88, 90, 108

Knight, Edward, prompter, compiler of scripts for KM 245: Court privileges extended to 245

Kyd, Thomas, dramatist 64, 74, 86: background 46: shares lodgings with CM 47: lodgings searched 71: 'heretical conceits' found 71: arrested and possibly tortured 71: death of 71, 86: **Plays:** *The Tragedie of Soliman and Persida* 46, 117, 121: *Spanish Tragedy,* 46–49, 121, 175, 176, 180: ;possibly most popular play of era 46: established vogue of revenge tragedy 46: probable author of *ur-Hamlet* 47: dating 48, 49

Langley, Francis (1548–1602) entrepreneur, 271, builds Swan Theatre 111; legal action against William Wayte and William Gardner (fl 1595–1608) 113: license of Swan Theatre withdrawn 125: suspected of fencing diamond 125
Laud, William, Archbishop of Canterbury 256, 277, 282
Lawes. William, composer, *The Triumph of Peace* 265
Lee, Anne, legal actions against by William Wayte 113
Lee, Sir Henry (1533–1611) Queen's Champion, at Garter ceremony 140
Lindsay. Sir Robert. diplomat 179
Lopus, Roderigo, physician, convert from Judaism to Christianity 118, appointed physician to Queen 118, charged with attempted poisoning by Earl of Essex 118, condemned and executed 118
Loquart, Hans, merchant, 35
Lowin, John, actor 52, 167, 175, 227, 251, 273: background 167: possible son of 221: apology to MoR for presenting *The Spanish Curate* without a license 244: plays Belieur in *The Wild Goose Chase* 266: Bosola 237: Falstaff 236
Lucy, Sir Thomas, landowner, reputed clash with WS 48
Lyly, John, writer, 31, 157: Secretary to Earl of Oxford, holds sublease of BT 9: and Marprelate controversy 57, 58: hopes of preferment 59: Member of Parliament 59: **Works**: prose romance, *Euphue, or The Anatomie of Wits* 9: plays, *Campaspe.* 31: *Gallathia* 31 *Midas* 114: *Mother Bombie* 59: *Sappho and Pluto,* 31 *The Woman in the Moon* 59: tract, *Pappe with a Hatchet* 58
Machiavelli, Niccolo, political philosopher, *The Prince* 69, 70, 184, banned in England, 69: influence on English writers 69, 70
Manningham, John, law student, anecdote about WS and Richard Burbage 68
Maria Ana. Spanish Infanta, proposed as bride for Prince Henry 237: on Henry's death, proposed as bride for Prince Charles 237: distaste for Prince Charles 239
Marlowe, Christopher, 64, 74, 86, 102, 103: writer, background 37, 131: at Cambridge University 38: recruited as secret agent 38: homosexuality 38, 43, 44, 68, 69, 72: atheism 38, 40: contemporary criticism of 39: violence of 43: tried for murder and discharged 43: appeals for protection from.43, bound over to keep the peace 43: William Corkins, tailor, alleges assault by 43: shares lodgings with Kyd 47: supposed attack by Greene 60, 61: and Dutch Church libels 71: warrant for arrest 71: intended flight to Scotland 71: killed in brawl 71: inquest on 72: accounts of death 72, 73: WS's tribute to 73: **Works:** translations, Lucan's *Pharalia.* Ovid's *Eligies* 38: **plays,** *Dido, Queen of Carthage* (with Thomas Nashe) 38, 39, , 43: *Dr Faustus* 39–43, 68, 97, 168: supposed appearance of devils during performances 41, 168: *Edward II* 38, 64:, 68, 69, 110: influence of Machiavelli on 69: *Tamburlaine the Great* 39, 40, 43, 68, 71, 97, 119, 176, as 'Turk Plays, 44, parodied by WS 44: *The Jew of Malta* 39, 43, 68, 69, 82, 119, 250: stereotype of Jews 40, 117: poems, *Hero and Leander* 38, 43, 44, 73:: *Passionate Shepherd to his Love* 73
Marston, John (1576–1634) poet and playwright 103: nickname of 103: sharer in BT 198: War of the Theatres 148–152, 159: flees from arrest after *Eastward Ho!* 176: quarrel with BJ 148, 149, 199: recorded in Newgate Prison 197: takes Holy Orders 199: **Works:** poems:, *The Metamorphosis of Pigmalion's Image* 103, *Thr Scourge of Villanie* 200. ordered cto be bunt by public hangman 103: likely author of *The SilverMine* 197, 198: **plays** *Eastward Ho!* 151, 176, 180, 197: *Histriomastix* 103, 149: *Jack Drum's Entertainment* 134, 135, 150: *The Malcontent* 117, 118, and corruption in high places 175, 198:, induction to 175: *Parasitaster, or The Fawn* 198, parallels with Court of King James 198: *The Dutch Courtesan* 199, satire on Puritans 199: *The Insatiable Countess,* onstage beheading in 221: *What You Will* 150
Massinger, Philip, dramatist 250, 263: in jail 217: collaboration with JFl 224; **Works:** plays: *The Beggar's Bush* 224, 225: *The False One* 231: *The Honest Man's Fortune* 205: *The Honour of Women* 245: *The Little French Lawyer,* source 224: *The Laws of Candy* 222: *The Picture* 205, 236: *The Prophetess* 224, echoes of *The Tempest* in 224: *The Sea Voyage,* based on William Strachey's account of his voyage 224: *The Spanish Viceroy* 231, 244, 245, anti-Spanish theme contributes to war fever 244, presented without license 244, apology to Master of Revels 244: *The Roman Actor* 251, 252: *The Tragedy of Sir John Oldenbarnevelt* 219–221, 231:: *The Virgin Martyr,* onstage beheading in 221
Massingham, John, diarist, on death of Queen Elizabeth 164

Matthews, Sir Toby, diplomat, 125
Maurice of Nassau, Prince, at Siege of Ostend, 104: brings about downfall of Johan van Oldenbarnevelt 220
Meade, Jacob, waterman, partnership with PH to build HT 216
Medici, Francisco de, Grand Duke of Tuscany 195
Medici, Marie de, Queen of France, marries Henri IV 195, slaps face of King's mistress 194–197
Meres, Revd Francis, author, on death of CM 72: on Henry Chettle 107, Richard Hathwaye 108, Henry Porter 108, BJ 121
Meyrick, Sir Gilli, conspirator, commissions LCM to perform Richard II 161: trial and execution 162, 163
Middleton, Thomas, playwright 76, 215, comment of BJ on, 108: background 110: legal disputes 110: hostility to lawyers 110: 'Honourable Entertainments' for City 110, 239: City's first paid Chronologer 110: flees from arrest 241, 242: confined to Fleet Prison 242:addresses flippant petition to King 242: decline and death 242, 275 **Works:** pageants, *The Triumph pf Truth* 110: *The Triumph of Health and Prosperity* not well received 24: masque *The World Tost at Tennis* 118: plays: *Anything for a Quiet Life* 239: *The Changeling* 235, popularity of 235: *A Chaste Maid in Cheapside* 204: *The Meeting of a Gallant at an Ordinarie* 138:: *A Game at Chess* 237–239, 245, background to 237–239, satire on Spanish Match 239: probably KM's greatest commercial success 237, 240, 242, 273: closed down by authorities 240, 241, represents serious phase in decline of theatre 242, 243: *The Lady's Tragedy* 227: *The Puritan* 215: *No Wit, No Help like a Woman's* 278: *The Roaring Girl* 131, 132: *The Spanish Gypsy,* source 224: *The Witch* 184
Milulin, Grigory Ivanovich, Russian Ambassador, at Court performance 143
Milton, John, scrivener, executor of RB 227, possibly father of poet 227
More, Sir Thomas, statesman, and Ill May Day riots 95: play of 95, 96: proclaimed saint and martyr 95
More, Sir William, administrator, leases Blackfriars Priory to William Farrant, 8, 9: repossesses building 31
Montchrestien, Antoine de, French dramatist: kills opponent in duel 196, flees to England 196: *L'Ecossaise* 196
Morley, Thomas, composer, *First Book of Ayres* 143
Moulton, Prof Ian, scholar, on disturbances in London, 24, 25
Mulcaster, Revd Richard, High Master of St Paul's School: introduces English as language of education 157: begins standardisation of English spelling 157: codifies rules of football 157
Munday, Anthony, writer and spy (?) , 23, 167, 224, 275: devises pageants for Lord Mayor's Show 18: collaborates on plays 32: background 32: possibly government agent 32: and Marprelate controversy 57, 58: hand in *Sir Thomas More* 95: witness against Catholic priests 95: satirised by BJ 124 **Works**, memoir, *The English Romayne Life,* 32: plays *Fidele and Fortunis* 32: *John a Kent and John a Cumber* 97, 123: *The Downfall of Robert Earl of Huntingdon* 99, 101: *Sir John Oldcastle* 137, 152: translation *The Strangest Adventure that Ever Happened* 46
Murray, Sir James, courtier, informs King of his lampooning in *Westeard Ho!* 176
Myles, Robert, City Alderman, partnership with John Brayne 12: alleged murderer of John Brayne 15, 30: fracas with Burbages 30, 31
Nashe, Thomas, author.36, 80, 271: extols acting of Knell, Tarlton, EA and Bentley 17: on theatre audience 20, 21: on 'Ned Allen' 37: influential pamphleteer 38: reference to *ur-Hamlet* 47: and Marprelate controversy 57, 58: supposed attack by Greene 60, 61: on historicsl plays 64: order for arrest and flight after Isle of Dogs affair, 125: on hostility of City Corporation to theatre 135: death 104: **Works**, satire, *Pierce Penniless* 17, 20, 21, 37, 38: plays *Dido, Queen of Carthage* 38, *The Isle of Dogs* 103, 124, 125, 162: official outrage caused by 124, 125, 191: erotic poem, *The Choice of Valentines* 38, 39: preface to *Menaphon* 47: pamphlet, *An Almond for a Parrot* 87: erotic poem, *The Choice of Valentines* 38, 39: preface to *Menaphon* 47: pamphlet, *An Almond for a Parrot* 87
Nicholls, Allen, Constable, appeals for protection from CM 43
Ogilby, John, steward and dancer, appointed MoR for Viceroy 278: opens Ireland's first theatre 278: *The Merchant of Dublin* (now lost) 278
Oldcastle, Sir John, Lollard, original of Sir John Falstaff 135, 138: life of 136: becomes Protestant hero 136, 138

Oldenbarnvelt, Johan van, statesman, trial and execution subject of play by Fletcher and Massinger 219 -221
O'Neill, Hugb, Earl of Tyrone, signs treaty with Essex 160
Orsini, Virginio, Duke of Bracciano, at Court performance 143
Osrler, Thonasine (née Hemminges), marries William Ostler 205: theatre shares due to her seized by father 205: sues father 205
Ostler, William, actor, with Children of the Chapel 204: joins KM 204: 'the Roscius of these times' 205: marries Thomasine Heminges 205: sharer in GT and BT 205: parts played 205, 237: death 205, 237
Owens, Margaret E., scholar, on on-stage beheadings 221
Page, William. publisher, hand cut off 1579 for distributing *The Discovery of a Gaping Gap* 177
Parker, Matthew, Archbishop of Canterbury, 38
Parker, William, 4th Lord Monteagle, conspirator, commissions LCM to perform Richard II 161
Patrons of Players: Robert Brydges, 4th Baron Chandos, 80: William Cavendish, Marquis of Newcastle, commissions BJ to create masques in honour of King 277: John de Vere, 16th Earl of Oxford, 3: Edward de Vere, 17th Earl of Oxford, 3: obtains sublease of BT 9: loses favour of Queen 9: re-forms OM 11: Ambrose Dudley, 3rd Earl of Warwick, 1: Edward Somerset, 4th Earl of Worcester 106, 162: captured by Essex rebels 162: William Somerset, 3rd Earl of Worcester, 32: Ferdinando Stanley, Lord Strange, (1558–94) 38, 88: claim to throne 33: succeeds as Earl of Derby 49: suspected murder of 82: William Stanley, 6th Earl of Derby 88
Paul, St. *Epistle to the Corinthians* 186, 187
Peacham, Revd. Henry, on Richard Tarlton, 11
Peckham, Sir Edmund, proposes marriage for son 13
Peckham, Sir George, adventurer, marries Susan Webbe, 13
Peele, George, writer, 64, 159: devises pageant for Lord Mayor's Show 19: **Plays:** *The Batel of Alcazar* 45: *The Famous Chronicle of King Edward I* 44, 100, 101
Penry, John, Puritan, University Preacher at Cambridge 57, involvement in Martin Marprelate controversy 57: charged with sedition and executed, 58
Percy, Henry, 9th Earl of Northumberland, Registrar, at Garter ceremony 140: papers of 143
Perkins, Richard, actor, 274, praised by John Webster 182: joins QHM from KM 250: part played 250: compared to EA by Thomas Heywood 250
Philip II, King of Spain, seizes Portuguese throne 45, 46
Philip III, King of Spain 237, death 239
Phillips. Anne, widow of AP 205, marries John Witter 205, death 205
Phillips, Augustine, actor and musician 126, 166, 169, 230: background 87, trains apprentices 87: becomes sharer in company 87: leaseholder of GT 143: commissioned by Essex conspirators to present *Richard II* 161: questioned before PC 162: financial role in company 174: will of 87, 166, 195, 230: jig, *Phillips, His Slipper* 87
Pickering, Lewis, undergraduate, places scurrilous poem on coffin of John Whitgift 177: brought before Star Chamber, fined., imprisoned and pilloried 177: *The Lamentation of Dickie for the deathe of his brother Jockie.*
Poley, Robert, agent, witness to death of CM 71
Platter, Thomas, Swiss visitor 21
Plowden, Sir Edmund, lawyer 104
Pope, Thomas, actor 34, 87: performs before rulers of Denmark and Saxony 79: appointed sharer 87: leaseholder of GT 143
Porter, Endymion (1587–1649) diplomat, intervenes with Charles I about WD's *The Wits* 262: obtains pardon for WD on murder charge 263
Pym, John, Parliamentarian, arrested by King 238
Prynne, William, Puritan, alleges most actors 'professed Papists 244: condemns women actors 264: proceedings against 265, 266: severe sentences 265, 266; admires Stephen Hammerton 266: *Histrio Mastix* 40, 264, 265, ordered to be burnt by public hangman 265
Radclyffe, Thomas 3rd Earl of Sussex, Lord Chamberlain, 12
Raleigh, Sir Walter (c1553–1618), Roanoke venture 110: prisoner in Tower 170: execution 238: *Discoverie of Guinea* as source of *The Tempest* 208

Rhodes, John, wardrobe master at BT 245, Court privileges extended to 245
Rice, John, actor: as boy actor 230, 231: in Thames pageant 23: parts played 231: apology to Master of Revels 245:'clerk' at St Saviours 231
Robinson, Edmund, miller's son, invents stories of witchcraft 268–9
Robinson, Richard, actor, 251, as child actor 227, 228: trains apprentices for KM 206: marries Winifred Burbage 227: administrative role in company 227: cross dresser 227, 228: parts played, Cardinal in *Duchess of Malfu* 237, Aesopus in *The Roman Actor* 251, the Hermit in *The Deserving Actor*257: apology to Master of Revels 244
Rossiter, Philip, lutenist, takes over lease of Whitefriars Theatre 203 complainant against PH 217
Rowley, Samuel, playwright 247: masque, *The World Tost at Tennis* 118: play, *When You See Me, You Know Me* 97
Rowley, William, actor and playwright, player of fat clown roles 226: role played 233 joins KM 239: probably wrote and played role of Fat Bishop in *A Game at Chess* 240, 241: apology to MoR 245: death 246 **Works:** *All's Lost by Lust* 226: *The Changeling* 235, popularity of 235: *Hymen's Holidays* (now lost) 226: *The Fool without Book* (now lost) 226: *Keep the Widow Waking* (now lost) 222: *A Knave in Print* (now lost) 226): *The Maid in the Mill* 226: *A Shoemaker a Gentleman* 226: *The Spanish Gypsy,* source 224: *The Travails of Three English Brothers* 106: *The Witch of Edmonton* 232–5, 268
Russell, Lady Elizabeth, noblewoman, opposes conversion of Blackfriars Priory to theatre 133
Russell, Francis, 4th Earl of Bedford, owner of Covent Garden Estate 267
Sackville, Thomas, Earl of Dorset, courtier and playwright, *Gorbuduc,* 4, 63, 264: introduces blank verse into drama, 4 : member of peace delegation 174: creates Salisbury Court Theatre 264
Sebastian, King of Portugal, death of 45: legend of 45
Shaa, Robert, actor, seeks sureties of peace against Christopher Beeston and Robert Pallant 106: arrested after *Isle of Dogs* affair 125
Shakespeare, Anne, wife of WS 48, 108
Shakespeare, John, glover, father of WS 131, awarded coat-of-arms 149
Shakespeare, Susanna, daughter of WS, before Consistory Court 189
Shakespeare, William, actor, playwright and poet 3, 4, 33, 34, 74, 80, 81, 91, 102, 110, 171, 203: known as 'Will 36: Aubrey on 48, 49: arrival in London 47, 49: background 47, 48, 131: supposed attack by Greene 49, 59, 60: as actor 49, 69, 108, 126, 167: rejection of slavish adhesion to classics 49, 52, 56, 88, 193: on acting 52, 53, 80: invokes Warwickshire roots 56: sources 63, 64: relation to earlier plays 64: and Divine Right of Kings 65: and class system 69: influence of Machiavelli on 69, 70: history plays as propaganda for the House of Tudor 70, 71: tribute to CM 73: assessor of plays for company 76: becomes sharer in company 86: godfather of WD 87, 260, 261: unchallenged as greatest living playwright 86, 88, 89: wealth 86: gives characters life beyond the stage 91–93 antipathy to mob rule 91, 96: hand in *Sir Thomas More* 95, 96, 111:comedies as response to 'Great Dearth 111: legal actions against by William Wayte 113: knowledge of Judaism 118: recommends *Every Man in his Humour* for performance 125: Oldcasstle controversy 135–138, 141: leaseholder of GT 143, 144: War of the Theatres 151, 152: wariness of crossing authorities 174: on child actors 151, 152, 174, 175: witness in court case 210: collaboration with JF 210:, on *King Henry VIII* 97, 210, 211: retirement from stage 212, 213: possible decline in powers 213: last will and testament 218: possible desire to publish complete works 218: death 218: continuing popularity of plays 236: suggested he 'died a Papist' 243 **Works:** FF 56, 79, 87, 141, 211, 229, 230: **plays,** *As You Like It,* 53, 7, 101, 102, 143: cult of melancholy in 116: and class structure 132: date of 143: *Cardenio* 210, not a success 210: *Comedy of Errors* 50, 56, 59, 229: *Cymbeline* 206, 208: *Hamlet,* 4, 50, 52, 69. 105, 119, 143, 153–157, 174–176, 184, 204, 219, 230, 242, 253, 271:: influenced by *Spanish Tragedy,* 47: cult of melancholy in. 114: on children's companies151, 152: various versions 153, 154: *Henry IV, Part 1* 136, 139: *Henry IV, Part 2* 42,, 43, 104, 137–139, 149: *Henry V.* 4, 44, 52, 53, 65, 104, 105, 131, 135, 136, 160, 230, possibly first play performed at Globe Theatre 144: *Henry VI, Part 1* 64, 65, 271: element of phlegmatic in, 122: *Henry VI, Part 2,* 64–66, 83, 136: *Henry VI, Part 3,* 60, 64–67, 69: *Julius Caesar* 146–149, 154: *King Henry the Eighth* 97, 210, 211–213, and destruction of GT 211: *King John,* 64: *King Lear* 24, 34, 185- 188, 247: *Love's Labours Lost* 62, 179, 230: *Macbeth* 42, 69, 154, 182–185, 229, 268: *Measure for Measure* 187, 199, 226, 229: Simon Forman on 183, Francis Beaumont on 183,

apparent haste in writing 183, interpolations 183, 184: *Merchant of Venice* 6, 42, 55, 118–120, 226: *The Merry Wives of Windsor* 132, 139–141, 229: *A Midsummer Night's Dream* 36, 37, 62, 112, 141, 169, 229, 259: cult of melancholy in. 114: *Much Ado About Nothing* 79, 105, 201, 230, 236: cult of melancholy in 116: *Othello* 174, 208, 219: *Pericles* 77, as collaboration with George Wilkins 188, 211: *Richard II*, performance commissioned during Essex rebellion 161–163: *Richard III* 67–71, 80, 154, 163, 184: *Romeo and Juliet* 79, 91–94, 104, 132, 230:: *The Taming of the Shrew* 55, 56, 201220, relation to *The taming of a Shrew* 55: *The Tempest* 50, 206–210, 213, 229: *Timon of Athens* 81, 188, 263: *Titus Andronicus* 49, 50, 82, 83, 230, 253: *Troilus and Cressida* 271: *Two Gentlemen of Verona* 48, 55, 229: *Twelfth Night*, 3, 143, 215, 229, 236, cult of melancholy in, 114–116, 122, 143: *The Two Noble Kiinsmen* 210, 211: *The Winter's Tale* 62, 206, 208: *A Yorkshire Tragedy* (attributed) 74–77: FF 56, 79, 87141, 211, 229, 230, compilation of 229. publication of 229, 230: cost of 230: Second Folio, Charles I annotat6es copy of 246: **poems,** *Rape of Lucrece* 86, *Sonnets* 168: *Venus and Adonis* 86, 103

Shank, John, actor, takes over skinny man roles 205, background 205, part played 205: trainer of boy actors 206, sues over apprenticeship of John Thompson 237: apology to Master of Revels 244

Sharpe, Richard, actor, parts played 257, creates title role in *The Duchess of Malfi* 237: reprises it 237: apology to MoR 245:

Shirley, Sir Anthony, Sefavid Ambassador, 107, 188

Shirley, James, dramatist, 263: Anglican priest 250: convert to Catholicism 244, 250: *Love Trick*, performed by LEM at Cockpit Theatre 250: joins troupe in Dublin 278: **Works:** masque, *The Triumph of Peace* 265, cost of 266: plays: *Love's Cruelty* 206 *The Cardinal* 206: *The Doubtful Heir* 281: *The Gentleman of Venice* 278: *The Maid's Revenge* 250: *The Politician* 278: *Rosiana* 278, 281: *St Patrick for Ireland* 278–9: verse*A Prologue there to the Irish Gent.*279

Sidney, Sir Robert, Chamberlain 137

Singleton, Hugh, reprieved from sentence for printing *The Discovery of a Gaping Gap* 177

Skeres, Nicholas, agent, witness to death of CM 71

Slater, Martin, actor, in Scotland with Lawrence Fletcher 165: attempts to form company with Aaron Holland 180: cofounder of Whiteftiars Theatre 203

Soer, Dorothy, lodging house keeper, legal actions against by William Wayte 113

Somers, George, Admiral, shipwrecked on Bermuda 207: death of 207

Spalatro, Maeco de Dominis, renegade Archbishop, satirised in *A Game of Chess* 240, 241

Spencer, Gabriel, actor, arrested after *Isle of Dogs* affair 125: kills James Feake 126: challenges BJ to duel 126: killed by BJ 126, 127

Spencer, Robert, 1st Baron Spencer, diplomat 172

Stewart, Ludovic, 2nd Duke of Lennox 197, 257, 261

Stowe, John, antiquarian, 1: on Richard Tarlton, 11: on Bear Gardens 39, on death of Ferdinando Stanley 82: on the Bridewell prison 180: *Survey of London* 143

Strachey, William, voyager, theatre buff and writer, account of wreck of *Sea Venture* on which *The Tempes* and *The Sea Voyage* are based 207, 208, 224

Street, Peter, carpenter and builder, assists in demolition of TT 142, 143: probable designer of GT 143

Stubbs, John, Puritan, attacks putative royal marriage 177, hand cut off for 'seditious writing' 177, 198: *The Discovery of a Gaping Gap*

Stukeley, Sir Thomas, adventurer, reputed som of Henry VIII, 44; Battle of Lepanto 45, death 45: as English folk hero 45

Suckling, Sir John, dramatist, 281;Tribe of Ben' 249: in attempted coup 282: suicide of 282: *Aglaura* 259, cost of 259: *The Goblins* 259, 281

Swanson, Eliard, actor, recruited by KM 236, 237: parts played 236, 237, Aretimus Clemems in *The Roman Actor* 251: Bussy d'Ambois 236, Othello 236: apology to MoR 245

Tarlton, Richardm clown, 48, 78, 87, 131: fame of 10, 11, 25: favourite of Queen 11: joins QM 16: early 'superstar' 17: as Master of Fence 26: jig of 25: last will and testament 54: death of 54: how he 'deceived an innholder' 54, 55: recommends Robert Armin as succeessor 79, 80: incident with spectator at Norwich 90: *Tarlton's Jests* 17, 25, 26, 54, 55, 79: *The Seven Deadly Sins* 26, 33–36, 96, 106, 236

Taylor, Joseph. actor, 227, 230: with children's companies 204: complainant against PH 217: replaces RB as lead actor with KM 219, 236: :shortness of stature 219: parts played Bussy d'Ambois 236: the Duke in *The Deserving Favourite* 257: Face 219, Ferdinand 219, Iago 219, Mirabel in *The Wild Goose Chase* 266, Mosca 219, Hamlet 219, Paris in *The Roman Actor* 251: Truewit 219: apology to Master of Revels for presenting *The Spanish Curate* without license 244

Tilney, Edmund, MoR 83, given regulatory powers over theatre, 25, 83: closes theatres 58: tolerant attitude towards theatre 83: censors play of *Sir Thomas More* 96

Tomkyns, Nathaniel, politician, on performance of *The Late Lancashire Witches* 269–70

Tooley, William, merchant 35: widow's marriages 35

Topcliffe, Richard, torturer, interrogates BJ 127

Tourneur, Cyril, soldier and dramatist, on expedition against Cadiz 246: death 246: *The Atheist's Tragedy or The Honest Man's Revenge* 246, 247

Turnor, Richard, arbiter in Brayne/Burbage dispute 13

Ulrik, Duke of Holstein, proposed as patron of theatre company 180

Valois, Margaret de, Queen of France, marriage to Henri IV annulled 195

Van Buchel, Aernout, antiquarian, makes unique drawing of Swan Theatre 112

Vavasour, Anne, Maid of Honour, impregnated by Edward de Vere, 9

Vereyken, Louis (fl 1604) Hapsburg diplomat, leads delegation to England 137

Villiers, George, Duke of Buckingham, favourite of James I 239; accompanies Prince Charles to Spain 239

Wallace, Charles, scholar, 26, 12

Walsingham, Sir Francis, warned of weak structure of theatres 10: forms QM 16: creates espionage system 38: Protestantism of 63: Matlowe seeks refuge with 71

Warburton, John, bibliophile, cook destroys mss of over 50 plays 245

Wayte, William (fl 1596) High Sheriff, legal actions against WS. Langley and others 113: dubious character 113

Webbe, Susan. marriage to George Peckham, 13, 14: dies in childbirth, 14

Webster, John, dramatist, 278.devises pageants for Lord Mayor's Show 18: on RBT 182:**Works** additions to *The Malcontent* 175: *Duchess of Malfi* 203, 204, 219, 231, 253, gives offence to Venetian visitor 219, first printed play to list cast 237: probably co-author of *A Game at Chess* 237: *Keep the Widow Waking* (now lost) 222, 232: *Westward Ho!* 176: *The White Devil* 181, not well received 182, as contemporary satire 182: revival of 1619 226: possibly *The Witch of Edmonton* 232

Wentworth, Henry, MoR 9, 10

Wenrworth, Thomas, Earl of Strafford, Lord Deputy of Ireland 278, 280, impeached for High Treason 282

Westcott, Sebastian, musician, 4

White, Margaret, widow, allegedly raped by Christopher Beeston 106, 107

White, Thomas, clergyman, attacks theatre 10

Whitehorn, Timothy, lawyer, AP's executor 205

Whitelock, Bulstrode, lawyer, organises *The Triumph of Peace* 265, 266

Whitgift, John, Archbishop of Canterbury, Martin Marprelate controversy 57: censor 103: scurrilous poem on 177

Whyte, Rowland (fl 1596–1626) letter writer 137, 139: on Garter ceremony 140

Wilkes, Revd William, Chaplain to King 199, BJ on 199

Wilkins, George, publican and author, **works:** novel, *Pericles* 77: plays: *The Miseries of Enforced Marriage* 74, 188: *Pericles,* collaboration with WS 188: *The Travails of Three English Brothers* 106, 188

Wilson, Robert, clown and playwright, 27: probable author of *The Pedlar's Prophesy* and *The Three Ladies of London and The Three Lords and Three Ladies of London,* 2: joins QM 16: prodigious output 109: contributor to *Sir John Oldcastle* 137

Winwood, Sir Ralph, Clerk to PC, receives complaint about Revels Children 176: as Ambassador to France, obtains injunction against presentation of play about Mary, Queen of Scots 196:

Wolfe, Reginald, printer, conceives idea of Universal Cosmology 63: employs Raphael Holinshed and William Harrison as assistants 63

Witter, John, marries Anne Phillips 205, deserts her 205, sues Hemminges and Condell 205
Woodford, Thomas, cofounder of Whitefriars Theatre 203
Wotton, Sir Henry, diplomat, impressed by production of *King Henry VIII* 211, 212: describes destruction of GT by fire 212
Wriothesley, Henry, 3rd Earl of Southampton, 39, member of 'Essex Circle' 62: patron of WS 62, 86: joins Essex plot 160: tried for treason 162, 163: condemned to death and reprieved 162, 163: rehabilitation 174, favourite of Queen 174

INDEX OF PLACES

America, Florida, 44: Massachusetts Bay Colony 18 , Sir Richard Saltonstall (1586–1661) founder of 18: Roanoke Colony 110: Virginia 207, Jamestown 207
Bath, Abbey 89, Guildhall 89
Berkshire, Eton 140, 141: College 48: Windsor, 240: Castle 140, 141: Frogmore 140: Garter Inn, 141: St George's Chapel, 4, 140, 141: garter ceremony at 140, 141: legend of Herne the Hunter 141
Bermuda, *Sea Venture* wrecked on 207
Bohemia, Estates throw off rule of Holy Roman Emperor 238: Elector Palatine accepts crown 238. popular revolt 238: invaded by Hapsburg forces 238
Bolsover, Castle 277
Bristol, Guildhall 89
Cambridge 89, 102: Puritanism in 40: River Cam 102: University, 4, 12, 36, 57, 71, 105, 108, 190, 201: Colleges: Caius 108: Christ's 4, 38, 40: Emmanuel, founded by Puritan, Sir Thomas (Mildmay 1540–1608) 18, 103: St John's 36, 38, 102, Parnassus plays at, 102: Trinity 180: Vice Chancellor 12
Carlisle, Moot Hall 217
Cheshunt, Theobald's House 245
Cornwall, Spanish raid on, 111: Mousehole, Newlyn and Penzance, Spanish raid on 111
Denmark 42, 157, Copenhagen 42, Elsinore 79: English actors in 79
Devon 222, Barnstaple 89, Exeter 41
Droitwich, St Peter de Witton Church 88
East Anglia 82
Essex 263, Braintree 90, 263, Brentwood, 21, Chelmsford 90, Colchester, 4
France, 230 Wars of Religion 62: Protestant refugees from 71: Rheims, English Catholic Seminary 32, 104
Germany, Palatinate, The 211: Saxony, Christian I, Elector of (1560–91), English actors play before 79
Hampshire 199
Holland 57, 79, 263: Protestant refugees from 71
Ireland, 44: Essex expedition to, 144: independent Parliament established 280: Dublin 144, Castle 278: the Pale 278: St Werburgh Street Theatre 278–9, 281, closed by Lords Justices 280: Kilkenny, General Assembly at 280
Italy 106, Florence: Ottaviano Lotti (fl 1608) Florentine agent 197, alludes to King's penchant for young men 197: Padua 182: Rome. 106, 179: English College 32, 95, 104, 138: Savoy, Duchy of 210: Venice 45, 107, 240: Molin, Nicolo (fl 1605) Venetian Ambassador, on King and Puritans 178, 179: Ghetto, 119
Jerusalem 106
Kent 185, Canterbury, 3, 43: Guild of Shoemakers 37: King's School 37: Chiselhurst, Scadbury Manor 71: Deptford, 'safe house in, 71: Dover 89:, King's Men in 185: Shakespeare Cliff 185, 186: Straits of, 22: Eltham Palace, 4, Faversham 89. Folkestone 89: Greenwich, 163, Royal palace of Placenta 124, Ship Tavern 269: Hythe 89, Maidstone 89: New Romney 89: Sandwich 54: Tonbridge: School, 9: theatre in 134
Lancashire 268, Lancaster 268, Manchester 58: Pendle, Witch Trials 268–9:
Lincolnshire 108, 178: Scrivelsby 178, village green 178

London, 1, 2, 35, 54: riots in 24, 25, 94, 95, 102, 105, 111, 271–2: Lord Mayor's Show 18, 19, 268: Jews in 118: expansion of 267

buildings: Aldgate 162: Bermondsey Abbey 111: Bethlem Hospital (Bedlam) 81, Bishop's Gate 81: Blackfriatrs Priory 8, 0, 132, 134, acquired by French Ambassador 243: chapel becomes London's most important mass centre 243:the 'fatal vespers', disaster in which many worshippers killed 243, 244: Clerkenwell Priory, 25: City Walls, 3, 6, 80, 81, 264: Crosby Place 80: Durhan House 174: Ely House 265: Essex House 161, 162: Holland's Leaguer 270–2: Holywell Priory 6, 7, 13, 14: 107, 108: granted to Henry Webbe, Gentleman Porter, (c1595–1553) 13: bought by Christopher Bumsted 13, 14, bought by Giles Allen 13, Edmund Peckham, (b 1555), claims ownership of 14: Leicester House 79: Ludgate 162: Old Bailey 127: Royal Mint 79: St Bartholomew's Hospital 114, 118: St. James' Palace, 4, Smithfield Market 216: Somerset House 173, 256, 265: Tower of London 13, 170, 171, 179, 265, 266, 282: Whitehall Palace 174, 186, 207, 262, 280, Banqueting House 174, 265, 266, 275: Chapel, 174: Winchester Palace 271

churches and parishes, Chapel Royal 211: Dutch Church 71, 'mutinous libels' posted upon 71, 95: St Ann's 189: St. Botolph's 32, 167, 246: St Giles 157, 167, 226: St Gregory by St Paul's 32: base of Children of Paul's 157: St. Helen's 80: St Lames' 246: St Laurence Pountney 88: St. Leonard's 54, 134, 218, 227: St Saviour's 153, 231: St Mary Aldermanbuty 88: St Mary-le-Strand 36: St. Mary's, Newington Butts 242: St Mary Overie 246: St Martin-in-the-Fields 267: St Paul's Cathedral, 4: St Paul's, Covent Garden 267: St Saviour's 32, 33, 231, 236: St Stephen's 15, 110: St Stephen Walbrook 35: Temple Church, 13, 200: City Corporation, hostility to public performances, 3, 6, 18, 83, 84, 134: bans performances in inns 111

Inns, Angel 81: Black Bull 81, Catherine Wheel 81, The Devil and St Dunstan. 249, Apollo Room at 249: Dog 249: Dolphin 81, George 13, 15: Green Dragon 81, Mermaid Tavern 201, Friday Club at 201, 207, 249: Nag's Head 102: Pegasus 102: Pye Inn 32, Sun 249: Triple Tun 249: White Hart 81, Wrestlers 81

Inns of Court, 11, 12, 21, 265: Gray's Inn, 50, 96: Inner Temple 201: Lincoln's Inn, 52, 94, 265: Middle Temple 149, 199, 222: Temple 102

Livery Companies, Drapers 242: Goldsmiths 143, 167, 203, 273: Grocers 35, 88: Leathersellers 35: Merchant Taylors 230 , 231m, 266, Great Hall of 266: Mercers 143: Stationers 104, 153, 262; William Aspley (c1569–1640) stationer, holder of WS copyrights 230, partner in FF project 230: John Benson (d 1667) 262: Cuthbert Busby (fl 1596) 64: Walter Burre (fl 1607) on *The Knight of the Burning Pestle* 194: Humphrey Moseley (d 1661) 245, seeks to publish *Cardenio* 210: Thomas Pavier((d 1623), publisher of WS 76:John Smethwick (c1577–1641), holder of WS copyrights 230, partner in First Folio project 230: Thomas Walkley, (fl 1618–58) 259

Stationers' Register 45, 50, 55, 69, 76, 83, 87, 98, 104, 105, 131, 143, 154, 193, 245, 246, 273: Tylers and Bricklayers 110, 127

Lord Mayors: Dixie, Sir Wolstan, (1525–84), opposition to theatre 18: Martin, Sir Richard (c1534–1617), Puritanism of, 18: request from Blunsdon to license Cross Keys as winter base 84, 85: Pipe, Sir Richard (1515–1587) 22: Pullyson, Sir Thomas, (1530–1617), attempts to pull down The Theatre and the Curtain 27: promulgates strict restrictions on theatre 27–29: Saltonstall, Sir Richard (c1521–1601), hostility to theatre 24: Webbe, William (d 1599), regards Edmund Tilney as obstacle to closing theatres 83: Woodroffe, Sir Nicholas, on theatre, 23, 24

Prisons, Bridewell 71, 143, 180, 196: Clink 108: Fleet 178, 241: Gatehouse 170, 270: King's Bench 107, 108, Marshalsea, 61, 125, 127, 129, 170, 281: Newgate 198, 232, 269: Poultry Counter, 02: Wood Street Counter 102

River Thames 112, 133, 143, 161, 170, 171, 231, 260, 275: boatmen on, 176: in flood 246: Frost Fair 274

Schools: Christ's Hospital 22, Merchant Taylors' 46, 48: St Paul's 48, 58, 59, 147, 276, John Harrison, John fl1581–1596) High Master 58, 59

Streets and districts: Aldgate, 4:, 162 Austin Friars 71: Bankside 32, 87, 111, 113, 143, 201, 236, 271: Bell's Inn Yard, 6: Bishopsgate, 6, 17, 32 , 80, 81, 112: Bucklersbury, 3, 7: Chancery Lane 265: Cheapside 102, 201, 263: Clerkenwell 180, 188: Coleman Street, 15: Covent Garden 267:

Cow Gate 188: Curtain Close, 10: Dowgate Ward 37: Fenchurch Street, 161, 170: Finsbury Fields 271–2: Fleet Street 102, 264: Golding Lane 238: Gracechurch Street, , 6: Hog Lane 43: Holburn 265: Holywell Street 6, 10, 12, 54: Horseshoe Alley 143: Hoxton Fields 126: Isle of Dogs 124: Liberty of the Clink 33, 143, 271: Lincoln's Inn Fields 272: London Bridge 9, 143: Ludgate Hill, 6, 8: Maiden Lane 143: Mile End, 3: Newington Butts, 9: Paris Gardens 87, 111, 121: Poplar 124: Queenhithe 260: Ram Alley 102: Ratcliffe 58: Shoe Lanr 102: Shoreditch, 1, 6, 21, 54, 143, 236: St Paul's Churchyard 102: St. Paul's Cross 132, 161: Southwark 33, 108, 111, 113, 126: The Sparagus Garden 273–4: Spitalfields 118, The Strand 161, 264, 265: Tover Hill 144, 282: Tyburn 58, 127, 163, 232: Wapping 272: Whitechapel, 6, 13: Whitehall 140

theatres: Bear Garden 10, 60, 114: collapse of seating at 10, 19: bought by EA 39: description by Johannes de Witt 112, bears at, 206: demolished 216: Bel Savage, 6, 18, fencing bouts at 25: Bell, 6, 18

Blackfriars: 1st Blackfriars 8, 9: subleased to John Newman 8: lease passes to Anne Farrant (fl 1581) 8: repossessed by Sir William More 31: lease bought by James Burbage 132, 133: conversion to theatre opposed by neighbours 133: leased by Henry Evans and Nathaniel Giles 134: social superiority to public playhouses 135, 194: admission prices 135: boy's beautiful singing at 152: 2nd Blackfriars: 205, 206, 210, 231 236, 251, 252, 254, 255, 259, 262, 264, 277: opened by RB 203, sharers 203, 205, 236: John Rhodes wardrobe master at 245: first appearance of actresses on English stage 256

Boar's Head, 6, 88: Bull, 6, 18: *Famous Victories*, , , at 17: Cockpit (Phoenix) 224, 235, 250, 253. 264, 277, 281, built as arena for cockfighting 231, converted into indoor theatre 231:burnt down by mob 232, 272: rebuilt and renamed 232: Cross Keys, 6, 18: use by Lord Chamberlain's Men as winter base 83:: Queen Anne's Men at 232: French actors perform at 256: Curtain, 10, 19, 95, 120, 171, 226, 236: Henry Lanman (fl 1585), owner of 10: warning of weak structure of 10: attempt to pull down, 27: possible temporary home of Lord Chamberlain's Men 143: demise 236: Drury Lane 210: Fortune, 131, 171, 236, 238: created by Peter Street 147, cost of 147, description of 147, raucus audiences at !80, outmoded productions at 180: destroyed by fire 221: rebuilt by Alleyn 222:

Globe, 1st theatre: 21, 56:, 76, 87, 105, 166, 167, 171, 180, 205, 231, 236, 260: lease of 143: site 143, 144: design of 143: Brend, Sir Nicholas Brend (1564–1601) freeholder of site 143: William Leveson (d 1621) mercer and Thomas Savage (c1552–1611), goldsmith, trustees of 143: opening 144: Simon Forman sees plays at 182, 183, 206: destruction by fire 212, 217, 221: 2nd theatre, 219, 242, 252, 255, 270–1, 281: building of 215: represents challenge to PH 216, 217: closed by PC 241: closed by Parliament 282

Hope 226, , building of 216, venue for both theatre and baiting 216, unsavoury smell of 216, , 231: Newington Butts 9, 56, 83, 271: closure of 83, 97: Red Bull, 44, 84, 181, 182, 226, 231, 232, 273: theatre built as large as the Globe 180: reputation for rowdiness 180, Queen Anne's Men at 181, 232 John Webster on 182: French actresses at 256: Red Lion, 3, 6, 9: first theatre since Roman times, 3: not a success, 4:influence of design, 4: Rose 32, 37, 39, 56, 82–84, 106, 112, 122, 123, 167: boom after plague 97, 98: one of only two licensed theatres after Isle of Dogs affair 125: Salisbury Courtt, 235., 273–4, created by Thomas Sackville 264: condemned by William Prynne 265: Swan 111, 113, 121, 124, 216: description and sketch by Johannes de Witt 112, 143: license withdrawn after Isle of Dogs affair 125: possible temporary home of LCM 143: falls into decay 271: Salisbury Court 235:

The Theatre, 1, 2, 3, 13, 19, 24, 26, 47, 49, 83, 112: lease signed 6, 7: building of 7–10: warning of weak structure of, 10: George Clough (fl 1590), attempts to seize possession of 15: public disturbances at 12, 95: ownership of, 13, 14: fencing bout at 25: attempt to pull down 27: riot at 27: disputes over lease 14, 15, 82, 132, 134, 142: one of only two licensed theatres after Isle of Dogs affair125

Whitefriars 191, 204: foundation of 203: closure 204

Middlesex, Edmonton 232: Hampton Court, King's Men at 169: tapestries at 169: Court masque at 171

Morocco 45

Moscow 143

Netherlands 219, Amsterdam 248, Flushing 139, Haarlem 221. Leiden 221: The Hague 219: Utrecht 221
Norfolk 34, 108, 159: King's Lynn 79, 81, New Buckenham 34: Norwich, 21, 36, 105: Church of St Peter Mancroft in 34: Red Lion Inn, incident with actors at, 90: Great Yarmouth 124:
Northamptonshire, 172, Althorp 172, Fawsley 58, Northampton 177
Nottinghamshire: Nottingham 89, King raises standard at 282: Welbeck 277
Oxford, 26, 89, 176, 191, John Davenant Mayor of, 261: Cornmarket 260: St, Martin's Church 260, Salutation Tavern 260
University, 2, 36, 105, 190, 265: Lincoln College 261
Oxfordshire 48, Thame 48, 88, 90
Portugal, Antonio. (1531–95), claimant to throne 45, 46
Rye 81, 89, 201
St Alban's 250
Scotland 42, 57, 182, 217: as refuge for Dissenters 71: Scottish Parliament 99: Dirleton Castle 165: Edinburgh 127, 165, 182, 277, Castle 280: Linlithgow, silver mine in 197: 42: Robert Bowes (c1535–97), English Ambassador, on North Berwick witch trials 42: George Nicholson, (fl1577–1612) English Ambassador, reports on hostility to theatre in 65
Shrewsbury 89
Spain, Spanish Armada 62, 111: peace delegation from 175, regarded as England's natural enemy 238, Cadiz, expedition against 140
Spanish Netherlands, peace delegation from 175, Antwerp 35: Ostend, siege of, 104
Stafford 89
Suffolk 136, Dunwich 89: Ipswich 89
Surrey 57, 113, 271, Croydon 177, 178: Dulwich 168, 213, College of God's Gift 251: East Molsey 57, Ewell, 113, Mortlake 169, 205: Nonsuch Palace 160
Wales 162
Warwickshire 56, 58, 109, 26, Barton-on-the-Heath and Wincot , mentioned by Shakespeare, 56: Coventry 58, 89: mystery cycle 4, 119: Hartshill, 109: Kenilworth Castle, 3: Nuneaton 109: Stratford-upon-Avon, 3, 47, 48, 86, 133, 210, 213: King's New School 48: Vicar's Court 99, 189
Westminster 18, 171: Abbey 22, 245, 271, 275: market place 177: St. Maegaret's Church 260: School, 4, 48, 120
Wiltshire 169, Barford St Martin 199: Marlborough, Guildhall 89, White Hart Inn, 89: Wilton 89: Wilton House, KM at, 169
York 8

INDEX OF SUBJECTS

Acting Companies, 1–4, 6, 9: skills of actors 18, 157: on tour 89, 90: adaptability of 89: success of childrens' companies 151, 152: impressment of children into 159, 160: actors lost to adult Companies replaced by former child actors 204: earnings of child actors 231
Admiral's Men, at Rose Theatre, 1581 32, 45, 84, 99, 106, 108, 122, 123, 128, 221, 231: as Lord Howard's Men 6, 162: become Nottingham's Men 221: perform at Court 6: uses teams of writers 32: association with Lord Strange's Men 33, 37: one of only two Companies licensed to perform in London after *Isle of Dogs* affair 125: perform play of *Sir John Oldcastle* 137: become Prince Henry's Men 166
Children of Blackfriars (previously Children of the Revels 121, 194, 198: imprisoned in Bridewell 196: move to Whitefriars Monastery 203: become Children of the Queen's Revels 203
Children of the Chapel Royal, 4, 8, 38, 134, 147: War of the Theatres 150, 151, 150: William Hunnis d 1597) Master of 8: power of Master to summarily recruit boys 157
Children of Paul's, 4, 3, 176, placed in abeyance 58, 59: resume playing 157, 200: in War of Theatre 159: base at St Gregory by St Paul's 157: cease to perform 200
Children of the Queen's Revels 203, 204
Children of the Revels 191, 201 noted for satire, violence and lewdness 174, 176, 178, 179, 194: baiting of royal Establishment: taken over by Robert Keysar 194: become Children of Blackfriars 194, 176, 179, 180: steal *Spanish Tragedy* from KM 175: performers committed to Bridewell 180

Children of Windsorl 4: annual play before Queen 4
Derby's Men (formerly Strange"s Men) 9, 49: death of patron, 82, as basis of LCMen 82, 83, 86: continuation under 6th Earl 88, 83, 96, 98, 110
Duke of York's Men, foundation of 226: becomes Prince Charles' Men 226:
Elector Palatine, or Palsgrave's Men 221, 238, 264, 273: lose scripts and costumes in fire at Fortune Theatre 221, 222
Hunsdon's Men.)1572–1592) 26
King and Queen's Young Company (Beeston's Boys), founded by Christopher Beeston 281, passes to William Beeston 281
King's Mem 56, 76, 169, 191, 201, 202, 204, 205, 210, 252–254, 259, 262, 276–7: granted Royal Charter by James I and become KM 166, 171: sharers 205: perform at royal wedding celebrations 211: replace RB 219, 236: unchallenged supremacy 221, 236: wait on Spanish delegation 173, 174: steal *The Malcontent* from Revels Children 175: *A Game at Chess* greatest commercial success 237, 239: present *The Spanish Viceroy* without license 245: apologise to Master of Revels 244, 245: privileges at Court extended 245: receive patronage of Charles I 250: taking subsidies for performing courtier's plays 259
King's Revels Children, founded by Richard Gunnell and William Blagrave 264
Lady Elizabeth's Men 131, 205, 216, 224, 231, 237: formation of 204, receive royal patent to play in London 204: complaint against PH 216, 217: accompany King on progress to Scotland 217: Christopher Beeston sole owner of 235 – become Queen of Bohemia's Men 250
Leicester's Men, 1–3, 10, 16, 24, 27, 33: secure Royal Patent, 1, 2
Les Comediens du Roi, French King's acting troupe 256, perform in London 256
Lord Arundel's Men 27
Lord Berkeley's Company, involved in fracas at Gray's Inn, 96
Lord Chamberlain's Men, 34, 83, 97, 104, 112, 140, 152, 154: mode of work, 32: value to of Hunsdon as patron 83–85: re-formed as 'super-troupe' 86: number of sharers expanded 86: close-nit family structure of company 87, 88: tours 89: possibly performing at the Swan Theatre 113: become Lord Hunsdon's Men after death of Patron 134: revert to orevious title 140: War of the Theatres 151: and Essex rebellion 161–163: last performances before Queen 164 : granted Royal Charter by James I and become King's Men 166
Lord Chandos Players, 80
Lord Hunsdon's Men, 6, 26: title revived after death of 1st Lord Hunsdon 134: revert to previous title 140
Lord Strange's Men, (later Derby's Men) 60, 97, 98: begin staging dramatic performances 33: association with Admiral's Men 33, 37: and Marprelate controversy 58: RB with 68
Oxford's Men, oldest acting troupe, 3, 17, 31, 32: re-formed by 14th Earl 11: in brawl at Inns of Court, 11, 12: at Cambridge University 1
Pembroke's Servants, 3, 49, 55, 69, 98, 121, 124, 205, on tour 81
Prince Charles' Men 219, 231, 232, 237, 266, 273: difficulties after King withdraws patronage 250: involvement in costly legal actions 273
Prince Henry's Men 131, 168, 171, 221, sharer 205: become Palsgrave's Men 238
Queen Anne's Men, formerly Worcester's 166, 171: wait on delegation from Spain 173, 174: at Red Bull Theatre 18, 232: at Cockpit Theatre 232: renamed Revels Company 232
Queen Elizabetth's Men (later King's Men) 16, 17, 27, 36, 37, 54, 63, 81, 82, 84, 205: foundation as milestone in theatrical history 16, 17: effect of legal restrictions on 28: petition PC 28: brawl at Thame 48: incident in Norwich 90: perform at court 91: tour in Ireland 278
Queen Henrietta's Men 206, 253, 274, 277, founded by Christopher Beeston 250; first production, *The Maid's Revenge* 250: sell off James Shirley's scripts 280
Queen of Bohemia's Men (formerly LEM) 255
Sussex's Men, 3, 16, 17, 49, 6, 73, 82, 98: Richard Tarlton with 11
Warwick's Men, members poached by Edward de Vere 11
Worcester's Men 32, 35, 111m167: third company licensed to play in London 106: Will Kempe joins 106, 152: become Queen Anne's Men 166

Anglicanism 62, 118, 157, 178, 179, 219, 240, 266, 281–2: Book of Common Prayer 280

Anonymous book, pageant, pamphlets, tracts and verse *The Children of the Chapel Stript and Whipt,* 4: *The Country's Censure on Ben Jonson's New Inn* 255: *The Delivery of the Lady of the Lake,* 3: *Greene's Funeralls* 61, 62: *The Jolly Brown Man* 273: *Leicester's Commonwealth* 118: *Newes from Scotland* 42: *News from Holland* 220: *Strange newes of the Retourne of Dom SEBASTIAN* 46: *Upon Mr James Shirley His Comedy...* 278

Anonymous plays

Arden of Faversham 73, 74: possible authorship 74: *The Blacke Smiths daughter,* 2: *The Most Famous Chronicle History of Leire King of England and his Three Daughters* 54, 82, 83: *The Dead Man's Fortune, 'platt' of* 15, 16: *Fair Em, the Miller'd daughter of Manchester* 33: *The Famous history of the life and death of Captaine Thomas Stukeley* 45: *The Famous Victories of Henry V,* 17, 63, 64: William Knell and Richard Tarlton in 17: Sir John Oldcastle character in 136, 137: *Gammer Gurton's Needle,* 4: *The Grecian Comedy* 97: Ur-*Hamlet 47,* 83, 153: *The History of Murdrous Michael* 73: *The Jew,* 6: *A Knack to Know an Honest Man* 97: A *Knack to Know a Knave* 50, 56, 97, 98: *The Life of Long Meg of Westminster* 98: *The Maid's Metamorphosis* 159: *The Pilgrimage to Parnassus* 78, 102: *Ptolemy* 6: *The Puritan* 215: *The Rebellion of Naples* by 'TB', features on-stage beheading 221: *The Return from Parnassus* 46, 78, 79, 102–104: The *Return fron Parnassus, or The Scourge of Simony* 104–106: *The Raigle of King Edward III,* attributed to WS 64: *The Rich Cabinat* 18, 19: *Robin Hood and the Friar* 99, 100: *The Silver Mine* 197: *Sir Clymon and Sir Clomdyes* 54: *The Story of Samson,* 3: *The Taming of a Shrew* 55, 56, 83: *Tooley* 6: *The Troublesome Raign of John, King of England* 54, 63, 66: T*he True Tragedie of Richard the Third* 63: *The Wise Man of West Chester* 97: *The Wisdom of Doctor Dodypoll* 159: *A Yorkshire Tragedy* 73–78: attributed to WS 76 77

Battles, and conflicts: Alcazar 45, 46: Bishop's War 280: Bosworth 70: Lepanto 45

Classical Unities 50, 5156: abandoned by WS 49, 52, 56, 62: BJ on 51, 167: Philip Sidney on 51, 52

Courts: Chancery 30, 31: Clerkenwell Sessions, 12, 22: Consistoty Court 189: Coroner's Court 15, 72, 126: Court of High Commission 272, 276–7: Court of Orphans, 35: Court of Requests 143, 205, 227, 266: Middlesex Sessions, 43: Star Chamber 57, 176, 177, 178, censures Henry Evans 159: William Prynne before 265, 266

East India Company 222

Essex Rebellion, 160–162, 196, Sir Charles Danvers (1568–1601) part in 162: Sir Charles and Sir Jocelyn Percy (fl 1601) commission LCM to perform Richard II 161: Thomas Smythe (1558–1625) Sheriff of London, and 161, 162

Gunpowder Plot 179, 183, 188

Holy League 44

Humours, theory of 121, developed by Hippocrates 121: developed as physiological theory by Aelius Galenus (Galen) 121, 122: humours comedies 122–124

Islam 44, 45, 119

Jews and Judaism , 119, alleged skill in preparing poisons to use malignantly 117, 118: expulsion from England 118. case of Dr Lopus 118: WS's knowledge of 118, 119: population in London 118

Martin Marprelate controversy 57, 58: and Thomas Cooper (1517–94), Bishop of Winchester 57, Sir John Harte, Sir John (d 1604) on 58

Masques 171, 172, 266: as monarchy's celebration of itself 172: costs of 173: reach new levels of extravagance in reign of Charles I 246,

Melancholy, Cult of, 114, in drama, 114, 115: and the role of the outsider 116

Order of the Garter 140

Parliament:, annual grant to King 237, 267: in dispute with King 238, 239: dissolved by King for eleven years 267: Petition of Right 280: Grand Remonstrance 281: Actors' Remonstrance 282: Westminster Hall, 246

House of Commons, Proclamation on royal wedding infuriates King 238: Bill of Attainder against Thomas Wentworth 282

House of, Lords 24

Statutes of Scandalum Magnatum 177: Poor Laws. 1: Witchcraft Act 42, 182, 232

Plague, 54, 81, 89: closes theatres 24, 81, 82, 191, 203, 204, 230, 246, 263, 274: believed causes 81: and *Romeo and Juliet* 91: Thomas Dekker on 153: coronation postponed by 167–170

Platonism, cult of, 258–260
Privy Council, 169: concerns about playhouses 9, 10, 23, 24, 33, 58, 71, 95, 111, 175, 176, 180: agrees to pulling down of theatres 27: petitioned by Queen's Men 28: intervenes for CM 38: orders closure of RT 83: closes playhouses 124, 241: opposes conversion to theatre of Blackfriars Priory 133, 134: examines AP 162: examines Edmund Robinson 270
Prostitution, 21, 270–1
Protestantism 62, 63, 71, 212: Religious sects: Arminians 219, 220: Brownists 58, Henry Barrow 1550–93), executed for sedition 58: John Greenwood 1556–93), executed for sedition 58: John Udall (c1550–92, charged with sedition, dies in prison 58: Calvinists 219: Church of Scotland, opposition to theatre 165: Bishop's War 280: Lollards 135, 136: Puritans, 9, 11, 16, 18, 70, 81, 99, 100, 102, 137, 177, 178, 239, 281–2: opposition to theatre 19, 213: background to 19, 252: concept of predestination 40: Marprelate controversy 57, 58: relations with King 178, 179: mockery of in theatre 199, 213, 214: Thomas Beard(d 1632), on death of Christopher Marlowe 72, 73: Thomas Bywater fl 1605), presents King with book about his errors 179: imprisoned in Tower 179: William Perkins(1556–1602), advocate of doctrine of double-predestination 40: John Rainolds, opposition to theatre in *The Overthrow of Stage Plays* 18: John Stockwood, (d 1610) Headmaster of Tonbridge School 9: preaches against theatre 9, 10: Separatists 58, 71
Revels Office, 25, 98, 99, 133, 143, 174, 175, 196, 220, 222, 224, 241, 24
Roman Catholicism 44, 45, 73, 104, 118, 127, 136, 138, 183, 215, 219, 224, 237–241: Dissolution of the Monasteries 13, 111, 271:
stringent laws against 179, 189, 240; the 'Fatal Vespers' 243, 244: actors and 244: Feast of Corpus Christi, 6: William Allen, Cardinal (1532–94) 104
Orders: Augustinian Sisters 6: Carmelites 62, Dominicans (Blackfriars) 8: St John 271: Society of Jesus, 127, 183, 240, 241: Edmund Campion(1540–1581) priest, 95: assists Raphael Holinshed 63: Henry Garnett (1555–1606) priest, possibly alluded to in *Macbeth* 183: *A Treatise on Equivocation* 183: Wright, Thomas (1561–1624), priest, possibly received BJ into Catholic Church 127
Papacy: 104: Sixtus V (1521–1590) Pope 104: Papal Bull *Quoniam Divinae Bonitati*
Sports and Pastimes: bear baiting 39, 113, 125: chess 240: dance: Selinger's Round 78: Declaration of Sportsn 1618 267: animal baiting 268: bowls 268, fencing, 25, 26: football 157: banning of 24: Maying 100, 268: Morris Dancing 90, 105, 106, 268 swashbuckling displays 125: Whitsun-Ales 268
'University Wits' 36–38:
Theatre, social mobility of 131, potential profits from imvestment in 203, 204, 216: beheading on stage, 221: types of drama – Chronicle History plays 62–70: as version of events 63, 70, 71: City Comedy, 128–132, 215: definition of 128: *The Alchemist* 128: *An Englishman for my Money* 128, 129: *The Roaring Girl* 131, 132: Iberian themes, 222–224: Morality plays, 4, 46: *Everyman*, 4: *The Castle of Perseverence*, 4: Mystery plays, 4, 52, 237, Coventry cycle, 4, 119: role of Herod 119: Place realism 266, *Bartholomew Fair*266: *The Late Lancashire Witches.* 268–70: Robin Hood plays 99–102, 165: anathema to Puritans 99, 100: tradition of randy friar 100, 101: 'Turk Plays', 44–47: definition of 44 *Tamburlaine* 44, *The Battel of Alcazar* 45, *Soliman and Persido* 46, *Captain Thomas Stukeley* 46: *A Christian turn'd Turk* 203
Treaty of Perpetual Peace and Alliance, 1604 174
War of the Theatres 148–152, 157: 56, 131, 150, 175, 178–180, 195–197:
Witchcraft, 42, 43, 182, 232: in *Macbeth* 182, 268: *The Witch of Edmonton* 232–3, 268: *The Late Lancashire Witches.* 268–70
Xenophobia, in *An Englishman for my Money* 128, 129: *Grim the Collier of Croydon,* 115, 116: in *Sir Thomas More* 116, in *The Pedlat's Prophesy*